Oman

Residents' & Visitors' Guide

there's more to life...
ask**explorer**.com

Oman Residents' & Visitors' Guide 2012/1st Edition
1st Edition 2012 ISBN 978-9948-450-29-0

Front Cover Photograph – Mutrah Corniche – Pete Maloney

Printed and bound by Emirates Printing Press, Dubai, United Arab Emirates.

Explorer Publishing & Distribution
PO Box 34275, Dubai
United Arab Emirates
Phone   +971 (0)4 340 8805
Fax   +971 (0)4 340 8806
Email   info@ask**explorer**.com
Web   ask**explorer**.com

Welcome…

…to the **Oman Residents' & Visitors' Guide**, your complete resource for visiting or living in one of the world's most intriguing and varied countries. Backed by a decade of insider knowledge, travel and off-the-beaten-path exploring, this guide is packed with everything you need to know about Muscat and beyond, from the lowdown on entry visas, currency and choosing a hotel room, to the issues that face residents who make Oman home. Red-tape to restaurants, housing to hobbies, entertainment to exploring, and shopping to socialising… it doesn't matter whether you're staying days, weeks, months or years, this guide will help you make the most of your time in the Sultanate of Oman.

Oman is a modern, thriving country – one that is constantly growing and changing – however, it is also a country that remembers and respects its past and its traditions. We can only fit so much exhaustive information on to these pages, so make ask**explorer**.com your digital companion to life in the Middle East. There, you'll find news, information and reviews of the latest places to stay and things to do in Oman and the rest of the GCC.

And don't forget that Explorer publishes hundreds of maps and activity guides that help to make the good life in Oman, and in the neighbouring UAE, even better. Head to ask**explorer**.com/shop to get your hands on these.

In your hands, in the glove box, in your rucksack; on your laptop, iPad or iPhone… wherever you're going and whatever you're doing, be sure to take us with you.

There's more to life...
The Explorer Team

  ask**explorer**.com

Off road.
But never out of reach.

Stay connected with our extensive network.

Visit www.omantel.om or call **1234**

In Oman, life begins at 2,000 meters

You don't have to travel far to experience cool temperatures and some of Arabia's best landscapes. Just outside of Muscat, you'll find Al Jabal Al Akhdar and Jabal Shams, among Arabia's highest mountain plateaus, where summer is mild and terraced gardens overflow with crops, fruit trees and vines.

Enjoy a day trip to the Hajar Mountains from Muscat or Nizwa, or stay at one of our many resorts and getaways.

Beauty has an address

At 2,000m in the Hajar Mountains, I am far from the hustle and bustle of everyday life. Now I am looking at distant horizons, reflecting on how beautiful life can be.

Al Jabal Al Akhdar, Hajar Mountains

SULTANATE OF
OMAN

Ministry of Tourism

The world's finest Watches, Jewellery Fashion Accessories and Luxury Mobiles

ROLEX | Cartier | Chopard | PIAGET | IWC SCHAFFHAUSEN

MIKIMOTO THE ORIGINATOR OF CULTURED PEARLS SINCE 1893 | VERTU | TUDOR TUDORWATCH.COM | ORIS

GP GIRARD-PERREGAUX | Bell & Ross | CARAN d'ACHE OF SWITZERLAND

Khimji's WATCHES

Al Ufouq Building, Shatti Al Qurum
Tel: +968 24 699 173, Fax: +968 24 699 171, Toll free 800 75000,
Email: krwatchs@omantel.net.om, www.khimjiblog.com.

OMAN

Beauty has an address

AIR

Let your senses fly

You never forget the best things

When you combine the world's ultimate in-flight experience and Muscat - one of the most attractive destinations in the world - the result is magical. Make Oman your destination or stopover.

Beauty has an address - Oman

CONTENTS

VISITOR **HIGHLIGHTS**

EXPERIENCE ALL THE AMAZING SIDES OF LIFE
IN THIS FASCINATING COUNTRY WITH OUR
TOP OMAN CHECKLIST.

OMAN
VISITORS'
CHECKLIST

01
GO UNDERGROUND
Oman's caves provide a mystical underground world containing glittering stalagmites and stalactites, white gypsum crystal and underground lakes. These underground treasures are there for you to explore. See Caving (p.238).

02
HIKE THE PEAKS

The spectacular mountain scenery of Oman, with its miraculous staircases crisscrossing the peaks, is paradise for those who like exploring the country by foot. The cooler climate in these higher areas can be a relief after the heat of the plains and coast.

03

BE AMAZED BY THE MUSEUMS

The Natural History Museum in Muscat is a fascinating tour of Oman's wildlife, while a trip to the Bait al Zubair Museum offers a glimpse into the past. See Discover Muscat (p.154).

04

FOLLOW THE FRANKINCENSE TRAIL

In ancient times, frankincense – a resin obtained from trees found in the Arabian Penninsula – was more valuable than gold because of its aromatic fragrance and relative scarcity. Oman was a producer and you can follow the historical tracks of this heritage in Dhofar (p.200), or sample the product in one of the souks.

05

STROLL THROUGH THE CITY OF GOLD

Muscat is full of examples of gilt-inspired architecture; as you wander the city streets you'll find many buildings with a golden glow. The Oman International Bank in Al Khuwayr, for example, has huge front doors that are plated in 24 carat gold.

06

DRIVE THE WADIS

Oman's wadis (dry gullies carved through rock by rushing water) offer spectacular driving opportunities for off-road enthusiasts. It can be hard navigating the narrow tracks, but if you need a break you can have a swim in one of the freshwater pools.

8

07
VISIT THE GRAND MOSQUE

The grandeur of the Sultan Qaboos Grand Mosque strikes you as soon as you see it, and inside it is just as magnificent. One of the largest in the Arab world, its highest minaret reaches almost 100m. The mosque is open to visitors between 08:30 and 11:00, Saturday to Thursday (p.159).

08
BASK ON THE BEACH

Oman has a long coastline and many beautiful beaches. Qurm Beach, stretching from the Crowne Plaza to Azaiba and beyond, is particularly popular. Most beaches are public, although the five-star beach hotels (p.66) have their own private beaches.

09
TAKE TO THE WATER

The beautiful Gulf of Oman has some amazing diving and snorkelling spots, best pointed out by one of the dive centres (p.263), although many hotels and major tour operators (see p.185) run activities including surfing, sailing and fishing.

10
DISCOVER THE PAST

Oman is one of the region's most ancient and longest inhabited countries. Step out of the towns and cities, and you'll find all manner of beautiful monuments to the country's culture, religion and heritage.

11
CARRY ON CAMPING

You can pitch your tent just about anywhere for a night out under the stars. Choose from the white beaches, the rocky mountains or the desert dunes, set up camp, and then just relax and enjoy your surroundings.

12

TUCK INTO OMANI FOOD

Enjoy the taste of Omani food, as well as traditional dining customs. Menus vary from spicy to mild, with delicious fish, meat and vegetarian options. Dishes are usually served with rice, and lunch is often the main meal of the day.

13
GO ON SAFARI

Experience the adventure of driving up and down golden sand dunes, riding a camel, watching the unique desert sunset, dancing with belly dancers, and falling asleep under the stars before waking up to a vivid red sunrise. See Tour Operators (p.185).

SEARCH FOR SINDBAD

Don't miss out on a trip to Sohar, the birthplace of the legendary Sindbad the Sailor. The Sohar Fort Museum, located in the fort, is the ideal place to learn all about Sohar's history. The museum touches subjects from geology and anthropology to historic trading.

15
RIDE A CAMEL

Ride on the back of the traditional 'ship of the desert'. Being atop an ungainly, yet surprisingly graceful, camel is one experience you won't forget in a hurry. If you'd prefer to keep your distance, get involved in the competitive camaraderie as a spectator at a camel race.

16

SET SAIL ON A DHOW

Watch these traditional boats being hand built in the yard in Sur. Each dhow takes as long as 12 months to build but can last for more than 100 years. To enjoy a trip, several tour operators (p.185) offer cruises on traditional dhows.

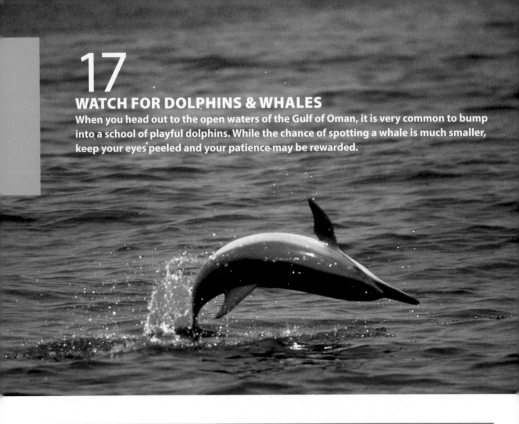

17

WATCH FOR DOLPHINS & WHALES

When you head out to the open waters of the Gulf of Oman, it is very common to bump into a school of playful dolphins. While the chance of spotting a whale is much smaller, keep your eyes peeled and your patience may be rewarded.

18

TAKE TO THE MOUNTAINS

Avid mountain bikers will love pedalling along the tracks that wind their way through Oman's rocky mountains, the wadis and along the coastline. There are easier tracks for beginners while even the most hardcore bikers will find testing routes. See Mountain Biking (p.257).

19

SHOP THE SOUKS

Experience the sounds, smells, sights and tastes of Oman at the local markets. It's the ideal opportunity to mingle with the local people, practise your bargaining skills and sample the local street cafe cuisine.

20

MARVEL AT THE TURTLES

A trip to see the nesting turtles is a must. Watching these huge creatures lumber up the beach to lay their eggs, then make their way back into the sea is to experience nature at its most miraculous. You are virtually guaranteed a sighting at Ras Al Jinz (p.176, 203).

OMAN **PROFILE**

OMAN PROFILE

One of the Middle East's oldest nations, today's Oman is a fascinating mix of old and new, of ancient traditions and modern culture.

OMAN OVERVIEW

Situated in the south-eastern quarter of the Arabian Peninsula, the Sultanate of Oman is bordered by the Kingdom of Saudi Arabia to the west, Yemen to the south-west and the United Arab Emirates (UAE) to the north-west. Its official total land area is 309,500 square kilometres, making it the third largest country in the peninsula. Mountain ranges and a narrow strip of coastal plains break up a topography that is predominantly made up of valleys and deserts. Oman's spectacular coastline, some 2,000km long, extends to the Gulf of Oman and the Arabian Sea as well as the Indian Ocean.

The country is divided into eight administrative regions: three governorates (Muscat, Dhofar and Musandam) and five regions (A'Dakhliyah, A'Dhahirah, Al Batinah, Al Wusta and A'Sharqiyah). Each region is further divided into smaller 'wilayats' (districts) headed by a 'wali' (district governor). The capital of the country is Muscat.

Musandam, known as the 'Norway of Arabia' because of its majestic fjords, lies at the furthest east point of the Arabian peninsula and is separated from the rest of the country by the UAE. It is an area of great strategic importance, lying south of Iran and controlling the main navigable stretch of the Strait of Hormuz, through which 90% of the world's crude oil passes. An Omani enclave also lies in the small village of Al Madha in the UAE.

Off the coast, there are several islands, the largest of which is Masirah Island in the southeast. It is a strategic entry point from the Arabian Sea to the Gulf of Oman, and houses military facilities used by the United States, although nowadays it is perhaps more notable as a hotspot for the region's watersports enthusiasts.

Oman's countryside is among the most stunning and varied in the Gulf region. It features 'sabka' (salt flats), 'khwars' (lagoons), oases, and stretches of sand and gravel plains dominated by stark mountains of rock and brownish-green ranges of ophiolites. The Hajar Mountains are the largest range, stretching from Musandam through the UAE to northern Oman, and rising to 3,000m at Jebal Shams, the country's highest peak. This countryside is crossed by 'wadis' (riverbeds), which are formed by the force of torrential water during the rainy season.

Oman is home to a large part of the seemingly endless Rub Al Khali (Empty Quarter) desert, which continues into Saudi Arabia and the UAE. The other main desert is the Ramlat Al Wahaybah (Wahiba Sands), home to nomadic Bedouin tribes. In contrast, the Dhofar region in the south is renowned for its green, tropical appearance and monsoon season with relatively high rainfall. It is one of the few places in the world where the frankincense tree grows; ancient trade in this resin features prominently in Oman's history.

Most of the population lives along the coast, on the Al Batinah plains and in the Muscat metropolitan area, but Oman's city centres are virtually devoid of skyscrapers, unlike many other cities in the region.

FLAG IT UP

The flag of Oman comprises three equal horizontal bands of white (top), red (middle) and green (bottom) with a thicker vertical red band on the hoist side. White stands for peace and prosperity, red for the battles fought against foreign invaders, and green for the fertility and greenery of the land. Centred at the top of the vertical band (in white) is the nation's emblem, an Omani 'khanjar' (dagger) and belt, superimposed on two crossed swords.

Stout, pretty, whitewashed buildings sit alongside ornate mosques, low-rise hotels and luxury villas.

Oman is proud of its ancestry and traditions, and rightly so. The country has a long list of cultural attractions to be explored. From crumbling forts and ancient cities, to lively souks and fascinating museums, Oman has the history that many other GCC nations lack.

Population

A national census is taken roughly every 10 years and the most recent was held in December 2010, putting the population of Oman at 2,773,279, compared to 2,340,815 in 2003. 70.6% are Omanis and 29.4% are expatriates. There are 1.02 Omani males to every female , an indication of a demographically stable community. However, in respect of the total population, due to the dominance of male expatriates who outnumber female expatriates by six to one, there are 1.39 males to every female.

35.3% of the Omani population is under 15 years of age, and 61.2% is between the

OMAN FACT BOX

Coordinates – 21º00´ North 57º00´ East.
Borders – 410km with UAE, 676km with Saudi Arabia and 288km with Yemen
Total land area – approx. 212,460 sq km
Total coastline – 2,092km
Highest point – 2,980m (Jabal Shams)
Time Zone – UTC + 4

ages of 15 and 64. The average age for Omanis is 23.9 compared to 22.4 in 2003 and 20.4 in 1993. 47.4% of the labour force is Omani (50.7% in 2003) while 52.6% is expatriate (49.3% in 2003), thus there has been an increase in the expatriate workforce. 53.3% of Omanis work for the government, but private sector employment for Omanis increased from 27.4% in 2003 to 39.7% in 2010.

In 2010, 75% of the population lived in urban areas compared to 71.5% in 2003. Today, 28% of the population lives in Muscat.

In 1970, the life expectancy was 40 years. Today Omani males have a life

Mutrah Corniche

expectancy of 72.2 years and females of 75.4, compared to the global life expectancy of 68 years for males and 72 years for females.

Muscat Governorate has seen great progress in education over the last 10 years. Illiteracy among Omanis is now 12.2% compared to 17.7% in 2003 and 31.8% in 1993. Thus great progress has been made in this area. The average size of an Omani household in Muscat is 7.8 members.

HISTORY

Archaeological evidence suggests that an early form of civilisation existed in Oman at least 5,000 years ago. The name 'Oman' is said to come from the Arab tribes that migrated to the area from a place in Yemen called Uman. The Omanis were among the first Arabs to embrace Islam, back in 630AD, and the country became an Ibadhi state (following the Ibadhi sect of the Muslim religion) ruled by an elected religious leader, the Imam.

Omani architecture

From the first to the third centuries, Oman was a prosperous seafaring nation, but tribal warfare over the election of a new Imam halted this expansion and Persian forces invaded the coastal areas. The Portuguese followed, arriving by force in 1507, with a view to protecting supply lines to the east and constraining Oman's trading power. They were driven out of their main bases, first from Hormuz in 1622, and eventually from Muscat in 1650, by Sultan bin Saif Al-Ya'arubi. This event marked the start of full Omani independence, making the country the oldest independent state in Arabia.

From the 1600s to the 1800s Oman vied with both Portugal and Britain for trade in the Gulf and the Indian Ocean. During the Ya'aruba Dynasty (1624–1744), Oman entered an era of prosperity and many of its great buildings and forts were built.

The history of Oman has always been a struggle for economic and political power between the interior (ruled by an Imam), and the coastal areas and Muscat (ruled by a Sultan). In 1744, Omani tribes elected Imam Ahmed bin Said, founder of the present Al Busaidi Dynasty. He expelled the Persian invaders, united the country, restored Oman's fortunes and moved the capital from the interior to Muscat. He also adopted the title of Sultan, which remains to this day.

The Omani empire reached the height of its power in the mid 19th century under Sayyid Said bin Sultan. He extended control all the way to Zanzibar and Mombassa in Africa, and to parts of Persia, Pakistan and India. Sayyid Said established political links with France, Britain and the United States, making Oman the first Arab state to establish relations with the USA. When Sayyid Said bin Sultan died the empire was split between his two sons. One became the Sultan of Zanzibar and the other the Sultan of Muscat and Oman.

Sultan Said bin Taimur came to power in 1932. He was able to enforce his rule over the interior, partly with the backing and encouragement of the British who needed stability in order to search the interior for oil. However, after establishing his rule, the Sultan became progressively more isolated, closing the nation's borders and shielding his country from the influences of the outside world. Eventually the only contacts were through the Sultan's mainly British advisors and certain well established trading links.

TRADING ON ITS LOCATION

Oman's geographical position on some of the world's most important trade routes between Africa and Asia has given it a unique dimension. From the first to third centuries, the southern part of the country was one of the wealthiest regions in the world due to the ancient trade in Arabian horses and the world's purest frankincense. Oman became a prosperous seafaring nation, sending dhows to Africa, India and the Far East.

In the 1960s, a serious new threat arose from Dhofar. By 1965, the Dhofar rebellion was underway, led by the communist Dhofar Liberation Front and aided by South Yemen through the Chinese. On 23 July 1970, a day henceforth celebrated as Renaissance Day, Sultan Qaboos bin Said overthrew his father, Sultan Said bin Taimur, to assume power. He was only 30 years old at the time but already had a strong vision for his country. Born in Salalah on 18 November 1940, he is the only son of the late Sultan Said bin Taimur

and is eighth in the direct line of the Al Busaidi Dynasty. He spent his youth in Salalah, where he was educated until he was sent, at the age of 16, to a private school in England. In 1960, Sultan Qaboos entered the Royal Military Academy at Sandhurst as an officer cadet, where he reputedly discovered a love for classical music. After military service in Germany he studied local government administration in England and went on a world tour, before returning to Salalah for six years. He devoted this time to studying Islam and Omani history. The Sultan married in 1976 but later divorced. He has no children.

Using the new oil wealth, Sultan Qaboos immediately set about transforming Oman and modernising the infrastructure. In 1970, Oman had only three primary schools, 10 kilometres of paved roads, two health centres, no infrastructure to speak of, and a per capita income of less than $50 a year.

Today, it is peaceful, stable and relatively prosperous. The Sultan is a strong yet

OMAN TIMELINE

1508	Oman falls under Portuguese control
1659	The Ottoman Empire takes control of Oman
1744	Ottoman Turks are overthrown by Ahmed bin Said of Yemen, who becomes Imam and starts the leadership of the Al Busaidis, which remains to this day
1890	Areas of Oman come under British Protectorate (as part of the Trucial States)
1962	Oil is discovered in Oman
1970	Sultan Qaboos comes to power as the Sultan of Oman
1971	Oman becomes a member of the United Nations and the Arab League
1975	Sultan Qaboos defeats Dhofar rebellion
1981	Oman joins with other Gulf countries to form the Gulf Cooperation Council (GCC)
1984	The first branch of Oman International Bank opens its doors
1986	Sultan Qaboos University opens
1996	Sultan Qaboos issues a decree clarifying the laws of royal succession and granting basic human rights for all citizens of Oman
1997	Two women are elected to the Consultative Council
1999	Oman and the United Arab Emirates settle their border disputes
2000	Oman joins the World Trade Organisation (WTO)
2003	All Omani citizens over the age of 21 are given the power to vote
2004	The first female government minister is appointed; a royal decree grants foreigners the right to purchase freehold property in certain developments in Oman
2006	Oman signs a free trade agreement with the USA
2007	Cyclone Gonu hits Oman causing the death of more than 50 people and creating damage costing approximately $4 billion
2009	Gulf Cup of Nations (football) is won by Oman for first time
2009	First residents move into The Wave
2010	Muscat holds the Asian Beach Games
2011	The Royal Opera House Muscat opens

benign leader, drawing his people into the modern world but at the same time preserving much of the character and heritage of his country, making Oman a unique place to visit.

ROYAL FAMILY

Oman's system of government is an absolute monarchy, and hereditary through the male line of Sayyid Turki bin Said bin Sultan of the Al Busaidi Dynasty, the great great grandfather of the present ruler, Sultan Qaboos bin Said. Sultan Qaboos bin Said is the Head of State and Supreme Commander of the Armed Forces. He is also Prime Minister, Defence Minister and Foreign Minister, although the day-to-day running of these and other ministries is performed by a Council of Ministers. The political and economic capital, and seat of government, is Muscat.

Given Oman's history of warring factions, it would have been difficult to put in place any kind of long-lasting economic, social and political reforms without some form of constitution. In November 1996, Sultan Qaboos passed the Basic Laws of the State. It is not actually a constitution in the official sense, but it does outline a series of

basic human rights for Omani citizens. More importantly, it defines the rules of succession, as the Sultan has no children.

The Basic Law provides for a bicameral legislature presided over by the 'Majlis Oman' (Council of Oman). It consists of the 'Majlis A'Shura' (Consultative Council) whose members are elected by Omani citizens to represent the various wilayats, and the 'Majlis Al Dawla' (State Council) whose members are appointed by the Sultan.

Oman's legal system is based on Islamic Shariah law and English common law, with ultimate appeal to the Sultan. Capital punishment is rare and subject to review by judicial and religious authorities. The Sultan has reportedly said that his country is not yet ready for full parliamentary democracy, implying that he considers this as the way forward. Nothing has been publicly finalised, although in November 2002 every Omani citizen over 21 years was granted the right to vote.

In his 39 years of rule, the Sultan has been an extremely capable, far-sighted and benign leader, held in high regard by his people. This is most apparent in their reactions when he travels around the various wilayats on his annual 'Meet the People' tour.

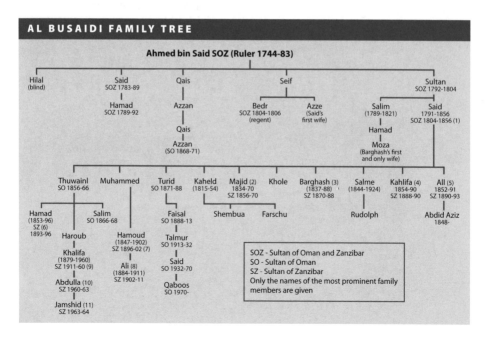

AL BUSAIDI FAMILY TREE

Ahmed bin Said SOZ (Ruler 1744-83)

SOZ - Sultan of Oman and Zanzibar
SO - Sultan of Oman
SZ - Sultan of Zanzibar
Only the names of the most prominent family members are given

CULTURE & LIFESTYLE

As you explore the many sides of Oman, you'll find that the local people are warm and welcoming. Oman's historical position on an important trade route means that the Omani population has been exposed to many different cultures over the centuries, and locals are generally tolerant, welcoming and friendly. Because of the active efforts of the government to increase local participation in the workforce, a large percentage of jobs are held by Omanis, so you have more opportunities to interact with the locals than you might elsewhere in the region.

Visitors are generally able to roam freely in the souks and villages, and may be pleasantly surprised by genuine offers of coffee. Perhaps the only exceptions are mosques and the Lewara quarter, adjacent to the Mutrah Souk in Muscat, where many Shi'a Muslims live.

As you travel deeper into the interior the people become more conservative but no less hospitable. The forbidding mountains and formidable deserts have kept them isolated from external influences so a foreign face becomes a welcome diversion. To get a quick overview of Oman, its traditions and its people, spend some time in one of the many excellent museums in the Muscat area (see p.162).

Oman's distinctive culture is influenced by Islamic traditions and regional heritage. Islam is more than just a religion: it is a way of life that governs everyday events, from what to wear to what to eat. Unfortunately, Islamic fundamentalism and its recent links to terrorism has caused some misunderstanding of this hugely popular religion and of Muslim countries and culture in general. In reality, Islam is a peaceful and gentle religion that is followed by millions of faithful Muslims around the world.

Most Omanis follow the Ibadhi sect, named after its founder Abdullah bin Abadha. Ibadhism is regarded as 'moderately conservative' and a distinguishing feature is the choice of a ruler by communal consensus and consent. Some Omanis are Sunni Muslims and live primarily in Sur and the surrounding areas, and in Dhofar. The Shi'a minority live in the Muscat-Mutrah area.

The basis of Islam is the belief that there is only one God and that the Prophet Mohammed is his messenger. There are five pillars of the faith (the

Inside Sultan Qaboos Grand Mosque

'hadith'), which all Muslims must follow – the Profession of Faith (a statement of the belief, as above), Prayer, Charity (giving of alms), Fasting (during the holy month of Ramadan) and Pilgrimage. Every Muslim, if possible, is required at least once in their lifetime to make the pilgrimage or 'Hajj' to the holy city of Mecca (or Makkah) in Saudi Arabia.

Additionally, a Muslim is required to pray five times a day, facing Mecca. The times vary according to the position of the sun. Most people pray at a mosque, although it is not unusual to see them kneeling by the side of the road if one is not near. It is not considered polite to stare at people praying or to walk over prayer mats. The modern call to prayer, broadcast through loudspeakers on the minarets of each mosque, ensures that everyone knows it's time to pray. Prayer timings are also published in local newspapers. Friday is the holy day. Other religions are recognised and respected, and followers are free to practise their faith.

The official language is Arabic, but English is widely spoken, and most of the road signs and menus are bilingual.

Ramadan

Ramadan is the holy month in which Muslims commemorate the revelation of the Holy Quran. For 30 days, Muslims are required to fast during daylight hours, abstaining from eating, drinking and smoking. In the evening, the fast is broken with an Iftar, or feast. The start date of Ramadan is determined by the sighting of the moon and usually falls 11 days earlier than the previous year.

Non-Muslims are requested to respect this tradition and refrain from eating, drinking and smoking in public places, even in their cars, between sunrise and sunset, although most hotels will provide screened rooms for those not fasting. Be aware that bars are closed for the entire month and the sale of alcohol is prohibited. Ramadan ends with a three-day celebration and holiday called Eid Al Fitr, or 'Feast of the Breaking of the Fast'.

Other Places Of Worship

Good Shepherd Protestant Church
Ghala, 24 692 464
Holy Spirit Catholic Church Ghala,
24 590 373, *holyspiritchurchoman.com*
Krishna Temple 24 798 546
Protestant Church In Oman Ruwi,
24 799 475, *churchinoman.com*
Salalah Christian Centre Salalah,
23 235 727
Shiva & Bajrangbali Temple Muscat,
24 737 311
Shree Ganesh Temple Ruwi,
24 798 548
Sts Peter & Paul Catholic Church Ruwi,
24 701 893, *ruwichurch.org*
St Anthony's Church Sohar,
26 841 396, *soharchurch.org*
St Francis Xavier's Church Salalah,
23 235 727
St George Orthodox Church Sohar,
26 843 892
Tamil Full Gospel Church Ruwi,
24 700 484

WORKERS' RIGHTS

In 2006, Oman made some changes to its labour laws, making it something of a leader within the region. Workers are now permitted to form labour unions and to carry out peaceful strikes. Oman will also punish employers who are found guilty of labour law violations or employing forced labour.

COMMERCE

Forty years ago, Oman was an economically poor nation but it is now a middle-income developing country with a vibrant economy, free universal welfare services and impressive infrastructure. Real GDP growth has been averaging 5% annually over the past 20 years. In recent years, Oman has experienced deflation thanks to government subsidies securing essential consumer items such as fuel and grain and lower import prices in local currency terms.

Endowed with modest oil reserves, Oman aims to create a viable non-oil economy by shifting economic emphasis to tourism, agriculture, fisheries, mining and light industry, while continuing aggressive development of natural gas to offset depleting oil production. Oman's main export partners are Japan, South Korea, China, Thailand, Taiwan, Singapore and the USA. The main import partners are the UAE, Japan, India, the UK, the USA and Germany.

In its foreign relations Oman maintains a stance of non-alignment and non-interference in the affairs of other countries, but is committed to Arab unity. Since taking power in1970, Sultan Qaboos has managed the extremely tricky task of maintaining friendly relations with just about everyone.

In recent years Oman has developed into a backroom mediator in solving the more politically volatile issues of the region. It was testimony to the Sultan's unique position on the world's stage when, in October 1998, he was presented with the International Peace Award by former US president Jimmy Carter, and in 2001, the Peace Prize from the Jewish-American Committee.

Oman belongs to the World Trade Organisation (WTO), the International Monetary Fund (IMF) and various pan-Arab economic groups, like the Arab Gulf Cooperation Council (AGCC) and the Indian Ocean Rim Association (IORARC) – Oman is in fcat a founding member of both. It is not a member of the Organisation of Petroleum Exporting Countries (OPEC) – although its pricing policy tends to follow that of OPEC fairly closely. At around 40%, oil remains the largest contributor to GDP. Most of Oman's estimated recoverable oil reserves (5.5 billion barrels) are located in the northern and central regions.

OMANISATION

Efforts to diversify the economy also include 'Omanisation', or a gradual replacement of the expat workforce with Omani nationals. This means that all companies must employ a certain percentage of Omanis. Around 40,000 young Omanis enter the job market each year, some with skills and some without. Government training schemes are in place to give nationals the necessary skills. By 2020, the government aims to have at least 95% of public sector jobs filled by Omanis, and at least 75% of private sector jobs.

Most of the major embassies or consulates are located in the Shati Al Qurm area and the Al Khuwayr diplomatic area. A few are in the Ruwi commercial business district (CBD). For a list of embassies and consulates, see p.340.

TOURISM DEVELOPMENTS

Oman is the essence of Arabia: stunning and unspoilt landscapes, rich marine life and a culture honed by the desert sands. A Ministry of Tourism was established in 2004, underscoring tourism's importance to the new economy; and the slow growth in the sector is considered a good thing, since it has allowed for more time to expand services and hotels to meet the demands of the modern traveller. The country is a successful model of how modernisation can be achieved without giving up the local cultural identity. Oman's more than 500 forts, castles and towers are awesome tourist attractions, as are the international dune rallies, yacht races and annual festivals like the Muscat Festival and the Salalah Tourism Festival in Salalah. For more information on Oman and what it has to offer, visit omantourism.gov.om.

Fast-paced developments are a Middle East phenomenon, and Oman is no exception. Key projects include the upgrade of both Seeb and Salalah airports (omanairports.com) and Blue City, a new coastal resort. The Wave (thewavemuscat.com) has become an exclusive residential beachfront community and is part of a huge development that includes a marina, luxury hotels, a golf course, retail outlets and recreational areas. Almost all the best-known hotel chains are present. There are currently around 100,000 beds, with hotels continually upgrading their offerings to better attract business travellers.

Blue City
Al Sawadi
bluecityoman.net
This ambitious project will create a whole new city over 32 square kilometres. The resort city will integrate tourism and residences, and will be home to around 200,000 people. Facilities will include a golf course, a tourist village and heritage museum, a sports stadium, luxury hotels, two hospitals, a university, a harbour for cruise ships and plenty of shopping opportunities. Construction began in 2006.

Duqm
Salalah
In a bid to attract tourists and citizens, the industrial oil town of Duqm is undergoing massive development. The project will include an airport, hotels, residential complexes, a refinery, free trade zone, power station, health facilities, shops, schools, recreational facilities, dry dock, commercial port and a shipbuilding yard. This coastal town also benefits from pleasant weather so it is hoped the area will develop into a maritime getaway destination. Duqm will open in phases.

Muscat Hills Golf & Country Club
As Seeb
muscathills.com
Muscat's first green golf course opened in early 2009, with 18 holes and a state-of-the-art clubhouse. The RO 20m development also incorporates luxury villas, available for freehold purchase, some of which are already occupied. Call 24 510 065 for more information.

Villas on The Wave

Oman Botanic Garden
Al Khawd
oman-botanic-garden.org
Oman Botanic Garden, an impressive 420 hectare project run by the Diwan of Royal Court, will be an education and conservation attraction showcasing over a thousand species of Oman's plants. Divided into huge plots which reflect the climate and landscape of various areas in Oman, visitors will experience everything from arid desert to cool forests. There will also be a mini village that demonstrates local skills, plus exhibitions, displays and education facilities. Currently a building site, the garden welcomes booked groups only to view its progress; the project will open to visitors in the not too distant future.

Salalah International Airport
Salalah
omanairports.com
New runways will be constructed to improve facilities at this airport, which is used predominantly for cargo but also for passenger flights, particularly during the khareef season. The upgraded airport will have a capacity of two million passengers a year. Work on the runways began in 2006 and the first phase is expected to be complete at some point in 2012.

The Wave
As Seeb
thewavemuscat.com
This multi-million dollar venture will see the staggered completion of four zones of entertainment, leisure and residential facilities. The development involves significant land reclamation and will eventually spread for over seven kilometres along Oman's coastline near Muscat. Facilities will include a golf course, hotels and spas, conference facilities, a marina, a shopping centre, and a range of residential options available for purchase by both Omanis and expats. Phased construction of The Wave began in 2006 and several developments are already open, with more to follow in the years to come.

Yenkit
Yiti
yenkit.com
This 9.4 square kilometre area, approximately 20km south-east of Muscat, will be a hub for visitors to Oman. The $2 billion project, with its unique coastal location, will offer several hotels, an eco-friendly resort, 18-hole golf course, beaches, diving destinations and a hilltop residential village with traditional architecture.

Salalah Beach
muriya.om
Spread over an area of 15.6 million square metres with 8.2km of beach front, Salalah Beach is 20km from the Salalah airport. This integrated tourism complex will comprise high-end luxury freehold apartments and villas, its own shopping and retail outlets, five 5-star hotels and two marina boutique hotels (Juwaira and The Lagoon boutique hotels), two 18-hole PGA golf courses, a 200-berth inland marina and marina town, restaurants and cafes. World class hotels such as Club Med, Rotana and Mövenpick Hotels & Resorts have been designed to enhance the atmosphere of the area, each capitalising on the beauty of the coast with easy access to the beach.

Jebel Sifah (ITC)
jebelsifah.com
Jebel Sifah is an integrated tourism complex (ITC) and is one of Muriya's key

Stay connected
n Oman

Join the leading operator and enjoy our extensive
coverage of fixed, mobile and internet services.

Visit www.omantel.om or call us on **1234**

DEVELOPING A NATION

Muriya is the developer that is shaping a lot of Oman's future leisure and tourism offerings. The company is a joint venture between the government-owned Omran and Orascom Hotels & Developments. Most of Muriya's projects include lifestyle elements, such as marinas, golf courses and retail, and if you're looking to buy a home in Oman, it is one of the few developers offering 'freehold' properties, which can be owned 100% by foreigners.

developments. The goal is to create a tranquil haven-like resort town 45 minutes from downtown Muscat. Jebel Sifah is a scenic destination, flanked by sandy white beaches and turquoise waters on one side, and the majestic Hajjar mountain range on the other. The appeal of Jebel Sifah lies in its close proximity to the capital. The drive from Muscat is a lovely one, passing peaceful fishing villages and offering views of the mountains and the sea all the way along. There are also a number of ferries and tours that make the trip by sea. The 6.2 million square metre Jebel Sifah resort is home to everything from apartments and villas, to an 18-hole PGA golf course. There are due to be four 5 star hotels (a Four Seasons Hotel & Resort, Banyan Tree Hotel & Resort and a Missoni Hotel are planned for along the beachfront), while Sifawy boutique hotel has already opened its doors to guests. One of the most ambitious elements is the 100-berth 'inland marina' and marina town, which will become a social hub, with retail venues, restaurants and cafes. Real estate here is freehold.

THE FUTURE

After a decline in tourism in 2009, due to the global economic downturn, the Sultanate of Oman hopes to post positive growth in tourist numbers over the coming years. Until now, Oman's strategy has focused mainly on upmarket tourism, encouraging wealthy holidaymakers to savour the delights of an 'exclusive' destination; backpackers were a rare sight in Oman. However, tourists are now looking for cheaper travel and better deals and, accordingly, Oman is becoming more accessible to a range of travellers.

In 2010, the Omani government unveiled a five year strategic plan for the development of travel and tourism with the aim 'to develop tourism as an important

and sustainable socio-economic sector in the sultanate in a manner that reflects the sultanate's historic, cultural and environmental heritage, and sense of traditional hospitality and values'. Areas of tourism that are being developed include adventure tourism and geo-tourism. To encourage adventure tourism, the ministry has sponsored the installation of several via ferrate routes in Oman. These are mountain routes with fixed wire cables, metal rungs and ladders, allowing adventurous walkers and climbers to ascend steep rock faces in relative safety. There are now three via ferrate in Oman, located in Grand Canyon, Snake Canyon and Bandar Khayran.

The 3rd global geotourism conference was held in Oman in November 2011. At the conference, Dr. Mohammed al Mahrooqi of the Geological Society of Oman stated that the 'unique geology/geomorpholgy in the country forms a golden opportunity for the development of outstanding geo-tourism'. These unique areas include some of the world's largest cave chambers, some of Arabia's highest mountain ranges, and remarkable geological features associated with plate tectonics.

Muscat being the Capital of Arab Tourism 2012 has given the country a great opportunity to increase its recognition as a high quality tourism destination. The Royal Oman Opera House, for example, has attracted attention as the first opera house in the Gulf, as well as the only one of its kind in the world, offering such a giant occupancy to a huge range of spectators; ticket prices are kept deliberately low to make them affordable to almost everybody. Oman is also set on attracting international sporting events to the country, such as February's Tour of Oman, which not only promotes cycling within the Sultanate but also attracts a large number of visitors.

THE ENVIRONMENT

With its extremely diverse terrains and rich marine life, Oman plays an important environmental role in the region.

Oman has been named one of the world's top 10 most environmentally committed countries and is party to international agreements on biodiversity, climate change, desertification, endangered species, hazardous wastes, marine dumping, Law of the Sea, whaling and ozone layer protection. In 1984, it became the first Arab state to create a ministry dedicated to environmental issues; environmental protection laws have been in place since 1974.

At the Earth Summit in 1989, Sultan Qaboos established the biannual Award for Environmental Conservation, the first Arab prize to be awarded in this area. Various organisations have been formed to protect the environment, as well as to educate people on the importance of environmental issues and the protection of human health. 2001 and 2002 were declared Years of the Environment.

The Sultan has always been committed to an extensive 'greening' programme of his cities. Highways are lined with colourful bougainvillaea, grassed areas, palm trees and flowers, all maintained by an army of workers who also pick up the litter on the roadside. It's no surprise then that Muscat Municipality received the UN Public Services Award for cleanliness in June 2003.

The Sultanate aims to protect endangered wildlife species by establishing nature reserves, while working together with local communities to ensure their success. The turtle breeding beaches at Ras Al Hadd and Ras Al Jinz

are protected sites, as are the Daymaniyat islands, which form a bird sanctuary to which entry is restricted during the breeding season.

Also, the beaches of Masirah Island are internationally recognised as a breeding site for turtles, among which the most prominent species include the Loggerhead, Olive Ridley, Green and Hawksbill. The Environment Society of Oman has since 2006 carried out a series of tracking projects with the involvement of local communities to monitor the movements of turtle populations across the Sultanate. Wadi Al Sarin, one of Oman's oldest reserves, is home to the Arabian tahr, while Jebel Samhan in Dhofar is a refuge for the Arabian leopard. Saleel Park is a nature reserve inhabited by gazelles and rare trees. Hunting and killing of any wildlife is strictly prohibited and carries stiff penalties.

Despite these significant efforts, there are still some serious environmental threats facing the Sultanate, such as groundwater pollution, rising soil and water salinity, desertification and beach pollution from oil spills. In 2007, the Arabian Oryx Sanctuary on the Jiddat Al-Harasis became the first ever nature reserve to be delisted as a UNESCO Heritage Site, following widespread poaching and, according to UNESCO, the decision by Oman to reduce the size of the area by 90%. For more information, contact the Environment Society of Oman (environment.org.om).

VISITOR ESSENTIALS

OMAN ESSENTIALS

From culture and customs to climate and area codes, all that you need to prepare for your trip of a lifetime in Oman.

GETTING HERE

The capital of Oman, Muscat is located at the crossroads of Europe, Asia and Africa, so it is an easily-accessible city. Most European cities are only seven hours away. However, Muscat's proximity to larger Middle East hubs, like Dubai, Abu Dhabi and Doha, means that you might have to connect via another Gulf city.

Muscat International Airport is located approximately 20 minutes from the main part of Muscat. It is a comfortable, modern airport that also offers domestic flights to Salalah and Khasab (Musandam). Salalah and Khasab airports handle limited international flights. The country's national carrier is Oman Air, which operates direct flights to various regional destinations. To contact Oman Air, call 24 531 111 or visit their website at omanair.com.

Flying to either Salalah or Khasab (Musandam) cuts down a full day's journey from Muscat to 90 minutes and is the quickest option if you don't plan to camp or visit the many attractions along the way. Oman Air offers three daily flights from Muscat to Salalah, and flights to Khasab four times a week.

Driving from the UAE to Oman requires a border crossing. From Dubai, the border crossing used most frequently is Hatta, while from Abu Dhabi it would be Burami. On the UAE side, passports must be shown which will be stamped with an exit stamp. For non-residents of Oman a visa must be purchased at the border crossing into Oman. The cost of the visa is RO 20.

DUTY FREE ALLOWANCES

- **Two bottles of alcohol per non-Muslim adult over the age of 21 (maximum two litres)**
- 'Reasonable' quantity of perfume
- Maximum 400 cigarettes
- Five DVDs

*These figures can all alter according to your country/nationality.

Cruise ships visit the ports at Mutrah, most frequently between the months of November to March. These cruise ships come from various parts of the world as part of a tour package purchased in the various countries where these cruises start from; the ship operators will almost always look after any visa issues.

VISAS & CUSTOMS

Visas

A passport (valid for at least six months and with enough blank pages) is required for all visitors, except nationals of Bahrain, Kuwait, Qatar, the United Arab Emirates and Saudi Arabia who hold national identity cards; and holders of a Macau (SAR) Travel Permit. Visa requirements have been greatly simplified as the country welcomes increased tourism. However, regulations should always be checked with your Oman Embassy or Consulate before travelling.

Tourists wishing to enter Oman are grouped, depending on their nationality. For each country, different procedures and terms of the visa apply. Check the website rop.gov.om to see which rules apply to you.

There are five types of visa that are of interest to visitors: tourist visa (RO 5); passengers ship tourist visa (free for up to 24 hours; between 24 and 96 hours costs RO 5): visa for foreign residents of GCC states (RO 5), and common visa facility with Dubai (no fee).

Arriving passengers who are eligible for visa on arrival are able to make visa payments at the Travelex foreign exchange bureau located in the immigration arrival hall. Payments are accepted in most currencies or you can pay by credit card. An automatic receipt will be issued to the traveller. This receipt is then presented at the immigration desk where the visa will be issued.

The varied sights of Oman's capital

For all visas, there is a stiff penalty of RO 10 per day if you overstay your welcome. This will be charged at the control point when you leave the country. In extreme cases you may not even be allowed to leave Oman until you have applied for an extension.

Customs

No customs duty is levied on personal effects brought into Oman. It is against the law to import narcotics, firearms (including toys and replicas) and pornography. There is no restriction on the import or export of any type of currency, although Israeli currency is prohibited.

If you enter the country by air, your bags are x-rayed before you leave the airport and opened if there are suspect items. Up to five videos or DVDs can be brought into the country although they may be temporarily confiscated for the material to be checked. You will be given a receipt to collect them at a later date and anything offensive will be erased (unless it's the whole thing, in which case you won't get it back).

If you enter Oman by land, which basically means driving in from the United Arab Emirates, your bags may well be searched at the Oman customs post. It is illegal to bring any alcohol into the country by road.

Health Requirements

No health certificates are required for visitors coming into Oman, except for those who have recently been in a yellow fever-infected area. If this is the case, you will need a certified vaccination at least 10 days before arriving.

Travellers from Africa may be spot-tested for malaria upon their arrival. Vaccinations for Hepatitis A and B, and typhoid are recommended. Check the World Health Organisation website at who.int.

Pets

It is not advisable to bring your pets on holiday with you, as there are strict quarantine rules – various vaccinations and health certificates from the Department of Health, as well as from your own vet, may be required. Your pet may also be subject to a six-month quarantine period although, strictly speaking, this is not required when coming in from a rabies-free country.

GETTING AROUND IN OMAN

The most popular way to get around Muscat and to the interior cities of Nizwa, Sur and Sohar is by car. If you don't own a car, you can hire one or make use of the many taxis available.

Oman's highways are of an excellent standard and international traffic symbols are in use. Major roads usually have two to four lanes, with intermittent roundabouts (traffic circles) at busy intersections. If you are new to the roads, be aware that drivers on the inside lane have priority over those entering the roundabout, so don't be surprised if someone jumps from the inside lane to the exit, cutting you off in the process. Further into the interior, the quality of roads is reduced to graded tracks that often seem to branch out in every direction. These tracks are often bumpy, hence the popularity of 4WDs.

Road signs are almost always in both English and Arabic, as are street and house numbers. However, people tend to rely on landmarks rather than road names to give directions. Landmarks are usually shops, hotels, petrol stations or distinctive buildings. To confuse matters further, places are sometimes referred to by a nearby landmark, rather than their real name.

Omani taxi driver

Driving

Car Rental

You'll find all the main rental companies, plus many local firms, in Muscat and Salalah. The larger, more reputable firms generally have more reliable vehicles and a greater capacity to help in an emergency. Make sure that you get comprehensive insurance and that it includes personal accident coverage. Most international and foreign licences are accepted.

If you are using a rental car and you're caught speeding or commit some other driving offence, don't think you'll get away with it because you're a tourist. Tickets for speeding and parking offences can be charged to your credit card, sometimes weeks after your departure.

Parking

In most cities in Oman, parking is readily available and people rarely have to walk too far in the heat. Increasing numbers of pay-and-display parking metres are appearing around Muscat. These areas, mostly around Qurum and Mutrah, are clearly marked with a blue signboard and cost 60 baisas for every half hour. Meters operate from 08:00 to 13:00 and 16:00 to 21:00, Saturday to Thursday.

Parking is free on Fridays and public holidays. If you haven't purchased a ticket, you don't display it properly or you fail to renew an expired ticket, you may be unlucky enough to receive one from the police for RO 3. Try to have loose change (25 and 50 baisa coins) with you since there are no automatic change machines available.

Petrol/Gas Stations

Petrol stations in Oman are numerous and are run by Shell, Oman Oil and Al Maha. Most offer extra services, such as a car wash or a shop selling the usual necessities like bread and milk, cigarettes and newspapers. Most visitors will find petrol far cheaper than in their home countries – prices range from 120 baisas per litre for Super (98 octane), 114 baisas per litre for Regular (95 octane) and 146 baisas per litre for diesel.

Speed Limits

Speed limits are clearly marked and are usually 60, 80 or 100 km/h within the Muscat area, and can be 120 km/h on roads to other parts of the Sultanate. When entering a built-up area the speed limit can drop suddenly from 120 km/h to 80 km/h, so keep your eyes peeled for signs and speed traps. The roads have both fixed and moveable speed traps which are activated by travelling over nine kilometres above the speed limit.

Accidents

If you are involved in a traffic accident, call 9999 to report the incident to the ROP, and wait for them to arrive. If the accident is minor (nobody has been injured) and the vehicles are blocking the road, then you should move them to a safe spot nearby; in more serious incidents, leave the vehicles where they are and wait for the police to arrive. Unfortunately, when you have an accident in Oman you become the star attraction as the passing traffic slows to a crawl with rubberneckers. In the event of a road accident where medical assistance is required, the police will arrange an ambulance to the nearest hospital.

Blood Money

If you are driving and cause someone's death, you may be liable to pay a sum of money, known as 'blood money', to the deceased's family. The limit for this has been set at RO 5,000 per victim and your car insurance will cover this cost (hence the higher premiums). However, insurance companies will only pay if they cannot find a way of claiming that the insurance is invalid (such as if the driver was driving without a licence or, for example, under the influence of alcohol). The deceased's family can, however, waive the right to blood money if they feel merciful.

Taxis

Taxis are very common, are always driven by an Omani national and all provide seatbelts. They are white with distinctive orange stripes, but not all are metered so be prepared to arrange the price before you get in – and don't be afraid to negotiate. If you are going somewhere by taxi, it is a good idea to ask someone to write the address for you in Arabic, just in case your driver speaks little English.

Buses

There is a reasonable public bus service in Muscat. The Oman National Transport Company (ONTC) has a fleet of buses and coaches servicing the whole of Oman. The buses cover all areas of Muscat and timetables, destinations and route numbers can be found at the bus stops (marked with a red bus on a green sign) at the side of the road. Make sure you have the exact change ready.

Cycling

While you won't see many tourists cycling their way around Oman, it can be an enjoyable way to see the country. There are no designated bike lanes, so the busiest parts of Muscat and the highways are best avoided if you're on two wheels. However, in the quieter areas there are some good riding spots and you'll probably see parts of Oman that you might miss in a car.

In the hotter months there is a higher risk of heat exhaustion, dehydration and sunburn, so take the necessary precautions.

Walking

Muscat is spread out over a long, thin area between the mountains and the coast, and therefore is not the easiest place to explore on foot. However, if you limit your exploring to specific 'pocket' areas, you can cover quite a lot of ground on foot.

A walk around Qurm Park or along Qurm Beach is highly recommended for some beautiful sights in this tranquil and picturesque suburb. During low tide hordes of people walk or jog along the stretch of beach between the Crowne Plaza and the Grand Hyatt.

You can also explore the Mutrah area on foot, taking in the corniche, the famous Mutrah Souk and the port. A wander around the old town of Muscat is fascinating for its insight into life in simpler times – the ramshackle houses and narrow streets are a huge contrast to the turquoise and gold splendour of the Sultan's palace. The roads in this area follow a confusing and convoluted one-way system, so exploring on foot is easier than by car.

If you don't mind doing some walking of a slightly more serious nature you could always tackle the trekking paths through Oman's mountains. The *Oman Trekking Explorer* features 12 spectacular trekking routes of varying degrees of difficulty, and with a little bit of effort (and a good pair of boots), you'll be rewarded with some amazing views of the country. Most of the routes follow trails through the Hajar Mountains, but there is a route from Riyam to Mutrah that is easy to follow.

Obviously the heat in summer, with daytime temperatures of over 40°C, makes walking a sweaty experience. After sunset it does cool down and a walk can be pleasant, but still a bit on the warm side. From October to March the temperatures are perfect for being outdoors.

Boats

There is a ferry service running between Muscat and Musandam. The two catamarans that make the trip are incredibly fast, completing the journey in less than five hours. The ferry runs from Shinas to Khasab. For more information, contact the National Ferries Company on 800 720 00 or visit nfc.om.

There is also a daily ferry from Shanab to Masirah Island (this is the only way that travellers can get to the island). The ferry only leaves at high tide (so you might have to wait a while) and the crossing takes around 90 minutes.

At various points along the coast it is possible to hire fishing boats or dhows for day trips to hidden bays or, for instance, along the coast of Musandam. If you are just looking for a quick boat ride, head for Bandar Al Jissah Beach, where you will find a crowd of crusty old seafarers touting for willing passengers – for about RO 5 they will take you on a half-hour trip around the coastline.

Vehicle Leasing Agents

Al Maha Rent A Car 24 603 359, *alhajiryoman.com*
Al Masky Rent A Car 24 595 241, *almaskry.com*
Al Miyasa Rent A Car 23 296 521
Avis Oman 24 510 342, *avisoman.com*
Budget Rent A Car *> p.43* 24 683 999, *budgetoman.com*
Dollar Rent A Car 24 562 877, *dollaroman.com*
Europcar 24 487 777, *europcaroman.com*
Global Car Rental 24 697 140
Hertz 24 521 187, *nttomanhertz.com*
Mark Rent A Car 24 782 727, *marktoursoman.com*
Sixt 24 482 793, *sixt-oman.com*
Thrifty Car Rental 23 211 493, *thrifty.com*
Value Plus Rent A Car 24 817 964, *valueoman.com*
Xpress Rent A Car 24 490 055, *sunnydayoman.com*
Zubair Leasing *> p.IFC* 24 500 842, *sayarti.com*

Discover

Oman

with the right wheels

Oman is full of delightful surprises. The best way to discover them is with Budget Rent A Car.

With six branches across the country, we offer you a 1800-strong fleet of European, American and Japanese cars, from 4WDs to luxury vehicles and practical cars. And an equally diverse range of services, to fulfil all your needs on the road.

For the right car at the right price, call us.
Explore Oman in top gear!

| Short-term rental | Long-term lease | Chauffeur service |
| Guided tours | Trips to the interior areas |
| International car hire reservations at special prices |

Budget
Car Rental

FEMALE VISITORS

Women should face few, if any, problems while travelling in Oman. It is generally safe to walk unescorted in well-lit and well-populated areas in Muscat and Salalah. However, travelling alone in the interior is not recommended. Ladies are also strongly advised to avoid taking the orange and white taxis if they are alone as there have been cases of harassment.

Single female travellers who don't want extra attention should dress modestly and avoid lower-end hotels. When travelling to the interior, always keep on hand a long-sleeved shirt and long skirt or an abaya, in case you have to cover up quickly. No matter what, most foreign females receive some unwanted stares at some point, particularly on the public beaches, but it tends to be out of mere curiosity rather than anything more threatening or sinister.

Generally, if you can ignore it you'll save yourself a lot of aggravation. If that doesn't help, call the police on 9999.

TRAVELLING WITH CHILDREN

Oman is a very family-friendly place and kids of all ages will have a great time. There are a handful of well-developed parks, such as Al Qurum Natural Park and Al Sahwa Park in Muscat, both of which have specific areas for children with climbing frames and slides. There are also numerous amusement centres, like the big one found right next to Qurum National Park.

There are endless other activities, particularly in the winter, for those who love nature and adventure. Many families go out at weekends to camp and explore Oman's many wadis, beaches and mountains.

Hotels and shopping malls (p.294) are generally well geared up for children, offering everything from babysitting services to kids' activities and small play centres. Restaurants (p.308), on the other hand, have children's menus but tend not to have many high chairs; it's best to ask when making reservations. Discounted rates for children are common.

Meanwhile, the Muscat Festival (muscat-festival.com) also offers all sorts of fun-filled activities for the whole family. The Discover Muscat (p.154) and Beyond the City (p.192) sections of this book will give a better idea of what there is to do for kids.

PEOPLE WITH DISABILITIES

Most of Oman's hotels have wheelchair access and toilet facilities for people with special requirements. There are also reserved parking spaces in most car parks. Some places do have wheelchair ramps, but often with incredibly steep angles. Always ask beforehand if somewhere has wheelchair access and make sure to get specific explanations – an escalator is considered wheelchair access by some.

The airports cater fairly well for disabled passengers. Request a wheelchair facility with your respective airline at the time of booking your flight and you'll be met off the plane by a wheelchair and a porter who will assist you right through the wheelchair-friendly terminal building. When departing, request a porter and a wheelchair at the check-in counter – the service is free of charge and the porter will escort you to the aircraft if required.

Unfortunately, disabled visitors may find the rest of Oman more challenging. Pavements are not always in good condition and Oman is still a country where the car is king, making it fairly pedestrian unfriendly, whether you are disabled or not. There are pedestrian walkways which are wheelchair friendly, but getting to those walkways is often far from easy.

The country's malls, by contrast, are almost all well equipped for disabled visitors with ramps, elevators and disabled toilets. There are parking spaces available for disabled drivers at most malls (although they are often occupied by other drivers!).

CLIMATE

Oman's climate varies considerably with the different regions, but sunny blue skies and warm temperatures can be expected most of the year. The best time to visit Oman is in winter, between October and April, when temperatures average between 25°C and 35°C during the day and about 18°C at night.

The north is hot and humid during the summer, with temperatures passing 50°C during the day in June and July, and averaging about 32°C at night. Humidity can rise to an uncomfortable 90%. The 'gharbi' (western) wind from the Rub Al Khali can raise coastal town temperatures by another 6°C to 10°C.

The interior is usually hotter than the coastal area, often reaching 50°C in the shade. In the mountains, night temperatures can occasionally fall to -1°C with a light dusting of snow. Rainfall is infrequent and irregular, falling mainly between November and March. Average annual rainfall in the Muscat area is 75mm, while rainfall in the mountains can be as high as 700mm.

The southern Dhofar region usually has high humidity, even in winter. Between June and September the area receives light monsoon rains, from the Indian Ocean, called the 'khareef'. The area around Salalah is lush and green and at certain times of the year is swathed in a cooling mist – it's hard for visitors to reconcile this image with the usual Arabian landscapes of forbidding deserts and rocky, inhospitable mountains.

Information on local weather and meteorological conditions is available by dialling 1103.

DRESS

Most Omanis wear traditional dress during work and social hours. Men wear an ankle length, collarless gown with long sleeves (dishdasha) that is usually white. Women, meanwhile, cover their normal clothes with a full-length, black cloak-dress (abaya) in public. Modern women will often wear trousers or a long skirt underneath. You can still see women, usually in the interior but also in Muscat, wearing the 'burkha' (mask) that covers the brow, cheekbones and nose.

Dress Code

Although Oman is a Muslim country, there is no need for women to wear head scarves or veils or dress in floor-length, long-sleeved garments. However, respect for local customs is recommended, and it is better to dress a little bit more conservatively than you might in your home country. Lightweight summer clothing is suitable for most of the year, but something slightly warmer may be needed in the evening for the winter months. In winter and summer, be sure to take some sort of jacket or sweater when visiting hotels, as the air conditioning can reach arctic temperatures.

Short, revealing or tight clothing can be worn, but it will attract a lot of unwelcome attention. It is always best to keep shoulders and knees covered in public, but you can show some more skin in hotel bars, clubs and restaurants. On the beach, topless sunbathing is a definite no-no.

Man in dishdasha

Attitudes in rural areas are usually a lot more conservative than in the cities. You will also have to dress appropriately if you visit the Sultan Qaboos Grand Mosque – long skirts or trousers and long-sleeved shirts for ladies, with neck, chest and head covered, and long trousers for men.

FOOD & DRINK

Traditional Omani cuisine is fairly simple; typically, rice is cooked with beef, mutton, chicken or fish, which has been marinated in a blend of herbs and spices. The country's restaurants serve up a range of excellent cuisine, particularly locally caught seafood. Both meat lovers and vegetarians will find plenty of choice on local menus.

Omani meals are eaten with the right hand. The main meal is usually eaten at midday, while the evening meal is lighter. Salads are quite simple – lettuce, cucumber and tomatoes served with a slice of lime for dressing. Maqbous is a saffron coloured rice dish cooked over spicy meat. Skewered meats (kebabs) are often served with flat bread (khoubz). Harees is a staple wheat-based dish with chicken, tomato, seasoning and onion. Fish and shellfish are used widely in dishes such as mashuai – whole spit-roasted kingfish served with lemon rice.

Omani 'halwa' is a popular dessert made of eggs, palm honey sugars, water, ghee and almonds, flavoured with cardamom and rosewater. These ingredients are blended and cooked to form a sweet, dense block with a delicious flavour and consistency. Traditionally, the making of halwa is very much a male preserve, with recipes being handed down from generation to generation.

It is during Ramadan that one can sample Omani food at its best. Dishes, such as shuwa, arsia (lamb with rice) and mishkak (similar to kebabs), are mainly served during Eid celebrations. Shuwa is elaborately prepared by seasoning a large piece of meat (often lamb) and wrapping it in banana leaves, sacking and then burying it in a pit on top of red-hot coals. The meat is left to cook slowly over a couple of days in the embers and when unwrapped, is tender and succulent. Many hotels set up a Bedouin-style tent outdoors in the winter months – this is an ideal opportunity to sample authentic Omani cooking. However, the Bedouins themselves enjoy a far more limited diet, depending on where they are travelling. Their standard fare is usually camel meat (dried or boiled), served with rice.

The serving of traditional coffee (kahwa) is an important social ritual in the Middle East. Local coffee is mild with a taste of cardamom and saffron, and is served black without sugar. It is served with dates, to sweeten the palate between sips. It is considered polite to drink about three cups of the coffee when offered (it is served in tiny cups, about the size of an egg cup).

Other favourite local drinks are laban (heavy, salty buttermilk) and yoghurt, which is often flavoured with cardamom and ground pistachios. Fresh juices, made on the spot from fresh fruits (mango, banana, pineapple, pomegranate), are delicious and very cheap. In particular, the mixed fruit cocktail should not be missed.

Shawarmas (lamb or chicken carved from a rotating spit, then rolled in flat bread with salad) are sold in small shops throughout Oman. If you don't eat meat, you can try a vegetarian version of this delicious, inexpensive snack made with foul (a paste made from fava beans) or falafel (deep-fried balls of mashed chickpeas). Salads like fattoush and tabbouleh are cheap and healthy. Don't miss out on trying the ultimate Arabic dessert – umm ali (similar to British bread and butter pudding) is made with milk, bread, nuts and raisins and it is delicious.

However, you can eat your way around the world in Oman – there is a huge choice of international cuisines thanks to the cosmopolitan mix of nationalities living here. Not only can you feast on exotic foods in the numerous five-star hotels, but you can also find cheaper options (like shawarmas and falafel) at the many street cafes and independent restaurants. You'll also find all the obligatory fastfood outlets such as McDonald's, KFC and Pizza Hut. Browse through the Going Out section (p.304) for some pointers on where to find the kind of cuisine you love.

TIPPING

Many hotels and restaurants automatically include a service charge of at least 8% (check the bottom of your bill). This is in addition to the government tax of 9%. However, none of this is likely to end up with your waiter, so a tip of a few hundred baisas is greatly appreciated. The same applies for petrol pump attendants and taxi drivers, hotel porters, and generally anyone providing a service.

ELECTRICITY & WATER

Electricity and water services are provided by the Omani government, although there are plans to privatise them eventually. The electricity supply is 220/240 volts and 50 cycles and there are few shortages or stoppages. Power cuts – lasting from a few minutes to several hours – do occur every now and then but rarely pose a major inconvenience.

The socket type is the three-pin British system but many appliances are sold with two-pin plugs, so you will need adaptors. Hotels usually have a generous supply of adaptors or, alternatively, you can pick them up cheaply at any supermarket or corner shop.

The mains tap water is purified eight times and is fine to drink but can taste chlorinated, so it is usually more pleasant to drink bottled water. Locally-bottled mineral or desalinated water is a cheap alternative and there are many brands available. Bottled water is usually served in hotels and restaurants – make sure the seal on the bottle is unbroken.

DOS AND DONTS

Although Oman is a fairly liberal Arab country, there are a few things to watch out for. When taking your holiday snaps, adhere to signs banning photography and always ask permission when taking photos of local citizens. If the answer is 'no', respect that and don't push it. It's illegal to drink alcohol in public places and the penalties are harsh. The same goes for drink driving and for drunk and disorderly behaviour. Be warned that it is illegal to bring alcohol into Oman by road. If you don't want unwelcome attention, dress conservatively. This is even more important in rural areas where you'll be considered as offensive if showing too much skin, so cover up shoulders and knees.

Pork

Pork is taboo in Islam. Muslims should not eat, prepare or serve pork. For a restaurant to serve pork, it should have a separate fridge, preparation equipment and cooking areas. Supermarkets also require pork to be sold in a completely separate area. You can buy pork mainly from Al Fair supermarkets, but you have to find the walled-off pork section first. All meat products for Muslim consumption have to be halal – this refers to the method of slaughter. As pork is not locally farmed you will find that it is more expensive than many other meats. However, after a few Friday brunches with chicken sausages and beef bacon, you will be surprised how easy it is to have a fry up without pork.

Alcohol

The attitude to alcohol in Oman is far more relaxed than in some other parts of the Middle East. The government grants alcohol licences to hotel outlets and independent restaurants, plus a few clubs, but alcohol cannot be purchased in local supermarkets. Permanent residents who are non-Muslims can easily get liquor supplies under a permit system from the Royal Oman Police. However, it is illegal to carry alcohol around, the only exception being when you are taking your purchases home directly from the liquor shop or airport duty free. Keep your receipt as this gives you the right to transport alcohol. It is also illegal to resell alcohol to others. If you have an accident while driving under the influence of alcohol, the penalties are high and, in addition, your vehicle insurance will be invalid. Alcohol is not served during Ramadan, even in hotels, except for guests.

Shisha

Smoking the traditional shisha (water pipe) is a popular and relaxing pastime that is enjoyed throughout the Middle East. It is usually savoured in a local cafe while chatting with friends. They are also known as hookah pipes or hubbly bubbly, but the proper name is nargile. Shisha pipes can be smoked with a variety of aromatic flavours, such as strawberry, grape or apple, and the experience is unlike normal cigarette or cigar smoking. The smoke is 'smoothed' by the water, creating a much more soothing effect. Smoking shisha is one of those things that should be tried at least once while you're in Oman, especially during the evenings of Ramadan, when festive tents are erected throughout the city and filled with people of all nationalities. You can buy your own shisha pipe from the souks, and once you get to grips with putting it all together you can enjoy the unique flavour anytime you want. See Shisha Cafes (p.327).

Photography

Normal tourist photography is allowed and in some parts of the country, actively encouraged. However, taking photographs near government buildings, religious institutions, military installations, ports and airports is not allowed, and you will see signs prohibiting photography in certain areas. Always ask permission when taking photos of local citizens – the Arabic phrase 'mumkinshura, min fadlak?' meaning 'may I take your picture please?' Children and men will usually oblige but local women may not, especially if the photographer is male.

PDAs

Not a reference to the handheld gadget but to public displays of affection: these are not looked on favourably in the region, and anything more than an innocent peck on the cheek will at best earn you disapproving looks from passersby.

Appropriate Attire

While beachwear is fine on the beach, you should dress more conservatively when out and about in public places. If in doubt, ensuring that your shoulders and knees are covered is a safe bet. A pashmina is always useful for the journey home or in case the air conditioning is set to 'deep freeze'.

Meeting People

Long handshakes, kisses and warm greetings are common when meeting people in the Middle East. It's normal to shake hands with people when you are introduced to them, although if you are meeting someone of the opposite sex, be aware that a handshake may not always be welcome. It's best to take your cue from the other person and not offer your hand unless they first offer theirs. It's polite to send greetings to a person's family, but can be considered rude to enquire directly about someone's wife, sister or daughter. You may see men greeting each other with a nose kiss; this is a customary greeting in Oman but is only used between close friends and associates and you should not attempt to greet someone in this way.

CRIME & SAFETY

Staying Safe

While street crimes are uncommon in Oman and violent crimes rare, a healthy degree of caution should still be exercised. Keep your valuables and travel documents locked in a safe, and don't leave tempting items like mobile phones or portable computers in plain sight in a parked car, particularly in hotel car parks.

When in crowded areas, be discreet with your money. As with anywhere in the world, just remain vigilant and know what's going on around you. It is always a good idea to carry your mobile phone and a camera (if you don't have one on your phone), so that you can call for help if necessary and take pictures of the offender. You should report such cases to the police immediately. The golden rule is to never let your guard down, even when your surroundings seem safe.

If you leave any personal possessions in a local taxi you will be unlikely to receive it back. If this happens in a registered taxi from a private taxi company though, you needn't worry as the drivers are usually trustworthy and will even drop your phone or bag back to you the next day. Giving the driver a tip to show appreciation for their honesty is a good idea in this situation.

Drinking & Driving

The Royal Oman Police exercises a strict zero tolerance policy on drinking and driving. It is illegal even to transport alcohol around Oman, except from the airport (or liquor store if you're a licence holder, see p.85) directly to your hotel or home.

If you are caught driving under the influence of alcohol, you will spend 48 hours in jail and receive a fine of up to RO 75. On your second offence, the jail time increases to 72 hours and the fine to RO 150. If you get caught a third time you will be given a RO 300 fine and deported to your home country. Being drunk and disorderly in public carries similar charges to drinking and driving.

Thankfully, taxi drivers are unlikely to report your inebriated state to police as long as you don't cause any trouble.

TIME ZONES & BUSINESS HOURS

The Sultanate of Oman is four hours ahead of UCT (Universal Coordinated Time, formerly known as GMT), and there is no summer time saving. When it is 12:00 midday in Muscat it is 08:00 in London, 13:30 in Delhi and 17:00 in Tokyo (not allowing for any summer time saving in those countries).

Social hours vary in Oman – some people get up early, some stay up late, and some do both. Some businesses still close for a long afternoon break – this is known as 'split shift'. Standard split shift hours are from 08:00 to 13:00 and then from 16:00 to 19:00 (for offices) or 22:00 (for some shops). However, most private sector offices will work a straight shift, usually 08:00 to 17:00 or 18:00. The weekend is traditionally Thursday afternoon and Friday (the holy day), but a few organisations close all day Thursday and Friday.

Government offices are open from 07:30 to 14:30, Saturday to Wednesday. Bank hours are usually 08:00 to 12:30, Sunday to Thursday. Smaller shops and souks are generally closed between 13:00 and 16:00 and usually remain closed on Friday mornings. The Mutrah Souk closes at 20:00 (although some shops start closing from 19:30). Many shopping malls also close for a long lunch, although Markhaz Al Bahja and Muscat City Centre both remain open throughout the day. Supermarkets are generally open all day, seven days a week.

Working hours at embassies and consulates vary but are generally 08:00 to 13:00 or 14:00. Most are closed on Thursdays and Fridays, but leave a contact number on their answering machines in case of emergencies.

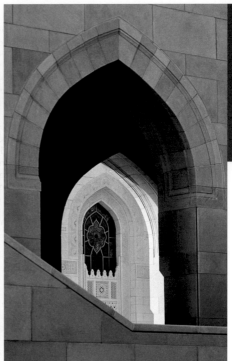

Ramadan

During Ramadan, work hours in most public and private organisations are reduced by two to three hours per day, and business meetings may be difficult to arrange. Muslims in the private sector may work only six hours per day and government offices close at 14:00 or earlier. Many private offices start work an hour or so later and shops are open until 22:00 or 24:00. Most restaurants are closed during the day. The Ruwi district in Muscat and more popular shopping malls are usually crowded, even at night, and parking can be hard to find.

TELEPHONE & INTERNET

Oman Mobile, Nawras and Friendi all offer a pre-paid mobile phone SIM card kit that is compatible with any freed handset. These kits range in price from RO.3 upwards. You can buy top-up cards in supermarkets, petrol stations and smaller shops, as well as prepaid phone cards for use on any landline phones or payphones. Internet cafes can be found in most shopping malls in the bigger cities and some restaurants.

Apart from the mobile phone network which has four providers, all other telecommunications are provided by Oman Telecommunications Company (Omantel). National call charges are based on the area to which the calls are made. International direct dialling is possible to over 170 countries and surprisingly enough the charges are often reduced rather than increased. Rates are published in the telephone directory and the Omantel website (omantel.om).

All telephone numbers in Oman have changed from six digits to eight. If you see a landline number that is still six digits, simply add 24 before the number if it is in Muscat, 23 for Salalah, 25 for Nizwa or Sur, and 26 for Sohar. If you are still in doubt, call 1318 for directory assistance.

Public pay phones accept phone cards. Cards are available in values of RO 2, RO 3 and RO 5 from petrol stations, supermarkets and some smaller shops.

Area Codes & Useful Numbers

Billing information 24 632 124
**Car breakdown
 services (AAA)** 24 605 555
Directory enquiries – international 143
Directory enquiries – national 198

Electricity 154
Fire Department 9999
Fault reports 192
GSM helpdesk 196
International operator 195
**Royal Oman Police
 Capital area** 24 560 099
**Oman Investment and
 Finance Company** 24 162 222
**Oman country code
 (landlines & mobiles)** 968
Omantel call centre directory 1318
Speaking clock 140
Water emergency 153

Internet

As you'll notice from the quality of many local websites, the internet isn't as popular in Oman as elsewhere in the world. According to 2010 figures from the International Telecommunication Union (ITU) 41.7% of the country has access to the internet. The sole internet service provider is Omantel and all sites are accessed through its proxy server. The proxy blocks any sites that are considered offensive to religious, moral, political or cultural sensitivities.

There are various Wi-Fi spots around Muscat where you can enjoy high-speed internet access on your laptop without the need for a phone connection. New Wi-Fi sites are being added all the time, and you can find a list of outlets on omantel.om. Wi-Fi is currently available at selected outlets in the Al Bustan Palace, The Chedi Muscat, Grand Hyatt Muscat, Intercontinental Muscat, Park Inn Hotel, Al Harthy Complex, Al Arimi Complex, Al Qurum Complex, Sabco Commercial Centre, Qurum City Centre, Muscat City Centre, MSQ Centre, Zakhir Mall, Jawharat Al Shatti Complex, Oasis by the Sea, Oman International Exhibition Centre, Radisson Blu Hotel, and Knowledge Oasis Muscat. All you need to do is buy a prepaid Ibhar card (available in denominations of RO 3, RO 5 and RO 15) and log in.

NEWSPAPERS & MAGAZINES

You can get a wide selection of English and foreign language press in Oman in bookshops, petrol stations, supermarkets, hotel bookshops and grocery shops. However, prices are usually higher than what you're used to and often a few days late. *The Oman Daily Observer*, *Times of Oman*, *Muscat Daily* and *Oman*

More Home Broadband
or everyone

t started with 2Mbps and unlimited usage for
) Rials per month with Omantel Home Broadband.

sit www.omantel.om or call us on **1234**

عمـانتل
Omantel

Tribune (200 baisas each except *Muscat Daily* at 100 baisa) are the four daily English newspapers. *The Week* and *Hi* are free weekly tabloids that come out on Wednesday and Friday respectively, and found on branded stands throughout Muscat.

Newspapers and magazines are available from bookshops, supermarkets, petrol stations, grocery shops and hotel shops. There are no street sellers at present. You will probably be provided with one of the local papers in your room if you are staying in a good hotel.

While these newspapers aim to keep Oman's English-speaking residents abreast of news and events in the region, the editorial quality can be somewhat dubious.

As is the case across the region, Oman's newspapers operate under the heavy hand of editorial self-censorship. This means that you will rarely read anything negative about the country, which can result in a false sense of security regarding crime and personal safety.

Foreign daily tabloid newspapers, mainly American, Asian, British, French and German, are available in hotel bookshops and supermarkets, although they are usually a lot more expensive than they are back home and a few days out of date. They will also be without extras like supplements and gifts. Hobby magazines, such as computing, photography, sports and women's magazines are also available, but are very expensive. Although the Press Act supposedly allows freedom of speech, the public media exercise rigorous self-censorship. Recent events in the country following the Arab Spring protests have resulted in new media laws prohibiting the publication of stories relating to national security. The internet is monitored and any site deemed offensive to the religious, moral, cultural or political principles of the country will be inaccessible. Publications are also censored for political, moral, religious and cultural reasons, and you'll often find that certain images or articles have received the infamous 'black marker' treatment. Many expats stock up with glossy magazines every time they travel,

and then distribute them among their friends upon their return. There are a number of decent publications available in English. Most are published in Oman and cover a variety of topics: *Signature*, *Al Mara* and *Crème de la Crème* cover lifestyle, while *Oman Economic Review* and *Business Today* cover business. Regional magazines such as *Emirates Women*, *Hello: Middle East*, *OK: Middle East*, *Grazia: Middle East* and *Arabian Business* are also available.

Further Reading

There is a huge range of books available about Oman, from glossy coffee-table books showcasing the natural beauty of the country to specialist hobby books and travel guides. If you have an interest in the history of the region, which has grown from barren desert to rapidly developing cities over a relatively short period of time, you will appreciate *Arabian Sands* by the great explorer Wilfred Thesiger. It is a pictorial account of his crossing of the Empty Quarter with a group of Bedouins in the early 60s. *The Maverick Guide to Oman* by Peter Ochs is an excellent travel guide if you are visiting Oman independently (not as part of a tour group).

To find your way around the less well-travelled areas of Oman, and see things that not all visitors get to see, get a copy of the *Oman Off-Road Explorer*. It is the ultimate accessory for any 4WD, and contains trip plans and maps for 26 adventurous routes (all marked with GPS coordinates and points of interest). If you prefer to do your off-roading by foot, the *Oman Trekking Explorer* features 11 trekking routes (each with a separate route card), a trekking handbook and an area map.

Websites

With internet usage becoming more and more popular in Oman, there is an increase in the number of local websites available. The table lists websites that are particularly useful.

chamberoman.com Oman chamber of Commerce and Industry
gcc-sg.org What the GCC is all about
kom.om Knowledge Oasis Muscat – Oman's IT park
mm.gov.om Muscat Municipality
mocioman.gov.om Ministry of Commerce and Industry
moneoman.gov.om Ministry of National Economy

EMBASSY INFO

One really useful website, wherever you are in the world, is embassyworld.com. Here, you'll find a complete list of phone numbers for national embassies and consulates, including Omani embassies abroad and foreign missions in Oman.

FINGER ON THE PULSE

For a real insider's point of view on what's happening in Oman, check out some of the blogs written by local residents. For starters check out muscati. blogspot.com and muscatmutterings.com. Oman Forum can contain interesting links to articles and blogs, or debates on points of interest, and can be found at omanforum.com.

muscatmall.com Online shopping
nawras.om Internet and telephone services provider
oeronline.com
Oman Economic Review
oite.com Oman International Trade Exhibitions Centre
omanet.om Ministry of Information
omantel.om Internet and telephone services provider
omantel-yellowpages.com Online Yellow Pages
omantourism.gov.om Ministry of Tourism
tenderboard.gov.om Tender board

TELEVISION & RADIO

Television

Oman TV (Channel 6 in Muscat and Channel 10 in Salalah) is the only local television channel in Oman. The shows on this channel are mainly Arabic, although you'll get the occasional film or series in English. The daily English news broadcast is at 20:00, and news in Arabic is shown at 01:00, 09:30, 11:00, 14:00, 17:00 and 22:00.

There is a wider choice of programmes offered by satellite TV, ranging from international entertainment and films to sport, cartoons and current events. Most leading hotels have satellite television for guests, and it is usually quite straightforward for a resident to have it installed (see p.107).

There are several sports bars around Muscat that show important games (usually football, cricket and rugby) on their big-screen TVs. Premiership football, for example, is shown regularly in the Al Ghazal Pub inside the InterContinental (p.68).

TVs are in PAL format (UK standard), so certain videos will not work unless you have multi-system equipment. However, almost any TV, VCR or DVD player you buy in Oman is multi-system and will work anywhere in the world.

Radio

Oman has a number of commercial radio stations, broadcasting mostly in Arabic. Hi FM (95.9 FM) is the most popular English-language station, with current music, competitions and upbeat DJs. You can listen online at hifmradio.com, where you can also find the programme schedules and find out more about the station. A new radio station is Merge 104.8; the station is the first to try to mix traditional Omani culture with its modern society, playing old and new tunes in both English and Arabic.

The government-owned English language radio station (90.4 FM in Muscat and Salalah) plays a mixture of news, talk shows, classical music and modern music. The station operates daily from 06:00 to midnight and the schedule is printed in the local newspapers. It is also available online at oman-tv.gov.om.

News headlines, weather forecasts and a list of pharmacies on duty are read out frequently on air in between the somewhat limited playlist. If you have broadband, then you can tune in to various international radio stations on your computer, or even download a pre-recorded 'podcast'.

The BBC World Service broadcasts on 15575 Hz between 07:00 and 14:00. If you want to hear Arabic music, tune in to 89.0 FM and 107.7 FM.

Oman Information

destinationoman.com All about Oman and getting there
hifmradio.com English language radio station
myoman.com Information and pictures

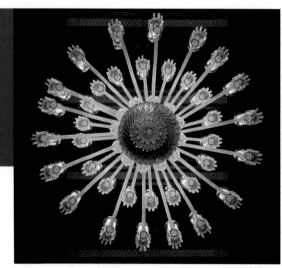
Details of Sultan Qaboos Mosque

In cities like Muscat and Salalah, most road signs and restaurant menus appear in both English and Arabic; however, in remoter areas, you may see considerably less English.

Learning a few words of Arabic will be useful, especially outside the cities. See p.55 for the Basic Arabic table. Arabic isn't the easiest language to pick up (or to pronounce), but if you learn the usual greetings you're more likely to receive a warmer welcome. Most Omanis appreciate the effort and will help you with your pronunciation. Just give it a try – it certainly won't hurt and it definitely helps when dealing with officials of any sort.

Face To Face

Omanis greet profusely on meeting and parting, and it would be polite to return the gesture with a friendly remark (master those greetings) or a handshake. Unlike the firm western handshake (a sign of aggressiveness), the handclasp is light and may be followed by placing the hand over the heart to show sincerity.

Some Muslims prefer not to shake hands with the opposite sex, so when meeting an Omani man or woman, wait until they offer their hand before you go in for the handshake.

Light cheek-to-cheek kissing between men is also common, but reserved for family and close friends. Avoid bad and forceful language and discussing local politics with casual acquaintances. It is considered impolite to ask someone about their origin or birthplace.

Arabic Family Names

Arabic names have a formal structure that traditionally indicates the family and tribe of a person. Names usually start with that of an important person from the Quran or someone from the tribe. This is followed by the word 'bin' (son of) for a boy and 'bint' (daughter of) for a girl, and then the name of the child's father. The last name indicates the person's tribe or family. For prominent families Al, the Arabic word for 'the', comes immediately before it. For instance, the ruler of Oman is Sultan Qaboos bin (Al) Said.

When women get married, they do not change their name. Family names are very important here and extremely helpful when it comes to differentiating between the thousands of Mohammeds, Ibrahims and Fatimas.

newsbriefsoman.info News and comments about Oman
nizwa.net Environment and culture, plus many links to the Oman websites
omanaccess.com Up to date community guide to Oman
omanforum.com Interactive forum on a variety of topics relevant to Oman
omanglobe.com News about the Middle East
omannews.com Oman News Agency; daily updates
omanobserver.com Daily newspaper
oman-radio.gov.om Oman radio broadcasts schedule
oman-tv.gov.om Oman TV programmes schedule
outpostoman.com Outpost Expatriate Network, for expats living or relocating abroad
rop.gov.om Royal Oman Police – visa information and viewing traffic fines
timesofoman.com Daily newspaper
radiomerge.fm English language radio station

LANGUAGE & CUSTOMS

Arabic is, of course, the official language in Oman, although English is widely spoken, particularly in the main towns and cities.

Other commonly heard languages include Urdu, Baluchi, Swahili, Hindi and a number of other Indian dialects.

BASIC ARABIC

General

Yes	*na'am*
No	*la*
Please	*min fadlak (m) / min fadliki (f)*
Thank you	*shukran*
Please (in offering)	*tafaddal (m) / tafaddali (f)*

Greetings

Greeting (peace be upon you)	*as-salaamu alaykom*
Greeting (in reply)	*wa alaykom is salaam*
Good morning	*sabah il-khayr*
Good morning (in reply)	*sabah in-nuwr*
Good evening	*masa il-khayr*
Good evening (in reply)	*masa in-nuwr*
Hello	*marhaba*
Hello (in reply)	*marhabtayn*
How are you?	*kayf haalak (m) / kayf haalik (f)*
Fine, thank you	*zayn, shukran (m) zayna, shukran (f)*
Welcome	*ahlan wa sahlan*
Welcome (in reply)	*ahlan fiyk (m) / ahlan fiyki (f)*
Goodbye	*ma is-salaama*

Introductions

My name is...	*ismiy...*
What is your name?	*shuw ismak (m) shuw ismik (f)*
Where are you from?	*min wayn inta (m) / min wayn inti (f)*
I am from...	*anaa min...*
America	*ameriki*
Britain	*braitani*
Europe	*oropi*
India	*al hindi*

Questions

How many / much?	*kam?*
Where?	*wayn?*
When?	*mataa?*
Which?	*ayy?*
How?	*kayf?*
What?	*shuw?*

Taxi Or Car Related

Is this the road to...	*hadaa al tariyq ila...*
Stop	*kuf*
Right	*yamiyn*
Left	*yassar*
Straight ahead	*siydaa*
North	*shamaal*
South	*januwb*
East	*sharq*
West	*garb*
Turning	*mafraq*
First	*awwal*
Second	*thaaniy*
Road	*tariyq*
Roundabout	*duwwaar*
Signals	*ishaara*
Close to	*qarib min*
Petrol station	*mahattat betrol*
Sea/beach	*il bahar*
Mountain/s	*jabal/jibaal*
Desert	*al sahraa*
Airport	*mataar*
Hotel	*funduq*

Accidents & Emergencies

Police	*al shurtaa*
Permit / licence	*rukhsaa*
Accident	*haadith*
Papers	*waraq*
Insurance	*ta'miyn*
Sorry	*aasif (m) / aasifa (f)*

Numbers

Zero	*sifr*
One	*waahad*
Two	*ithnayn*
Three	*thalatha*
Four	*arba'a*
Five	*khamsa*
Six	*sitta*
Seven	*saba'a*
Eight	*thamaanya*
Nine	*tiss'a*
Ten	*ashara*
Hundred	*miya*
Thousand	*alf*

ANNUAL EVENTS & PUBLIC HOLIDAYS

Oman hosts a number of annual events, some of which have been running for years. Here are some of the most popular.

PUBLIC HOLIDAYS

The Islamic calendar starts from the year 622AD, the year of Prophet Muhammad's migration (Hijra) from Mecca to Al Madinah. Hence, the Islamic year is known as the 'Hijri year' and, when written, dates are followed by the letters AH (AH stands for Anno Hegirae, meaning 'after the year of the Hijra').

As some holidays are based on the sighting of the moon and do not have fixed dates on the Hijri calendar, Islamic holidays are more often than not confirmed less than 24 hours in advance which can be a little confusing for those new to the region. Most companies send an email to employees the day before, notifying them of the confirmed holiday date. Some non-religious holidays are fixed according to the Gregorian calendar.

It should be noted that the public sector often gets additional days off for holidays where the private sector may not (for example on National Day the public sector gets two days of official holiday, whereas private sector companies take only one day). This can be a problem for working parents, as schools fall under the public sector and therefore get the extended holidays, so your children will usually have more days off than you do. No problem if you have full-time home help, but if not then you may have to take a day's leave.

The main Muslim festivals are Eid Al Fitr (the festival of the breaking of the fast, which marks the end of Ramadan) and Eid Al Adha (the festival of the sacrifice, which marks the end of the pilgrimage to Mecca). Mawlid Al Nabee is the holiday celebrating the Prophet Muhammad's birthday, and Lailat Al Mi'raj celebrates the Prophet's ascension into heaven.

Eid Al Fitr is a three-day holiday that celebrates the 'Feast of the Breaking of the Fast' at the end of the holy month of Ramadan. Later in the year, Eid Al Adha, meaning 'Feast of the Sacrifice', is a four-day holiday that marks the end of the annual pilgrimage to Mecca. The ritual traditionally involves the slaughtering of many animals and the giving of alms and food to the poor. The holiday is celebrated 70 days after Eid Al Fitr. Lailat al Mi'raj celebrates the Prophet's ascension into heaven.

Oman's National Day is on 18 November, as is His Majesty's Birthday. Celebrations take place with parades, fireworks, camel races and bullfights going on throughout the country. Over the summer months, Renaissance Day commemorates the accession of His Majesty Sultan Qaboos to the throne.

The table opposite lists the holidays and the number of days they last. This applies mainly to the public sector, so if you work in the private sector you may get fewer days per holiday.

Muscat Festival
JANUARY/FEBRUARY
Various locations, 80 077 222
muscat-festival.com
This is a 22 day event that is designed to showcase Oman's vibrant history and culture, as well as providing a boost to tourism in the sultinate. Organised by Muscat Municipality and running throughout January and February, the festival sees traditional dances, camel races, concerts, sporting and educational events held in different venues throughout Muscat. Some hotels and shopping centres run discounts to coincide with the festival.

PUBLIC HOLIDAYS

	2012	2013
Mawlid Al Nabee (1 day)	4 Feb (Moon)	24 Jan (Moon)
Lailat Al Mi'raj (1 day)	17 Jun (Moon)	05 Jun (Moon)
Renaissance Day (1 day)	23 Jul (Fixed)	23 Jul (Fixed)
Eid Al Fitr (3 days)	19 Aug (Moon)	08 Aug (Moon)
Arafat (Haj) Day (1 day)	25 Oct (Moon)	14 Oct (Moon)
Eid Al Adha (3 days)	26 Oct (Moon)	15 Oct (Moon)
Islamic New Year's Day (1 day)	15 Nov (Moon)	05 Nov (Moon)
National Day (1 + 2 days later in the month)	18 Nov (Fixed)	18 Nov (Fixed)
New Year (1 day)	1 Jan (Fixed)	1 Jan (Fixed)

Tour Of Oman

FEBRUARY

Various Locations, tourofoman.om
A preliminary to the gruelling European bicycle season, the Tour of Oman takes place over four days and uses the natural assets of Oman to their full. From flat and open sprints, to gruelling mountain climbs, the tour is regarded as a significant challenge to both riders and teams. Fans line to cheer on the peloton along the routes which appear in newspapers in advance.

Wadi Bih Run

FEBRUARY

The Golden Tulip Hotel & Resort, Dibba
wadibih.com
Each year, a couple of hundred teams (consisting of five members) head for Dibba to take part in one of the region's most unique sporting events – a 72km relay race along Musandam's most famous wadi and back. Runners compete one at a time, while the rest of the team follow in their 4WD. When all the teams (not to mention the handful of hardy souls who do the whole thing solo) are out in the wadi, it makes for a truly spectacular sight – especially as some run in fancydress. The race starts and ends at the Golden Tulip Dibba, with prize giving and festivities taking place around the pool.

Rally Oman

MARCH/APRIL

Various locations, omanauto.org
Oman's premier motorsport event is usually held in March or April (although related events take place throughout the year) over three days on 260km of timed gravel special stages around Muscat, with a three kilometre timed spectator stage at Maidan Al Fateh in Wattayah. International rally teams compete with local talent for victory. Family entertainment is also on offer including a freestyle motorcross competition, music concert and parachutists. Entrance is free.

Khanjars used in traditional celebrations

Fahal Island Swim
MAY
Various locations
muscatswimming.com
Petroleum Development Oman has been hosting this challenging, yet fun, competition every May since 1989. Brave competitors get up at 06:00 to swim four kilometres from Al Fahal Island to the Ras Al Hamra Recreation Centre beach. Anyone can participate; swimmers just need to fill in the entry form, pay the fee of RO 5 and organise boat support.

Fete de la Musique
JUNE
Various locations
ambafrance-om.org
Club Fete de la Musique, a traditional French festival of music which is organised by the French Embassy, is held every year on June 21. During the 2011 event, the embassy organised a concert by Racha Arodaky as part of an increased focus on the event.

Renaissance Day
JULY
Various locations
Held on 23 July each year, this day commemorates the accession of His Majesty Sultan Qaboos to the throne. The event is marked by a variety of festivities and a holiday for both the public and private sector.

Salalah Tourism Festival
JULY
Salalah
salalahfestival.com
Held each year in Salalah, from mid-July to the end of August, to celebrate the monsoon season . There are music and dance performances from different regions of Oman, the exhibition and sale of Omani handicrafts, and sports events. It is a chance to witness rare performances such as the Zanooj dance, which involves a cast of thousands.

Wahiba Challenge
NOVEMBER
Wahiba Sands
pdorc.com
Usually held in early winter, once the warmest months of the year have passed, this motorsports event involves competitors crossing the Wahiba Sands, from east to west, in a 4WD. The event is

organised by Ras Al Hamra – Off Road Adventure Club; the club emphasises that it is not a race, but rather a test of skill and endurance. Participants have to pick their ways across 31 dune ridges in the space of 60km! More information is available from the website.

Reunion d'Aventures Bike & Run
DECEMBER
Muscat
Reunion d'Aventures is the only major adventure-nature endurance competition which brings together contestants of different levels in a single event, but who share the same passion for nature, sport, exertion, team work and unexpected, unpredictable situations. For further details email omanadventure@aol.com.

Muscat Home Show
DECEMBER
Muscat
muscathomeshow.com
Covering everything from residential properties for sale, to interior design, fixtures and fittings, and the latest appliances, this is one of the biggest trade shows to take place in Oman.

Exhibitions
ALL YEAR ROUND
Oman International Exhibition Centre, 24 512 100
omanexhibitions.com
With the increasing importance of MICE (Meetings, Incentives, Conferences, Exhibitions) tourism to Oman, the government-owned Oman International Exhibition Centre has seen a full calendar lately. It is located a stone's throw from the Seeb International Airport and is adjacent to the Golden Tulip Seeb Airport Hotel. See their website for a monthly listing of exhibitions.

PDO Musical & Social Events
ALL YEAR ROUND
Various locations, 24 677 321
pdorc.com
The Ras al Hamra Recreation Club conducts a year-round calendar of events including sports, music and social welfare for members, and regularly ventures out in the community on for special events and occasions. Contact RAHRC (PDO club) office (24 677 321) for information.

Clockwise from top left: Royal Opera House Muscat, Muscat festival, camel racing

Camel Racing
DURING PUBLIC HOLIDAYS AND
NATIONAL DAY
Various locations,
omantourism.gov.om
Time spent watching this traditional
sport is never wasted as it is truly an
extraordinary experience. Races are spread
over several days, with different sprints
organised daily for different age groups of
camels. The camels are bred and trained
for racing; those with Omani bloodlines are
the most coveted. Winners can fetch up to
RO 250,000. Camel races are held at tracks
in As Seeb, Salalah, the interior and Batinah
regions during public holidays and National
Day celebrations. Admission is free.

Classical Music, Ballet & Opera
SEASONAL
**Royal Opera House Muscat,
Shati Al Qurm, 24 403 300**
rohmuscat.org.om
Opened in October 2011, and the first
location of its kind in the region, the
Royal Opera House hosts a variety of
classical music performances and recitals
throughout the year. The first season saw
Placido Domingo, Andrea Bocelli and the
Mariinsky Ballet all perform. Muscat's high
society comes out to parade on such events,
making the shows some of the most sought
after in town. Tickets for performances start
from around RO 15 for upper tier to RO 75
for a box, depending on the show.

Omani handicrafts

Bullfighting
DURING WINTER
**Barka, Seeb, Sohar & Al Sawadi
Various Locations**
In the true sense of the word, two
gargantuan Brahmin bulls butt heads and
lock blunt horns sumo-style until one of them
stumbles, flees or is knocked out of the arena.
Human handlers restrain over-aggressive
bulls rather than incite them, as the bulls
here are bred for fighting and winners can
fetch up to RO 2,500. Matches start at around
16:00 during the winter months in Barka and
As Seeb. Admission is free.

Horse Racing & Show Jumping
DURING WINTER
Muscat, 244 904 24
Oman is famous for its pure-bred Arabian
horses, which originate from Zad-ar-Raakib,
the stallion given by the Prophet Solomon
to the Azd tribe. The Oman Equestrian
Federation (24 490 424) organises the
Annual Royal Meeting national show
jumping competitions every winter, and
the Royal Equestrian Show every five years.
Both of these events take place at the Enam
Equestrian Grounds in Seeb.

Terry Fox Run
DATE VARIES
**The American International School
Of Muscat, Ghala**
terryfox.org
Each year, millions of people around the
world gather to raise money for cancer
research in the Terry Fox Run (named after
the courageous Canadian, Terry Fox, who
lost a leg to cancer and attempted to run
across Canada to raise funds and awareness).
Terry Fox Runs are casual affairs, and you
can complete the run on a bike, with a pram,
or even on rollerblades. The date of the
Oman Terry Fox Run changes each year so
check the website for details and organiser's
contact details.

Extreme Sailing Series
(TBA)
Various locations
extremesailingseries.com
Racing catamarans zip along the blue
waters just off the Omani coast, with
numerous World Championship and
Olympic sailors competing in this viewer-
friendly international sailing series. Two
Omani boats, called The Wave Muscat and
Masirah, regularly compete in the Extreme
Sailing Series.

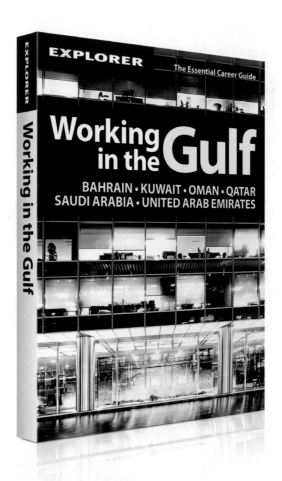

PLACES TO **STAY**

PLACES TO STAY

Luxury resorts, business hotels, apartments, cabins and even a spot of camping – Oman has something, and somewhere, for everyone.

HOTELS

Oman has no shortage of places to stay, from luxury hotels to hotel apartments, rest houses, officially approved campsites and even desert camps for tourists. However, the cheap and cheerful market is limited, so try some of the smaller hotels or rest houses for more competitive rates. Visitors can expect attractive promotions during the summer months when occupancy rates are lower. However, during peak times, such as the khareef in Salalah or festival time in Muscat, it can be difficult to find a room, and advance booking is a must.

Hotels In Al Awabi

Jabal Akhdar Hotel
Sayq Plateau Jabal Al Akhdar
25 429 009
Map **1 F4**
Perched 2,400m up on Jebel Akhdar ('the green mountain'), this sleepy hotel offers a friendly welcome to weary travellers and, although not luxurious by any means, it has everything a tired and hungry explorer could need for a night. Plus, the breakfast is hearty enough to set you on your way for another day of hiking, biking or off-roading.

Al Bustan Palace, A Ritz-Carlton Hotel

Hotels In Al Musanaah

Millennium Resort Mussanah
Wudam Al Sahil Al Musanaah
26 871 555
millenniumhotels.com
Map **1 F4**
The sprawling beachfront Millennium Resort offers 74 furnished apartments and 234 spacious rooms with large windows that let in the natural light and allow for great panoramic views of the 54 berth private marina. The resort also has two restaurants, one of which overlooks the delightful marina. There are many places of interest between 25km and 100km from Barka; for diving fanatics, the amazing Daymaniyat Islands offer coral gardens and numerous tropical fish, and are just a 10km boat ride away.

Hotels In Barka

Al Sawadi Beach Resort & Spa
Al Sawadi Jct 9kms Barka
26 795 545
alsawadibeach.com
Map **1 F4**
Visitors have the option of staying in one of the chalet-style rooms, or bringing a tent and camping on the private stretch of beach that enjoys access to the resort's ample facilities. Those facilities include a swimming pool and gym, mini golf, and tennis and squash courts. Watersports like windsurfing, waterskiing, jetskiing and kayaking are all available. The dive centre offers PADI courses, and organises regular dive trips.

Hotels In Khasab

Golden Tulip Khasab Hotel Resort
Khasab Main Rd Khasab **26 730 777**
goldentulipkhasab.com
Map **1 E1**
The Golden Tulip Khasab is situated in a small cove, right at the foot of Musandam's imposing mountains. Visitors can choose from guest rooms and suites, or opt instead for one of the independent chalets. The eating and drinking options here include a coffee shop, a nice pool terrace bar, a standard restaurant, the Oriental Café tent and Darts pub. There's a swimming pool and children's play area, and the hotel is extremely active in organising diving, fishing and dhow cruising trips for guests.

Khasab Hotel
Nr Khasab Airport, Musandam Khasab
26 730 271
khasabhotel.net
Map **1 E1**
A small, friendly place located in the centre of town, the hotel has a swimming pool and an international restaurant, with rooms split between the older poolside wing and a newer building. It's quite basic but clean and perfectly fine for a night or two.

Hotels In Muscat

Al Bandar
Shangri-La's Barr Al Jissah Resort & Spa
Al Jissah **24 776 666**
shangri-la.com
Map **1 G4**
Apart from the 195 rooms (all with balcony or terrace), the stunning Al Bandar also has eight food and beverage outlets, making it just as popular with residents as it is with tourists. In the heart of the Barr Al Jissah Resort, it has a souk area selling upmarket brands, art and crafts. A large swimming pool snakes around the hotel, with sunbeds immersed in water so that you can relax in cool comfort. There is also a Jacuzzi and a kids' pool.

Al Bustan Palace, A Ritz-Carlton Hotel
Nr Al Bustan R/A, Al Bustan St Haramil
24 799 666
ritzcarlton.com
Map **2 L4**
This award-winning hotel nestles in a coastal oasis of 200 acres, fronting rugged mountains and with its own private beach. The elegant Arab theme of the lobby carries over to its 250 suites, all with private balconies. There are four international restaurants, including one of the best Chinese restaurants in Oman (p.313).

Al Husn
Shangri-La's Barr Al Jissah Resort & Spa
Al Jissah **24 776 666**
shangri-la.com
Map **1 G4**
Resembling an Omani fort and built with luxury in mind, Al Husn is an escape from everyday life. Each of the 180 bedrooms has a balcony or terrace and bathrooms are designed to ensure you can see the sea from your bath (which your butler will run for you, should you so wish!). Al Husn has a private gym, a beach, an infinity pool and a library, as well as some excellent restaurants and bars.

Al Waha

Shangri-La's Barr Al Jissah Resort & Spa
Al Jissah **24 776 666**
shangri-la.com
Map **1 G4**
This is the largest of the hotels within Shangri-La's Barr Al Jissah Resort, with 302 bedrooms. Designed for families, kids will love the Little Turtles club, where they can play in air conditioned comfort or outdoors when temperatures allow. The hotel has numerous swimming pools, including a rubber-cushioned toddlers' pool and a kids' pool in the shape of a mushroom. Baby sitting services are available and adults are equally well served by the resort's eclectic mix of restaurants and bars.

The Chedi Muscat

18th November St, North Ghubra 32
Al Ghubrah Ash Shamaliyyah **24 524 400**
chedimuscat.com
Map **2 E3**
This beautiful and elegant hotel, regularly voted as among the world's very best, is designed for relaxation and pampering. Guests have the choice of 119 rooms or 32 private villas from which to contemplate Muscat's Hajar Mountains and the azure waters. There are spa facilities, two infinity pools, poolside cabanas and a private beach. The snappily-titled The Restaurant (p.321) offers excellent contemporary Asian and Mediterranean cuisine.

Crowne Plaza Muscat

Off Qurum St Al Qurm **24 660 660**
ichotelsgroup.com
Map **2 H2**
Located on a cliff overlooking Al Qurm town and beach, this hotel has one of the best views in Muscat. The pool seems to spill on to the beachfront below, which can be accessed by steps from the hotel gardens. It has three restaurants, including the excellent Iranian eatery Shiraz (p.324). There is a popular health club within the hotel.

Golden Tulip Seeb

Exhibition St Hay Al Urfan
24 510 300
goldentulipseeb.com
Map **2 C3**
This handy hotel is located just 1.5km from Muscat International Airport. Guests can enjoy private beach facilities (just a short hop across the road), and a host of other leisure facilities within the

hotel. There are 177 rooms, including six luxurious suites. Le Jardin restaurant serves international buffet cuisine 24 hours a day, and there is a bar where a live band performs most nights.

Grand Hyatt Muscat

Way 3032 Hay As Saruj **24 641 234**
muscat.grand.hyatt.com
Map **2 G2**
The decor is often described as 'Disneyland meets Arabia', but most of the Hyatt's 280 rooms have amazing sea views, while the hotel has a delectable range of dining options: Tuscany for Italian fare; Mokha Café for casual all-day dining; Marjan Beachfront Restaurant & Bar for food and drinks with a view, and the lively Copacabana nightclub (Muscat's most happening night spot, p.327).

Hotel Ibis Muscat

Azaiba Dohat Aladab Rd Al Khuwayr
Al Janubiyyah **24 489 890**
ibishotel.com
Map **2 F3**
This three star hotel is a 10 minute drive from the airport, just off the main Sultan Qaboos Highway in the Al Khuwair district. The hotel offers a restaurant, 24/7 snack service, laundry, business centre and fitness facilities. There are also four small meeting rooms available with complimentary Wi-Fi. Places of interest in the vicinity include the Grand Mosque, Qasr Al Alam Royal Palace and Al Jalali Fort.

InterContinental Muscat

Al Kharjiya St Hay As Saruj **24 680 000**
intercontinental.com
Map **2 G2**
The InterCon, as it's known, is popular with expat locals for its outdoor facilities, international restaurants, and pubs with regular live bands. Alfresco restaurant Tomato is a must-try, as is Trader Vic's with its legendary cocktails. Some of the 265 rooms have views of Qurm Beach.

Oman Dive Center

Bwn Qantab & Barr Al Jissah, Bandar Jussa Al Jissah **24 824 240**
Map **1 G4**
Nestled in a sheltered cove, this popular collection of barasti huts offers charming – if a little rustic – accommodation. Perfect for water babies, boat and diving trips can be arranged and the alfresco restaurant will keep your energy levels up.

Oman's hotels cater to all tastes and budgets

Park Inn By Radisson Muscat
Sultan Qaboos St Al Khuwayr
Al Janubiyyah **24 507 888**
parkinn.com
Map **2 F3**
In the main business district of Al Khuwair, the Park Inn is conveniently located just 15 minutes from Seeb International Airport and five minutes from the diplomatic area and beach. An appealing option, the biggest draws are the hotel's rooftop swimming pool and the state-of-the-art fitness centre, although guests in the 175 bright rooms and seven suites will also enjoy the mountain views, and snacks and drinks in the RBG bar and grill.

The Platinum
Nr Oman Oil Petrol Pump Al Khuwayr
Al Janubiyyah **24 392 500**
theplatinumoman.com
Map **2 F3**
One of the latest additions to Muscat's hotel scene, The Platinum is aimed predominantly at Gulf and Arab visitors (both in terms of architecture and its being unlicensed) and has 85 rooms and suites, a fine dining restaurant and Arab cafe, as well as a swimming pool, gym and steam room.

Radisson Blu Hotel, Muscat
Way 209 Al Khuwayr Al Janubiyyah
24 487 777
radissonblu.com
Map **2 F3**
Just 15 minutes from Muscat airport, this 142 room hotel stands out in the Al Khuwayr business district. Some rooms boast mountain views. Although predominantly a business hotel, there's a good health club and the steakhouse is a big draw for residents, as are the variety of lively bars.

Sheraton Oman Hotel
Street 40 Ruwi **24 772 772**
starwoodhotels.com
Map **2 K3**
One of the city's landmark hotels, the Sheraton is well located near to all the main tourist attractions. Its restaurants and bar are varied and excellent, attracting many locals as well as tourists. The hotel also has indoor and outdoor pools, a well-equipped gym, tennis courts, Jacuzzis and saunas. At the time of going to print, the hotel was undergoing extensive renovations, but was set to reopen by the end of 2012.

Sifawy Boutique Hotel > p.71
45km from Muscat Jebel Sifah
24 749 111
sifawyhotel.com
Map **2 F3**
Sifwa Boutique is a newly opened upmarket resort offering 55 air-conditioned rooms, including 30 suites, all opening onto private balconies with amazing coastal views. The resort is about 45 minutes from Muscat in a remote marine village, although the resort boasts two restaurants, an outdoor pool area, and a fitness centre as well as organising small shopping and nightlife events. Various other activities, such as scuba diving, snorkelling and tours, can also be organised.

Sifawy Boutique Hotel

SO, WANNA GO CAMPING?

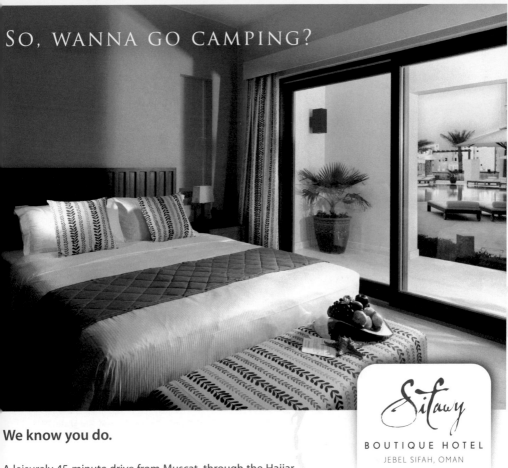

We know you do.

A leisurely 45-minute drive from Muscat, through the Hajjar mountain range, leads you to Oman's newest, and first, marina hotel; Sifawy. An away-from-it-all marina front hotel located within the Marina Town of Jebel Sifah. With 30 suites and 25 rooms, the ambiance is intimate, personal and warm.

Enjoy the beautiful scenery. Splash in the outdoor Jacuzzi. Relax and get pampered by the pool. Dine at the marina and explore a pristine world of beaches and sunshine. Come & discover Oman's newest Hotel.

Sifawy

BOUTIQUE HOTEL
JEBEL SIFAH, OMAN

SIFAWY BOUTIQUE HOTEL,
NOW OPEN IN MARINA TOWN, JEBEL SIFAH.

24749111 | RESERVATIONS@SIFAWYHOTEL.COM
WWW.SIFAWYHOTEL.COM

JEBEL SIFAH
A MURIYA DEVELOPMENT

Six Senses Zighy Bay

Hotels In Musandam

Six Senses Zighy Bay > p.73
Zighy Bay, Musandam Daba
267 355 555
sixsenses.com/sixsenseszighybay
Map **1 E2**
Located in one of Musandam's most secluded coves, this uber-luxurious resort may have been designed in a rustic style but it offers nothing but relaxed extravagance. Made up of individual pool villas, like all Six Senses resorts the focus here is on pampering. Expertly prepared dinners can be enjoyed from the comfort of your own villa – each villa also has its own splash pool – or from the mountainside restaurant with its breathtaking views of the bay. The spa treatments available are, of course, also of the highest quality. This is a hideaway like no other.

Hotels In Nizwa

Al Diyar Hotel
Nizwa **25 412 402**
aldiyarhotel.com
Map **1 F5**
Located just outside Nizwa city centre, this hotel offers a relatively comfortable but uncomplicated stay, with basic facilities that include a swimming pool, a gym, a Lebanese restaurant and an internet cafe.

Single, double and triple rooms and suites are available.

Falaj Daris Hotel
Nr Nizwa Souk Nizwa **25 410 500**
falajdarishotel.com
Map **1 F5**
Set amidst nicely landscaped gardens, with two outdoor pools, a play area and a gym, Falaj Daris Hotel is decently appointed if basic, with 55 rooms, two suites, and a few creature comforts like a restaurant, bar, aircon and satellite TV. It's also just a couple of minutes' drive from the town centre.

Golden Tulip Nizwa Hotel
150 kms from Muscat, Nr Hajar Mountains Nizwa **25 431 616**
goldentulipnizwa.com
Map **1 F5**
The Golden Tulip Nizwa benefits from a picturesque setting with landscaped gardens and the Hajar Mountains in the distance. There are 40 guest rooms, all with private access to the central swimming pool. The Birkat Al Mawz restaurant serves international cuisine and the hotel has two comfortable bars.

Hotels In Salalah

Crowne Plaza Resort Salalah
Al Khandaq St, Dahritz Salalah
23 238 000
ichotelsgroup.com
Map **4 K8**
Set in a private garden beside the sea, this hotel features 119 rooms and nine suites. There are three pools, kids' facilities and entertainment, health and fitness facilities and a miniature golf course. Guests have three restaurants to choose from, including the excellent Dolphin Beach Restaurant that offers alfresco dining with stunning views of the white sands and Indian Ocean.

Hamdan Plaza Hotel
Al Wadi St Salalah **23 211 025**
hamdanplazahotel.com
Map **4 F7**
Although not a luxury resort, this three-star hotel certainly fits into the 'comfortable' category, with a variety of rooms and suites, gym and pool, and Wi-Fi throughout. There's an international and an Oriental restaurant on, with drinks available in rooms. It also has a great location near the ocean and airport.

nature is your playground

SIX SENSES
Zighy Bay

For reservations: +968 26735 888
Zighy Bay, Musandam Peninsula, Sultanate of Oman
www.SixSenses.com/SixSensesZighyBay
Facebook.com/SixSensesZighyBay | Twitter.com/ZighyBay

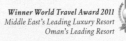

Winner World Travel Award 2011
Middle East's Leading Luxury Resort
Oman's Leading Resort

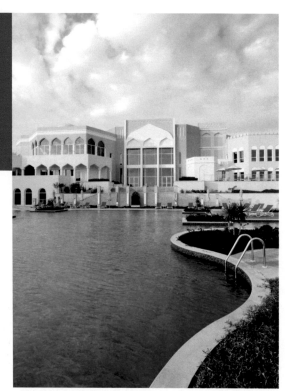
Salalah Marriott Resort

more athletically inclined, there are tennis courts, diving facilities, an outdoor pool and a well-stocked gym. The resort is just 25km from the Unesco site of Khor Rori.

Hotels In Sur

Sur Plaza Hotel
Sur Main Rd Sur **25 543 777**
omanhotels.com
Map **1 H5**
A few kilometres from Sur, this hotel is a perfect base from which to explore the surrounding area, including the turtle nesting sites at Ras Al Hadd and Ras Al Jinz. The hotel offers 108 well-appointed guest rooms, and has a swimming pool, health club and gym. Dining options include Oysters Restaurant, and two bars.

OTHER PLACES TO STAY

Hotel Apartments
Al Khuwair Hotel Apartments Al Khuwayr Al Janubiyyah, 24 697 171, *safeerhotel.net*
Beach Hotel Apartments Shati Al Qurm, 24 696 601, *omanbeachhotel.com*
Dhofar Park Inn International Salalah, 23 292 272
Esra Hotel Apartments Khasab, 26 730 562, *khasabtours.com*
Hala Hotel Apartments Ruwi, 24 810 442
Khuwair Hotel Apartments Al Khuwayr Al Janubiyyah, 24 789 199
Manam Hotel Apartments Al Wutayyah, 24 571 555, *manamhotel.com*
Nuzha Hotel Apartments Darsayt, 24 602 355, *safeerhospitality.com.om*
Safeer Hotel Suites Al Khuwayr Al Janubiyyah, 24 691 200, *safeerintll.com*
Samharam Tourist Resort Salalah, 23 211 420, *shanfarihotels.com*
Seeb International Hotel As Seeb, 24 543 800, *seebinternational.com*
Sohar Hotel Apartments Sohar, 24 703 844

Guest Houses
Al Qabil Rest House 25 581 243
Extra Divers Villa Khasab, 26 730 501, *musandam-diving.com/villa*
Ghaba Rest House Muscat-Salalah Highway, 99 358 639

Hilton Salalah Resort
Sultan Qaboos St Salalah **23 211 234**
salalah.hilton.com
Map **4 D9**
This is the only five-star hotel in Dhofar and also one of the newest. Its simple Omani-style exterior hides a luxurious domed lobby and mirror-like marble floors. Its beachfront location, 12km from Salalah centre, allows guests to truly get away from it all and enjoy the hotel's facilities. There are three international restaurants, two entertainment outlets, a health spa and a doctor on call.

Salalah Marriott Resort > *p.75*
Salalah Beach Mirbat **23 268 245**
marriottsalalahresort.com
Map **1 C11**
This five star resort is located an hour from Salalah. It has 170 rooms and 67 suites with balconies overlooking the pool, beach and Indian Ocean. There is a wide range of facilities and activities within the resort, with the health and wellness centre and spa particularly popular. For the

CAMPING

Camping is an extremely popular pastime among both the Omani people and the expat community, thanks mainly to it being extremely easy, with few rules about where you can and can't camp. Should you be tired and need a place to catch 40 winks after a long day of driving or hiking, it really is as easy as pulling off the road, finding a suitably flat place and pitching your tent.

Beach and wadi camping (never camp in the wadi bed itself as flash floods can occur even when you least expect them) are best in winter, because their low altitudes mean the summer months are just too hot. The mountains, however, can be lovely during the summer months, because at altitude the temperatures remain lower for longer. Also, it is advisable to shy away from the mountains during the coldest months (November to February) as temperatures can drop to below zero; believe it or not, it has even been known to snow on Jebel Akhdar and Jebel Shams.

The most popular beach areas to camp in are Tiwi, Fins, Ras Al Jinz and Bandar Khayran. Tiwi and Fins are easily accessed by car, but both can be quite busy, especially during holiday weekends, so it is best to leave early to secure your space on the beach. You can't simply arrive and erect your tent in Ras Al Jinz, as much of the beach is a protected nature conservation area, so you'll need to head for the allocated camp site which is a fair distance from the actual beach.

The easiest way to get to Bandar Khairan, meanwhile, is by boat. You should find a boat at Qantab and it will cost about RO5, but it is always best to negotiate the price with the boatman first. The boatman will take you and your luggage to a small secluded beach, where you will be able to stay for as long as you want. Arrange a time for the boatman to collect you; be sure to pay him on the return journey.

Camping near wadis is as easy as driving down the wadi in your 4WD, stopping, and then finding a comfortable but raised place on the banks well above the wadi where you can pitch your tents and spend the night. In the *Oman Off-road Explorer*, you'll find several routes dedicated to some of the more picturesque wadis in Oman. Although they are all worth a visit, some of the best to visit and camp at are Snake Gorge, Wadi Al Abyadh and Wadi Dhaiqah.

Jebel Akhadar and Jebel Shams also have places for camping and, again, as with any mountain camping, try to do it during the spring to autumn months. The main problem with mountain camping is pegging your tent down, so remember to take a hammer with you for knocking pegs into the dirt or, alternatively, rocks or bags and buckets of sand can help you weigh down and secure your tent.

Finding good camping equipment in Oman is just as straightforward as finding a campsite. There are numerous outlets that sell camping gear, with the best place arguably the Sultan Center which has everything you could ever need for one night of roughing it through to a full week of luxury camping. Carrefour and Lulu's also stock good ranges of camping equipment.

The dome style tent, in various sizes, is the most readily available, although you will find some small, mountain style hiking tents here and there if you look carefully. Gas bottles and all the accessories that go with them can also be purchased in all of the stores mentioned.

If you prefer traditional barbecuing when out camping, you can either build a small fire using whatever you can find in the area along with some kind of grill or, easier, take a small barbecue and the necessary charcoal or wood with you. Again, Carrefour and Lulu's will have everything you need from the BBQ to lighter fluid and utensils.

In conclusion, camping is one of the great Omani experiences, as you are not hampered by the rules and regulations that you would face in most other countries. It is a taste of something more real and basic, in that you won't readily find a camping spot with electricity and you're unlikely to see anyone towing a caravan or trailer. All that is necessary for a great, and cheap, weekend is a full cooler box, a tent, a barbecue and a sense of adventure.

1000 Nights Camp

Bidiyyah **99 448 158**
1000nightscamp.com
Map **1 G5**

Located in the heart of the Wahiba Sands, 1000 Nights is camping with more than a touch of luxury thrown in. Tents, although based on traditional Bedouin tents, are semi-permanent with shared bathroom services. There's even an onsite pool,

ON THE DESERT TRAIL
You can't live in, or even holiday in, Oman without experiencing the vast, dramatic majesty of the desert; waking up to a fierce red sunrise between a set of dramatic dunes is a unique Arabian experience. But, if adventure is something you think is best served up, well, by others, then there are plenty of 'luxury camping' venu-es (such as the Desert Nights Camp, pictured) scattered throughout the Wahiba Sands, offering everything from proper toilet facilities to restaurants and bars.

restaurant with terrace and a conference centre. All the nearby desert activities make it as popular for teambuilding as for adventurous family holidays.

Al Areesh Camp
Wahiba/Sharqiyah Sands Al Qabil
92 402 414
areeshcamp.com
Map **1 G5**
The campsite at the Al Areesh resort in the Wahiba Sands allows you to get away from it all in a peaceful 'back to nature' environment – while still enjoying a good level of luxury, certainly by any camper's standards. The camp consists of 12 tents with camp-style beds. Meals are prepared on site and cooked over open fires.

Al Naseem Camp
Wahiba Sands Bidiyyah **99 328 858**
Map **1 G6**
This is a great base camp if you plan to go turtle watching, because it is just four minutes away from the Ras Al Jinz nature reserve. And it's even greater if you're the type of camper who needs running water, flushing toilets and hot showers nearby – Al Naseem has all of these, as well as electric lighting, soft mattresses (single beds only), and continental breakfasts! What makes it really special is the spacious entertainment area, covered in palm fronds, where you can dine and lounge on carpets and cushions in true Omani style.

Al Raha Tourism Camp
Wahiba Sands Bidiyyah **99 343 851**
alrahaoman.com
Map **1 G5**
This desert camp in the Wahiba Sands offers visitors a chance to sample a tourist-friendly version of Bedouin life – as well as to dabble in some dune buggy driving, dune bashing in 4WDs, sandboarding and, of course, go on a camel ride. Accommodation is in clean but basic concrete rooms with an attached toilet, or Bedouin-style tents with communal bathrooms. The meals are generally buffets, set out beneath the stars in an open courtyard that is also the venue for live music and entertainment.

Desert Camp
Wahiba Sands Bidiyyah **99 311 338**
Map **1 G5**
Desert Camp lies about 220km from Muscat and is a good opportunity to get a taste of Omani hospitality. You can choose to sleep in a Bedouin tent, but they have single bedrooms and rest rooms for men and women available too. Breakfast and dinner are included. Dinner usually takes place under the stars where you're often treated to traditional music. Various activities available in the camp include dunebashing, camel rides, desert cycles for the kids, or even a desert crossing on foot with an experienced guide.

Desert Nights Camp
Nr Sand Coloured Mosque, 11 km from Al Wasil Bidiyyah **92 818 388**
desertnightscamp.com
Map **1 G5**
The ultimate chic camping experience, this camp is around two hours from Muscat in the Wahiba Sands and gives visitors a taste of Bedouin life and a slice of luxury. The 30 tents boast en-suite bathrooms, aircon and mini bars, while there's an onsite restaurant and bar, as well as traditional camp fire entertainment. Ideal for the adventurous, visitors can enjoy everything from henna tattoos and star gazing to camel safaris, dune bashing, quad biking and excursions to Wadi Bani Khalid.

Jabel Shams Base Camp
Nizwa Jabel Shams **96 566 600**
jabelshams.com
Map **1 F5**
Perched on the mountainside of Jebel Shams – the Gulf's highest peak at around 3,000m – this camp is ideal for adventurers looking to scale the summit or explore the amazing hiking trails that wind across the range. There are 15 Bedouin-style tents with shower and toilet facilities, six family rooms, a 'wild' camping area and even a restaurant and BBQ terrace. The views are, understandably, among the best you'll find anywhere in the Middle East.

Safari Desert Camp
25km from Al Ghabbi, Wahiba Sands Bidiyyah **92 000 592**
safaridesert.com
Map **1 G6**
Another permanent camp that uses Bedouin-style tents, each with its own attached toilet facilities. Located in the Wahiba Sands, there are several activities on offer here, such as henna by the camp fire and dinner in the majlis BBQ restaurant, while several excursions can also be arranged.

explorer

there's more to life...

FOR ADVENTURE SEEKERS

EXPLORER 26 ADVENTUROUS ROUTES

UAE OFF-ROAD

UAE

off-road

GPS

EXPLORER 26 ADVENTUROUS ROUTES

OMAN OFF-ROAD

Oman

off-road

GPS

Sponsored by

askexplorer.com/shop

  askexplorer

LIVING IN **OMAN**

LIVING IN OMAN

Everything you need to consider, do, and apply for if you've decided it's time for a new life in the Sultanate of Oman.

CONSIDERING OMAN

While some expats come to live in Oman for a fixed term, there are many thousands of foreigners who stay for much longer periods and are in no hurry to move. And it's not hard to see why: sunshine almost every day of the year, great leisure facilities, a beautiful mix of scenery (ocean, mountain, desert, greenery), luxurious hotels and their top-notch in-house restaurants, and a pace of life that is neither too hectic nor too boring. And to top it all, the salaries are tax-free.

This said, moving to a new country nearly always involves an element of stress. However, once you get over the initial culture shock, most expats discover that Oman is a relaxed and friendly country; it is modern (and developing all the time), and yet it still retains a certain charm from the past that is unique to the region.

One of Oman's greatest assets is its people, who are warm and welcoming, and who have a long history of fascinating traditions. You'll also find a large group of friendly expats, and before you know it you'll meet loads of people. Remember that rules and regulations change frequently in this part of the world, so keep your eye on the local press and be prepared for the unexpected.

NOT THE BEST, NOT THE WORST

Mercer's 'Quality of Living' index measures the quality of living for expatriates based on 39 criteria grouped into 10 categories. This entails assessing the degree to which expatriates enjoy the standard of living in each host nation, factoring in the interaction of political, socio-economic and environmental factors in the host location. In 2011, Mercer ranked 221 cities throughout the world. For 'quality of living', Muscat ranked 101st while, for 'personal safety', it ranked at an impressive 29th position, mainly due to its internal stability and low crime levels.

BEFORE YOU ARRIVE

Some people love expat life and take to it like a duck to water, but there are equally a few who never manage to adjust. Therefore, it is not always a good decision to cut all ties with your home country (like selling your property and closing your bank accounts) before you've tested the waters for a year or so. However, you will need to get your financial affairs in order, particularly if you have to continue paying tax in your home country.

If you have accepted a job offer in Oman, most of the administrative tasks will be taken care of by your employer, but you might still want to visit the country before you take up your post to look at houses and schools. If you have children of school-going age, you will need to start investigating schools straight away. There are not many schools to choose from and with Muscat expanding all the time, some schools are running out of places in certain age groups. See p.136 for a rundown of the nursery, primary and secondary schools in Muscat.

If you negotiate your contract well, you will have made provision for shipping costs – both for when you arrive and when you leave. If you are staying for more than a year, it is probably well worth it to ship out some of your belongings, as this can make you feel at home sooner.

If you are seriously considering moving to Oman, there is lots of paperwork to be taken care of but your employer will almost always do this on your behalf – leaving you to worry about more important things like whether you've got enough summer clothes in your wardrobe.

It's a good idea to get a big batch of passport photos taken before you arrive. You will need countless passport photos over the coming months, as just about every procedure requires at least one. You'll also need plenty of passport copies.

Mutrah Corniche

It is unusual for people to arrive in Oman on a visit visa to look for work – most people already have jobs lined up before they arrive. However, if you are coming to Oman to look for work, do your research before you arrive. Contact recruitment agencies and sign up with online job sites as far in advance as possible. There may also be agencies in your home country that specialise in overseas recruitment.

WHEN YOU ARRIVE

The list of things you'll have to deal with in the first few weeks can be a little daunting, and you may well be in for a lot of form filling, queuing, and coming and going. Try not to let it spoil your first impressions of the country though, because hopefully you'll soon be a fully fledged resident enjoying your new life, and all that boring bureaucracy will be a distant memory.

For many procedures you'll have to produce your 'essential documents'. At the very least, these are:
- Original passport
- Passport copies (including photo page and visa page)
- Passport photos
- Copy of labour card (if you are working)
- Copy of sponsorship certificate for non-working residents

Some nationalities also need to get a health certificate from their home country, stating that they are free from illness and not carrying any communicable diseases.

RESIDENCY VISAS

For foreigners to live and work in Oman, they must usually be sponsored by an employer or family member. To obtain a residency visa as an employee, you need a local sponsor and a labour permit from the Ministry of Manpower. The requirements vary by nationality and are subject to change at short notice, so it's always best to check with your embassy.

Once your employer sponsors you, you can then arrange sponsorship for your family members. Two family sponsorship options are available: a family joining visa or a family residence visa. Children under the age of 21 years can be sponsored. Expats may also be eligible to apply for a Contractor Visa or an Investor Resident Visa – refer to the website of the Royal Oman Police (rop.gov.om) to get the latest information on visitor visas, residence permits and employment, investor or student visas.

Residence Visa

Before getting a visa you must get a no objection certificate (NOC). This is an official document stating that neither your Omani sponsor nor the government has any objection to your entering the country. There are two types of residence visas – one for employment (when you are sponsored by your employer) and one for residence only (when you are sponsored by a family member).

Your sponsor should organise everything related to your visa, including payment. On arrival your company's PRO or your sponsor will take you to the Royal Oman Police (ROP) station on Death Valley Road to be fingerprinted. Those working must have labour clearance and an employment residence visa; spouses and family members are each issued with a 'joining family' residence visa. It is illegal to work on a joining family residence visa, even part time. If you wish to work you must get an employment visa. If you are working for the same sponsor as your spouse, exchanging the visa is usually a simple process. If you obtain a job elsewhere, you must transfer sponsorship to your new employer and go through the whole process from the beginning. Your new sponsor will do what's necessary.

It is advisable, if possible, to try to avoid doing this (or anything which requires the involvement of government departments) during Ramadan, when everything tends to slow down until after Eid, by which time there will be a huge backlog. The ROP is located near Muscat Private School on Madinat A'Sultan Qaboos Street (Death Valley Road), and the phone number is 24 600 099.

Most expats seeking employment or applying for residency in Oman must have a health certificate from their home country, stating that they are free from illness and not carrying any communicable diseases. UK citizens are currently exempt, although this could change at any time.

Sponsorship By Employer

Your employer should handle all the paperwork, and will usually have a staff member (who is thoroughly familiar with the procedure) dedicated to this task alone. This staff member is usually called the PRO, which stands for public relations officer. After your residency is approved, they should then apply directly for your labour clearance. You will need to supply the essential documents (p.83) and your education certificates. You must have all your certificates attested by a solicitor or public notary in your home country and then by your foreign office to verify the solicitor as bona fide. The Oman embassy in your country of residence must also sign the documents. While this sounds like a run around, it is much easier if you get this done before you arrive in Oman.

Family Sponsorship

Once you are sponsored by your employer, you can then arrange sponsorship for your family members. Again, most employers will help you with this task. If yours doesn't, the process can be lengthy and tedious. There are two family sponsorship options available – a family joining visa or a family residence visa.

A family joining visa is for your spouse and children only (children cannot be older than 21 years).

The family residence visa is for relatives that do not fall into the family joining visa category, such as siblings or elderly parents. Brothers and sisters of the resident must be younger than 18 years, and a document must be provided stating that there is no other family income outside Oman. People on family sponsorship may not work in Oman, paid or unpaid. Once a visa has been granted, the holder has up to six months from the date of issue to enter Oman. The visa is valid for two years from the date of entry. This visa is renewable and allows multiple entries.

DRIVING LICENCE

Visitors may drive a hired or borrowed car on a valid international or home country licence for up to three months but, if you're staying for longer, you'll need to transfer your driving licence into an Omani one. You must be a resident to apply for a driving licence. Residents from many countries, including the UK and US, may simply exchange their national licence for an Oman one at Death Valley Road traffic police headquarters. To do this, you will have to have an eye test, and pay the fee of RO 20.

The following documents are required for a licence exchange:
- A licence exchange form bearing your sponsor's signature and the company stamp
- A copy of your passport and residence permit

POLICE PORTAL

The Royal Oman Police website – rop.gov.om – is an excellent site where you can find either online applications or step-by-step procedures for many of the confusing red tape matters you'll face in Oman. There, you can do everything from learning how to get a UAE road visa or a Police Clearance Certificate, to reading safety tips and regional information, or even paying traffic fines and enquiring about your visa status.

- Your original (home) driving licence along with a copy. The foreign licence must have been issued at least one year back
- Blood group certificate

If you're not from an 'exchange' country and need to apply for an Omani licence, you'll need to be at least 18 years old, free of any handicap that could hamper your ability to drive, and you'll need to pass the eyesight test. You then require:

- Two passport photos
- An application form
- A copy of your ID card or passport
- A letter of no objection from your sponsor
- A blood group certificate
- A copy of your residence permit

Your company PRO should take you to the police station and help you through the process of licence exchange or test booking. Always carry your driving licence when driving; you may be fined if you fail to produce it during a spot check. Driving licences are valid for 10 years and can be renewed at traffic police HQ on Death Valley Road.

LIQUOR LICENCE

If you want to buy alcohol you'll need a liquor licence and only non-Muslim residents in possession of a labour card are allowed to apply. Equally, for married couples, only the husband can apply, and his wife cannot use the licence to buy alcohol unless he works in the interior. Licences are valid for two years, but can't be used outside of the city in which they were issued.

Your liquor licence permits you to buy a limited amount of alcohol each month; this allowance is calculated based on your salary, and is usually not more than 10% of it. You can apply for a larger allowance if you feel you've certain extraordinary circumstances (for example, if your job entails corporate entertaining).

WHEN YOU LEAVE

Before jetting off, there are certain things that have to be wound up before you leave Oman for good. You will have to disconnect your electricity and water supply (p.104) and get your security deposit back from your landlord (minus any damages).

You will also have to sell your car – not always an easy task, and used car dealers have learned to smell a departing expat a mile away, so be prepared for some very low offers.

You will probably then need to ship your household contents back home, and sell whatever you are not taking with you. The more notice you can give the shipping company, the better. For a list of companies, see p.103.

If you are selling loads of stuff, you can put a notice up on the community noticeboards (they can be found near Al Fair supermarkets in MSQ centre and Sarooj Centre). Alternatively, arrange and advertise a garage sale or list your items on sites such as omanbay.com or muscatads.com.

COMBAT CULTURE SHOCK

Knowing as much about Oman as possible before you get here is a good way to help reduce culture shock. This book, of course, is one of the most comprehensive sources of information, but you may also find the websites listed on p.52 of some interest.

HOUSING

If you are arriving in Oman on a full expat package then accommodation is usually included in your employment contract. Some companies provide a cash allowance to spend on rent, some let you choose a property and then they liaise directly with the landlord and make the payment on your behalf, and some companies provide staff accommodation on a compound. Most expats find themselves living in the capital, Muscat, where good quality apartments can be found all over the city. The main areas are Muscat, Mutrah, Ruwi, Wattayah, Qurm, Shati Al Qurm, Madinat Sultan Qaboos (MSQ), Al Khuwayr, Ghubbrah, Azaibah and Seeb. Muscat's hilly terrain means that people living on the top floors usually have a great view, while expat families more commonly prefer one of the many villas. The cost of accommodation is relatively high and, as the city is spread out over a large area, it pays to consider commuting distances when choosing where to live.

RESIDENTIAL AREAS

Once you have received confirmation that you are relocating to Oman, it can be difficult to choose which residential area you would prefer to live in.

Of course, your budget may affect your decision, and you may decide to live in an area that is a little further out of town and therefore a bit cheaper. You should also consider closeness to schools (if you have children) – the traffic situation in Muscat is gradually worsening with the rising population and you don't want to get stuck in a jam every morning on your school run.

Also important is the proximity of entertainment venues – if you've got an exorbitant taxi fare to pay every time you go out anywhere it might deter even the most social of butterflies.

That said, every area of Muscat has its advantages and disadvantages, and with Muscat being a relatively small city you should be able to get to most places in less than half an hour, no matter where you live.

The following pages will give you some insight into the various residential areas, but remember that nothing beats getting in the car and exploring on your own.

Latest Muriya development

ON THE SHOPPING TRAIL...

THE ULTIMATE SHOPPING ADVENTURE
THE ONE-STOP SHOPPING DESTINATION
FOR ALL YOUR WANTS AND NEEDS

مركز البهجة
Markaz Al Bahja

Family Friends & You

Location: Seeb | Tel.: 24540 200 | Timing: 10am - 10pm
www.albahja.com

MUSCAT
RESIDENTIAL AREAS

Gulf of Oman

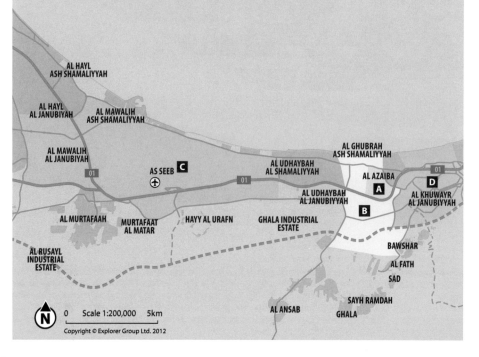

AL HAYL
ASH SHAMALIYYAH

AL HAYL
AL JANUBIYAH

AL MAWALIH
ASH SHAMALIYYAH

AL MAWALIH
AL JANUBIYAH

01

AS SEEB **C**

AL GHUBRAH
ASH SHAMALIYYAH

AL UDHAYBAH
AL SHAMALIYYAH

AL AZAIBA

A

01

D

AL UDHAYBAH
AL JANUBIYYAH

AL KHUWAYR
AL JANUBIYYAH

01

B

AL MURTAFAAH

MURTAFAAT
AL MATAR

HAYY AL URAFN

GHALA INDUSTRIAL
ESTATE

BAWSHAR

AL RUSAYL
INDUSTRIAL
ESTATE

AL FATH

SAD

SAYH RAMDAH

N

0   Scale 1:200,000   5km

AL ANSAB

GHALA

Copyright © Explorer Group Ltd. 2012

Gulf of Oman

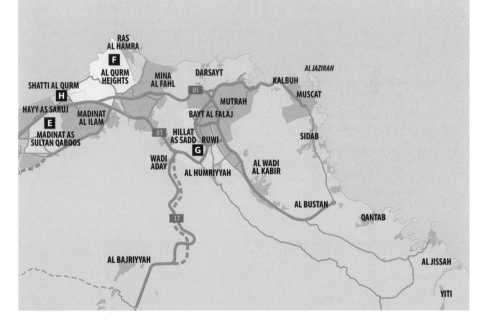

AL AZAIBA
Map 2 E3

Al Azaiba merges with Al Ghubbrah to the east and As Seeb to the west and is mostly a residential area but is fast becoming a business district.

Best Points
The beautiful long stretch of beach is a big plus.

Worst Points
There are not many shops or amenities. This is changing however because of its growing popularity.

Accommodation
Large villas on the beach are sought after and prices are very steep. Old and new villas are available with gardens or paved areas and maid's accommodation. Some landlords can smell a naive expat a mile away and may quote you an inflated price if they think you don't know better, so do some price comparisons before you agree to anything.

Shopping & Amenities
There are plenty of shops in neighbouring areas to keep you in stock of everything, but nothing of note locally apart from a few large car dealerships and service centres which line the road parallel to the highway, and the Al Safeer supermarket. The TSC supermarket is nearby as well as the recently opened Al Fair, both located on November 18 Street.

Entertainment & Leisure
Endless sandy beaches will keep you busy outdoors. There is not much in the way of dining or nightlife in the area, but it is a short drive to some great restaurants in neighbouring areas.

Healthcare
There are no clinics or hospitals to speak of in the area, although you'll find plenty of medical facilities a short drive away.

Education
Nurseries are popping up all over the place.

Traffic & Parking
Al Azaiba is mostly a residential area, so you won't face too much frustration on the roads. Parking is easy to find. However, there is ongoing construction which might lead to diversions and occasional delays.

Safety & Annoyances
Lurking youths 'hanging out' and stray dogs roaming around are the two main annoyances, but as long as you pick your neighbourhood carefully you should be fine. Stray dogs are usually dealt with by the ROP.

AL GHUBRAH ASH SHAMALIYYAH & BAWSHAR
Map 2 E3

This area covers a large expanse from the beach to the mountains and is in easy reach of many businesses and the main Sultan Qaboos highway.

Best Points
The scenery in Bawshar is fantastic.

Worst Points
Peak-hour traffic congestion and ongoing road works make this a hotspot for traffic jams.

Accommodation
Accommodation is mainly two-storey villas, with a few apartment blocks above the shops and businesses in Ghubbrah. Rents are lower in Bawshar and you have the advantage of a spectacular view of the sand dunes and mountains. Oasis Residence has some options for shopping, eating out, plus a bakery and health club. The Dolphin Complex is also popular with families because of the leisure club facilities (including pool, tennis court and gym), the safe outdoor play area for kids and licensed restaurant.

Shopping & Amenities
The biggest and best supermarket in Muscat – Lulu Center – is located just off the Bawshar Roundabout, between Bawshar and Ghubbrah. There is also a variety of small shops in Ghubbrah selling everything from fabrics to fertiliser. While this means you can usually buy essential items at all hours, it also results in a certain amount of traffic congestion, particularly at peak times.

Entertainment & Leisure
There are three hotels in the area: the Bowshar Hotel, Park Inn and The Chedi. The Bowshar is basic and not a particularly great haunt for western expats, while The Chedi is spectacular in its understated Zen-

like architecture and superbly decadent restaurant. The Chedi also has one of Oman's most popular and luxurious spas. Park Inn is a great business hotel with a rooftop pool and several restaurants.

Healthcare
Muscat Private Hospital – the main healthcare choice for expats – is here. It offers a complete range of inpatient and outpatient facilities, and has a 24-hour emergency room (24 583 600). Al Raffah Hospital also offers surgical, inpatient, outpatient and diagnostic care (24 618 900 /1/2/3/4). See p.142 for more information.

Education
There are various Arabic and Indian schools in the area, but no education facilities for western expat children.

Traffic & Parking
The Ghubbrah Roundabout has undergone construction to ease the flow of heavy traffic, which usually congests the area. The smaller 'Sail' roundabout is now a junction for the same reason. At peak times (mornings, lunch times and evenings) you might find a few traffic backups that could delay you for five minutes or so.

Safety & Annoyances
Construction in Ghubbrah can really slow down traffic.

AS SEEB
Map 1 G4
This is not usually the first choice for expats when looking for a home, mainly due to the distance from the city centre and all the facilities they will probably desire (such as schools and medical services). However, many are now moving to the area due to lack of accommodation in other parts of town and low prices.

Best Points
Lower rents and larger houses, and some of Muscat's best shopping right on your doorstep.

Worst Points
The out of town location means lots of time in the car and expensive taxi fares.

Accommodation
Rents are a little lower this side of the airport, and villas are spacious with more

likelihood of a small garden or paved area outside. If you don't mind travelling a few extra minutes in the car, this is a great opportunity to live in a much bigger villa at a lower price.

Shopping & Amenities
It doesn't get much better than having Muscat's two largest shopping malls right there on your doorstep. Markaz Al Bahja (p.297) and Muscat City Centre (p.297) both have all the large shops you will need, and you will also find plenty of smaller local shops in As Seeb town and Seeb souk itself. As Seeb is home to all the city's main garden centres, which are actually all located in a row on the same street. Park at one end and walk down.

Entertainment & Leisure
There is a cinema in Markaz Al Bahja Centre, as well as a superb play area that will keep your kids busy all year round. This is particularly useful during summer, but it's also popular during the cooler months, when there is plenty of white sandy beach nearby to have fun on, as well as a beachpark. The Golden Tulip Seeb is predominantly a business hotel, although it does have a few restaurants, including one on the roof which is an excellent venue in winter. The hotel has some good leisure facilities. The Seeb International Exhibition Centre is nearby.

Healthcare
The area is home to various small clinics offering private outpatient treatment to all nationalities. It is also the location of the Sultan Qaboos University Hospital, which is not usually available to expats unless you require treatment that is not available at one of the city's private hospitals.

Education
Sultan Qaboos University is in this area, and, although it is a reputable education institution, it is currently only for Omanis. It is, however, an establishment that hires quite a few international lecturers and hosts a lot of sporting events. The Caledonian College of Engineering is open to all nationalities and offers a variety of under and postgraduate courses.

Traffic & Parking
Traffic can be busy around the airport area, but a recently-added flyover has helped and it is much calmer in As Seeb town

and in Al Hail. The highway can become a bit of a racetrack beyond the airport, so keep your wits about you. Also beware of stray goats crossing in front of you. On the whole though, the roads in the area are good.

Safety & Annoyances
The crime rate is reportedly rising here, but it is still very low. Be sensible with protecting yourself and your property as you would anywhere else. While you may be able to hear the odd plane taking off at the nearby airport, this should not be too much bother.

AL KHUWAYR AL JANUBIYYAH
Map 2 F3
Al Khuwayr is fast becoming one of Muscat's most desirable places to live. Your neighbours are likely to be predominantly Omanis or expats from the subcontinent, and they tend to keep to themselves, apart from some of the children who will think nothing of using your parked car as a goal post.

Best Points
The beautiful mountain backdrop with Taimur mosque and reasonable rents.

Worst Points
Traffic congestion, particularly during peak times near the roundabout.

Accommodation
Al Khuwayr offers mainly two-storey villas, but also many apartments in the business district which runs along the road parallel to the highway.

Shopping & Amenities
There are some big-name electrical shops, local home furnishing stores, clothing stores and art supply stores located along the slip road and off the Al Khuwayr Roundabout towards Madinat Sultan Qaboos. There is also a Mars hypermarket and a Rawasco supermarket in central Al Khuwayr.

Entertainment & Leisure
The Radisson Blu is superbly located, although its famed view of White Mountain and Taimur mosque has now been blocked thanks to a raised highway. The hotel houses bars and restaurants, with the excellent Tajin Grill (p.309) proving particularly popular. There's also a swimming pool to keep you entertained.

Opposite the hotel are a number of shisha cafes (try Kebab King) with their plastic tables and chairs spilling out onto the pavement, which sell food and fresh juices outside. These are very popular with locals and expats alike, and a great place to spend a cool evening with friends, watching football or politics on the big-screen TV.

Other notable hotels include the Park Inn by Radisson, which is licensed, while the City Seasons, Hotel Ibis and Platinum have a variety of restaurants. The service road running parallel to Sultan Qaboos Highway also has a wide selection of restaurants and diners to choose from (no alcohol).

Healthcare
There are many small clinics offering a variety of medical treatments. Badr al Samaa Polyclinic offers general healthcare.

Education
Al Khuwayr is home to the College of Technology, which seems to be expanding at an alarming rate judging by the number of cars parked within a one-kilometre radius of the campus. Unfortunately, it is not open to expat students. The ABA school here offers the international baccalaureate syllabus as part of its well-regarded primary and secondary education courses.

Traffic & Parking
The flagrant disregard for parking regulations around the mosque at prayer time can be interesting and even amusing – it's amazing to see just how far people will go to avoid having to walk any distance. The roundabout becomes a car park and all roads leading from it are lined on both sides with double-parked vehicles.

Safety & Annoyances
Some of the younger residents and students like to practise 'doughnuts' and other noisy tricks in their cars and beach buggies when most people are trying to sleep. Be mindful of occasional random acts of vandalism that include spray painting on cars and vehicle damage. Women should probably not walk alone at night in this area.

MADINAT AS SULTAN QABOOS

Map 2 G3

Fondly known as 'Little Britain', this area is extremely popular with western expats, the diplomatic corps and young families.

Best Points

MSQ is a tranquil, leafy suburb that comes with a great range of amenities.

Worst Points

Traffic in the mornings and around the Home Centre junction, plus escalating rents.

Accommodation

MSQ has a mixture of older villas with established gardens, swanky new apartments with pools, and garden courts. It is one of the areas most sought after by expats, due to its proximity to the British School and the ABA School, and it has soaring rental prices to reflect the fact.

Shopping & Amenities

It's all here – there is a large Al Fair supermarket (with a pork room), an off-licence, a travel agent, a vet, a medical centre, huge furniture shop Home Centre, Tavola, Busy Bees and much more.

Entertainment & Leisure

There's a Pizza Hut, a Starbucks, and an interesting restaurant with local flavour and a jungle theme: Kargeen Caffé (p.317). You've also got a great Mexican in the centre – Pavo Real (p.321) is an authentic and lively venue with all the right ingredients (tequila included) for a fabulous night out. Apart from the lively atmosphere throughout the week, Pavo also hosts a legendary karaoke night on Mondays. Just across 'Death Valley Road' is the superb ladies' salon Diva (p.151) and Bamboo Spa (24 640 222). D'Arcy's and Costa Coffee are popular with ladies of leisure, and if all the great dining outlets leave you feeling like you've overindulged, you can burn it all off in Adam's Gym.

Healthcare

The Medident Centre (p.142) offers general medical care, as well as dentistry and prenatal care. It is staffed by expats.

Education

This is the location of the renowned British School Muscat, one of Muscat's best schools (p.138). The British School provides high quality education for children from the age of 3 right up to A-levels, and follows the English National Curriculum. It is also a community meeting point for all kinds of activities from Scottish dancing to karate. MSQ is home to a few embassies and the British Council, which holds a range of English language courses for non-English speakers. The British Council also offers CELTA courses for people wishing to teach English as a second language. Nurseries such as Bright Beginnings (p.136) and Abu Abnan (p.136) offer activities and daycare.

Traffic & Parking

Parking can get a little busy around Al Fair, but there are other parking areas dotted about so you will never have to walk far. Traffic at the junction near Home Centre can hold you back, so avoid lunch times if possible. Morning drop-off time around schools and nurseries can also be tricky.

Safety & Annoyances

Due to the popularity of the area with young families, there are ladies with prams everywhere so watch your driving.

AL QURM (INCLUDING QURM HEIGHTS)

Map 2 H2

Al Qurm is home to a mixture of residential and commercial buildings, and it is safe to say that this is one of the most desirable areas in which to live (and the most expensive).

Best Points

Due to its hilly setting, Qurm has some amazing views.

Worst Points

The traffic around Qurm junction can get quite congested at peak times.

Accommodation

Qurm features mainly large villas set amid undulating slopes; therefore your chances of landing a villa with a view are high. This is also the location of the Petroleum Development Oman housing compound (complete with its private leisure facilities). Shati Al Qurm is the epitome of luxury living, with huge white villas spaced out along quiet suburban streets. However, unless you are a foreign diplomat, a wealthy local or an overpaid chief executive, it may be out of your budget.

Shopping & Amenities

Shopaholics will enjoy living in Qurm, as it is home to four large shopping centres, including Qurum City Centre (p.298). In the area, you'll find big-name brands, a host of fabric shops, a fancy dress shop, a pet shop, a selection of banks and three big supermarkets, including a Carrefour in Qurum City Centre.

Entertainment & Leisure

There is no shortage of leisure options in the area. You'll find a selection of restaurants and bars, some of which are in the Crowne Plaza hotel (which also boasts a health club and a great swimming pool). Kids will be able to spend hours in Marah Land (p.177), and you could spend many a cool evening strolling around the adjacent Al Qurum Natural Park (p.170). In terms of beaches, you've got Al Marjan beach and the long stretch of beach running from Qurm to Azaiba and beyond.

Healthcare

Qurm is home to the Al Hayat Polyclinic (p.142), Al Masaraat Clinic and various smaller clinics.

Education

Muscat International School (p.138), offering an international curriculum to both local and expat children from kindergarten to A-Level, is in Qurm.

Traffic & Parking

There is a healthy amount of free parking around the shopping centres, although in some areas a 50 baisa ticket is required. Traffic can get congested around the Qurm junction.

Safety & Annoyances

The 'PDO Pong' is sometimes noticeable if the wind blows in a certain direction. This is just an odour from the PDO petrochemical plant, and it is harmless.

RUWI

Map 2 J3
Ruwi is home to the Central Business District areas of Muscat. Ruwi High Street comes alive in the evenings as people throng the streets and the roadside cafes.

Best Points

You can pick up a good range of fake designer items here.

Worst Points

There is a lot of traffic throughout the area.

Accommodation

As Ruwi is predominantly a business area, accommodation is mainly in the form of low-cost apartments.

Shopping & Amenities

Ruwi is fantastic for little fabric shops and pirated DVDs. There is a KM Trading Centre, popular amongst locals and expats with many shops selling sunglasses, jewellery and cheap clothing.

Entertainment & Leisure

Star Cinema (p.306) shows Arabic and Indian film releases. The City Cinema (p.306) is also a good option for subcontinent releases, and if you feel like sampling some authentic Pakistani kebabs and flat bread step across to the restaurant opposite. There are also plenty of roadside Indian and Arab restaurants in the area where you can get a decent curry or a tasty shawarma for pocket change. The Golden Oryx (p.316) is an excellent dining venue, serving up Chinese and Thai food in an authentic setting (although diners should note that the restaurant no longer serves alcohol). The Al Falaj Hotel houses Muscat's first Japanese restaurant, the newly opened Nuts and Bolts offering late night partying. Another top-floor bar in the hotel also holds a fantastic view of the nightlights of CBD. The Sheraton is currently being refurbished.

Healthcare

The Badr Al Samaa (p.142) and Kims Oman Hospital (p.142) are located near Ruwi Christian church, and there are also several homeopathic clinics, a Chinese herbal medicine clinic and various smaller clinics dotted around the area.

Education

Ruwi is home to the Pakistan School (p.138), but there are no educational establishments offering English or American curricula.

Traffic & Parking

Traffic is very busy and parking can be a problem. You may find a spot on one of the roads behind Ruwi High Street, or near Lulu Centre (Darsayt).

An Omani Home

Safety & Annoyances

With all the comings and goings of the local businesses in the area, and the resulting traffic, Ruwi can be noisy. Do remember to dress conservatively when walking around, especially near the High Street. This applies to both men and women.

SHATI AL QURM

Map 2 G2
Shati is home to the embassies and their staff, and is a highly desirable area near the beach and official offices.

Best Points

The area is close to a beautiful beach and a wide range of leisure options.

Worst Points

The beach gets busy, especially during low tide. Lifeguards are not always on hand and retreating tides can be strong.

Accommodation

Unfortunately, living in Shati Al Qurm is simply out of most people's reach. The area is characterised by huge, sprawling villas with stained glass windows and surrounded by mature trees and rows of private parking spaces for the numerous cars that residents possess. There is also an apartment block above Bareeq Al Shatti mall (p.296) but, again, it is certainly on the pricey side.

Shopping & Amenities

There is plenty here: the Al Sarooj Plaza houses a big Al Fair and a selection of smaller shops. Next to the centre there is a Shell petrol station with a large 24 hour convenience store. Bareeq Al Shatti mall (p.296) is a great spot for a coffee while Jawharat A'Shati (p.296) is a handy shopping complex with restaurants, a post office, some souvenir shops, a WH Smith store, a party balloon outlet, a card shop and a nail bar for that all-important manicure.

Entertainment & Leisure

City Cinema, Shatti Al Qurum is always popular at weekends – it shows all the current Hollywood releases, although censors do remove any scenes that contravene Islamic sensibilities. The Al Deyar restaurant has a collection of outside tables and offers shisha and snacks late into the night. Another place to visit is Café Barberra, next to the cinema, which is good for a quick, tasty bite. Future Gym is next door and is well equipped for both men and women. There is also ten pin bowling in nearby Al Masa Mall (p.300), and Ayana Spa (p.149) is the place to head for massages and beauty therapies.

The beach is a stone's throw away and popular for football, walking and jogging. Starbucks, Costa Coffee and Darcy's Kitchen all have outdoor seating areas that are great for watching the world go by.

The InterContinental Muscat (p.68) has an excellent choice of restaurants and bars, as well as one of the best health clubs in the city.

Healthcare

Muscat Eye Laser Center (p.145) is nearby, as are Precision Dental Clinic (p.145) and The American Dental Centre (p.145). VLCC (24 695 157) offers dietary and skincare consultancy and treatments. If it's cosmetic surgery you're after, Emirates Medical Center p.142) is located in Al Sarooj Plaza.

Education

Al Zumurrud Montessori Kindergarten (9228 5849) is located in a bright, modern villa in Shati Al Qurm, just past the Grand Hyatt. The kindergarten has a high staff-to-child ratio.

Traffic & Parking

There are many places for parking near the shops and cinema and also near the hospital. Traffic is not a problem but you may wait a while at roundabouts during rush hour.

Safety & Annoyances

Bad car parking can result in scratched paintwork and there are lots of local youths cruising in their cars which can be intimidating.

MAIN ACCOMMODATION OPTIONS

Your employer may provide a house or apartment for you, but if they provide you with an allowance instead, you will be able to choose what type of accommodation is suitable. The following options are available:

Apartment/Villa Sharing

You can cut your accommodation costs in half by sharing an apartment or villa

Get your local
Prepaid Starter Pack
from the leading mobile operator

Join the leading operator and enjoy our extensive mobile coverage in Oman.

عمـانتل
Omantel
Mobile

with colleagues or friends. It's also a great way to avoid those long, lonely nights of feeling homesick and wondering what all your mates back home are up to – especially if you've only made the move to Muscat fairly recently.

Some villas are so big that, even if you've got numerous house mates, you should still be able to find a quiet corner. To look for shared accommodation or find a suitable housemate, check the notice boards outside supermarkets.

Standard Apartment
Apartments can be found all over the Muscat area and vary from tiny studio apartments to vast penthouses. Muscat's hilly terrain means that people living on the top floors usually have a great view. Rents are usually between RO 350 and RO 1,350 per month.

Villa
Whether your budget stretches to a luxurious four-bedroom palace overlooking the beach in Qurm, or a more modest villa in outlying areas such as Azaibah or Seeb, you should find something to fit your budget. If your villa has a swimming pool, central air conditioning, covered parking, electric gates, a big garden or outside maid's quarters, the price will be higher.

HOUSING ABBREVIATIONS
BR – Bedroom
C A/C – Central air conditioning (usually included in the rent)
D/S – Double storey villa
En suite – Bedroom has a private bathroom
Ext S/Q – Servant quarters located outside the villa
Fully fitted – Includes major appliances (oven, refrigerator, washing machine)
Hall flat – Apartment has an entrance hall (entrance doesn't open directly onto living room)
L/D – Living/dining room area
Pvt garden – Private garden
S/Q – Servant quarters
S/S – Single storey villa
Shared pool – Pool is shared with other villas in compound
W A/C – Window air conditioning (often indicates older building)
W/robes – Built-in wardrobes

A garden court is a group of small, semi-detached villas built around a communal garden (often with a swimming pool). There are quite a few of these found in the Madinat Sultan Qaboos area. Villas currently rent from RO 600 to RO 6,000 per month, depending on size and location.

Serviced Apartments
Serviced apartments are fairly expensive and, therefore, more suited to shorter stays. Some people live in serviced apartments for a month or two until they find the house they want, or while they await the arrival of their family members or furniture shipment.

Apartments can be rented on a daily, weekly, monthly or yearly basis and are fully furnished right down to the last detail, with a cleaning and laundry service included. The main contacts for serviced apartments are ASAS Oman (24 571 509), Al Noorah Gardens Guest House (24 697 203), and Safeer Hotel Suites (p.74).

FINDING A HOME
If you drive around Muscat, you'll see a good number of 'To Let' boards hanging up outside available properties, so, if you already have a preferred area in mind, this is a good way to look for a house. By doing this, you may also be able to rent directly from the landlord and therefore avoid paying agents' commission. However, a reliable estate agent can save you a lot of time and effort by arranging viewings of several suitable properties.

Look out also for properties nearing completion. Although they may not have a sign outside, try and find the watchman who will give you the landlord's number. You can also browse the classified ads in the local newspapers, or keep an eye on supermarket noticeboards.

If you do choose to use an agent, you have the choice of local agencies or the bigger, internationally recognised names. Many people can organise an estate agent through their company PRO, but it is always wise to check that the recommended agent is a registered real estate broker, authorised to conduct leasing in Muscat.

Reputable agencies will not only show you a selection of suitable properties, but they will also assist you with the paperwork and ensure that the required municipality

Your global property partner in Oman

Residential & Commercial Leasing

Local & International Property Sales

Market Research

Feasibility & Best Use Studies

Valuations & Appraisals

Property Management

Real Estate Consultancy

Relocation Advisory Services

Call +968 24699773
muscat@hamptons-int.com
www.hamptons-int.com

UAE . UK . Saudi Arabia . Oman . India . Egypt . Morocco . Italy . Seychelles . Monaco

procedures are followed. Landlords should pay the agent's commission and you should bear no cost or 'finder's fee'.

Real Estate Agents

Al Habib & Co 24 700 247, *alhabibonline.com*
Al Qandeel Real Estate Services 24 643 800, *alqandeel.com*
Better Homes 24 699 334, *bhomes.com/oman*
Cluttons & Partners 24 564 250, *oman.cluttons.com*
Eamaar Real Estate 24 647 666, *eamaar.com*
Gulf Property World 24 697 588, *gpw-oman.com*
Hamptons International > *p.99* 24 699 773, *hamptons-int.com*
Hay Al Rahbah Property Management Services 24 694 088, *assarain.com*
Hilal Properties > *p.101* 24 600 688, *hilalprp.com.om*
OmanHomes.com 24 488 087, *omanhomes.com*
The Wave, Muscat Rentals 24 534 649, *thewavemuscat.com*

BUYING PROPERTY

Expats being able to buy property in Oman is a relatively new phenomenon – until the relevant change in the law was announced by royal decree in 2006, non-nationals could only rent accommodation. Expats can still only buy property within areas designated as 'integrated tourist complexes' or ITCs. ITC licences are granted by the Ministry of Tourism, and have so far been approved for The Wave, Muscat Golf and Country Club, and the Muriya Jebel Sifah project. Properties within these complexes can be bought to live in or for investment purposes, meaning that you can buy one to let out to a third party. You are also permitted to sell your property at any time after the construction is completed.

It is important to note that in the event of the death of a property owner, the laws regarding transfer of ownership are governed by the laws of that person's home country. It is essential to have a valid will in place if you are considering purchasing property in Oman. If no heir applies to inherit the property within one year, the Ministry of Tourism will manage the property for 15 years, after which time ownership reverts to the Government of Oman.

Mortgages

Since the government announced that expatriates would be entitled to purchase freehold property in certain developments, some of the banks have started offering mortgage options to expats. Mortgage conditions are different for expats as opposed to locals, especially in terms of how many years you can repay your loan for and how much deposit you have to put down. The mortgage industry is still in its infancy, and as more freehold residential developments near completion, there will be more on offer.

Property Developers

Eamaar Real Estate 24 647 666, *eamaar.com*
Muscat Hills Golf & Country Club 24 510 065, *muscathills.com*
Oman Tourism Development Company SAOC (OMRAN) 24 391 111, *omran.om*
The Wave, Muscat 24 545 428, *thewavemuscat.com*

RENTING

Although foreigners have recently been given the legal right to purchase property on certain developments in Oman, renting remains the main option for accommodation. In Oman, rent is usually paid annually and not monthly. This is good news for the landlord, but bad news for tenants who often have to come up with a sizeable lump sum to cover their rent for the whole year. If your company provides you with an annual accommodation allowance, then they will usually cover your rent upfront. If not, it's worth negotiating for your employer to pay the upfront sum, which you can then pay back on a monthly basis through salary deductions.

There remains a steady demand in the rental market (especially for better quality properties). The golden rule is that if you see a house you love, sign on the dotted line as soon as possible or someone else will snap it up.

Rents vary considerably depending on the size and location. As of 2012, the average rent for a two-bedroom apartment in Muscat ranges between $1,000 and $1,500 (RO 385 and RO 578) per month. Sharing accommodation provides a cost-effective way of living, if you don't mind giving up some of your privacy, but

be aware that mixed cohabitation is illegal unless you are related to your housemates.

Apart from your rent (paid annually), you will face additional costs when moving into a new house. These might include:
- A 3% municipality tax
- A security deposit (refundable when you vacate the premises, minus any damages)
- A deposit for your water and electricity accounts

If you are renting a villa with a garden, your water costs will be higher since the grass and plants will need watering every day in Oman's hot climate.

The Lease

Your lease is an important document and will state, in addition to the financial terms, what you are liable for in terms of maintenance and what your landlord's responsibilities are. It is important that you (or your company PRO, who may have more knowledge about the pitfalls of rental contracts) read through the lease and discuss any points of contention before you sign it. You may be able to negotiate on certain clauses in your contract, such as how many cheques you can use to pay your annual rent, who is responsible for maintenance, and how much security deposit you should pay.

The entire leasing process in Muscat is governed by well-drafted legislation and the lease is prepared on a standard municipality form. The standard lease, which can have minor changes made to it, is normally for one year (which is automatically renewable unless three months' notice is given before expiry by either the landlord or the tenant). Annual rent for villas is often requested in advance in one cheque, although it is sometimes possible to agree with the landlord that six months' rent is paid upon signing of the lease and the remainder of the amount by post-dated cheque.

To take out a personal lease (in your name, not your employer's name), you need to be a resident. The landlord will need a copy of your passport (with visa page), a no objection letter (NOC) from your employer, a copy of your salary certificate, a signed rent cheque and up to three post-dated cheques covering the remainder of the annual rent (the number of cheques depends on your landlord). If the rented property will be in your employer's name, then the landlord needs a copy of the company's trade licence, a passport copy of the person signing the rent cheque, and the rent cheque itself.

It is the landlord's responsibility to register the lease with the relevant municipality. The registering of leases showing rental at less than the real amount is against the law, and it is also a big risk for tenants, who will have no protection in the event of a dispute.

The landlord must ensure that the house is in good condition before you move in, so don't sign the lease until he has made the improvements you think need to be done (like painting, filling in wall holes, regrouting bathrooms and servicing the air conditioning units).

Rent Disputes

It goes without saying that there are distinct advantages to keeping friendly relations with your landlord. There are no hard-and-fast laws protecting the tenant and therefore it pays to stay on your landlord's good side. If you have a disagreement with him that reaches a stalemate, the Ministry of Justice (24 697 699 / 800 77 777) will assist.

MOVING

Moving house can be stressful, especially if you are moving to a new country. You can reduce the stress by planning the move well, and enlisting the help of a professional moving service. When moving your furniture to or from Oman, you can ship it by air or by sea. Airfreight is quick, and is good for small consignments and the essential things you can't live without. But to move a whole houseful of furniture you need to arrange a container by sea, and this will take several weeks. You can get a 20 or 40 foot container, depending on how much stuff you are moving. If you're really lucky and you know someone moving at the same time as you, you could share a container. Either way, ensure that you use a reputable company to pack your goods and make all the arrangements. If you are moving to Oman in the height of the summer (July or August), bear in mind that your belongings will travel at sustained high temperatures in the container ship, so some of your plastic items may warp and your china might have little surface cracks from the heat. A reputable moving company should be able to offer you advice on how to minimise damage by using proper packaging, therefore a company with a wide international network is usually the best option.

When your shipment arrives in Muscat you may be called to the customs department so that you can be present when your crates are opened. This is done to ensure that you are not bringing anything illegal or inappropriate into the country. Someone from your company (such as the PRO) may be able to stand in for you, and you will only have to go if something suspect is found. The process can be exhausting, because the search can take a few hours, often out in the heat, and you will have to watch your carefully packed boxes being unceremoniously rummaged through.

Smooth Moves

- Get more than one quote – some companies will match lower quotes to get the job
- Make sure that all items are covered by insurance
- Make sure that you have a copy of the inventory and that each item is listed
- Don't be shy about requesting packers to repack items if you are not satisfied
- Take photos of the packing process, to use for evidence if you need to claim
- Carry customs-restricted goods (DVDs, videos or books) with you: it's easier to open a suitcase in an air-conditioned airport than empty a box out in the sun

Relocation Experts

Relocation experts offer a range of services to help you settle into your new life in Oman as quickly as possible. Practical help ranges from finding accommodation or schools for your children to connecting a telephone or information on medical care. In addition, they will often offer advice on the way of life in the city, putting people in touch with social networks to help them get established in their new lives. Sununu Muscat (99 800 613; sununumuscat.com)

CUSTOMS

Customs officers may retain certain items such as CDs, DVDs, books and even photo albums, for further investigation. You will get these items back once they have been checked, although it may take several weeks.

is a relocation specialist that can help to ease your move to Oman in a number of ways.

Removal Companies

Gulf Agency Company (GAC)
24 477 800, *gac.com/oman*
Inchcape Shipping Services
24 701 291, *iss-shipping.com*
Khimji Ramdas Shipping 24 706 501, *khimji.com*
Middle East Shipping & Transport Co
24 790 024,
suhailbahwangroup.com
Yusuf Bin Ahmed Kanoo & Co
24 712 252, *kanooshipping.com*

FURNITURE SHOPPING

If you are a new arrival in Oman and moving into a new home, chances are that you will need to buy some furniture. Most properties are unfurnished, and that means not only will you have no furniture, but in most cases you will have no electrical items or white goods either (not even a cooker), and not all villas have fitted wardrobes.

Oman is home to several big furniture shops so no matter what your tastes are, you'll find something you like. A lot of furniture is locally or regionally made, and is often extremely ornate. Simpler styles can be found in ID Design (Markaz Al Bahja) and Home Centre (Centrepoint). The world-famous Swedish furniture store IKEA is just a few hours down the road in Dubai, so you can load your car up with flat-pack furniture.

Second-Hand Furniture

The population of Muscat is fairly transitory, with people coming and going all the time. As a result there is quite a busy second-hand furniture market, so keep your eyes on the supermarket noticeboards. Look out also for adverts for local garage sales, where families will sell all the stuff they are not taking with them at rock-bottom prices.

UTILITIES

Water and electricity services are supplied by the government and are generally efficient and reliable. There is no mains gas service but bottled gas (LPG) is available for cooking. Power cuts – lasting from a few minutes to several hours – occur every now and then but rarely pose a major

HOT WATER

The water in your cold taps gets so hot in summer that you can turn off your water heaters – in fact this is the only way to get cooler water, since your hot water unit is usually inside the house, away from the sun's glare. You know winter's coming when you have to turn the water heater on again!

inconvenience. It helps to have a stock of candles and torches handy, just in case. Utility bills are paid at Oman Investment & Finance Company (OIFC) or through your bank or ATM. To use the ATM service, you have to register your details by phone (the bank will have the number). Once you are registered, it means you can pay your bills outside banking hours, without having to stand in queues. The bank transfer system is slower than paying directly to OIFC so allow a few extra days so that you don't get disconnected. Wherever you pay, make sure your bill is stamped and that you keep it for reference – you may need it for proof of payment at a later date.

Electricity
The electricity supply in Oman is 220/240 volts and 50 cycles. Sockets correspond to the British three-pin plug but many appliances are sold with two-pin plugs, so you will need lots of adaptors (available in any supermarket or corner shop) – better still, change all the plugs.

Water
Though some water comes from natural wells, there is not enough to service the country's needs so most of the supply is from the sea, processed at the desalination plant at Al Ghubbrah. The main supply of water is very reliable but not all of Muscat's residential areas are connected to it. If your house is not, you will have to rely on a water bowser to fill up your tank every two or three days. Water trucks for domestic use are blue (the green ones carry non-potable water, for municipal garden watering and industrial use) and they are everywhere – just flag one down or ask your neighbours which 'water-man' they use. You will often see several trucks filling up at one of the water wells dotted around the city. Expect to pay around RO 25 a month for truck water. Oman Oasis will deliver (800 71222).

If you are connected to the main supply, keep an eye on your bills and water meter;

if you have an underground leak within your property boundary you could be held responsible for a hefty bill, even if you weren't aware of the leak. In the heat of summer, it's unlikely you'll have the chance to take a refreshing cold shower. Water tanks are usually located on the roof, where they are heated to near boiling point by the sun, and you can't even stand under the shower because it's so hot. Between April and October, the only way to get a cool shower is to turn off your water heater, and use the hot water tap.

Oman's water is safe to drink as it is purified eight times. However, it is heavily chlorinated (which affects the taste) so most people prefer to drink one of the many locally bottled mineral waters. Apart from the coffee shops, all restaurants will supply bottled water. If in doubt, ask for a sealed bottle to be brought to your table. You can get 20 litre bottles of purified water for use at home, either with a hand pump or a water cooler. These are available from shops and supermarkets, and you pay a RO 6 deposit per bottle, and refills cost RO 1. Alternatively, get a company to deliver the water to your house.

Rubbish Disposal & Recycling
The rubbish disposal system in Oman is efficient – it has to be, because the health hazards of mounds of domestic waste festering in the sweltering heat would be too great. Large metal containers (skips) are placed at regular intervals along residential streets and you just chuck your daily rubbish bags into them. Skips are emptied regularly by rubbish trucks (although not before the local 'bin cats' have had a good rummage).

There is a landfill site at Al Amerat – previously waste was just dumped in the desert. Unfortunately, there are no recycling systems at present, the argument being that it would be too expensive to implement and educate people on how to use it effectively.

Sewerage
All properties in Oman have septic tanks, which must be emptied regularly by one of the yellow sewerage trucks. The cost for having a septic tank emptied is between RO 10 and RO 14 each time, and you'll probably have to get it done about once a year (you'll know when it's time from the smell). If you need to order a sewerage truck, the easiest way is to call the number

APARTMENTS ARE COOL...

You can expect a higher A/C bill in a villa – not only is it probably bigger than your average apartment, but many apartment buildings include air conditioning costs in the rent. Oman doesn't have mains gas but there are many suppliers of bottled gas. Gas canisters are available in various sizes, and you pay RO 15–20 as a deposit, and RO 3 per refill. Gas is delivered to houses by orange trucks that drive around residential areas. If you need gas, just flag one of the trucks down; popular times for the gas run are late mornings, early evenings and on Fridays. Once you've found a supplier, get his mobile number and you'll be able to call him whenever you need more gas. Most will deliver any time up to 21:00.

on the back of one of the yellow tankers, or ask a neighbour. Alternatively, call Oman Wastewater Services Company (800 77111). The Oman Wastewater Services Company (haya.com.om) is currently undertaking a RO 350 million sewerage recycling project.

TELEPHONE

Mobile Phones

In 2005, Nawras began operating as an alternative mobile phone service provider in Oman, ending the monopoly held by the government-owned Oman Telecommunications Company (Omantel). Friendi Mobile and Renna mobile services came to the market in 2009, offering great coverage and flexible packages including prepaid recharge cards for amounts as low as 500 baisas. SIM cards start at RO 2 and users can call fellow Friendi customers for 39 baisas, 24 hours a day. Customer service is offered in a number of languages including Arabic, English, Malayalam, Hindi, Urdu and Bengali. For help with your GSM, voicemail, SMS or other mobile services, call 1234 (toll free). Friendi, Oman Mobile, Nawras and Renna offer a huge range of services and it might be difficult to choose the provider you like best. The companies usually have information desks in various malls, so go along for a chat with one of their representatives or see p.107.

Bill Payment

Telephone bills are sent monthly and include rental charges and call costs. Only international calls are itemised on the bill, although the number of local and mobile calls and text messages is listed. You can pay your landline bill at the Omantel office in Al Khuwayr (behind Al Zawawi mosque, next to the ice rink) which is easy and efficient, and the best way to ensure continuity of service. You can also pay through some banks (such as Bank Muscat or HSBC) or through the ATM, but these services have a processing time of up to 10

days. You can check your GSM and internet bills on Omantel's website. Apply online for a PIN and just log in to find out how much you owe (for more information on paying your landline and mobile bills for Omantel, see their website – omantel.om). If you do not pay when you receive your bill, Omantel will helpfully send an email reminder. If you ignore that, they will cut you off without further warning. Landlines continue to receive calls for several days but outgoing calls will be barred. If you do get cut off, take your bill to the Al Khuwayr office, pay all outstanding debts and a reconnection fee of RO 1, and your service will be reconnected immediately. Always keep your bills and receipts for proof of payment. If you are a Nawras post-paid GSM subscriber, you can pay your bills at certain banks, online, through your ATM, over the phone, or at a Nawras store. See their website (nawras.om) for more information.

Missing Mobile

Lost your mobile? Call 1234 to temporarily or permanently disconnect your number. You will have to provide the number of the document that you presented when you applied for your SIM card (probably your passport or labour card). To replace the SIM, you'll need to go to a branch of Oman Mobile with your essential documents in hand and a fee of RO 7. As soon as you have the new SIM card, your old one will be permanently disconnected. You can keep the same telephone number.

No Mobile When Mobile

It is against the law to use a mobile phone handset while you are driving, so if you like to talk behind the wheel you should use a hands-free kit. Failure to do so can result in you being pulled over and given a spot fine of RO 70.

INTERNET

As you'll notice from the quality of many local websites, the internet isn't as popular in Oman as elsewhere in the world. The sole internet service provider is Omantel and all sites are accessed through its proxy server. The proxy blocks any sites that are considered offensive to religious, moral, political or cultural sensitivities.

When you sign up for an internet account with Omantel, you will be given an email address. It will be an eight-character

NO NAUGHTY SITES

While using the internet in Oman you will have to do so under the watchful eye of a proxy. Sites that are considered harmful to the political, religious, moral or cultural sensitivities of the country are inaccessible.

THURAYA

Omantel offers the Thuraya system – a satellite-based GSM (mobile phone) service that is valuable for emergency communication when travelling outside standard GSM range. Although Oman's populated areas have GSM network coverage there are still empty spaces with no reception. If you're a regular camper and wadi basher, you may consider it worth buying a Thuraya phone – especially if you travel with small children or need to be accessible at all times for some reason. Thuraya currently provides access to 99 countries in Europe, the Middle East, Africa and Asia. The handset costs around RO 300 and doubles as a GPS receiver.

user name, along with the Omantel suffix (username@omantel.om). You can access the internet from any Omantel landline, using a computer and a 56Kbps modem. To get connected using your own landline (or one in your company's name), you need to apply at Omantel. There are several Omantel Customer Service Outlets in Muscat – check the website for details of the one closest to you. You'll need to hand over a completed application form, copies of your passport, visa and labour/resident card (plus the originals, just in case), and a letter from your sponsor. There is also a registration fee of RO 10. The monthly charge for internet connection is RO 2, and each hour's surfing is charged at 18 baisas. You can have one email address – yourname@omantel.om. If you need extra email space, it costs 20 baisas per megabyte. If you register for a PIN on the Omantel website, you can also access your Omantel email account from any computer anywhere in the world. Omantel now offers packages for corporate web hosting. If you need assistance with the internet, you can call 1313 toll free. Broadband (ADSL) is available in many areas of Muscat, and use of broadband services is increasing all the time.

Log & Surf

This facility allows you to surf the internet without a contract or subscription to Omantel. All you need is a computer with a modem, and a phone line. The charge will be billed to the line you are connecting from. To connect, just double click on 'My Computer', then on 'Dial-up Networking' and then on 'Make a New Connection'. Type in 'Omantel' for both your username

and password, dial 1312 and click connect. Charges are a little higher – 25 baisas per minute from a landline and 50 baisas per minute from a mobile (to access the internet using your mobile you need to subscribe to the data service, for an extra RO 3 per month).

Satellite TV

Thank goodness for satellite TV! Satellite offers an enormous choice of programmes and channels, and most expats have at least one satellite provider. You will need to pay for any equipment you need (dish and decoder) as well as installation. You can usually choose from a number of packages depending on what kind of programmes you like to see – the advantage being that you don't have to pay for things you won't use (for example, if you are not interested in watching sport, you can subscribe to a package that does not include any sports channels). There are quite a few 'free-to-air' satellite channels, and to view these you need to get the dish and decoder but then you pay no subscription fees. However, most of these channels are not in English. Equipment can be bought from main dealers or any of the small electrical shops. Second-hand dishes and decoders are often advertised on supermarket noticeboards and in the classifieds. The majority of dealers will offer installation. Many apartment blocks have satellite systems already fitted. If not, ask your landlord about a cost-share system.

Telephone, Internet & Satellite TV Providers

Firstnet 26 844 076, *firstnettv.net*
Friendi Mobile 98 400 000, *friendimobile.om*
Nawras 95 011 500, *nawras.om*
Omantel *> p.iv-v, 31 51, 97, 323* 24 474 000, *omantel.om*
Orbit Showtime Network 24 489 277, *osnetwork.com*
Renna 800 73 662, *rennamobile.com*

HOUSEHOLD INSURANCE

As you probably won't own your house in Oman, it's easy to take a more relaxed attitude to household insurance. The sultanate is very safe and the crime rate extremely low, but burglaries do occur and, if they do, it's predominantly expat residential areas that are targeted. Many national and international insurance companies have offices in Muscat, offering all the standard services – check the Yellow Pages for details. To take out a policy you will need confirmation of your address, your passport, a list of household contents and valuation, and invoices for any items over RO 250.

DOMESTIC SERVICES

Having maintenance done in your villa or apartment is usually just a case of making a quick call to the landlord. He is responsible for any plumbing or electrical work (unless otherwise stated in your lease), and will probably use a specific maintenance company every time. This is good if they know what they are doing, but landlords will often go for 'cheaper' rather than 'better'.

If you need some work done that your landlord won't pay for, you can use the services of a plumber, electrician or handyman. The table below lists companies specialising in carpet cleaning, carpentry, plumbing, painting and electrical services, although these companies may also offer other services too. Often word of mouth is the best way to find a trustworthy company that shows up on time, does the job that needs doing, and doesn't charge you an arm and a leg.

Domestic Services Providers

Al Ahid Trading & Contracting
24 817 509
Al Wadi Al Kabir Carpentry
24 812 856
Bahwan Engineering Co 24 597 510
Cape East & Partners, 24 496 469
International Sanitation Co
24 592 351
London Cleaning & Maintenance
24 478 341
National Electrical Contractors
24 571 363, necoman.com
Ocean Centre , 24 707 833
Ruwi Furnishing 24 521 118
Shafan Trading 24 692 058
Specialised Technical Contractors
24 788 640
West Coast Trading 24 535 680

DOMESTIC HELP

One of the perks of expat life is how common it is for people to have domestic help. Most expat families have some sort of home help, whether it's a full-time, live-in housemaid, or a part-time ironing lady. Most domestic helpers come from India, Sri Lanka, Bangladesh, Indonesia, Pakistan or the Philippines, and the only restriction in terms of nationality is that you are prohibited from employing someone from the same country as you (or someone related to you).

Azooz Manpower (24 831 448) and Friends Manpower Services (24 489 268) are two domestic help agencies in Oman. When you employ a domestic helper, you must sponsor them and provide accommodation. Most villas have servant quarters (an independent room, usually fairly small, with a private bathroom). You have a duty of care to your domestic helper, and you must make all the arrangements (and payments) for their residence visa, medical test and labour card. You are also obliged to pay for their medical bills and provide them with a return flight to their home country every two years. The visa will cost you RO 20 and the labour card will cost you RO 70. It is up to you what salary you want to pay your domestic helper and there is no stipulated minimum wage. However, part-time helpers (two to four hours per day, five days a week) usually earn RO 70 to RO 100 per month, and full-time helpers (eight hours a day, six days a week) usually earn RO 100 to RO 120 per month. If you hire a full-time, live-in helper, you should be clear with them at the beginning what duties they will be responsible for, including any evening babysitting. Part-time helpers usually charge extra for babysitting (RO 1–1.5 per hour).

Sponsoring a maid is   a substantial financial commitment so make sure you have the right person. The best way to find a good helper is by word of mouth, so keep your ear to the ground in case a 'friend of a friend' is going back home and leaving behind their loyal, trustworthy maid who is good with pets and kids. You could also look on supermarket notice boards and in newspaper classifieds, but remember to check references if you are taking on someone unknown. There are several reliable maid agencies who can recommend a good maid and in some cases, help you with the paperwork.

Laundry Services

Although there are no self-service laundrettes, there are numerous laundries in Muscat. As well as dry cleaning and laundry, they all offer an ironing service. If you have specific cleaning or ironing instructions, make sure these are noted when you drop off your laundry – creases in trousers, for instance, are standard, so speak up if you don't want them pressed into your jeans.

Compensation policies for lost or damaged items vary. But even though some laundries may seem disorganised from the piles and piles of stuff behind the counter waiting to be ironed or collected, losses are rare. Some of the more upmarket laundry chains may offer a pick-up and drop-off service.

Laundry Companies
Al Tayyibat Services 24 695 599
Grand Sultanate Laundry 24 833 097
Ibn Iqbal Trading Est 24 540 082
Kwik-Kleen 24 816 749, *ashaoman.net*
Snowhite Dry Cleaners 24 597 085, *snowhite-oman.com*
Wadi Al Khuwair Laundry 24 695 825

POSTAL SERVICES
There is no postal delivery service to home addresses, so everyone gets their mail delivered to a post office box. All mail is routed through the Central Post Office and then distributed to post office boxes in central locations. Most people use their company address, but it is also possible to get an individual PO Box number – just apply through your local post office. The postal system is fairly reliable and efficient but on occasion parcels will be returned, deemed 'undeliverable' and you'll have to pay to get them back. There is a regular airmail service and an express mail service. Most leading courier services also have branches in Oman.

Postal services are provided solely by the government-operated General Post Office (GPO). The GPO is reasonably efficient, with standard airmail letters taking 10-14 days to reach the USA, Europe or Australia. The GPO offers an express mail service (called EMS), and letters posted using the EMS get delivered in half the normal time.

It costs 50 baisas to send a postcard anywhere within the GCC, 100 baisas to other Middle East countries, and 150 baisas to anywhere else. Letters cost from 50 baisas internally (15g maximum) and from 250 baisas internationally (10g maximum). Post office opening times vary, but most branches open at 07:30 and close at 14:00 from Saturday to Wednesday, and most also have a short evening session. They close at 11:00 on Thursdays and do not open on Fridays. The post offices inside the Al Harthy Complex (Qurm) and in As Seeb are open for longer hours.

Post Office Locator
Al Harthy Complex: (24 563 534)
07:30-14.30 & 19:00-21:00
Madinat Sultan Qaboos: (24 697 083)
08:00-14:00
Al Hamriya: (24 789 311)
08:00-14:00 & 16:00-20:00
Muscat: (24 738 547)
07:30-14:00 & Thurs 08:00-11:00
Mina al Fahal: (24 565 465)
08:00-14:00
Ruwi: (24 701 651)
07:30-14:30 & 16:00-18:00
As Seeb: (24 519 922)
08:00-15:00 & 17:00-24:00
SQU campus: (24 413 333 ext 3161)
8:00-14:00
JawaharatA'Shati Complex:
(24 692 181) 09:00 -13:30

Courier Services
The major international courier companies operate in Oman, although some may limit their deliveries to Muscat itself and not the entire sultanate. Aramex (aramex. com) provides a 'Shop & Ship' service, which sets up a mailbox for you in both the UK and the US. You pay a small fee to set up the mailbox, and then you can get online purchases delivered there. Aramex will then deliver the contents of your mailbox to you in Oman, at very reasonable rates. The amount you pay will depend on the weight of the shipment, but the rate is $15 for the first half-kilogram, and $9 for every additional half-kilogram. It's a great solution if you're shopping online and the company you are buying from doesn't ship to the Middle East.

Courier Companies
Aramex 24 473 000, *aramex.com*
DHL 24 520 100, *dhl.com*
Federal Express (FedEx) 24 833 311, *fedex.com*
TNT 24 477 870, *tnt.com*
UPS 24 683 943, *ups.com*

DRIVING IN OMAN

DRIVING IN OMAN

Compared to some other countries in the region, the driving on Oman's roads is fairly calm. However, there are still a lot of motorists who drive recklessly and with scant regard for the safety of pedestrians and other road users. The government promotes road safety with a number of high-profile campaigns such as the Salim & Salimah – Safe & Sound campaign (see salimandsalimah.org for more information).

If you are a new arrival in Oman and find the road conditions scary, the best advice is to get behind the wheel as quickly as possible. Your first few drives will be stressful but it won't take long to get the hang of defensive driving. The roads are monitored closely by the Royal Oman Police (ROP).

Drinking and driving is illegal – there is a zero-tolerance policy, so even if you've only had half a shandy or a bowl of trifle laced with sherry, don't get behind the wheel. Road blocks (where police pull drivers off the road and make them do a breathalyser test) are infrequent, but if you have an accident and you have any alcohol in your bloodstream, you are in very hot water. Not only will your insurance be invalidated, but you could face a hefty fine or even jail time.

Using your mobile phone while driving is prohibited, unless you are connected to a hands-free device. If caught, your fine could be as much as RO 70 (that's one expensive phone call). Always carry your driving licence with you. Failure to produce it in a spot check will result in a fine. If you have any queries on driving licences or traffic regulations, contact the ROP Directorate of Traffic on 2460 0099 or visit the website (rop.gov.om).

DRIVING LICENCE

Visitors do not need a temporary Oman licence to drive in Oman. All they need is a valid international licence or a licence from their home country (GCC and European nationalities only). The traffic law permits expatriates on a visit visa to drive rental cars for up to three months. Expats on employment visas, however, should have Oman driving licences.

The following driving licences are transferable in Oman without taking a driving test: GCC countries, Australia, Belgium, Brunei, Canada, Denmark, Finland, France, Germany, Ireland, Italy, Japan (after translation), Jordan, Lebanon, Luxembourg, Monaco, Morocco, New Zealand, the Netherlands, Norway, Spain, Sweden, Tunisia, Turkey, United States of America, United Kingdom.

Permanent Licence

To drive a light vehicle in Oman, you must be over 17 years of age (you have to be over 21 to drive heavy vehicles or trucks). Residents from many countries, including the UK and the US, can simply exchange their driving licence from their home country for an Oman licence. The only condition is that they have had the licence for one year or more. It costs RO 20 to transfer the licence, which can be done at the traffic police head quarters on Death Valley Road (near Muscat Private School). Take along essential documents (see p.83) and you will need to have an eye test done before you go.

Strangely, married women have to take their marriage certificate and a letter of no-objection from their husband. Your company's PRO will usually go with you to help you through the process. If you do not have a driving licence from one of the 'automatic exchange' countries, you will need to take a driving test. The first step is to obtain a learning permit – start by picking up an application form from the traffic police headquarters. To do this you'll need to take your essential documents (p.83) and RO 5. You will be given an eye test at the Traffic Police. Your next step is to find a good driving school. There are a few schools, but many instructors work individually and you will find them by word of mouth. They often operate out of Death Valley Road police HQ, although some will come to your house. They drive white cars with easily recognisable red diagonal stripes. There are female driving instructors for women, although no female test inspectors.

When your instructor feels you are ready to take the test, you will have to sit a three-part driving test, consisting of a reversing test, a road test and a Highway Code test. The first involves reversing between oil drums placed in two parallel rows barely wider than your car; you have to get it right first time and you can't take the road or theoretical tests until you've passed this test (known, with fear and loathing, as 'the barrels'). Once you've passed all three tests, you have to apply for your licence through the authorised driving school. The police are known to be strict in issuing new licences and this process can take several months. You'll need perseverance.

Oman driving licences are valid for 10 years and can be renewed at the traffic police headquarters. To renew your licence you will need a driving licence renewal form (stamped by your sponsor), your expired licence, a copy of your labour card and a passport copy.

Driving Licence Documents
- Licence Exchange form with signature and stamp of sponsor
- An NOC from your sponsor/company (in Arabic)
- Two photographs
- Passport and resident visa copy
- Original driving licence along with a photocopy (and translation, if requested by the Traffic Police)
- Blood Group Certificate

Additional Requirements For Female Applicants:
- NOC letter addressed to the Director of Licensing brought in person by the guardian or substitute
- If married, marriage certificate or birth certificate of a child
- If unemployed, a copy of husband's labour card and a letter from his sponsor/company

Driving Schools
Al Fursan Driving School 24 565 779
Morning Star Driving School 24 478 506
Muscat Driving School 24 781 123
Oman Driving Institute 24 596 921
Safety Line Institute 24 568 919

BUYING A VEHICLE
To own a car in Oman you must have a labour or resident card. If you decide to buy a car, you'll find that it is considerably cheaper to buy, maintain and run a car in Oman compared with most other countries. Every expat resident is allowed to own up to three vehicles. Whether you are buying a brand new car or a second-hand one, when it's time to close the deal you'll need to present certain documents.

You'll need your essential documents (p.83), a vehicle purchase form (available from the police station or the showroom), plus your valid driving licence and a copy. The vehicle purchase form should be signed by your sponsor or company, and then taken to your insurance provider. In the case of a private sale, the seller should be with you, as the car must be insured in your name before the registration can be finalised.

Once the car is registered, you will get a vehicle registration card (a 'mulkia'). You should always have the mulkia with you in the car, although many people keep a copy in the car and leave the original mulkia at home.

NEW VEHICLES
Most new car models are available through the main dealers. Many car dealerships have showrooms between the Al Wattayah and Wadi Adai Roundabouts, although there are others located all along the highway. Some dealers sell several makes of car. Don't forget to haggle – most dealers will offer a discount on the advertised price of a new car. The best time of year to get a good deal is during Ramadan, when all the dealers have promotions. Some dealers even offer a 'buy one, win one' raffle ticket that gives you the chance to win a second car. You'll also get a good deal if a new batch of cars arrives, as last year's models immediately drop in price.

The dealer will take care of all the paperwork involved in the car purchase on your behalf, including registration and arranging finance. They will also usually offer good warranties and free servicing for the first few years. Unless you are paying cash for the car, you will need to get a bank loan or leave a post-dated cheque for every month of the finance period (typically 12, 24 or 36 months). When you collect your car you will drive with green licence plates until the vehicle registration is complete.

New Car Dealers

Al Jenaibi International Automobiles
24 567 108, *bmw-oman.com*
Auto Plus 24 478 080, *autoplusoman.com*
Bahwan Automotive Centre 24 578 000,
saudbahwangroup.com
Daihatsu 24 579 092, *daihatsu.com*
European Motors 24 500 700, *em-oman.com*
General Automotive Company Al Azaiba,
24 500 500, *generalautomotive-oman.com*
KIA 24 550 200, *kiaoman.com*
Lexus 24 578 913, *lexusoman.com*
Mohsin Haider Darwish 24 523 200,
mhdoman.com
Porsche Centre Oman 24 492 544,
porsche.com
Proton Oman 23 210 143, *protonoman.com*
Shanfari Automotive Co 24 483 500,
shanfari.com
Suhail Bahwan Automobiles 24 560 111,
suhailbahwanautogroup.com
Towell Auto Centre 24 526 650,
towellauto.com
Toyota Oman 800 73 444, *toyotaoman.com*
Wattayah Motors 24 573 700,
wattayah.com
Zawawi Trading Company 24 562 077,
omzest.com
Zubair Automotive Group 24 500 000,
zubairautomotive.com

Used Car Dealers

Al Fajer Cars Al Ghubrah Al Janubiyyah,
24 491 111
Al Ittihad Cars Showroom Al Hayl Al
Janubiyah, 24 542 990
Al Jazeera Motors Madinat As Sultan
Qaboos, 24 600 127
Al Siyabi Used Cars Madinat As Sultan
Qaboos, 24 698 195
Audi Approved Plus 24 500 300,
audiapproved.com
Auto Plus Salalah, 24 478 080,
autoplusoman.com
Best Cars Al Wutayyah, 24 578 322,
bestcarsoman.com
Modern Cars Exhibition Ruwi, 24 786 011
Mohsin Haider Darwish Ruwi, 24 523 200,
mhdoman.com
New Zahra Trading Al Humriyyah,
24 833 953
Nissan Salalah, 23 214 784,
nissanoman.com
Popular Pre-Owned Cars Al Qurm,
24 560 111, *popularcarsoman.com*
Real Value Autos Ruwi, 24 560 518,
realvalueautos.com
Sayarti Quality Cars various, 24 500 333
Wattayah Motors Al Watayyah,
24 573 700, *vw-oman.com*

USED VEHICLES

With cars being relatively cheap, and
expats coming and going all the time,
the second-hand car market is thriving.
The main areas for used car dealers are
Al Wattayah, Al Khuwayr and Wadi Kabir,
although you'll find dealers in other
locations too.

The advantage of buying through
a dealer is that they'll arrange the
registration and insurance for you. In
general, dealers do not offer warranties,
unless you are buying a car that is still
protected under its 'new car' warranty.

Newspaper classifieds offer little in
terms of second-hand vehicles for sale,
except for Sunday's Times of Oman
supplement and the classified section of
The Week. Supermarket noticeboards are
a good source of cars for sale, and there is
the car souk at the Friday Market.

If you do buy a second-hand car
privately, it's a good idea to have it
checked for major faults and damage
before you buy. Reputable car dealers will
perform a thorough check-up of a vehicle
for about RO 15.

OWNERSHIP TRANSFER

To transfer a private vehicle into your
name you need to fill in a form, which
details the buyer's personal information
and bears the signatures of both buyer
and seller. The seller must appear
in person before the Directorate of
Licencing at the Traffic Police department.
If the seller still has a loan outstanding
on the vehicle the bank must give its
approval, and if the loan has been paid
the bank will issue a letter of discharge.
All transactions related to buying or
selling second-hand vehicles should go
through the Royal Oman Police.

VEHICLE IMPORT

If you are importing a vehicle, you need
to go with your shipping agent to the
port to get the import papers from the
port authorities (if you're lucky your
shipping agent will do this without you).
They'll give you a form with some details
of the car on it, such as engine number,
chassis number and date of production.
Depending on the age of the vehicle, and
the mood of the person assisting you, you

Driving in Oman

might have to pay tax. The next thing you need is insurance. Even though the car is not registered, you can insure on the basis of the engine number or chassis number to identify the car. The insurance company will give you a form, all in Arabic, which you'll need for the registration. The insurance company will fill in the form for you. You'll also need a letter from your sponsor to say they approve of you importing the vehicle.

The next step is to go to the Ministry of Commerce in Ruwi, behind the Lulu shopping centre. Take the vehicle export papers from the country of origin, the import papers from the shipping agent, the registration form in Arabic from the insurance company, the insurance papers, the sponsor letter, passport copies, your Oman driving licence, a copy of your labour card, and the original ownership papers. To be on the safe side, just take any document remotely connected with the vehicle, plus a few spare copies. After paying a fee of RO 1 you'll be given an approval form.

Armed with all your papers, your next stop should be the police station on Death Valley Road to have your car checked in the Annual Inspections section. Once your vehicle has been inspected, collect the inspector's report (from the small office in the inspection area) and proceed to the main office of the police station. Here, you'll have to present your documents before being directed to the customs counter (which is in the same room).

After customs, you'll be sent back to the inspector's office and this is when you'll have to pay a fee of RO 20 – remember to keep the receipt. You will then get your licence plates, which you'll take home to affix to your car.

The following day you should go back (to the same counter) and hand over the receipt (take all the other papers too, just in case). They will give you the final registration card, which is the same size as a credit card.

Finally, go back to the insurance company and give them the registration number and show them the card.

VEHICLE FINANCE

Many new and second-hand car dealers will be able to arrange vehicle finance for you, often through a deal with their preferred banking partner. Strangely, it is unusual to setup a direct debit to cover your monthly car payment, and instead you will have to write out a post-dated cheque for every month of the life of your loan, and submit them all at the very beginning.

So if you take a four-year car loan, you will have to write out 48 cheques before you can take ownership of your car. Always ask about the rates and terms of the loan, and then consider going to a different bank to see if they will offer you a better deal.

VEHICLE INSURANCE

You must have adequate insurance before you can register your car in your name. The minimum requirement is third party insurance, but fully comprehensive insurance is advisable. To insure your car you need copies of your driving licence, your labour or residence card, and the 'mulkia' for your car. In some cases the insurance company will want to inspect the car first.

It is simple and inexpensive to insure your car for the United Arab Emirates too, should you wish to drive across the border. Remember, your insurance will not be valid if your licence is not valid, or if you have an accident while under the influence of alcohol.

REGISTERING A VEHICLE

All cars must be registered and the registration must be renewed annually. The registration document is called the mulkia, and should be carried with you in the car whenever you drive. Along with your essential documents (p.83) the following documents are also required:

- New registration form filled in by the applicant or their representative and stamped by the sponsor
- Insurance certificate
- Proof of purchase certificate
- Copy of a valid driving licence
  There is a detailed list on the ROP website (rop.gov.om) of all required documents when registering your vehicle. Regulations can change overnight, so it is always a good idea to check what the

requirements are before you go. Additional documents are needed if you have imported your car or bought it at an auction.

If your car is 10 years old or older, it will need to pass a roadworthiness test. This involves an inspection to check that the chassis and engine numbers match those on the mulkia, that the lights and brakes work, that there are no smoke emissions, and the paintwork is not damaged or fading. Once the car has passed the test, you can proceed with registration. If your car fails the test, you must first fix any problems and start the process again.

TRAFFIC FINES & OFFENCES

If you are caught driving or parking illegally, you will be fined (unless the offence is more serious, in which case you may have to appear in court).

Around Muscat, there are a number of police-controlled speed traps, fixed cameras and mobile radar traps, which are activated by cars exceeding the speed limit by 9 km/h or more. Fines start at RO 10 and go up in increments of RO 5.

All traffic fines should be paid at the traffic fines section of the Death Valley Road police station. Your fines are 'banked' and you only have to pay them once a year when you renew your car registration, although you can quickly check whether you've received any fines online at rop.gov. om/trafficfine.

BREAKDOWNS

In the event of a breakdown, you will usually find that passing police cars stop to help you, or at least to check your documents. It is important to keep water in your car at all times – the last thing you need is to be stuck on the side of the road with no air conditioning and no water while you wait for assistance. If you can, pull your car over to a safe spot. If you are on the hard shoulder of a busy road, pull your car as far away from the yellow line as possible, display your red warning triangle and step away from the road until help arrives.

You can call the Arabian Automobile Association (AAA), a 24 hour breakdown service (similar to the AA in the UK). If you break down for any reason (even a flat tyre or if you run out of petrol), they will send a mechanic out to you as soon as possible. The number is 24 605 555 and often the operator on duty won't speak great English so be patient.

TRAFFIC ACCIDENTS

Oman has a relatively high rate of road accidents, and unfortunately the figures of death and injury on the roads increase every year. The government started a large road safety campaign in an effort to educate drivers about safe driving standards and how to reduce accidents. The name of the campaign is 'Salim and Salimah, Safe and Sound' (salimandsalimah.org), and the website contains a great deal of excellent information on accidents and road safety.

If you have an accident, don't move your car until the police arrive, even if you are causing a major road blockage. The police will usually arrive pretty quickly. In case of an accident, call 24 560 099 (don't call 9999, it is reserved for the Fire Department and emergency cases only). Expect a crowd of rubberneckers to gather around the accident – at least you'll have someone there who can translate from Arabic to English when the police arrive. The police will decide (on the spot) which party is responsible for the accident, and then all involved parties should go to the nearest police station.

In the case of minor accidents where there is no injury, you must move your car out of the way so that you don't cause a road blockage, and both parties can go to the police station together and report the incident and a decision made about who was responsible, and who has to pay.

If your car can't be driven, the police will arrange for it to be towed away. When you get to the police station you might have to wait around for quite some time, so be patient. You'll need to present your driving licence and mulkia (registration card). If any of your documents are invalid you will immediately be blamed for the accident. If your company has a PRO, it's a good idea to get him to come down to the station to help you translate and fill in the many forms. If there is a fine to be paid, the police will hold your licence until you've paid it.

The police will fill in an accident report and you will be given a reference number. The car must be sent to a garage that is approved by your insurance company. The garage is not allowed to carry out repairs to any vehicle without the police report. If you are in an accident where someone is hurt or killed, and the case goes to court, you will not be allowed to leave the country until the case is settled.

VEHICLE REPAIRS

By law, no vehicle can be accepted for repair after an accident without an accident report from the Traffic Police. Usually, your insurance company will have an agreement with a particular garage to which they will refer you. The garage will carry out the repair work and the insurance company will settle the claim. Generally, there is an RO 100 deductible due on all claims, but confirm the details of your particular policy with your insurance company.

Besides accidents and bumps, you may also have to deal with the usual running repairs associated with any car. Common problems in this part of the world can include the air conditioning malfunctioning and batteries suddenly giving up the ghost. If your air conditioning is not working well it is usually a case of having the gas topped up, which is a fairly straightforward procedure.

However, if something more serious goes wrong it can be very costly to fix, mainly due to labour charges as the mechanic may have to remove your dashboard to get access to the aircon. Car batteries don't seem to last too well in the heat, and it is not uncommon to come back from your holidays to find your car won't start.

Also, all the dealers do servicing of cars and repairs, but it does usually cost more if you do the repairs through a motor dealer service centre. Most cars are sold with a two to four year service plan that can be renewed every two years and this will generally keep any car in very good working order.

Vehicle Repairs

Al Khuwair Auto Maintenance Al Khuwayr Al Janubiyyah, 24 602 393
Balqees Trading & Contracting Wadi Kabir, 24 815 161
East Arabian Establishment Wadi Kabir, 24 815 161
Four Wheel Drive Centre Wadi Kabir, 24 810 962

WORKING IN OMAN

A good expat package in Oman remains a golden opportunity to experience a different culture, a relaxed lifestyle and eternal sunshine. But if you're thinking about working here, be aware that it's unusual for people to arrive in Oman on a visit visa to look for work – most people already have jobs lined up before they arrive.

Expat workers come to Oman for a number of reasons – to advance their careers, for higher standards of living, to take advantage of new career opportunities, or just for the experience of living in a new culture. Some people are seconded to Oman by companies based in their home countries, and some actively seek out opportunities for a new job that includes a place in the sun. Few arrive on the spot hoping to find a job when they arrive.

Although expat positions are still available, the main setback to finding a good posting is the highly successful Omanisation programme. Some organisations have achieved over 90% Omanisation, so less than 10% of their workforce is comprised of foreigners. But while Omanisation has closed off certain sectors of industry to expat jobseekers, you should still be able to find a job in sectors like oil, medicine and education.

If you're considering coming to Oman to look for work, do your research before you arrive. Sign up with online job sites as far in advance as possible and visit the websites of some of Oman's larger organisations to see if they have any vacancies.

It's also a good idea to pick up a copy of the Apex Business Directory of Oman (businessdirectoryoman.com), which contains information, addresses and phone numbers of most companies operating here. There may also be agencies in your home country that specialise in overseas employment, or you could try your luck in the neighbouring UAE, where some international recruitment firms have set up their Middle Eastern offices. Oman-based recruitment agencies for expat positions are virtually non-existent.

Sponsorship

As in most parts of the GCC, for foreigners to live and work in Oman, they must usually be sponsored by an employer or family member. To obtain a residency visa as an employee, you need a local sponsor and a labour permit from the Ministry of Manpower. Your sponsor will typically take care of all practical arrangements related to the application process. However, you may need to get a health certificate from your home country, stating that you are free from illness and not carrying any communicable diseases. The requirements vary by nationality and are subject to change at short notice, so it's always best to check with your embassy (see Directory on p.340).

Once your employer sponsors you, you can then arrange sponsorship for your family members. Two family sponsorship options are available: a family joining visa or a family residence visa. Children under the age of 21 can be sponsored. Expats may also be eligible to apply for a Contractor Visa or an Investor Resident Visa – refer to the website of the Royal Oman Police (rop.gov.om) to get the latest information on visitor visas, residence permits and employment, investor or student visas.

Working Hours & Benefits

If you're new to the GCC, you'll quickly become aware of the split-shift phenomenon. Traditionally, companies start work a little early, break for a long lunch (usually three hours), and return to work for a late-afternoon session. Split-shift timings are usually 08:00 to 13:00 and 16:00 to 19:00.

Not all companies follow these hours however, and many work a 'straight shift' with a short lunch break. Indeed, most private sector companies now work straight shifts from 07:00 to 16:00, as do several government organisations, which tend to operate from 07:00 to 14:00.

The official weekend days are Thursday and Friday, but many sectors are now moving to a Friday-Saturday weekend in line with neighbouring countries like the UAE. Public holidays are declared by the government. Most are religious holidays and therefore are governed by the Hijri (lunar) calendar. Holiday can't be declared until the new moon has been seen by the Moon Sighting Committee so you won't know the exact day or duration of the holiday until the moon is sighted the night before.

During Ramadan, all Muslims and people working in government organisations have reduced working hours. Some private sector companies also reduce the hours, at times also for non-Muslim employees.

Omani labour law grants new mothers their basic salary for six weeks following birth. Paternity leave is not a recognised right, but this is at the discretion of your employer.

Business Culture & Etiquette

Although it is an up-and-coming modern city, Muscat is still an Arab city in a Muslim country, and this affects every aspect of daily life, including how business is done. Even if your counterpart in another company is an expat, the head decision maker is often an Omani who could possibly have a different approach to business matters. Your best bet when doing business in Muscat for the first time is to watch closely, have loads of patience, and make a concerted effort to understand the culture and respect the customs. Don't underestimate your

Corniche at night

business contacts or assume that you have a better way of doing things than them – Omanis can smell an arrogant expat a mile away and you'll soon find many business opportunities passing you by.

FINDING WORK

Expat workers come to Oman for various reasons, primarily because the salaries are great and there is no personal income tax. As an added bonus, the weather is sublime, it is a relatively safe country, and the lifestyle is easy. When weighing up the pros and cons of accepting an offer on Oman, remember that the Omani rial is pegged to the dollar. That said, despite the fluctuations of the US dollar against a number of major currencies, including the Japanese yen, the Euro and the pound sterling, the US dollar remains the primary reserve cash currency in the world and is expected to remain so for many years to come. Time has shown that pegging the Omani rial to the US dollar has stabilised its currency exchange.

You might find that currency fluctuations decrease the actual value of your salary package when you compare it to what you would earn in dollars, sterling or Euros back home. Nevertheless, there is no question that a good expat package in a good company in Oman is a golden opportunity to experience a different culture in a country where the sun always shines.

Finding Work Before You Come

It is better to have a job arranged before you come to Oman, as with a sponsor lined up all your paperwork will be taken care of on your behalf. If you fancy living in Oman for a few years and are on the lookout for a good opportunity, contact some reputable recruitment agencies in your home country who may have jobs available in this region.

If you want to do the legwork yourself, you have a number of options. You can 'cold-call' companies by sending out unsolicited CVs to targeted industries, although this is rarely the path to success. If you have friends or acquaintances in Oman, you can send them some copies of your CV and ask them to put out feelers for you. Or you can do some research on the internet to find out more about job vacancies in Oman. Try visiting the following websites: gulfjobsites.com, careermideast.com,

overseasjobs.com, ociped.com, and monster.com. Alternatively you could visit the websites of some of Oman's larger organisations to see if they have any vacancies. Try Petroleum Development Oman (pdo.co.om), British School Muscat (britishschoolmuscat.com), Muscat Private Hospital (muscatprivatehospital.com), Omantel (omantel.net.om), Nawras (nawras.om), or American British Academy (abaoman.edu.om).

If you are in the hospitality industry, try contacting the individual hotels directly (see a list of hotels on p.66). If you get a job offer, you will need to negotiate your employment package carefully to cover all bases. A good package covers housing, medical insurance, transport (either in the form of a company car or a car allowance), shipping or relocation costs, and education for your children.

Finding Work While You Are In Oman

Unless you have excellent contacts lined up before coming to Oman, don't expect to find work while you are on a visit visa. The slow pace of life means that decisions are not always made quickly.

There are no newspaper supplements for appointments, and any classified ads in the papers are usually targeted at Omanis or at labourers. When you arrive, pick up a copy of the Apex Business Directory of Oman, which contains information, addresses and phone numbers of most companies. You can find a copy at the Apex office in Ruwi (24 799 388).

If you have come to Oman with your spouse who is working and you wish to find a job for yourself, the options are limited unless you are in the teaching or medical professions. To find a job in these sectors, it's best to ask directly at schools, hospitals and clinics. The rigorous Omanisation programme does not permit an expat to hold a job that an Omani is qualified to do, which cuts out most administrative jobs and many others. If you are a well-qualified English teacher, then you should be able to find work as a teacher of English as a second language. There are several institutes offering English courses to non-native speakers, so call them to see if they have any vacancies.

Try the Polyglot Institute (p.140), ELS Language Centers (p.140), Modern Gulf Institute (p.140), British Council (p.140) and Salalah Language International (p.140).

Recruitment Agencies

Virtually non-existent, recruitment agencies generally cater for manual labourers from Asian countries. The only agencies that might offer more interesting expat jobs are those listed in the table. To register, check with the agency to find out if they take walk-in applicants. Most accept CVs via fax or email these days and will then contact you for an interview. The agency takes its fee from the registered company once the position has been filled. It is illegal for a recruitment company to charge job seekers for their services.

Employment Contracts

Accepting an expat posting can have its pitfalls, so before you sign your contract pay special attention to things like probation periods, accommodation, annual leave, travel entitlements, medical and dental cover, notice periods and repatriation entitlements.

Once you accept your offer, you will be asked to sign both an English and an Arabic copy of your contract. The Arabic copy is the one that will be referred to in any legal dispute between you and your employer, so if you have any doubts about the integrity of the company, ask a lawyer or Arabic-speaking friend to look through it. However, if there was ever a legal dispute, the court would want to know why there was any discrepancy between the English and Arabic versions in the first place.

It is worth reading through a copy of the Oman labour law before you sign your contract. Labour law takes precedence over your contract, so if your contract reads differently from the labour law it's worth noting why.

If you are sponsored by your spouse and want to work, you need to get an NOC from his employer before you can sign a contract with your new employer. Your employer will then apply for your labour card.

Labour Card

The old labour card, issued by the Labour Department, is a legal document certifying the employment status of an individual. If your employer is arranging your residency, your labour clearance should be processed directly after your residency has been approved. If you are on family residency and decide to work,

your employer (not your visa sponsor) will need to apply for your labour clearance. Your sponsor should supply an NOC. Women on their husband's or father's sponsorship are not allowed to work unless they have a work visa.

In 2005 the government began replacing labour cards with resident cards. The resident card uses biometric recognition and is multi-functional, holding personal details, driving licence, and emergency medical information. It can be used for electronic validation at immigration checkpoints, and can even serve as an electronic cash card for transactions at government organisations. Cards are issued by the Directorate General of Civil Status. You will need a completed application form, passport, medical certificate, labour clearance from the Ministry of Manpower (private sector workers) and two photographs. Non-working residents (family members) need a completed application form, passport, birth certificate, medical certificate and two photographs. Further information can be requested from the Directorate General of Civil Status, located on the Seeb Airport Roundabout.

Health Card

There is no health card as such in Oman. You will need to undergo a medical test as part of your residency process. This involves a blood test, taken at the Ministry of Health clinic in Ruwi, where they will test for infectious diseases (such as HIV and hepatitis) and blood type. Your sponsor will advise you on the procedure and perhaps even accompany you to the clinic to assist. When you get to the clinic you will find a very long queue, so to avoid waiting all morning you should get there as early as possible.

Some nationalities are required to produce a health certificate from their home country if they are entering Oman on an employment visa. This test will be a comprehensive report including x-rays and blood tests. Your sponsor should be able to advise you, or you can check rop. gov.om (the website of the Royal Oman Police) for more information according to your nationality.

Labour Law

The current version of the Oman labour law was promulgated in 2003. The law outlines everything from employee entitlements (end of service gratuity, workers' compensation, holidays and other benefits) to employment contracts and disciplinary rules.

The labour law is considered fair and clearly outlines the rights of both employees and employers. Labour unions and strikes are illegal, but adherence to the law is rigorously policed and disputes are adjudicated by the Labour Board. Copies of the labour law can be obtained from the Ministry of Manpower (manpower.gov.om) or viewed at directory-oman.com.

Labour Law

Al Ahlam Higher Education Services, 24 562 623, *ahlameducation.com*
CFBT Education Services & Partners, 24 692 004, *cfbtoman.com*
Ministry Of Commerce & Industry, 24 799 500, *mocioman.gov.om*
Ministry Of Manpower, *manpower.gov.om*
Ministry Of Social Development, *mosd.gov.om*
The Public Authority For Investment Promotion & Export Development (PAIPED), 24 623 300, *ociped.com*

CHANGING JOBS & BANS

In relation to the contract of work, article 46 of the Omani Labour Law states that 'the employer shall give to the worker, upon his request, at the end of the contract, an end of service certificate free of charge, wherein he shall state the date of the worker's joining the service, date of leaving it, the type of work he was performing, the wage and other remuneration and privileges, if any.'

Of course, the employee has to settle all bills, loans etc before he moves to a new job as it is usually the sponsor who would be liable for these in the case of non-payment. This forms the basis of the letter of release. Once this is done, the employee can freely move to a new company.

Your employer can no longer prevent you from taking up a job with another company. This has proved a great help to people wishing to change jobs. The company can no longer ban the person and people do not have to leave the country for two years as was previously the case.

FREE ZONES

Free zones are not as prevalent in Oman as they are in other Gulf states, but there are a few developments. A technology park called Knowledge Oasis Muscat (kom.om) is situated in Rusayl Industrial Estate (near Sultan Qaboos University) and offers 100% foreign ownership of businesses. You pay no personal income tax, you are exempt from foreign exchange controls, and you pay no tax on your company profits for the first five years.

There are three free zones and one special economic zone in Oman:
Al Mazunah Free Zone – strategically located in the south west of Oman on the Oman-Yemen border. *almazunah.com*
Knowledge Oasis Muscat – a public-private sector led technology park located 32km from Muscat. *kom.com*
Salalah Free Zone – in the south of the country. *sfzco.com*
Port of Sohar – a special economic zone. *portofsohar.com*

Setting Up A Business In Oman

Setting up a business in Oman can be a lengthy and arduous task. Firstly, you will need to find a suitable Omani sponsor, which is easier said than done. Obtain professional legal advice throughout and ensure all agreements are written down, not just verbal. It may be easier to set up in Knowledge Oasis Muscat (kom.om) or in Salalah Free Zone (sfzco.com).

Networking

While Muscat is still a relatively small city, networking is critical, even across industries. Everyone seems to know everyone and getting in with the corporate 'in-crowd' certainly has its benefits. Business acumen can, at times, be more important than specific industry knowledge and therefore it pays to attend business events and meetings. Make friends in government departments and this will often land you in the front line for opportunities. Because bad news is rarely made public in the newspapers here, staying tuned in to the business grapevine helps prevent wrong decisions. For in-depth information about business in Oman, refer to your local business group or the commercial attache at your embassy or consulate. The contact numbers can be found in the table below.

Networking

British Businessman's Forum,
99 360 263
British Council, 24 681 000,
britishcouncil.org/me
Business Information Centre,
24 494 500
Muscat American Business Council,
24 566 140, *mabcoman.com*
**Oman Chamber Of Commerce &
Industry,** 24 763 700,
chamberoman.com
**The Public Authority For Investment
Promotion & Export Development
(PAIPED),** 24 623 300, *ociped.com*
United Media Services SAOC,
24 700 896, *oeronline.com*

VOLUNTARY & CHARITY WORK

Voluntary work is widely available in
Oman and those who dedicate their
time to worthy causes are held in high
esteem. The Sultan Qaboos Award
for Volunteer Work acclaims three
individuals and three associations for
their contributions in voluntary projects
and the award, which is conducted by
the ministry of social development, aims
to promote the culture of volunteering
and its importance to both the family
and community, highlight the role of
associations and civil institutions, and
encourage social responsibility.

The Art Of Living Oman Chapter
24 789 859
artofliving-oman.org
The Art of Living is a multi-faceted,
not-for-profit educational and
humaritian NGO. Almost a decade in
existence, the Oman Chapter of the
Art of Living voluntary work includes
organising blood donations, fund raising
programmes and recycling drives.

Association Of Early Intervention For Children With Disability
18th November Rd, Villa 3215, Al
Athaiba 24 496 960
aei.org.om
This association serves children from
birth to 6 years, who are at risk or
disabled, with a comprehensive early
intervention programme that covers
social, medical, physical, academic and
therapeutic services.

Centre For Special Education – Indian School Muscat
Darsayt **24 707 567**
indianschoolmuscat.com
This centre supervises and teaches
children with special needs self-help skills,
arts and crafts, music and pre-vocational
skills. The teaching of the children is need-
based in small groups and an individual
education programme (IEP) is carefully
designed for each child. Volunteers are
given on-the-job training.

Dar Al Atta Society
daralatta.org
This is a voluntary non-governmental
organisation that seeks to provide
the less privileged members of society
with basics that secure them a decent
living. Its work includes monthly food
aid to needy families, reconstruction of
houses that are not fit for habitation and
providing emergency relief aid at times of
natural crises.

Environment Society Of Oman
eso.org
This is a non-governmental organisation
that aims to help conserve Oman's
natural heritage and raise awareness
of environmental issues. Activities
for members include participating in
hands-on projects and awareness-raising
activities to reduce litter, recycle waste,
and help keep the environment clean.

Oman Association For The Disabled
99 329 030
This is an NGO established to provide
support, education and recreational
activities for people with disabilities.

Oman Charity Club
96 655 800
This organisation is for expats living
in Oman who want to help the less
privileged in the country. Activities include
organising donations of clothes, toys and
games, and visiting poor villagers.

Oman National Association For Cancer Awareness
24 498 716
ocancer.org.om
The objectives of the organisation include
creating public awareness of all types
of cancer through community-based
programmes.

LEGAL & FINANCIAL ISSUES

Oman is an Absolute Monarchy with a bicameral system. The Head of State and Supreme Commander of the Armed Forces is His Majesty Sultan Qaboos Bin Said. Laws in Oman are issued by Royal Decree as primary legislation, or by Ministerial Decisions as secondary legislation. Oman has the following court system – Supreme Court, Appellate Courts, Courts of First Instance and Courts of Summary Jurisdiction. Each court is able to deal with matters relating to civil, commercial, labour, tax and personal (Shariah) law.

Although judges can practise either secular law or Shariah law, Shariah is the basis for all legislation as set out in the basic law (Royal Decree 101/96), which is in effect the constitution of Oman. Court proceedings are conducted only in Arabic. All official documents issued by the courts and used in proceedings must also be in Arabic.

The main legal issue likely to affect expats is property ownership (p.100). As a foreigner, this is limited to purchasing property within integrated tourist complexes only, such as The Wave and Muscat Golf and Country Club. Other issues where you might land on the wrong side of the law are linked to the rules of Islam: gambling is forbidden, and although you can drink under certain conditions are inviting trouble if you get drunk and disorderly in public places. Living with a member of the opposite sex who is not a family member is illegal.

There is one prison near Mabella and a new one is being constructed in Nizwa. Oman's prisons are best described as basic. Facilities are poor and hygiene is questionable. Your personal items (including shoes and belt) will be taken off you when you enter the prison and only returned when you leave. You may be allowed to make a phone call, or the prison may inform your sponsor or company PRO officer that you are in custody. For a first offence, bail can be paid after 48 hours

Omani currency

– the bail amount is usually somewhere between RO 50 and RO 75. If you can't afford the bail then you have to remain in custody. Your embassy will not be able to offer financial or legal assistance.

Alcohol & Drugs

Attitudes to drinking in this region are a bit stiffer than you might experience back home (popping into your corner shop for a six-pack is a definite no-no). However, compared to some of the other GCC countries, Oman has a fairly relaxed view of alcohol. Non-Muslims can drink in licensed bars and restaurants, at private clubs, and at various social events that are generously sponsored by major alcohol retailers. Muscat is not famous for its buzzing nightlife, but some hotel bars have extended their opening hours to 03:00 (thus brightening up the social scene a bit).

However, drunk and disorderly behaviour in public is frowned upon and fortunately most expats seem to respect this. If you want to buy alcohol for consumption at home, you need to apply for a liquor licence (p.85). Only non-Muslim residents with a labour card are allowed to apply. If you are married, only the husband can apply, and his wife cannot use the licence to buy alcohol unless he works in the interior. Licences are valid for two years, but can't be used outside of the city in which they were issued.

Your liquor licence permits you to buy a limited amount of alcohol each month. Your allowance is calculated based on your salary, and is usually not more than 10% of it. You can apply for a larger allowance under certain conditions (for example, if your job entails corporate entertaining). You can't 'bank' your allowance – you must either use it or lose it. Many expats have learned the benefits of stockpiling alcohol, particularly in the lead-up to Ramadan when liquor stores are closed for a whole month and bars do not serve any booze. It is illegal to drive around with liquor in your car, with the exception of transporting it from the liquor store to your home.

Drug offences usually result in serious sentences, and your time in prison can be anywhere from one month to 25 years, depending on the amount you were caught with, the type of drugs and the circumstances surrounding the arrest. In addition, your fine could be up to RO 20,000 and the court can even sentence you to death in severe cases. If you are caught with forbidden prescription medicines, it is important that you can produce the actual doctor's prescription for them. It will depend upon the judge's decision for what sentence you will receive, but it will again be severe.

Traffic Offences

If you are involved in an accident involving a fatality, you will be required to hand over RO 7,000 to the ROP, RO 5,000 of that being 'blood money' which will go to the deceased's relatives. The other RO 2,000 will be used for any medical bills or repatriation in case of an expat. It will be up to your insurance company to decide whether or not your insurance will cover the cost of this blood money. The court could take up to six months to finalise the sentence, so you may be allowed to continue working until your sentence is given. You will not however, be allowed to leave the country while your court case is pending.

Myths & Truths

- If you write a cheque that bounces, you will be given around a week to pay the amount (if it is your first offence). If you can't pay, you will be taken into custody.
- Be careful what stickers you place on your car – car stickers featuring donkeys (even if it is a national mascot of a particular region in your home country) are apparently illegal because the position of the sticker on the car indicates that anyone passing the sticker is a donkey themselves. You will receive a fine.
- Flogging does not happen in Oman.
- Pregnancy outside wedlock will result in deportation if you are caught.
- Smoking, eating or drinking in public places during Ramadan is considered highly offensive and can carry a jail term of up to three months.
- Unmarried men and women are not permitted to live together unless they are related (brother and sister, for example). However, before you rush down the aisle, rest assured that this law is rarely enforced. Just be discreet, and you should be fine.

Law Firms

Al Busaidy, Mansoor Jamal & Co
24 814 466, *amjoman.com*
Curtis, Mallet – Prevost, Colt & Mosle
24 564 495, *curtis.com*

BARTERING

Bargaining is a traditional part of doing trade in Oman and it is still widely used today, especially in the souks. You can sometimes end up paying half of the original asking price. A discount of 10% is usual, even in appliance stores, but not in supermarkets or department stores. It can also be a fun way to do business; vendors will square up to 'do battle', courteously offering their customers some kahwa, and in return customers should bargain hard. Start your negotiations by asking for the 'best price' and go from there.

Hafedh Al Mahrouqi & Co
24 799 755, omanilaw.com
Hamad Al Sharji, Peter Mansour & Co
24 780 333, sharjimansour.com
Jihad Al Taie & Associates 24 478 282
Said Al Shahry Law Office,
24 603 123, saslo.com
Said Al Shahry Law Office
23 289 833, saslo.com
SNR Denton & Co 24 573 000,
snrdenton.com
Trowers & Hamlins 24 682 900,
trowers.com

Insurance Companies
Al Ahlia Insurance Co SAOC
24 766 800, alahliaoman.com
Arabia Insurance Company
24 793 299, arabiainsurance.com
AXA Insurance Gulf 24 400 100,
axa.com
Dhofar Insurance Company (SAOG),
23 294 368, dhofarinsurance.com
Falcon Insurance SAOC 246 609 00,
falconinsurancesaoc.com
MetLife Alico 24 787 531,
metlifealico.com.om
Oman Qatar Insurance Company (SAOG)
24 700 798, qatarinsurance.com
Oman United Insurance Co (SAOG)
23 295 040, omanutd.com
Risk Management Services
24 704 004, rmsllc.com

MONEY

Cash is the preferred method of payment in Oman, although credit cards are accepted in larger department stores, restaurants and hotels. Cash and traveller's cheques can be exchanged in licensed exchange offices, banks and international hotels – as usual a passport is required for exchanging traveller's cheques. To avoid additional exchange rate charges, take traveller's cheques in US dollars if possible. Local cheques are generally accepted in business but not for personal purchases. If you are taking a lease for accommodation, it is likely that you will need to pay by cheque and supply post-dated cheques for the remaining period of the rent. There are no restrictions on the import or export of any currency. Israeli currency is prohibited.

Exchange Rates
Foreign Currency (FC) 1 Unit FC = RO RO 1 = x FC

Australia	0.40	2.49
Bahrain	1.02	0.98
Bangladesh	0.005	212.43
Canada	0.39	2.59
Denmark	0.07	14.46
Euro	0.51	1.94
Hong Kong	0.05	20.16
India	0.01	131.93
Japan	0.005	215.30
Jordan	0.54	1.85
Kuwait	1.39	0.72
New Zealand	0.32	3.17
Pakistan	0.004	235.63
Philippines	0.01	111.54
Qatar	0.11	9.46
Saudi Arabia	0.10	9.74
Singapore	0.31	3.26
South Africa	0.05	19.78
Sri Lanka	0.003	336.02
Sweden	0.06	17.25
Siwitzerland	0.43	2.35
Thailand	0.01	79.88
UAE	0.10	9.54
UK	0.61	1.63
USA	0.39	2.60

Source: www.xe.com 28 Mar 2012

EXCHANGE CENTRES
Money exchanges are found all over Muscat and Salalah, offering good service and exchange rates (often better than the banks). Exchange houses are usually open from 08:00 to 13:00 and 16:00 to 19:00, and often operate in the evenings and at weekends. Alternatively, hotels will usually exchange money and traveller's cheques at the standard (noncompetitive) hotel rate. At Seeb International Airport, there is a Travelex counter before immigration to facilitate visa payments.

Exchange Centres
Abu Mehad 24 566 123
Al Barzah Money Exchange 24 487 444
Gulf Overseas 24 834 182

BankDhofar credit cards

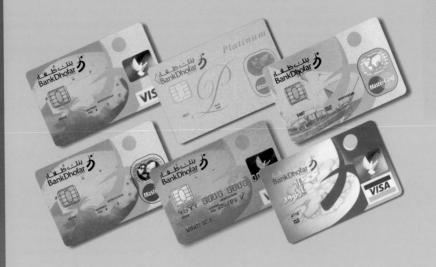

Shopping, travel and entertainment made easy

- Worldwide recognition
- Interest-free repayment period
- Emergency cash withdrawal facility
- Lost card protection
- Supplementary cards for family members
- Free Travel Insurance Cover
- Access to airport lounges worldwide

www.bankdhofar.com

Call 24 x 7
2479-1111

Hamdan 23 296 903
LaxmidasThariaVed 24 700 065
Modern Exchange 24 832 133
Oman & UAE Exchange Centre
24 584 358
Oman International Exchange
24 832 197
Oman United Exchange 24 794 305
Purshottam Kanji Exchange
24 713 338

LOCAL CURRENCY

The monetary unit is the Oman rial (RO or OR). It is divided into 1,000 baisas (also spelt 'baiza' making it a 3 decimal currency, not like most countries where it is a 2 decimal currency. Notes come in denominations of rials 50, 20, 10, 5, 1, 1/2 (500 baisas) and 100 baisas. Coin denominations are 50, 25, 10 and 5 baisas. Denominations are written in both Arabic and English.

It is best to take a few minutes to familiarise yourself with the currency, although shopkeepers are generally honest when giving you your change. The rial is tied to the US dollar at a mid-rate of approximately US$1 ~ RO 0.385, which has basically remained unchanged for a number of years.

The way prices are written can lead to some confusion. An item may be marked 'RO/OR.1,500'– the price could be one thousand five hundred rials or one rial and five hundred baisas. The value of the item will usually be obvious. For clarity in this book, prices are shown in a standard way: one rial and 500 hundred baisas will be shown as RO 1.500 and one thousand five hundred rials as RO 1,500, while 15 rials will be RO 15.

For an idea on what basic items cost in Oman, compared to your home country, see the cost of living table on p.127.

BANKS

The well-structured and ever-growing network of local and international banks, strictly controlled by the Central Bank of Oman, offers the full range of commercial and personal banking services. Transfers can be made without difficulty as there is no exchange control and the Oman rial is freely convertible to other currencies. There is a good range of international banks in Oman, all of which offer standard facilities such as current, deposit and savings accounts, ATM facilities, cheque

books, credit cards and loans. In addition, you could consider setting up an offshore account.

Bank headquarters are clustered in Ruwi, Muscat's central business district. There are branches all over Muscat and Salalah, and in major towns such as Nizwa, Sur and Sohar. Banking hours are usually 08:00 to 13:00 or 14:00 (Sunday – Thursday).

Main Banks

Bank Dhofar >*p.125* 24 791 111, *bankdhofar.com*
Bank Sohar SAOG 24 730 000, *banksohar.net*
BankMuscat (SAOG) 24 795 555, *bankmuscat.com*
Banque Banorabe 24 704 274
Central Bank Of Oman 24 702 222, *cbo-oman.org*
Habib Bank 24 817 142, *habibbank.com*
HSBC Bank Middle East Limited 24 799 920, *oman.hsbc.com*
National Bank Of Abu Dhabi 24 761 000, *nbad.com*
National Bank Of Oman (NBO) 24 811 711, *nbo.co.om*
Oman Arab Bank 24706265, *oman-arabbank.com*
Oman International Bank 24 682 500, *oiboman.com*
Standard Chartered Bank 24 773 666, *standardchartered.com*

ATMS

Most banks operate automatic teller machines (ATMs) that accept a wide range of cards. Common systems accepted around Muscat include MasterCard, Visa, American Express, Global Access, Plus System and Cirrus. ATMs can be found in shopping malls, at the airport, and various street locations in Muscat. Exchange rates used in the transaction are normally competitive and the process is often faster and easier than travellers' cheques.

CREDIT CARDS

Larger shops, hotels and restaurants in Muscat and Salalah accept major credit cards (American Express, Diners Club, MasterCard and Visa) and they will often have the card logos displayed at the entrance. However, if you are travelling in the interior, or are shopping at souks and smaller shops, cash is usually the only form of payment accepted.

TAXATION

Oman levies no personal taxes and withholds no income tax of any sort. However, the IMF is advising many Middle Eastern countries to introduce tax reforms to diversify their resources.

The lack of direct income taxation makes Oman a great place to save money. Currently, the only taxes expatriates are obliged to pay are the 8% service tax at food and beverage outlets in hotels, a 4% tourism tax, a 5% municipality tax, and a 3% tax on rental accommodation. There is also a tax on alcohol bought at retail shops, and on pork.

Before leaving your home country to take up an expat posting, you should contact the tax authorities to ensure that you are complying with the financial laws there. Most countries will consider you not liable for income tax once you prove that you are not resident in that country. But you might still have to pay tax on any income you are getting from your home country (for example if you are renting out your property or earning interest on a bank account).

Check with the revenue service of your country – the following websites may be helpful: UK (hmrc.gov.uk), USA (irs.gov), South Africa (sars. gov.za), Australia (ato.gov.au), Canada (craarc.gc.ca), New Zealand (ird.govt.nz).

Branch of BankMuscat

Cost Of Living

(Item or Activity Price/Cost)

Apples (per kg) RO 0.850
Bananas (per kg) RO 0.700
Bottle of house wine (restaurant) RO 12.000
Bottle of wine (off licence) RO 3.000
Burger (takeaway) RO 0.400
Bus (10km journey) RO 0.500
Can of dog food RO 0.450
Can of soft drink RO 0.150
Cappuccino RO 1.500
Car rental (per day) RO 20.000
Carrots (per kg) RO 0.790
CD Album RO 6.000
Chocolate bar RO 0.400
Cigarettes (per pack of 20) RO 0.750
Cinema ticket RO 3.200
Dozen eggs RO 0.920
Fresh beef (per kg)
RO 7.000 (ribeye); RO 10.900 (fillet)
Fresh chicken (per kg) RO 2.800
Fresh fish (per kg) RO 1.500
Golf (18 holes) RO 55.000 (non-affiliated visitors) RO 5.000 for driving range

House wine (glass) RO 2.500
Large takeaway pizza RO 7.000
Loaf of bread RO 0.800
Local postage stamp RO 0.050 correct
Milk (1 litre) RO 0.530
Mobile to mobile call (local, per minute) RO 0.055
New release DVD RO 7.000
Newspaper (international) RO 1.000
Newspaper (local) RO 0.200
Orange juice (1 litre) RO 1.000
Pack of 24 aspirin/paracetamol tablets RO 0.750
Petrol RO 0.120/Ltr
Pint of beer RO 3.000
Postcard RO 0.200
Potatoes (1kg) RO 0.500
Rice (1kg) RO 0.700
Salon haircut (female) RO 20.000
Salon haircut (male) RO 7.000
Shawarma RO 0.250
Six-pack of beer (off licence) RO 3.000
Strawberries (per punnet) RO 1.800
Sugar (2kg) RO 0.450
Taxi (10km journey) RO 3.500
Text message (local) RO 0.010
Tube of toothpaste RO 1.000
Water (1.5 litres, restaurant) RO 1.500
Water (1.5 litres, supermarket) RO 0.300
Watermelon (per kg) RO 0.600

FAMILY AND EDUCATION

FAMILY

Family life

Muscat and Oman are described by expats as ideal for family life. The general pace of life is relaxed and affordable home help is at hand. You should bear in mind, however, that arranging a spot in a good school can be a difficult task. If you have children of school-going age, you will need to start investigating schools as early as possible. There aren't many schools to choose from and with Muscat expanding all the time, some schools are running out of places for certain age groups.

MATERNITY

Many expats choose to give birth in Oman and do so without any problems. The main difference is that you will not have the same choices regarding your birth plan as you would probably have in your home country. You don't have the option of a home birth or a water birth, but straightforward births are expertly handled. If you do decide to travel home to give birth, you will need to check with your doctor regarding whether it is safe to travel at an advanced stage of pregnancy. Your doctor will usually give you permission to fly up to 34 weeks, but you should check with your airline about their restrictions and requirements for pregnant passengers.

If you give birth in Oman your only choice is to give birth in one of the private hospitals, unless you develop complications that can only be dealt with in a government hospital. In such cases you will be referred to the government hospital by the private hospital or clinic where you have had your prenatal care. Standards of care are excellent at both government and private hospitals, so don't worry if you are referred to a government hospital for your labour. It is possible to get private health insurance to cover maternity costs, although there is usually a specific time period which must have lapsed before conception – in other words, you usually have to have been on the insurance plan for a year or so before you fall pregnant. Prices for private maternity packages start from around RO 900 for a standard antenatal, delivery and postnatal package – this may include all your ultrasound scans, blood tests, and any extra tests or procedures you require.

Don't listen to any urban myths about having to go through labour without pain relief – the normal pain solutions such as gas and air, Pethidine and epidurals are common.

You will pay extra for Pethidine or an epidural, and if you end up having a caesarean section, that will cost extra too. Your husband is allowed to be in the delivery room with you, and so is an independent doula if you have one.

Once your baby is born you need to have the birth registered within two weeks and then set about getting a passport for him or her from your embassy. There may be extra paperwork if the mother was also born outside of her country of origin or if her embassy is not represented in Oman. For more information on registering a birth, see p.129.

The birth of an expat child should be registered within two weeks of the date of delivery. It is important to get all paperwork relevant to your new baby in order, particularly if you are planning to travel in the near future. You'll get an official birth certificate from the hospital where your child was born (it costs RO 6), and you then need to have this certificate stamped at the Ministry of Foreign Affairs Attestation Office (consular section – 24

MUSCAT MUMS

Having a baby in a strange town can be taxing, since you've probably left your support network (mum, sister, friends) behind. Muscat Mums is an amazing group that was set up to help new mums find their feet, and they welcome all new members. To find out more visit muscatmums.com. Another excellent resource is pregnantinoman.com.

699 500) in Qurm. Then you need to go to your embassy, where your baby will be issued with a passport, before applying for your baby's residence visa through the usual channels. If you are British you can register your child's birth with the British Consulate – this is not compulsory but it means your child will have a British birth certificate and will be registered at the General Registry Office in the UK. You do not have to do this immediately after the birth, but you should try to do it before you leave Oman for good. If you don't, and you subsequently lose your child's birth certificate, you can only get a replacement from the British Consulate in Oman. But if you do complete this procedure, you will be able to get a replacement birth certificate from the UK. Before the birth, it is worth checking the regulations of your country of origin for citizens born overseas (see p.340 for a list of embassies and consulates in Oman).

To register your child with the Oman authorities, you will need a completed application form, birth notification from the Ministry of Health (birth certificate), resident cards or passports of both parents, and the parents' marriage certificate. Legal responsibility for registering the child's birth rests with the father, although in his absence it may also be done in the order of their listing by any adult relative present at the birth, any adult residing with the mother, the doctor or any midwife who attended the event.

Even if your baby is born in Oman, it does not get Oman citizenship. It will take the citizenship of the mother or the father (or both). Speak to your embassy regarding citizenship rules for your baby.

Pregnant & Single?
While it is possible for single parents to sponsor their children here, having a baby out of wedlock in Oman is against the law. If you find yourself in this situation, you will need to make arrangements to have the baby outside of the country, or get married as soon as possible. For more information, see p.130.

Sole Custody/Single Parents
There are no problems for a single parent wanting to bring their child into Oman as long as their passport and documentation is in order. If you have sole custody of your child and wish to sponsor him or her, you may need a letter from the other parent

stating the child's name, passport number and nationality, and that they have no objection to the child living with you in Oman. The letter must be endorsed by the legal authority that issued the sole custody, and attested. If you have no way of contacting the other parent (or if they are deceased), then the attested divorce or sole custody paperwork (or death certificate) should suffice.

Antenatal Care
If you have your antenatal care in a private clinic, they will refer you to a hospital for delivery. Your gynaecologist will possibly be present at the birth. A doctor must deliver the baby – unlike in some countries where a midwife can perform a delivery in the absence of any complications.

If you are over 35 or you are seen as having a greater chance of having a baby with spinal or neurological birth defects, you will be offered a variety of tests to check for certain problems.

Postnatal Depression
A relatively high number of women suffer from postnatal depression to varying degrees. In serious cases it can be debilitating and can even result in you or your baby being in danger of injury.

If you are having your baby in Oman, you will probably be far away from the important emotional support of your family and friends back home, and this can increase your chances of suffering from PND.

Fortunately, there are now support outlets for mothers with PND, such as:

Al Harub Medical Centre 24 600 750
Healthy Minds Clinic 99 350 547
Jane Jaffer 99 314 230

Adoption
There are several orphanages in Oman, but it is still not clear whether expats are permitted to apply to adopt any of these children or not – the answer tends to depend on who you speak to.

Many couples find it relatively easy to adopt from outside Oman, for example, from Asia or the Far East. Once you have successfully met all the requirements in your adopted child's home country, you should have little trouble bringing your child back to Oman and applying for a residence visa. Check the regulations involved in securing your citizenship for your adopted child; your embassy will be be able to help with this matter.

Babysitting & Childcare

Childcare – the dilemma facing all working parents. Options are limited and there is no network of childminders like you might find in your home country. If you have a live-in maid, and you trust her with your children, then you have a round-the-clock babysitter. Alternatively you could pay your part-time maid an extra hourly rate (around RO 1.500) to babysit for you when you need her. Word of mouth is a great way to find a babysitter, whether it's a friend's maid or a responsible teenager needing pocket money. Domestic help agencies may offer babysitting services, although there is no guarantee you will be able to get the same person each time (which means leaving your child with a stranger). You could also try asking at nursery schools – often teaching assistants will baby sit in the evenings to make some extra money.

GETTING MARRIED IN OMAN

Since Oman law is governed largely by Islam, it is actually illegal for an unmarried couple to live together. It is even illegal to share a house with flatmates of the opposite sex who are not related to you. However, many couples do end up living together without getting into trouble – as long as you are discreet, you should be left alone to co-habit in peace.

The singles scene is not exactly swinging in Muscat and if you are single you may find yourself doing the rounds at endless family barbecues where everyone is married with children. But you never know – true love may be round the corner. It is not common for expats to stay in Oman to get married – the expense of flying all your family and friends out for a posh party in one of the many five-star hotels puts most people off. However, if you choose to have an Oman wedding, there are numerous options at your disposal.

BRIT OF BOTHER

Due to administrative restrictions, the British Embassy in Muscat is currently not able to conduct weddings. Contact the embassy directly (see p.340) for the latest updates.

The wedding packages at the Al Bustan Palace range from RO 25 per person to RO 50 per person. (based on a minimum of 300 guests but the hotel can arrange different packages for smaller weddings). Packages include a buffet with soft drinks, a wedding cake, a red carpet and a dance floor. The happy couple can enjoy a complimentary dinner on the night of the wedding as well as a two night stay in the executive suite with breakfast. However, there is no Bentley – or any car in fact – to transport the couple in style!

If you'd rather save your money for the honeymoon, you can have a civil service at your embassy or consulate and a more modest reception in a hotel ballroom or restaurant (depending on number of guests).

There are Catholic and Protestant churches in Muscat (Ghala and Ruwi) and Protestant churches in Salalah and Sohar. Protestants should contact the pastor at the office in Ruwi for an appointment (24 799 475/24 702 372). Both partners should be resident in Oman and must provide proof of their marital status, which can take the form of a letter from their sponsor or embassy. Partners from different countries must provide evidence from their respective embassies that they are free to marry. Widowed or divorced people must produce appropriate original documents indicating they are free to marry. Four witnesses, two from the bride's side and two from the groom's, must attend the wedding ceremony. Copies of the passport information page and visa of each partner must be provided. The church requires at least one month's notice to perform the ceremony and premarital counselling is recommended. The marriage certificate must be attested by both the Ministry of Foreign Affairs (consular section) Attestation Office and by the couple's respective embassies. There is no fee for the ceremony but a donation is welcomed. To marry in the Salalah or Sohar Protestant churches, contact the pastors (23 235 677 in Salalah or 26 840 606 in Sohar).

Catholics should contact the priest at the Catholic Church of Saints Peter & Paul in Ruwi (24 701 893) or at Holy Spirit Catholic Church in Ghala (24 590 373). The couple is expected to take instruction before the wedding ceremony takes place. You will need your original baptism certificates and a no objection certificate from your priest stating that you have

LOCAL WEDDINGS

If you get the opportunity to attend a local wedding, grab it! Local weddings in Oman are traditionally grand affairs, especially in terms of size – it is not uncommon for the guest list to reach figures of 200 or more. The ceremony takes place over two days, and includes traditional singing and dancing, as well as vast quantities of favourite local dishes.

not previously been married in a church. A declaration of your intent to marry is posted on the public noticeboard of the church for a period, after which, if there are no objections, the priest will fix a date for the ceremony. The parish priest will advise you of his fee accordingly.

Civil Weddings

Couples wanting a non-religious ceremony should contact their local embassy or consulate, as they may have regulations and referrals to arrange for a local civil marriage, which can then be registered at their embassy. See the list of embassies and consulates on p.340. Many people opt to hold their wedding receptions in Oman's plush hotels (p.66). Several hotels offer facilities for hosting weddings (see the table opposite for contact details).

The Paperwork

Marriages should be registered at the Department of Notary Public in Al Khuwayr within 30 days. To register your marriage, you will need a completed application form and the marriage notification (from the Ministry of Justice) or a marriage certificate authenticated by the Oman diplomatic mission in the country where the marriage took place (if not in Oman). If one of the newly-weds is an Omani, they should produce their resident card or passport and ID card, as well as an approval letter from the Ministry of Interior. A marriage can be registered by the husband or the wife, or by their fathers. Although the Department of Notary Public is part of the Ministry of Justice, it is not located in the same building in Al Khuwayr. The Ministry of Justice is located on Ministry Street, but the Department of Notary Public is located in Dohat Al Adab Street, one street down from the Radisson Blu Hotel. The phone number is 24 485 795, although few employees speak English, so it might be better to go in person. Opening hours are 07:30 to 14:30.

Wedding Accessories

When it comes to finding the perfect dress, there are literally hundreds of tailor shops dotted around Muscat. The best way to find a good one is to ask around, and it's always a good idea to try them out with a smaller job before you hand over your priceless fabric. See p.289 for a list of tailors.

For a list of wedding items such as stationery and florists, see Shopping p.266 and, for hair and make-up, see p.151.

Muslims

Two Muslims wishing to marry should apply at the marriage section of the Shariah Court in Wattayah. You will need two witnesses, both of whom should be Muslims. The woman does not need the permission of her father or brother to marry, unlike in some other Middle East countries. Passports and passport photocopies are required and you may marry immediately. The Shariah Court is located just off the Wattayah Roundabout, next to the Royal Oman Police (ROP) football stadium.

Hindus

Hindus can be married through the Shiva Temple (24 737 311), the Darsait Temple (24 798 548) and the Indian Embassy (24 698 291). Contact the Indian Embassy for further details.

Divorce

Unless you are married to an Omani, you may find it simpler to get divorced in your home country. Whether you choose to carry out the divorce in Oman or back home, you should contact your embassy first for guidance on the procedures and laws that apply to separation of assets, custody of children and legal status. While they may be able to provide some guidance, you should also contact a good lawyer in your home country, who will be able to advise on all aspects (for a fee, of course).

All divorces occurring in Oman need to be reported within 30 days from the date of the event. You will need a completed application form, divorce notification from the Ministry of Justice or divorce certificate authenticated by the Oman diplomatic mission in the country where the divorce took place. If one of the married couple is an Omani citizen, their resident card or passport and their ID card should be produced, along with an approval letter from the Ministry of Interior. Divorces are finalised at the Department of Notary Public (24 485 795).

DEATH CERTIFICATE & REGISTRATION

In the unhappy event of the death of a friend or relative, the Royal Oman Police (ROP) must be informed immediately. The ROP will make a report and you must also inform the deceased's sponsor, who is responsible for registering the death with the authorities. Death registration must be done within two weeks. To register the death, the sponsor should produce a completed application form (which you get from the ROP), a notification from the Ministry of Health, the ID of the deceased, the resident card or passport, and a letter from an official authority notifying that the burial has been carried out or that the body has been sent out of the country.

Remember that, in Muslim societies, bodies must be buried as soon as possible (in some cases, before sunset on the day of the death), so things can happen very fast. If there are any suspicious circumstances, the ROP will take photographs of the body. Post mortems, which are carried out at the ROP hospital in Wattayah, are only performed in the event of a suspicious or accidental death. In the case of an accident, doctors in the hospital will release the death certificate unless there is a post mortem pending, in which case the ROP will do so. The certificate is usually released to the sponsor. There is no charge for the death certificate, although it will not be released until all hospital bills are settled. Ensure that the cause of death is stated on the death certificate. From hospital, the deceased is taken to the mortuary.

In order to release the body, you or your sponsor must obtain a letter from the relevant embassy authorising the removal of the deceased from the hospital. This letter should be taken to the ROP, who will issue a letter for the hospital. You or your sponsor must arrange transport for the body, so you will need to buy a coffin and hire an ambulance. If you can't afford an ambulance, the deceased can be transported in your car.

If desired, you can transport the deceased to their home country. To do this you should talk to the relevant airline to enquire about their procedures (see the airlines table on p.341). You will need a release letter from your embassy, and the body will need to be embalmed. The ROP hospital charges RO 120 for embalming, and Khoula Hospital charges RO 100.

If you wish to perform a burial in Oman, you should get a letter to that effect from your embassy. Give this to the ROP, who will supply you with a letter for the hospital to release the body. Contact the church of your choice to perform the funeral service (see a list of churches on p.28). Your embassy will contact the municipality. For non-Muslims, there is a cemetery at PDO.

On a precautionary note, if you intend to stay in Oman for some time you should seriously consider making a will under Shariah law, particularly if you are married. If one partner dies, it is so much easier for the remaining partner to sort out legalities quickly. Otherwise, it can take a long time to resolve questions of inheritance of items that are in your partner's name – and you can't leave the country until it's done.

Making A Will

Just like having savings, getting household insurance and contributing towards some kind of pension scheme, having a valid will in place is one of those essential things that everybody should do. As an expat, it is strongly advisable to make your will in your country of residence so that local laws do not adversely affect it.

If you become a property owner in Oman, you must make sure that you have changed your will accordingly as Shariah law has a very different view on who inherits your possessions in the event of your death. A good Oman-based law firm will be able to assist you with a locally viable will.

PETS

There is a mixed attitude towards pets in Oman, so if you are an animal lover and have a pet, it is advisable to keep them under strict control at all times. There are cases of animal abuse, mainly caused by a lack of education on the proper care of animals.

The Animal Rescue Centre of Oman (ARCO) was set up with the aim of improving animal welfare in Oman. Its efforts to attain government recognition as an official charity are progressing. In the interim, the centre has put a halt to all its actions as, according to Omani law, this will jeopardise successful completion

of charity status. ARCO has temporarily handed over rehoming, fostering and the general info hotline to a few Omani nationals and international residents who are operating as an informal network of concerned people regarding the welfare of abandoned, stray and injured animals that are suffering on the streets of Muscat. For general info on how to donate money or your time call 95 504 303 or visit the Facebook page Animal Adoption and Fostering – Oman.

Cats & Dogs

It is a commonly held misconception that Muslims dislike dogs and this explains why there are some cases of animal cruelty in the Middle East. The Quran forbids the maltreatment of animals, including dogs, so the problem does not have a religious foundation. In the Arab culture in general, however, dogs are not held in high regard and are not usually seen as fluffy, lovable members of the family. On the other hand, there are many dog owners in Oman.

All dogs must be registered with the municipality and inoculations must be kept up to date. Puppies should be vaccinated at six weeks old and then annually. It is recommended that cats and dogs are sterilised to stop them from roaming (and adding to the stray population), although this is not compulsory.

Stray cats are a huge problem in Oman – they are often called 'string' cats because they are as thin as a piece of string. Every now and then the municipality has a crackdown where they round up and shoot or gas strays and it doesn't warn when this will happen, so it's best to make sure your pet wears a collar at all times.

If you do adopt a stray, make sure it is vaccinated, dewormed, and sprayed for fleas. Oman is not a rabies-free country, so be very careful. If you are bitten by a stray animal (cats can carry rabies as well as dogs), go to Accident and Emergency at Khoula Hospital (p.142) in Al Wattayah for an anti-rabies shot (only government hospitals have stocks of the vaccine).

Pet Shops

There is now quite a good selection of pet shops in Muscat. Conditions in which the animals are kept vary from shop to shop with Animal World (p.135) in the Al Araimi Complex arguably the best. The reputable shops provide papers for the 'pedigree' animals. You can pay up to RO

400 for a dog and RO 200 for a 'pedigree' cat (sort of Persian or Siamese without papers). These cats are locally bred – genuine pedigree animals, with papers, come from Eastern Europe and will cost you twice as much.

You can have your cat or dog vaccinated at the pet shop and the first set of jabs is free, but they don't give all the vaccinations your pet will need. It's better to pay a visit to a reputable vet who can provide the essential rabies vaccination and give your new pet a check-up. Grooming is available at most pet shops in Muscat.

Vets & Kennels

Although there are not a huge number of vets practising in Muscat, you can still find good quality healthcare for your pet. Most clinics offer grooming and pet boarding as well as assisting you in arranging the paperwork involved in bringing a pet to Oman and having it registered, or taking it home again.

Tafani Veterinary Clinic (p.135) is based in Al Azaibah, but they also offer a mobile vet service run by Louise. If your pet hates travelling in the car, or you'd prefer the vet to come to your home, Louise will pop round to treat your pet. One of the advantages of having a live-in domestic helper is that they can care for your pets while you are on holiday. Alternatively, you can book your pet into boarding kennels.

A newer addition to the list of places offering kennelling is Canadian Jebel K-9 Training and Services (p.135). This facility is centrally located in Bawshar and offers boarding for dogs, in-house training, behaviour modification classes and private and public classes.

Bringing Your Pet To Oman

There are a number of regulations regarding the importing of your pet, and the procedure involves its fair share of paperwork and time. Before you leave your home country, you need to make sure that all your pet's vaccinations are up to date and stamped in its veterinary record booklet (which should be in English). The rabies vaccination, in particular, should be up to date. Ask your vet which other vaccinations are required.

You will also need two health certificates from the vet in your home country: one should be dated no more than six months before your departure, and one should be obtained 10 days before your pet is due to travel. Check which airlines will carry pets, and book a space for yours.

With the help of your sponsor, you need to get a pet import certificate (RO 5) from the Ministry of Agriculture and Fisheries Animal Health Department (24 696 300). This certificate, along with a copy of the vaccination records and health certificates, should accompany your pet on arrival into Oman. Certificates must be produced at the airport on arrival of the animal to the quarantine office. If the authorities are not satisfied with the certificates, they can quarantine your pet for six months (so it is essential to check with your local vet and the Oman embassy in your home country about the exact requirements).

Clearing your pet at Seeb International Airport will take two to three hours. Although there are no special facilities for animals, they are placed in a special ventilated area where they won't suffer from the high temperatures.

Requirements For importing Cats & Dogs

- Dogs and cats must be fully vaccinated, including for rabies, at least one month and no more than 12 months before arrival in Oman.
- Dogs and cats must be at least 4 months old.
- The rabies vaccination sticker must be applied to the vaccination card.
- An import permit must be obtained from the Ministry of Agriculture before arrival. The permit is valid for one month.
- The original vaccination card and health certificate must travel with the animal, and they must be in English or have an English translation.

Pet Services

Animal World 24 561 211
Canadian Jebel K-9 Training & Services 99 419 595, *canadianjebelk9.com*
Creatures Pet Shop 24 563 721
Creatures Trading 24 563 721, *creaturestrading.com*
Pet Planet 24 533 487, *petplanet-oman.com*

Veterinary Clinics

Al Hossan Pet Surgery 99 310 035
Al Marai Al Omaniya 26 840 660

Al Qurum Veterinary Clinic 24 562 263, *muscatvets.com*
Capital Veterinary Centre 24 567 736, *vetoman.com*
Dr Fathy A Fadil 24 705 974
Muscat Veterinary Clinic 99 100 056, *mvc-oman.com*
Private Veterinary Clinic 24 560 459
Royal Vet Royal Stables 24420322
Samha For Veterinary Services 26 882 927
Tafani Veterinary Clinic 24 491 971, *tafani-vets.com*

Taking Your Pet Home

When you leave Oman you need to start the procedure for taking your pet home a few weeks before your departure. Check with your airline about their policy on pets – if your pet is small enough you may be allowed to take it as carry-on luggage, rather than as cargo.

The regulations for exporting your pet depend on the country you are taking them to, so check beforehand. The basic requirements are usually the same though. You will need a valid vaccination card which should have been issued not more than one year and not less than 30 days ago. You need to get a pet health certificate from the municipality or the Ministry of Agriculture and Fisheries (normally issued one week before departure). Contact your airline to find out the best place to get a travel box that meets their regulations (normally it is made of wood or fibreglass).

For more information, a vet or kennels in your destination country, or the airline you are using, can give you more specific regulations such as quarantine rules.

EDUCATION

Oman, and Muscat in particular, is home to several international schools catering to children of various nationalities. Government schools are for Omani citizens only, so if you are living in Oman as an expat you will have to send your child to a private school. While it is advisable to visit as many schools as you can to get an idea of the academic standards and extra-mural facilities, remember that it makes sense to stick to a national curriculum that fits in with your future plans. For example, if you will probably end up living back in the UK during some stage of your child's education, it is sensible to enrol your child in a school that teaches the English National Curriculum. If possible, have a chat to other expats to ask for their advice on schools. Try to visit schools during the school day and ask if you can see a class in progress. You will sometimes find that there are waiting lists for certain schools or nurseries, so register your child as early as you possibly can.

To enrol your child in a school, you will need to submit the following:
• School application form
• Passport photos of your child
• Copies of your child's birth certificate
• Up-to-date immunisation record
• Reports from your child's previous school (if applicable)

The school will inform you of any other documents they need, as well as any registration fees.

Children walk to school

NURSERIES & PRE-SCHOOLS

If you have a child of nursery age, you will find quite a lot of choice in Muscat. Facilities and standards vary enormously, as do the fees, so it is worth checking out a few different nurseries before you make your decision. Some nurseries accept children as young as six months, but this is the exception rather than the rule. There are often waiting lists for the more popular nurseries, so put your child's name down early if there is one you have your heart set on.

Nurseries are usually open in the mornings only. Some offer flexibility in terms of how many days per week your child will attend, so if you don't want your child to go to school for a full five days a week, you may be able to choose four, three or even two days a week. Different nurseries have different teaching styles – some encourage learning through play and some have a more structured curriculum. It is up to you to decide what system will be more beneficial to your child. Other factors to consider are child to teacher ratio, staff qualifications, and provision of extra services such as meals and transport.

Nurseries & Pre-Schools

Abu Abnan Nursery Villa 1679, Way 1932, Road 17, Madinat As Sultan Qaboos, 24 605 704, *abuadnannursery.multiply.com*

American British Academy (ABA) Al Khuwair Heights District, Al Khuwayr Al Janubiyyah, 24 605 287, *abaoman.edu.om*

The American International School Of Muscat Ghala St, Nr Church Complex, Al Ghubrah Al Janubiyyah, 24 595 180, *taism.com*

Art Of Living Nursery Villa 3701, Way 4032, Al Ghubrah Al Janubiyyah, 24 613 130, *artofliving-oman.org*

Bright Beginnings Nursery Way 1934, Villa 1908, Madinat As Sultan Qaboos, 24 699 387, *bbnursery.com*

Kids World Nursery House 9411A, Way 897, Mawaleh North, Nr The Wave Muscat, Al Mawalih Ash Shamaliyah, 99 254 455, *kidsworldoman.com*

Little Flowers Nursery Way 3032, Villa 169, Ruwi, 24 703 317, *nurseriesofoman.com*

Shared Glass collaboration with Fabrica 2011

MFA.DESIGN.

The only graduate design program in the Gulf region

www.qatar.vcu.edu/mfa

vcuqatar

virginia commonwealth university in qatar
جامعة فرجينيا كومنولث في قطر

مؤسسة قطر
Qatar Foundation

Little Gems Al Azaiba, Al Udhaybah Ash Shamaliyyah, 24 498 464, *littlegemsoman.com*
National Nursery Montessori Villa 1045, Way 2414, Qurum Heights, Al Qurm, 24 560 096, *montessorioman.com*
Oasis Kindergarten Al Khuwayr Al Janubiyyah, 24 691 348, *ok-oman.com*
Small Steps Nursery Way 4848, Villa 2979, Al Azaiba, 24 495 802, *ssnursery.com*
Tender Buds Nursery Way 2472, Villa 4472, Al Khuwayr Al Janubiyyah, 24 691 055, *nurseriesofoman.com*

PRIMARY & SECONDARY SCHOOLS

Standards of teaching in Oman's schools are usually high and schools tend to have excellent facilities with extracurricular activities offered. International schools will often employ teachers who have been trained in, and have teaching experience from, the country relevant to the curriculum.

The curriculum will probably be an important factor in choosing a school for your child – it makes sense to choose a curriculum that will make it easy for your child to slot back into a school in your home country (or in whatever country you might end up in one day).

Be aware that waiting lists can be very long so prioritise this when you confirm the move to Oman. A relocation company like Sununu Muscat (sununumuscat.com) can help.

Primary & Secondary Schools

American British Academy (ABA) Al Khuwair Heights District, Al Khuwayr Al Janubiyyah, 24 605 287, *abaoman.edu.om*
The American International School Of Muscat Ghala St, Nr Church Complex, Al Ghubrah Al Janubiyyah, 24 595 180, *taism.com*
Azzan Bin Qais International School Nr Dolphin Village Residential Complex, Bawshar St, Bawshar, 24 503 081, *azzanbinqais.com*
The British School – Muscat > *p.139* 19 Street, Madinat As Sultan Qaboos, 24 600 842, *britishschoolmuscat.com*
École Française de Mascate Way 5914, Al Feteh, Bawshar, 24 596 600, *efmascate.voila.net*

A LITTLE BIT OF BRIT

Teaching co-ed students from 3 to 18 according to the National Curriculum for England (from primary to GCSEs and A Levels), the British School Muscat is highly thought of for its high standards and is regularly inspected by the UK's strict OFSTED framework. As well as traditional classes, the school offers several additional language options, as well as being active in sports and the arts. However, BSM is more than one of the country's leading schools, and forms something of a social hub for the local expat community.

Indian School Al Ghubrah 4287 Way, Al Ghubrah Al Janubiyyah, 24 491 587, *indianschool.com*
Indian School Al Wadi Al Kabir Al Wadi Al Kabir, 24 816 633, *iswkoman.com*
Indian School Muscat, Darsayt, 24 707 567, *indianschoolmuscat.com*
The International School Of Chaueifat Muscat As Seeb, 24 534 000, *iscoman-sabis.net*
Muscat International School Madinat Al Sultan Qaboos St, Al Qurm, 24 565 550, *misoman.org*
Pakistan School Muscat 2519 Way, Off Ruwi St, Al Wutayyah, 24 702 489, *pakistanschool.edu.om*
The Sultan's School A'Soroor St, 3117 Way, Al Hail South, As Seeb, 24536777, *sultansschool.org*

UNIVERSITY & HIGHER EDUCATION

Over the past 10 years, there has been great investment in the expansion of higher education institutions (HEI) in Oman. Sultan Qaboos University (SQU) is still the largest government funded university but expatriate students are not permitted to apply. However, by 2011, there were 29 private institutions and colleges with an enrolment of some 35,000 students, with expatriates making up a substantial percentage. The Omani Ministry of Higher Education encourages these private HEIs to choose highly reputable universities as partners in academic affiliation agreements for the purpose of monitoring and improving quality, diversifying programme offerings, and increasing the prestige of the

The British School - Muscat

Tel: +968 24600842 Fax: +968 24601062
admin@britishschoolmuscat.com
www.britishschoolmuscat.com

A British Education For An International Future

At The British School - Muscat we encourage our students to
strive for excellence in all that they do, to prepare them as
global entrepreneurs and responsible citizens of the world

diploma/degree awarded by the HEI. Thus, students can be satisfied that they are getting a good quality level of education. These HEIs have also helped to introduce new courses to Oman. For example, Bayan College is the first university in Oman to offer degrees in media studies. Many students still choose to go abroad for their higher level education, but not as many as in the past.

There have been huge developments in the higher-education sector in neighbouring Dubai, so expat students living in Oman could always attend university there.

For more information, the following websites might be helpful: the American University in Dubai (aud.edu), the American University of Sharjah (aus.edu), the British University in Dubai (buid.ac.ae), Heriot Watt University Dubai (hw.ac.uk), the University of Wollongong (uowdubai.ac.ae) and Dubai Knowledge Village (kv.ae).

University & Higher Education

Bayan College Madinat Al Ilam, 24 691 183, *bayancollege.edu.om*

Caledonian College Of Engineering As Seeb, 24 536 165, *portal.cce.edu.om*

Gulf College Of Oman Al Khuwayr Al Janubiyyah, 24 600 665, *gulfcollege.edu.om*

GUtech – German University Of Technology In Oman Al Ghubrah Ash Shamaliyyah, 24 493 051, *gutech.edu.om*

Oman Medical College Sohar, 26 844 004, *omc.edu.om*

OVERSEAS STUDY

Dubai isn't the only regional education powerhouse. Abu Dhabi has a couple of higher education opportunities, such as a Paris-Sorbonne campus, while Qatar is hot on their heels. Virginia Commonwealth University Qatar (qatar.vcu.edu) focuses on creative qualifications in areas such as fashion design, graphic design, interior design, painting and printmaking. Northwestern University in Qatar (qatar.northwestern.edu), meanwhile, specialises in communications, journalism, and liberal arts, such as ethics, anthropology and sociology. Carnegie Mellon Qatar (www.qatar.cmu.edu) offers majors in biology, business and IT related subjects. These universities all boast the latest facilities and top-notch faculties, and they are becoming popular options for students who want to remain in the region to continue their higher education.

SPECIAL NEEDS EDUCATION

There are no dedicated schools in Oman for expatriate children with special needs. However, there are centres that accommodate both Omani and expatriate children as well as special support departments in some schools.

Special Needs Education

Association Of Early Intervention For Children With Disability, 24 496 960, *aei.org.om*

Centre For Special Education – Indian School Muscat, 24 707 567, *indianschoolmuscat.com*

Creative Center For Rehabilitation, 95 303 700, *ccr-oman.com*

LEARNING ARABIC

English is so widely used in Oman that you can get by fairly effortlessly without ever having to learn a single word of Arabic. However, some say that to enrich the cultural experience of your time in this part of the world, knowing some basic Arabic is helpful.

If you have children, there is a good chance that they will be learning some Arabic at school, so it can be useful to know a bit yourself. A good way to learn the language is to get a local tutor or join in a group lesson.

Language Schools

Berlitz Language Center 24 566 293, *berlitz.ae*

British Council 24 681 000, *britishcouncil.org/me*

ELS Language Centers 24 602 105, *elsoman.com*

Goethe Institut 24 496 013, *goethe.de/gulfregion*

Gulf Arabic Programme 25 640 078, *orbislingua.com*

Modern Gulf Institute, 24 542 737, *moderngulf.com*

New Horizons Computer Learning Centers 24 486 600, *newhorizons.com*

The French-Omani Centre 24 697 579, *ambafrance-om.org*

Polyglot Institute Oman 24 666 666, *polyglot.org*

Salalah Language International 95 628 825, *salalahlanguageinternational.com*

PREPARE TO LEAD IN THE WORLD OF MEDIA.

Report the news, launch websites, direct films, write scripts, produce television, lead corporate communications, manage public relations campaigns, or help governments develop media policies.

Find your voice at Northwestern University in Qatar. Degrees in Communication and Journalism.

www.qatar.northwestern.edu

NORTHWESTERN
UNIVERSITY
IN QATAR

مؤسسة قطر
Qatar Foundation

HEALTH AND WELLBEING

HEALTH

Expats and tourists are not entitled to use government hospitals but must instead register with one of the private hospitals or clinics, with the exception of expats requiring emergency treatment that is not available in private hospitals. If you are an expat and you do require treatment at a government hospital or clinic, you will be charged for their services. Muscat Private Hospital and KIMS Oman Hospital are clean and well-staffed with English speaking professionals. Most people who receive medical treatment in Oman can say their experience was a positive one. However, private medical care is costly, and visitors and non-residents are strongly advised to take out medical insurance.

Your employer may provide health insurance for you but it may be less than fully comprehensive. It is vital that you arrange insurance for yourself and your family as treatment here can be very costly. Dental and maternity cover are usually optional extras and not provided as standard.

Hospitals

Al Raffah Hospital 26 704 639, *asterhospital.com*
Badr Al Samaa Hospital 24 799 760, *badralsamaahospitals.com*
Khoula Hospital 24 561 571, *khoulahospital.com*
Kims Oman Hospital 24 760 100, *kimsoman.com*
Lifeline Hospital 26 755 900, *lifelineauh.ae*
Muscat Private Hospital 24 583 600, *muscatprivatehospital.com*
The Royal Hospital 24 599 000, *royalhospital.med.om*
Starcare Hospital 24 557 200, *starcarehospital.com*

General Practice Clinics

Al Azaiba Health Centre Al Azaiba, 24 497 233
Al Ghubrah Health Centre Al Ghubrah Al Janubiyyah, 24 497 226

Al Wadi Al Kabeer Health Center Wadi Kabir, 24 812 944
Bausher Polyclinic Al Qurm, 24 593 311
Muttrah Health Center Mutrah, 24 711 296
Ruwi Health Center Ruwi, 24 786 088

Specialist Clinics & Practitioners

Al Afaq Medical Diagnostic & Imaging Centre Ghala Industrial Estate, 24 501 162
Al Amal Medical & Health Care Centre Al Khuwayr Al Janubiyyah, 24 485 052
Al Hayat Polyclinic Sohar, 26 845 104, *alhayatclinic.com*
Al Lamki Polyclinic Al Khuwayr Al Janubiyyah, 24 489 563
Al Massaraat Medical Centre Al Qurm, 24 566 435
Al Rimah Medical Centre Ruwi, 24 700 515
Apollo Medical Centre Al Humriyyah, 24 787 766, *apollomuscat.com*
Atlas Star Medical Centre Ruwi, 24 811 743, *healthcare.atlasera.com*
Dr Maurice Al Asfour Specialised Medical Centre Al Qurm, 24 560 673
Elixir Health Centre Al Qurm, 24 571 800, *elixir-oman.com*
Emirates Medical Center Salalah, 23 212 145, *emc-oman.com*
Hatat Polyclinic Al Wutayyah, 24 563 641, *assarain.com*
IbnSina Hospital Al Amrat, 24 877 361
Lama Polyclinic Sohar, 26 751 128, *lamapolyclinicoman.com*
Medicare Centre Hay As Saruj, 24 699 082
Medident Madinat Qaboos Medical Centre Madinat As Sultan Qaboos, 24 601 668, *medidentoman.com*
Muscat Eye Laser Center Hay As Saruj, 24 691 414, *muscateye.com*
Muscat Private Hospital Bawshar, 24 583 600, *muscatprivatehospital.com*
Qurum Medical Centre Madinat Al Ilam, 24 692 898, *qurummedicalcentre.com*

Dr. Maroun Khoury
Consultant
Hematology/Oncology

Dr. Shah Numani
Consultant Nuclear
Medicine

Dr. Nidal Mahgoub
Consultant
Paediatrician
Hematology/Oncology

Dr. Salim Chaib-Rassou
Consultant Radiation
Oncology

In your battle **against cancer.**
Think of us as **your army.**

The Regional Center for Cancer Care at American Hospital Dubai

Cancer not only affects your health, but also your family and lifestyle. Understanding this, the American Hospital Cancer Care Facility offers a range of current Medical Oncology and Hematology services for adults and children. Our specialists are American Board Certified (or equivalent) and are supported by a team of expert staff trained in advanced cancer treatment techniques in the region.

Clinical Offerings

- Medical Hematology Oncology • Pediatric Hematology
- Oncology Radiation Oncology • Surgery • Palliative Care
- Multidisciplinary Approach

For more information, contact +971-4-377-6369

MOH 2238/2/1/31/31/12

AMERICAN HOSPITAL
D U B A I — المستشفى الأمريكي دبي

Delivering better health in the Middle East

www.ahdubai.com

The first hospital in the Middle East to be awarded
Joint Commission International Accreditation (JCIA)

The first private laboratory to be certified by the
College of American Pathologists (CAP)

ACCIDENTS & EMERGENCIES

If you have a medical emergency while in Oman, you can just turn up at the Khoula Hospital A&E department to be seen by a doctor. You may then be transferred to any private hospital of your choosing for further specialist treatment if required. Charges depend upon what kind of treatment you receive, but are not cheap, regardless of which medical centre you choose. A consultation with a doctor will set you back around RO 20, even before any medication or treatment is dispensed. Medical insurance is a must.

The ambulance service in Oman is fairly new and the fleet of vehicles with trained staff is still relatively small. Response times are not published so it's difficult to say how reliable a service it actually is. This may be due in part to the fact that other road users do not automatically move out of the way to let an ambulance through the traffic, or are already blocking the emergency lane. Some of the hospitals and clinics have their own ambulance service but again, may take some time to reach you. The golden rule is never to attempt to move an injured person, but in a place where ambulance response times are slow, you may have to weigh up the risks and decide whether it would be better to transport the victim to hospital in your own car.

PHARMACIES & MEDICATIONS

Most pharmacies are open from 09:00 to 21:00, Saturdays to Thursdays. Some do close for lunch between 13:00 and 16:00. Some pharmacies are open on Fridays from 16:00 to 21:00. There is always at least one pharmacy open 24 hours a day – this is done on a rota system so check the daily papers for details. Alternatively, call Muscat Pharmacy (24 702 542) or Scientific Pharmacy (24 566 601).

Pharmacies & Medications
Abu Al Dahab Clinic & Pharmacy 23 291 303
Hatat Polyclinic 24 563 641, *assarain.com*
Medident Madinat Qaboos Medical Centre 24 601 668, *medidentoman.com*
Muscat Pharmacy & Stores 24 814 501, *muscatpharmacy.net*
Muscat Private Hospital 24 583 600, *muscatprivatehospital.com*

Scientific Pharmacy 24 702 850
Sultan Qaboos University Hospital 24 147 777, *squ.edu.om*

MATERNITY CARE

Oman labour law allows working mothers to their basic salary, including allowances, for six weeks after the birth. If you have had a caesarean section, you may be granted extra leave depending on your doctor's recommendation. You are also allowed two hours a day for the hilariously titled 'milking time' for the next 12 to 24 weeks, so that you can go home and feed your baby. After these weeks, you will be required to return to work as you did before the birth, unless your doctor has recommended that you take extra time. Paternity leave is at the discretion of your employer, but it is not recognised as a father's right in Oman. Instead, it is common to take some of your annual leave if you want to spend time with your exhausted wife and new baby.

Maternity Care
Hatat Polyclinic Al Wutayyah, 24 563 641, *assarain.com*
Medident Madinat Qaboos Medical Centre Madinat As Sultan Qaboos, 24 601 668, *medidentoman.com*
Muscat Private Hospital Bawshar, 24 583 600, *muscatprivatehospital.com*
Sultan Qaboos University Hospital Salalah, 24 147 777, *squ.edu.om*

PAEDIATRICS

Most hospitals have full-time paediatricians on staff. Many private clinics also have paediatricians – the trick is finding one that both you and your child like. Ask around, call Muscat Mums (p.128) for a recommendation, or just try a few different ones until you find a good one.

Paediatrics
Al Lamki Polyclinic Al Khuwayr Al Janubiyyah, 24 489 563
Apollo Medical Centre Al Humriyyah, 24 787 766, *apollomuscat.com*
Atlas Star Medical Centre Al Ghubrah Al Janubiyyah, 24 504 000, *healthcare.atlasera.com*
Muscat Private Hospital Bawshar, 24 583 600, *muscatprivatehospital.com*
The Royal Hospital As Seeb, 24 599 000, *royalhospital.med.om*

Obstetric & Gynaecology Clinics

Advanced Fertility & Genetics Centre
Al Khuwayr Al Janubiyyah, 24 489 647
Al Massaraat Medical Centre Al Qurm,
24 566 435
Al Rimah Medical Centre Ruwi,
24 700 515
Apollo Medical Centre Al Humriyyah,
24 787 766, *apollomuscat.com*
Atlas Star Medical Centre
Al Ghubrah Al Janubiyyah, 24 504 000,
healthcare.atlasera.com
**Dr Maurice Al Asfour Specialised
Medical Centre** Al Qurm, 24 560 673
Hatat Polyclinic Al Wutayyah,
24 563 641, *assarain.com*
Medicare Centre Hay As Saruj,
24 699 082
Muscat Private Hospital Bawshar,
24 583 600, *muscatprivatehospital.com*

**Medident Madinat Qaboos Medical
Centre** Madinat As Sultan Qaboos,
24 601 668, *medidentoman.com*
Muscat Dental Specialists Hay As Saruj,
24 600 664, *muscatdental.com*
Precision Dental Clinic Hay As Saruj,
24 696 247, *precisiondentalclinic.com*
Qurum Medical Centre
Madinat Al Ilam, 24 692 898,
qurummedicalcentre.com
Scientific Polyclinic Al Qurm,
24 560 035
Sun Dental Centre Al Ghubrah Al
Janubiyyah, 95 961 234,
sundentalmuscat.com
Waneela Polyclinic Al Khuwayr Al
Janubiyyah, 99 314 365
Wassan Specialty Dental Clinic
Al Khuwayr Al Janubiyyah,
24 489 469, *wassandental.com*

DENTISTS & ORTHODONTISTS

Private dentistry in Oman is, like most other private medical services, of a high standard and you'll find many international practitioners, such as those at American Dental Center, which is operated by an Ohio-based consultancy. Not only does American Dental Center offer all the usual services (from cosmetic and orthodontics to implants and jaw repositioning) but it also houses several state-of-the-art offerings, like reduced radiation X-rays and the Whitesmile whitening system.

Prices in Oman tend to match the level of service (fairly high), and unfortunately most standard health insurance packages will not cover dental costs (except for emergency treatment required as the result of an accident). Most policies do offer the option of paying a higher premium to cover dentistry.

Dentists & Orthodontists

Al Amal Medical & Health Care Centre
Al Khuwayr Al Janubiyyah, 24 485 052
Al Essa Dental Clinic Ruwi, 24 797 406
Al Ghubrah Dental Clinic & Orthodontic
Ruwi, 24 597 708
American Dental Center *> p.147*
Hay As Saruj, 24 695 422, *adcoman.com*
Amira Dental Clinic Al Qurm,
24 565 477
Emirates Medical Center Mina Al Fahl,
24 604 540, *emc-oman.com*
Harub Dental Surgery Al Qurm,
24 563 814, *harubdental.com*

OPTICIANS & OPHTHALMOLOGISTS

There are plenty of opticians in Oman, with most outlets selling a range of sunglasses and prescription lenses. Most opticians offer free eye tests if you order glasses from them. Disposable contact lenses and coloured contact lenses are also available. Look out for special offers where you can get two pairs of prescription glasses for the price of one.

Opticians & Ophthalmologists

Al Ghazal Opticians 24 563 546
Al Said Optics 96 24 566 272
Grand Optics 24 558 890,
grandoptics.com
Muscat Eye Laser Center 24 691 414,
muscateye.com
Oman Opticals 23 293 714
Yateem Optician 24 563 716,
yateemgroup.com

ALTERNATIVE THERAPIES

Muscat is a cultural crossroads and many of its residents come from countries where traditional therapies are practised. There is a good balance of holistic treatments and orthodox western medicine available. Natural medicine can be effective and, because treatments are aimed at balancing the whole person, your therapist will need to know a lot about you. Be prepared to spend up to two hours on the first consultation so that your therapist can build a picture of your background and medical history. Alternative treatments can cost as much as western medicine.

While they rarely offer a quick fix, they work slowly and gently with the body's natural processes, so be prepared to stick with it to get a result. As always, word of mouth is the best way to find the most appropriate treatment. Some of the more common disciplines are listed below, but for general advice on a range of alternative medical treatments, contact the Al Kawakeb Complex Ayurvedic Clinic, Qurm (2449 4762, 2456 4101 or 2454 3289), or the All Season Ayurveda Clinic, MSQ (2447 5280).

Alternative Therapies

1st Chiropractic Centre Shati Al Qurm, 24 698 847
Acu-Magnetic Treatment Centre Al Khuwayr Al Janubiyyah, 24 487 828
Al Muthanna Ayurvedic Clinic 24 484 049
Al Nama Medical Centre Al Ghubrah Al Janubiyyah, 24 597 977
Al Salsabeel Herbal Center 99 389 547
Ayurvedic Clinic, 24 478 618
Chinese Massage Centre Al Ghubrah Al Janubiyyah, 99 890 804
Chinese Medical & Herbal Clinic Ruwi, 24 799 729
Noor Al Madeena Herbal Clinic Ruwi, 24 780 519
Roots & Herbs 24 799 097
Taimour Ayurvedic Clinic Ruwi, 24 799 689

Acupressure & Acupuncture

One of the oldest healing methods in the world, acupressure involves the systematic placement of pressure with fingertips on established meridian points on the body to relieve pain, soothe nerves and stimulate the body. Acupuncture is an ancient Chinese technique that uses needles to access the body's meridian points. The technique is surprisingly painless and is quickly becoming an alternative or complement to western medicine, aiding ailments such as asthma, rheumatism, and even more serious diseases.

Homeopathy

This form of treatment has been practised in Europe for 200 years. It is a safe and effective treatment for jump starting the body's formidable self-healing powers. Working at both the physical and emotional levels, it treats the whole person rather than the symptoms, using remedies derived from a variety of natural sources. Practitioners undergo rigorous training and many are also qualified western medical doctors. Homeopathic remedies are not available over the counter in Oman as they are in many countries, but there are several practising homeopaths and clinics.

Reflexology & Massage Therapy

Reflexology is another scientifically detailed method of bringing the body and mind back into balance. Based on the premise that reflex points on the feet and hands correspond to the organs and body systems, and that massaging these points improves and maintains health, reflexology works by stimulating the body's natural self-healing process. When considering reflexology, remember the following safety guidelines: do not eat right before your massage; keep drinking water during the course of your massage; and get your doctor's permission if you suffer from asthma, diabetes, a heart condition, kidney problems, high blood pressure or epilepsy.

While many spas and salons offer massage and reflexology, there are those which offer a more focused therapeutic approach to the holistic healing qualities of reflexology and massage.

Chakra & Crystal Healing Therapy

Chakras are the seven energy centres of the body and they make up a person's aura. The direction and intensity of the chakras' spin indicate your level of emotional health. Peter Emery Langille provides workshops on request that will teach you how to explore the attributes of each Chakra, how to visually diagnose your own chakras' condition, and how to rebalance your chakras using colour, crystal and light energy, and meditation. Call 92 605 102 for more information, or email lahave@canada.com.

Sports Injuries

Many expats lead active lives, working hard and then playing hard. But accidents and injuries do happen, so whether you get roughed up playing rugby, pull something in the gym, or simply trip over the cat, you'll be pleased to hear there are some excellent facilities to help you on the road to recovery.

AMERICAN DENTAL CENTER

Muscat

World Class Care

www.adcoman.com

An operation of American Int'l Dental Consultants Inc. USA

Al-Masa Mall, Shatti Qurum, P.O.Box: 458, P.C: 133, Muscat, Sultanate of Oman
Phone:+968-24695422, Fax +968-24695433 Email: Info@adcoman.com

Physiotherapy

If you're unfortunate enough to be on the end of a nasty injury or muscular skeletal illness and require physiotherapy, you'll find excellent and well trained care at Muscat Private Hospital (p.142) and the Physiotherapy and Rehabilitation Centre (24 605 115).

Back Treatment

Treatment for back problems is widely available through some excellent specialists. Chiropractic and osteopathy treatments concentrate on manipulating the skeleton in a non-intrusive manner to improve the functioning of the nervous system or blood supply to the body.

Chiropractic is based on the manipulative treatment of misalignments in the joints, especially those of the spinal column, while osteopathy involves the manipulation and massage of the skeleton and musculature.

Pilates is said to be the safest form of neuromuscular reconditioning and back strengthening available. Les Mills' Body Training System classes are also extremely effective, particularly BodyPump, BodyBalance and RPM. The Palm Beach Club at the InterContinental Hotel (24 680 000) has five Body Training System licences. A number of clinics offer therapeutic massage for back pain, and word of mouth is a good way to get a recommendation.

Cosmetic Treatment & Surgery

There are reputable options if you want a little 'touch-up'. Muscat Private Hospital (p.142) has resident plastic surgeons, and Emirates Medical Center (24 604 540) offers a huge range of treatments. They also have regular visits by specialists from around the world.

COUNSELLING & THERAPY

In addition to the normal pressures of modern living, expat life can have its particular challenges. Moving to a different culture can be stressful, even for the most resilient personalities. If you have moved to Oman with your spouse and aren't working, time can hang heavy on your hands. Although people are generally friendly here, they have their own busy lives and it can be lonely until you settle in. If you need someone to talk to there are places you can go for

support. The Al Harub Medical Center (24 600 750) in Shatti has both life coaches and psychotherapists available, while Muscat Private Hospital (MPH), University Hospital and Hatat Polyclinic can put you in touch with counsellors, psychologists and psychiatrists. The hospitals and clinics listed in the table either have excellent practitioners on their staff, or they can refer you to an appropriate counsellor or therapist.

SUPPORT GROUPS

One of the toughest parts of expat life is the loss of your immediate support network back home (friends and family). In 1992, Unicef together with the Ministry of Health set up CSG (Community Support Groups). With the help of the Omani Women's Association, CSG holds workshops and training to implement support networks throughout the region.

In addition, health centres, private clinics and hospitals are a good source of information for finding support groups.

Support Groups

Al Noor Association For The Blind 24 483 118
Alcoholics Anonymous *AAinArabia.org*
Association Of Early Intervention For Children With Disability 24 496 960, *aei.org.om*
Down Syndrome Support Group 24 496 960
Muscat Mums *muscatmums.com*
Narcotics Anonymous 99 264 347
Oman National Association For Cancer Awareness 24 498 716, *ocancer.org.om*

WELL BEING

For some, it takes little more than the soothing sound of the sea to relax mind and body. Even if that doesn't quite do the trick, mental and physical well-being is easily obtainable in Oman. Whether you choose to set the tone of your day with a morning yoga session, or you want to fix your weight, skin or hair, there are a number of centres that can help.

HEALTH CLUBS

Most health clubs offer workout facilities such as machines and weights, plus classes in anything from aerobics to yoga, while

some also have swimming pools and tennis or squash courts. Many of the beach clubs also offer some sports and gym facilities so are worth considering if you want the added bonus of the beach.

In addition to these, the Ras Al Hamra Club offers a wide variety of activities for PDO employees and members are sometimes allowed to sign guests in for specific occasions or events.

Remember that when using the changing rooms of your health club, some people may feel uncomfortable if you do not use the private cubicles. Respect the modesty that prevails in any Islamic country, and always remain as covered up as possible.

Health Clubs

Al Nahda Resort & Spa 26 883 710, *alnahdaresort.com*
Al Nama Medical Centre 24 597 977
The Health Club, 24 524 400, *ghmhotels.com*
Horizon Fitness 24 390 428, *horizonoman.com*
The Platinum Healthclub 24 392 500, *theplatinumoman.com*
The Spa 24 524 400, *ghmhotels.com*

SPAS

Ayana Spa
Al Sarooj Plaza Shati Al Qurm
24 693 435
ayanaspa.com
Map **2 G2**
Looking and feeling good is taken to a whole new level here at the Ayana Spa. The Balinese-inspired decor, with water features and soft background music, puts you in the mood for some pampering. There's a range of personalised treatments for body and hair to choose from (and they just happen to do wonders for your mind too), plus the usual manicures, pedicures and massages. Treatments from the Institute of Biologique Recherché care for every skin type and condition, while slimming programmes are executed by an expert team of professional aestheticians and therapists, using state of the art techniques and equipment.

CHI, The Spa
Shangri-La's Barr Al Jissah Resort & Spa
Al Jissah **24 776 828**
shangri-la.com
Map **1 G4**
Chi creates a perfect world where your mind and body are surrounded by luxury

and serenity, with smells and sounds all muted and mellow to ensure a totally restful experience. There are so many wonderful treatments on offer that it can be difficult to choose. The Aroma Vitality massage, however, comes highly recommended, leaving guests feeling both relaxed and rejuvenated after being tended on by professional therapists who fully embrace the serenity of the surroundings The Spa is like a little hideaway where guests can enjoy privacy and luxuriate in the spacious relaxation areas and private garden patios.

Eram Spa
Al Nahda Resort & Spa Barka
26 883 710
alnahdaresort.com
Map **1 F4**
This luxurious resort and spa in Barka is a haven of pampering for weary souls in need of some care. Whether you want to improve your fitness, lose some of those extra pounds, or just spend a few days of blissful relaxation away from the stresses of everyday life, Al Nahda's expert team of fitness and health specialists can help.

After checking into your beautiful villa or room, you can start your wellness programme and take the first step towards a better you. While at the resort, you can enjoy a healthy menu of spa cuisine, although a glass of wine or a big slice of chocolate cake are available, in case you lose your resolve. A minimum stay of three days is recommended.

Six Senses Spa > *p.73*
Six Senses Zighy Bay Daba
26 735 555
sixsenses.com/sixsenseszighybay
Map **1 E2**
A holistic oasis nestled into the mountainside, there are nine treatment rooms, a juice bar and two Arabian Hammams. The spa's wide-ranging menu of regional and signature treatments focuses on holistic and pampering therapies using natural products. Treatments are administered by skilled international therapists and specialist practitioners who combine eastern and western techniques with modern-day lifestyle programmes to balance the senses.

The Spa at The Chedi

The Spa

The Chedi Muscat Al Ghubrah Ash Shamaliyyah **24 524 400** ghmhotels.com
Map **2 E3**

The largest spa in Muscat is well equipped to invigorate your senses and sooth your soul. With 13 meditative spa suites (including double suites) and a spa lounge (where you can enjoy herbal tea while looking out on the ocean), this is the perfect place for an individual or a couple to relax. Embracing Eastern philosophy, spa rituals here originate from the healing traditions of places such as Bali, India and Tibet. Enjoy the Chedi jade massage, during which two therapists work in synchronised movements; or try a bio-rhythm envelopment for combating jetlag – it includes an energy body polish and a mud wrap or a bespoke facial for toning and moisturising. There is an extensive spa menu and manicure/pedicures are also available. Treatments are expensive but what you get goes a long way to restoring the beauty and balance of the body, mind and soul.

NUTRITIONISTS & SLIMMING

Unfortunately, there is no Weight Watchers or similar slimming group in Oman, so if you have a few pounds to shift, you're on your own. You might benefit from the various slimming treatments on offer at Ayana Spa in Shati Al Qurm (p.149) – depending on your needs, specialists recommend a combination of treatments such as ultrasonic treatment, lymphatic drainage, body sculpting massage and healthy eating programmes.

Apollo Medical Centre in Ruwi (p.142) has an obesity clinic aimed at helping you control your weight in a healthy way. While the clinic will focus on your eating habits and give you diet and exercise guidelines to follow, in severe cases of obesity they may prescribe certain medications.

VLCC Wellness Centres offers dietary plans and slimming programs from its locations in Shati Al Qurm (24 695 157) and Al Mawaleh (24 553 535) outside Muscat.

Most gyms have professionally trained staff who can advise you on a healthy eating plan along with an exercise regime. They will monitor your progress until you achieve the results you are after. For a list of health clubs, see p.149.

BEAUTY SALONS

Beauty salons in Oman offer a wide variety of treatments and one of the more unique experiences is to have your hands and feet painted with henna. This is a traditional art, mainly done for weddings or special occasions. The intricate patterns fade after two to three weeks. You can identify which salons offer henna painting by the pictures of patterned hands and feet displayed in their shop windows. All the major hotels have their own in-house styling salons, which are open to both guests and the general public. Some of the more popular private salons are listed below.

Beauty Salons

Angel Beauty Salon 24 698 511
Beauty Centre 24 602 074
Beauty Today 24 568 991
Crowne Plaza Resort Salalah 23 238 000, *ichotelsgroup.com*
Diva Hair & Beauty Salon 24 693 011
Hana's Hair & Skincare Centre 24 698 138
Hollywood Beauty Centre 24 568 292
Lucy's Beauty Salon 24 571 757
Muscat Beauty Salon 24 562 541
Nails 24 699 440
Raz Hair & Beauty 24 692 219
Signature Hair Salon 24 490 282
The Spa Bar For Men 24 698 681
Star Salon & Spa 24 693 436

HAIRDRESSERS

Oman has a wide range of options for getting your hair done – at one end of the scale there are small barber shops where men can get a haircut and relaxing head massage for under RO 2 (if you're feeling brave, opt for a cut-throat razor shave for a few hundred baisas more!). For ladies, there's a choice of basic cuts in a beauty salon (cut without blow dry should cost around RO 5 or less), and top-of-the-range hair care in a swanky hairdressers, where you could spend RO 30 or more.

Hairdressers

Al Hana Saloon Qurm Heights, 24 561 668
Angel Beauty Salon Shati Al Qurm, 24 698 511
Beauty Centre Shati Al Qurm, 24 697 585
Diva Hair & Beauty Salon Madinat As Sultan Qaboos, 24 693 011
Raz Hair & Beauty Ruwi, 24 692 219
Signature Hair Salon Al Azaiba, 24 490 282

DISCOVER MUSCAT

Although the pace of life may be slower and more relaxed in Oman, you'll still find plenty to do and see when you're in the mood for adventure.

The fabled land of Sindbad the sailor, Oman was on the must stop list of every explorer worth his weight in frankincense for centuries. Marco Polo is believed to have visited the area 50 years before famous Moroccan explorer Ibn Battuta, who started his pilgrimage to Mecca in 1325.

Omanis passionately treasure their heritage, and rightly so, as its rich history makes this beautiful land that much more magical. Take full advantage and be sure to stop and take in the abundant remains of ancient cities.

They don't call Muscat the 'pearl of Arabia' for nothing. Embedded in culture, with the city's diverse topography, its many museums, the famous souks and other commercial centres, a visit here allows you to discovery a friendly and modern city of juxtapositions.

There is no one place which you can visit to get a 'feel' of Muscat, the capital city. The areas are divided by low craggy hills and each part has its own distinctive character. The only way to do it is to get out and explore and take in all that it has to offer

If you have a touch of the wild wanderer in you, there's many an adventure to be had, from desert driving, wadi bashing, turtle watching and mosque tours to discovering ancient forts and heritage sites. Just call up one of the tour operators

listed later in this chapter (p.185) to make arrangements. If you can't find exactly what you're looking for, they'll happily tailor a trip to suit.

AREAS OF INTEREST

AL BUSTAN & SIDAB

The villages of Al Bustan and Sidab provide an interesting diversion from the main Muscat areas. Heading south along Al Bustan Street out of Ruwi, the spectacular mountain road takes you over the rise from Wadi Kabir, where you can see the village of Al Bustan nestled at the base of the hills with the sea in the background.

Just past the Sohar dhow landmark is the Al Bustan Palace Hotel, one of the most famous hotels in the Gulf. If you're not lucky enough to spend a night or two there, it's well worth making a reservation for a cocktail on the beach or dinner in the Beach Pavilion Restaurant and Bar (p.311).

From the Al Bustan roundabout, you can head up the coast towards the old town of Muscat. Along the way, you will find the scenic harbour area of Sidab. Fishing is the lifeblood of this area and traditions have been passed down through the generations. The Marine Science and Fisheries Centre is an academic institution that undertakes studies of different fish stocks, but it also has a small, interesting public aquarium and library where you can learn more about the area's aquaculture. On your way to Sidab you will pass Marina Bandar Al Rowdha and the Capital Area Yacht Club, both offering a chance to get closer to the ocean with all manner of marine activities for members and guests.

WHAT ABOUT SEEB?

Out near the airport, Seeb is where you'll find the Sultan Qaboos University, as well as two of Muscat's biggest and most popular shopping destinations. Seeb City Centre is the biggest shopping mall in Oman, with many different clothing shops and boutiques, as well as stores selling electronics, furniture and groceries. Marqus Al Bajar, meanwhile, is where, amongst other shops and eateries, Marks & Spencer is currently found, although it is set to move soon to Seeb City Centre.

Architectural touches to hidden coves

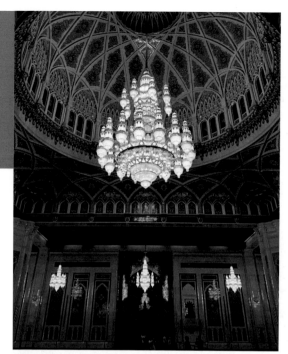
Sultan Qaboos Grand Mosque

AL KHUWAYR

Heading towards central Muscat from Seeb, Al Khuwayr is on the south side of the main road. It is home to a few ministry buildings, as well as some banks and embassies. There are some very impressive buildings to be seen in the area, most notably the head office of the Oman International Bank. The front doors are 10 metres high and plated in 24 carat gold; the interior is just as impressive. If you pass by early enough, you'll see the doors being polished every day. The architecturally splendid Zawawi Mosque is also found in this area, just off the main road. Al Khuwayr has its fair share of shopping opportunities; although there are no big shopping malls, there are plenty of other independent shops scattered around. Al Khuwayr Commercial Centre is billed as the area's obligatory souk, although it is more of a shopping centre.

AL QURM

The area known as Qurm (meaning 'mangrove' in English) lies in the centre of the greater Muscat area, stretching along the coast north of Madinat As Sultan Qaboos (p.93) and Ruwi (p.94). It is divided into two districts – Qurm and Shati Al Qurm – each of which has quite different characteristics.

Qurm is one of Muscat's main shopping areas and you'll find four of the main shopping malls here: Al-Araimi Complex (p.294), SABCO Centre (p.298), Al Qurum Complex (p.300) and Qurum City Centre (p.298). All are pleasant places to shop with a wide range of goods and services and plenty of free parking. The Jawharat A'Shati Centre in Shati Al Qurm is mainly a coffee-drinkers' hangout, thanks to the presence of Starbucks, Costa Coffee (across the road) and the very popular D'Arcy's Kitchen. New mall Bareeq-Al-Shatti (sometimes referred to as 'Shining Sahtti' is the place to find some exclusive boutiques along with another good variety of outlets to arouse the taste buds.

The largest park in Muscat – Al Qurum Natural Park & Nature Reserve – is one of the main attractions in this area. During the cooler months, you'll find many people heading to the park in the early evening; some strolling, some striding, some reclining and some enjoying picnics. While it may be smaller than the Al Qurum Natural Park, Qurm Heights Park is another enjoyable, grassy, shaded respite from city life.

Several of Muscat's biggest hotels are in this area, including the Muscat InterContinental (p.68), the Crowne Plaza (p.68) and the Grand Hyatt Muscat (p.68). All have great leisure facilities and, between them, they offer an excellent range of food and beverage outlets.

One of Qurm's main attractions is the Beach Promenade, although such is its appeal that it can become uncomfortably crowded during the last few hours before sunset and you'll have to look pretty hard to find yourself a spot in between all the informal football games and out of the way of passing joggers and walkers. However, it's a great place to witness an active slice of Muscat life.

BANDAR AL JISSAH & QANTAB

Further down the coast from Al Bustan, the mountains increase in height and the landscape becomes notably more rugged. However, this rocky coastline hides a number of beautiful secluded coves. These bays, most of which are reachable by the road that winds over the mountain, are home to the beaches of Qantab and Jassah, the Oman Dive Center (p.68) and the Shangri-La Barr Al Jissah Resort (p.172).

Many of the bays in this area have stretches of sandy beach sheltered by the rocky cliffs, and crystal clear waters that are perfect for snorkelling, diving and fishing. At Qantab Beach you'll find a number of friendly local fishermen offering to take you out fishing (for a price, of course).

A little further south is the Oman Dive Center, regarded as one of the top dive centres in the world. It offers dive training in a customised dive pool, and organises dive trips for certified divers.

The Shangri-La Barr Al Jissah Resort (p.172) has three distinct hotels: Al Bandar, the focal point of the resort; Al Waha, the largest of the hotels and the one that focuses on family fun and entertainment; and Al Husn, the ultimate luxury destination offering six-star service. The resort also offers some amazing food and beverage outlets in a beautiful setting.

is flanked by two forts overlooking the harbour: Jalali Fort and Mirani Fort. Both forts were built when Oman was under Portuguese control. The forts are rarely open to visitors due to their proximity to the palace and the fact that they are still in use by authorities. However, you are allowed to take photos of the exteriors.

The city wall of Muscat connects to mountain hills behind the old town of Muscat, along the natural bay. You can walk from the bay to the front side of the palace by passing the beautiful Al Khor Mosque, then turning left into Qasr Al Alam Street. Evidence of the city walls can still be seen – these walls used to completely surround the old town. You can also still see the three gates that were closed to protect the city from intruders.

At one of these gates you'll find the Muscat Gate Museum (p.164), which opened in 2001 and offers, among other attractions, a great view over the town from its roof. Within the old city walls you'll also find the Omani French Museum (Bait Fransa), and the Bait Al Zubair Museum is

Al Alam Palace

MADINAT SULTAN QABOOS

MSQ has a small retail and leisure area which is home to a few coffee shops, takeaway outlets like KFC and Pizza Hut, and a handful of other restaurants like the traditional Omani style eatery Karjeens, and popular Darcy's Kitchen (this is the second branch of Darcy's – the first is in Jawharat A'Shati). Otherwise, the area is predominantly a residential one, and it is considered to be something of a traditional expat stronghold. The British School is also located in this area, while the large American British Academy (ABA) international school is in a neighbouring suburb. Both these schools are well supported by expat families.

MUSCAT (OLD TOWN)

The old town of Muscat is situated on the coast at the eastern end of the Greater Muscat area between Mutrah and Sidab. It is a quiet and atmospheric place, based around its sheltered port which was historically important for trade.

The striking Alam Palace, home of Sultan Qaboos, was built on the waterfront in the 1970s and dominates the area. The palace located just outside the walls on Al Saidiya Street. Bait Al Zubair is well worth a visit to find out how life was for Omanis centuries ago (it was a lot harder than it is now).

MUTRAH

Mutrah rests between the sea and a protective circle of hills, and is neighboured by Qurm, Ruwi and the old town of Muscat. It has grown around its port, which today is far more vibrant than the port of the old town. One of Muscat's most famous shopping experiences lies here: the Mutrah Souk – always buzzing and renowned as one of the best souks in the region. It has recently undergone a bit of a facelift and some might say that this has diminished its authenticity; however it is still well worth a visit for the sheer choice of goods on offer. You'll find all the usual things like pashminas and tacky souvenirs, household goods and scented oils. But you'll also find plenty of tiny shops stacked to the ceilings with dusty Omani silver (a good rummage through might result in

a lucky find). Look out for the place with barrels of silver and beads as you'll also find photos of supermodel Kate Moss taken in the shop trying on the wares. There are shops selling some rare Omani antiques too, such as pots, leatherwork, silver scrolls and khanjars (traditional daggers). Mutrah Corniche shows how far Oman has come since the early 1970s. It runs for about three kilometres along the harbour, and is lined with pristine gardens, parks, waterfalls and statues. At the northern end, the old traders' houses and the Al Lawati Mosque showcase traditional architecture, complete with windtowers designed to capture the slightest whisper of breeze. You'll also find the fish market on the edge of the dhow harbour, where you can witness the hustle and bustle of the local fishing industry. Small fishing boats start returning with their catches at around 06:30, so get there early if you can. Right next to the fish market is an excellent fruit and vegetable market with a colourful range of exotic produce. With some good bargaining skills you should be able to save yourself some money compared with buying your produce in the supermarkets.

When the weather is not too hot, it is a pleasant walk from the souk area along the corniche to Mutrah Fort. Unfortunately, it is rarely open to visitors since it is still used by the authorities, although you are permitted to take photos. Further east you'll find the Al Inshirah restaurant and Riyam Park, where a huge incense burner sits on a rocky outcrop. Just behind Al Inshirah is an ancient watchtower overlooking Mutrah. The view at the top is lovely and well worth the steep climb.

RUWI

Less than 30 years ago, the valley (Wadi Kabir) in which Ruwi lies was completely undeveloped. Today, it is the bustling commercial district of Muscat, commonly referred to as the central business district (CBD). Wadi Kabir is the main artery, with all the main buildings found alongside it. Although there are plenty of modern buildings in the area, building regulations are restrictive and you won't find any obscenely tall skyscrapers. In fact, the tallest building is the Sheraton Oman (p.70).

Ruwi may not be a tourist hotspot, but it is worth a wander around for the charming little shops and all the streetside restaurants selling excellent

A mosque in Mutrah

Arab and Indian food at cheap prices. A good point from which to begin your exploration of Ruwi is the GTO Tower next to the main post office (almost in the centre of the CBD).

On the south side, you'll find Sultan Qaboos Mosque on Al Jaame Street, as well as the central bus and taxi stations and the clock tower. On the northern side of the GTO Tower, the Bait Al Falaj (in the army base) houses the Sultan's Armed Forces Museum (p.165). The National History Museum (p.164) can be found in Al Noor Street, in the north-west part of Ruwi. The Ruwi Souk (also known as Ruwi High Street) is the place to go for anything from souvenirs to diamond rings.

ART & CULTURE

HERITAGE & CULTURAL SITES

The mud brick and stone architecture of Oman's many ancient buildings is a constant reminder of the country's past. Whether you travel through the interior, the coast or the mountains, you are sure to happen across the remains of a fort or palace, with its own story to tell of Oman's defensive history. The government takes great care of these national treasures, and many of the forts, palaces and museums are either heavily restored or in the process of restoration.

OTHER CULTURAL SITES

Fish Market
Mutrah
Map **2 K2**
Just across from the Marina Hotel in Mutrah is the fish market. For a slice of bustling, local life, this market is well worth an early morning visit when you can watch as fish traders sell everything from shell fish to enormous tuna, all fresh off the boat, while everyone from housewives to restaurateurs tries to haggle down the prices.

Mutrah Souk
Nr Mutrah Corniche Mutrah
Map **2 K2**
This traditional Arabic market is one of the oldest preserved souqs in oman. Located on the cornice on Mutrah, the

The fish market

souq stores sell an abundance of gold and silver jewellery, while you'll also find gifts and keepsakes such as wooden carvings, ornaments and spices.
It is open Saturday to Thursday 10:00 to 13:00 and 16:00 to 22:00. On Friday, the market is open 16:00 to 22:00.

Sultan Qaboos Grand Mosque
As Sultan Qaboos St, Wilayat District
Al Udhaybah Al Janubiyyah
omantourism.gov.om
Map **2 E3**
Inaugurated by his majesty the Sultan in 2001, this mosque can accommodate up to 20,000 worshippers and consists of a main prayer hall, a ladies' prayer hall, covered passageways, a meeting hall and a library. A major feature is the handmade Persian carpet that took 600 weavers four years to complete. Open Saturday to Thursday 08:30 to 11:00. Entry is free but arrive early to avoid the crowds.

The Sultan's Palace
Old Muscat
Map **2 K2**
Located in Old Muscat, the palace itself may be closed to the public, but it is still well worth the visit to see the distinctive architecture of this landmark. It's also a popular spot for a photo opportunity just outside the main gates.

A NIGHT AT THE OPERA

One of Muscat's latest cultural offerings is a big draw to both tourists and residents, adding high culture to the capital's list of offerings.

With Sultan Qaboos bin Said Al Said being such a fan and patron of the arts and high culture, it was perhaps inevitable that a grand music venue would eventually be built in Muscat, and the idea behind the opera house first surfaced in 2001. However, construction on the WATG-designed Royal Opera House Muscat began in 2007 and was completed in 2011, when the doors to the huge venue – which has a capacity of 1,100 people – opened to the public. Combining Arabic architecture with the conventions of the traditional European theatre space, the Royal Opera House Muscat is, today, arguably the most advanced building of its kind anywhere in the world, boasting technology such as the state-of-the-art Radio Marconi seatback multimedia system.

This has so far attracted an impressive roster of performers that includes global superstars like Yo Yo Ma, Placido Domingo, Jose Carreras and the London Philharmonic Orchestra, along with Arabic offerings from Ammar El Sherei and Sonia M'Barek, for example. The stage is not only set for

operas but ballets, orchestral and individual performances.

Although the Royal Opera House Muscat does follow the traditions of formal dress (whether that's shirts and suits or dishdasha and massar), one of the most unique attributes is its commitment to keeping culture affordable for the masses. Although the very best seats at top tier events do fetch RO 55 or more, there are other seats available for just RO 3.

Aside from the theatre, the site houses an auditorium, a retail and restaurant area and delightful landscaped gardens. There's also an art centre, and education plays a key role here, with the Royal Opera House intended to be a place where creativity is nurtured, as well as a showcase for local and international art.

If you are not fortunate enough to be in town when there's a performance, or simply want a glimpse behind the curtain, there are now tours of the Royal Opera House Muscat available. For more information, an events calendar and to book tickets, visitrohmuscat.org.om.

FORTS & CASTLES

Forts were built primarily for military defencive purposes, but they also served as points of convergence for political, social and community activity. Therefore, some forts actually have palatial, luxurious interiors hidden behind their stark exteriors.

Despite the official opening times, it is not uncommon to arrive at a fort and find it is closed off for restoration. To avoid disappointment, check with the Ministry of Tourism (800 77799, omantourism.gov.om) in North Ghubrah or the Ministry of National Heritage and Culture (24 641 300, mhc.gov.om) in Al Khuwayr beforehand. Oman is renowned for its forts and there are hundreds around the country. Below is a brief selection of some of the best around Muscat but, for more information on others, most hotels have leaflets or booklets or you can check out the book, *Forts of Oman*, available in bookshops.

Al Hazm Fort Welayat Rustaq, *omantourism.gov.om*
Al Jalali Fort Old Muscat, *omantourism.gov.om*
Al Mirani Fort Old Muscat, *omantourism.gov.om*
Ar Rustaq Fort Wilayt Ar Rustaq, *omantourism.gov.om*
Bahla Fort Wilayt Bahla, *omantourism.gov.om*
Bait Al Maqham Al Falaj Quarter
Fazah Castle Batinah
Ibri Castle Ibri City, *omantourism.gov.om*
Jibreen Castle A'Dakhiliyah, *omantourism.gov.om*
Muttrah Fort Mutrah, *omantourism.gov.om*
Nakhal Fort Wilayt Nakhal, 26 781 384, *omantourism.gov.om*
Nizwa Fort Nr Nizwa Market, 24 588 849, *omantourism.gov.om*
Quriyat Fort Quriyat
Shinas Castle Wilayat Shinas
Sohar Fort Al Batinah, 26 844 758, *omantourism.gov.om*

MUSEUMS

The Oman government plays an active role in preserving the country's history, and museums are an important way of doing this. You can spend hours learning about the achievements of Oman's ancestors, most of which are impressive considering the often harsh circumstances they lived in, and in the process you'll gain valuable insight into the history of life in each specific area.

Entrance to museums costs very little, and you will generally find that information on exhibits is given in both English and Arabic. Opening times often change during summer, Ramadan (typically 09:00 to 13:00 Saturday to Wednesday), Eid and on public holidays, so try to call in advance to avoid a wasted journey. The Ministry of Tourism website (omantourism.gov.om) does now list the opening times for museums in the region.

Amouage > p.287
As Seeb **99 346 811**
amouage.com
Map **1 G4**
Not exactly a museum, but in fact the factory where the 'most valuable perfumes in the world' are produced. There is a fascinating guided tour during which the guide explain the entire perfume production process, as well as allowing visitors to sniff and test the fragrances. If you purchase a product (they make for great gifts or souvenirs) you also receive a special gift to remember your trip by. It's a really interesting insight into a company that has come to define modern Oman, as well as the ancient techniques still used. Traditional Omani coffee and dates are served during the visit. Entry is free. Open from 08:30 to 16:30, Sunday to Thursday.

Aquarium & Marine Science & Fisheries Centre
Nr Al Bustan Palace Hotel & Capital Yacht Club Haramil **24 736 449**
Map **2 L4**
This centre is located between the Al Bustan Palace hotel and the Capital Yacht Club. It showcases the rich and unique marine life that thrives in the Omani waters and along a coastline that measures nearly 3,165 kilometres. In cooperation with Sultan Qaboos University, the centre studies a range of marine species, with particular emphasis on the conservation of ecosystems and endangered species, including turtles. The aquarium has recently been renovated. Open 08:00 to 14:00 Saturday to Wednesday; 08:00 to 13:00 on Thursday; 16:00 to 19:00 on Friday. Entry is free.

Bait Adam
Building 2881, Way 2, Nr Madinat Al Sultan Qaboos Bridge Al Qurm
24 605 033
omanet.om
Map **2 H2**
Situated in Qurum, Bait Adam is in fact the creation of a single private collector, Lafif Al Bulushi. It boasts a rare and unique collection of artifacts from Oman's long history, all laid out across five themed galleries. Open Saturday to Thursday 09:00 to 13:30 and 16:00 to 19:00. Costs RO 3 per person.

Bait Al Baranda
Nr Fish R/A, Mutrah Corniche Mutrah
24 714 262
baitalbaranda.om
Map **2 K2**
This Mutrah museum recounts the history of Muscat, from its geological formation right up to the present day. It uses interactive technology that displays pictures of tectonic plate movements over the past 750 million years and showcases the activity that created the continents in the past, and how they will change over the next 20 million years. The museum also includes documentation of the Sultanate of Oman's history since its inception. Open Saturday to Thursday 09:00 to 13:00 and 16:00 to 18:00. Entry is RO 1 for adults and 500 baizas for children.

Bait Al Zubair
Al Saidiyah St, Old Muscat
24 736 688
baitalzubairmuseum.com
Map **2 L2**
A collection rather than a museum, Bait Al Zubair offers a fascinating insight into the Omani lifestyle and traditions, mixing ancient and modern. It is located in a beautiful restored house and each display is accompanied by excellent explanations and descriptions. The four major displays cover men's jewellery, khanjars and male attire; women's jewellery and female attire; household items including kitchenware, incense burners and rosewater sprinklers; and swords and firearms. There is a central photo gallery showing fascinating pictures from the 1920s up until the present day which are great for everyone from children to history enthusiasts.

Outside you'll find full-size recreations of stone-built Omani homes, a small souk, fishing boats and a flowing falaj. A gift

shop sells a variety of items and paintings, custom-made miniatures of the pieces on display and other museum souvenirs. Opening hours are 09:30 to 18:00, Saturday to Thursday and entry costs RO 1.

Children's Museum
Nr Qurum Natural Park Al Qurm
24 605 368
omantourism.gov.om
Map **2 H2**
Kids of all ages will enjoy this interactive science museum. Solidly built displays clearly explain holography, lasers, the human body, energy, faxes, computers and many other fascinations of daily life. Plenty of button-pressing, handle-turning, pedalling, balancing, jumping and running space for kids to exhaust themselves before lunch. This museum is popular and can get crowded on Thursdays. Entrance is free for children under 6, but costs 100 baisas for children aged 6 to 12, and 300 baisas for those aged 12 and over. The museum is open from 08:00 to 13:30 Saturday to Wednesday, and 09:00 to 13:00 on Thursdays (closed on Fridays).

Currency Museum
Central Bank of Oman Bldg, Nr HSBC Bank HQ Ruwi **24 796 102**
omanet.om
Map **2 J3**
Located in the head office of the Central Bank of Oman, in the CBD of Ruwi, the museum showcases modern and historic coinage, as well as a gallery of Oman's currency throughout the years. It is not limited to Omani currency. You can also see various colonial currencies that were in circulation in the early 20th century, as well as coins and notes of regional importance. Entry fee: 250 baisas. Opening hours: 08:00 to 15:00.

The Heritage & Culture Museum
Way 3123, Off A'Noor St, Nr Al Falaj Hotel Ruwi **24 701 289**
omantourism.gov.om
Map **2 J3**
A small but fairly comprehensive museum showing silver jewellery, ladies' costumes from around Oman, pottery, a selection of scale-built dhows, crockery, coffee pots, and guns. Additionally, there is a selection of unique items of furniture from the old palace in Muscat, clothes, pictures and medals from the Zanzibar rulers; as well as correspondence and pictures of the last

five sultans in the Al Said Dynasty. Your English-speaking guide will probably offer you the chance to sample the legendary Omani hospitality, by inviting you to have some traditional kahwa (coffee), halwa and dates afterwards. The museum is open Saturday to Wednesday 08:00 to 13:30 and Thursday 09:00 to 13:00. Entry costs 500 baisas for adults (or 300 baisas if with their family), 200 baisas for children and kids under 6 get in free.

Muscat Gate Museum
Al Bahri Rd, Mutrah Corniche
Mutrahomantourism.gov.om
Map **2 L2**
The Muscat Gate Museum, located on the Mutrah Corniche, is housed in a fort-like building on the road leading out of Old Muscat. Opened in 2000, it illustrates the history of Muscat, Al Alam St and Oman from ancient times right up to the present day, with a special display on the city's springs, wells, underground waterways, souks, mosques, harbours and forts. The awe-inspiring view from the roof over the

Natural History Museum

old town of Muscat is almost worth the visit alone. Open Saturday to Thursday, 09:30 to 11:30 and 16:30 to 19:00.

Natural History Museum
Ministry of National Heritage & Culture Complex, Off Al Wazarat St Al Khuwayr Al Janubiyyah **24 641 510**
omantourism.gov.om
Map **2 F3**
Housed within the Ministry of National Heritage & Culture, this is a fascinating and informative collection of exhibits on Oman's wildlife. You can see stuffed animals in their different natural habitats, many of which are unique to Oman and the Gulf region (such as the oryx and the Arabian leopard). The 'Oman Through Time' exhibition follows the history of Oman through fossils, and includes the development of oil and gas reserves. The separate Whale Hall should not be missed – it is dominated by the suspended skeleton of a 25 year old sperm whale. The quiet blue hall is filled with the sounds of whale and dolphin calls, and offers a wide range of information about the unique selection of whale species found off Oman's coast. The dolphin and whale skeletons that are displayed in the Whale Hall have all been recovered from Oman's beaches. If you visit during the winter months, you can tour the botanical gardens next to the museum. These carefully tended gardens feature indigenous trees, shrubs and flora, including frankincense, desert rose, henna and aloe. Entrance costs 500 baisas for adults, 200 baisas for children between 6 and 12 and 100 baisas for children under 6.

Oil & Gas Exhibition Centre
Seeh Al Maleh St, Nr Gate 2 Mina Al Fahl **24 677 834**
pdo.co.om
Map **2 H2**
Given to the Omani people as a gift from Petroleum Development Oman, the largest oil and gas production company in the country, this is a well designed interactive journey through the development, discovery, extraction and use of fossil fuels in Oman. Kids love the interesting displays that include seismic computer games, nodding donkeys and gigantic drill bits. A cafe serves light meals and refreshments. In 2000, a planetarium was built. It is open Saturday to Wednesday 07:00 to 12:00 and 13:00 to 16:00; and 07:00 to 12:00 on

Detail of Sultan Qaboos Grand Mosque

Thursday. Admission is free. Show timings at the planetarium vary, so call beforehand (24 675 542) or check the 'pdo and community page' on pdo.co.om.

Omani French Museum
Lane 9310, Qasr Al Alam St, Nr Al Alam Palace, Old Muscat
24 736 613
omantourism.gov.om
Map **2 L2**
This museum is on the site of the very first French Embassy, and it is a carefully preserved example of 19th century Omani architecture. It celebrates the close ties between France and Oman over the past few centuries. Although the museum exhibits have French captions, there are usually brief English translations. The ground floor of the museum features exhibitions on early French contacts, the history of Omani-Franco trade and on HM Sultan Qaboos' visit to France. Upstairs you'll find records, furniture, clothes and photographs of early French diplomats. One room holds not just regional Omani women's clothing, but also some antique French costumes. The museum is open from 09:00 to 13:00, Saturdays to Thursdays. Entrance costs 500 baisas for adults and 200 baisas for children aged 6 to 12. Children under 6 enter free.

Omani Museum
Al Alam St, Way 1566, Nr Ministry of Information Madinat As Sultan Qaboos
24 600 946
omantourism.gov.om
Map **2 G3**
The Omani Museum sits on top of Information Hill and is almost worth visiting for the view alone. It is run by the Ministry of Information and, although it is fairly small, it is very informative. It is the only museum in the capital city of Muscat that offers detailed archaeological information and artefacts. It also has displays on agriculture, minerals, trade routes, architecture, dhows, arts and crafts, jewellery and weaponry. The museum is open Saturday to Wednesday 08:00 to 13:30 and Thursday 09:00 to 13:00. Admission costs 500 baisas for adults (300 if with a family), 200 baisas for children aged between 6 and 12 and is free for children under 6.

The Sultan's Armed Forces Museum
Bait Al Falaj Fort, Mujamma St
Bayt Al Falaj **24 312 642**
omantourism.gov.om
Map **2 J2**
This showcase of Oman's military history is set in the main building and grounds

of the beautiful Bait Al Falaj Fort, which was built in 1845 to be the garrison headquarters for Sultain Said bin Sultan's armed forces. It features descriptions of the origins of Islam in Oman, tribal disputes and the many invasions of the coast by foreign powers. While these exhibits are a little on the dry side, the more recent military history is lavishly represented with uniforms, antique cannons, early machine guns, weapons confiscated from the rebels in Dhofar, models of military vehicles and planes, instruments, medals and even an ejector seat and parachute.

Outside you'll find exhibits of military hardware such as planes, helicopters, boats, rough terrain vehicles and the first car owned by HM Sultan Qaboos when he became Sultan – a Cadillac with inches-thick bulletproof glass. You can also have a wander around wartime field headquarters and a military hospital. A representative of the army, navy or air force will guide you around the museum, which is a definite must-do for military enthusiasts.

The museum is open Saturday to Wednesday 08:00 to 13:30; Thursday and Friday 08:00 to 13:30 and 15:00 to 18:00. Admission is RO 1 for adults and 500 baizas for children up to 18 years old.

ART GALLERIES

Art is valued highly in the Arab world, so galleries in the region tend to stock art of high quality and in various styles. Although Oman has no art museums, its art galleries do offer peaceful surroundings where you can browse or buy. Most of the galleries also offer a framing service.

Al Madina Art Gallery

145/6 Al Inshirah St Madinat As Sultan Qaboos **24 691 380**
Map **2 G3**
A one-stop shop for many different forms of art in Oman. It has regular exhibitions of watercolours and oil paintings, and also hosts many special events throughout the year. If you have some time to kill, have a browse through the ample selection of prints – you could be rewarded with an attractive piece of art for a lot less than you would pay for an original. Al Madina also stocks some interesting jewellery made from unconventional materials such as freshwater pearls or desert diamonds. And if a genuine Omani wooden chest is on your shopping list, this is the place to go if

you want to make sure you are buying an original and not one that has been made in India.

Bait Al Baranda

Nr Fish R/A, Mutrah Corniche Mutrah
24 714 262
baitalbaranda.om
Map **2 K2**
Nestled just off Mutrah Corniche, this modern art gallery hosts collections from both foreign and local artists. Previous exhibitions have included several works by recognised masters, such as the great Salvador Dali and Henri Matisse, among others. The gallery also houses a small coffee shop, perfect for whiling away an hour or two while considering the work you have perused.

Bait Al Zubair

Al Saidiyah St, Old Muscat **24 736 688**
baitalzubairmuseum.com
Map **2 L2**
Although strictly a museum of Omani culture and handicrafts, Bait Al Zubair does hold a number of temporary exhibitions during the year, primarily featuring works from local artists. Owned by the Zubair family, it opened in 1998 and is located near Al Alam Palace in old Muscat.

Bait Muzna Gallery

Al Saidiya St, Way 8662, HS 234
24 739 204
baitmuznagallery.com
Map **2 L2**
Set in a traditional house that was originally built as a home for a member of the royal family, this gallery showcases the work of local talent and organises a number of workshops for both Omanis and expats. Workshops are offered periodically (check website) and are provided by a number of qualified teachers, some of whom are successful international artists themselves. The gallery sells fine arts and antiques, and offers a framing service.

The Omani Society For Fine Arts

Hay As Saruj **24 692 090**
osfa.gov.om
Map **2 G2**
Consider this a community where artists meet, share knowledge and display their work. The society holds regular exhibitions, meetings and events where people can learn more about a particular art form.

OMAN, NATURALLY

For many, Oman conjures up an image of dry, sandy and inhospitable deserts and, although the rolling dunes certainly play their role in the country's stunning landscape, the sultanate actually has incredible flora and fauna for visitors to discover.

Oman has around 1,200 native plant species. Of the indigenous flora, date palms provide oases of green covering about 49% of Oman's cultivated area. The deserts are fairly barren but after a bout of rain they are dotted with wild flowers. Coconut trees, banana trees and other tropical fruit trees thrive well in the subtropical climate of Salalah.

Oman is home to the frankincense tree (Boswelia sacra), which grows only in Dhofar, the Wadi Hadhramaut in Yemen, and Somalia. They are short trees with a gnarled trunk and silver-green leaves. Incisions are made on the bark to collect the aromatic resin. For hundreds of years, frankincense was more valuable than gold and Dhofar frankincense was said to be the finest and purest in the world. It was used not only as a fragrance, but also to embalm corpses and as a medicine. The frankincense trade brought immense wealth and importance to southern Arabia – even Alexander the Great had plans to invade the area in order to control the trade at its point of origin.

Mangrove trees (Avicennia marina) used to cover large stretches of Oman's coast but have been threatened with extinction in many areas. Some of the most beautiful and dense mangrove forests today are found in the Qurum Nature Reserve in the heart of Muscat, and at Mahawt Island, 400km south of the capital. The Qurum Nature Reserve contains an important site where prehistoric fishermen exploited mangrove resources, and a nursery that produces seedlings for replanting. Thanks to urgent conservation measures, mangrove forests now cover about 1,088 hectares of Oman's coastline.

Oman has a wide variety of indigenous wildlife which includes many endangered species such as the Arabian oryx, Arabian leopard, Arabian tahr (a mountain goat now found only in Oman), Nubian ibex and humpback whale. Realistically though the only large animals you are likely to see are camels, donkeys and goats, often roaming dangerously close to the road.

Some 460 species of birds (of which 80 are resident) are found at different times of the year – an impressive number considering that Oman has vast areas of desert and no real forests. Millions of birds wintering in East Africa pass over Oman on their spring or autumn migration to Central Asia.

The waters off Oman are every bit as bountiful, making them extremely popular with divers. Around150 species of commercial shell and non-shell fish, 21 species of whales and dolphins, and a whole host of other assorted marine creatures are found in Omani seas. The humpback whale feeds and breeds in the rich waters off central and southern Oman. There are four breeds of sea turtle that come ashore to lay their eggs. The huge leatherback turtle is known to swim in the waters offshore but there are no records of it nesting in Oman.

The more popular nesting sites are Ras Al Hadd for green turtles, Masirah Island for the world's largest population of nesting loggerheads and the Daymaniyat Islands Nature Reserve – Oman's only marine reserve – for hawksbill turtles. Be aware that collecting live shells, turtle eggs and shellfish is forbidden in Oman. Several new varieties of seashells have been discovered on Oman's beaches.

The Oman Whale & Dolphin Research Group is dedicated to learning more about the habits and needs of whales and dolphins in Oman, and the risks they face. If you see any whales or dolphins while you are in Oman, please report the sighting –there is a special form on the website of the research group that you can fill in.

For more information, visit the Environment Society of Oman's webpage on eso.org.om.

PARKS, BEACHES & ATTRACTIONS

PARKS

In 'desert' countries such as Oman, the lack of lush greenery is something that you might miss from back home. Fortunately, Oman has a good selection of parks and gardens that are welcome patches of green. Parks are well looked after by the municipality, and usually include lawns, sandy play areas and playground equipment for children, and maybe a water feature or two. Before you load your bicycle, rollerblades or dogs into the car, check the park's policy on these – some might allow certain activities, while others don't. Entry to many of the parks is free.

Al Qurm Natural Park
Al Qurm St Al Qurm
omanet.om
Map **2 H2**

This sprawling park and nature reserve runs from the side of the main coastal road right down to the public beach. It is Muscat's main park, and features large lawns, a boating lake, water fountains and shady pergolas. It is the home of the Sultan's rose garden, a tranquil, fragrant area that is full of rose varieties from around the world. The large fountain shoots water up to 30 metres into the air, and it is even more impressive at night when it is lit up. The park incorporates a nature reserve, which is made up of tidal wetlands and mangroves. It's a great place for spotting migratory birds, and you can expect to see sooty gulls, white-cheeked

Al Qurm Natural Park

terns, crested terns and, at low tide, various herons and waders. There is also a mangrove nursery, which yields thousands of valuable mangrove tree seedlings every year. Children will enjoy the playground (no entry fee) and light refreshments in The Rose Garden Cafe. The park is also home to the City Amphitheatre, which seats up to 4,500 people and is a popular venue for events. Open Saturday to Wednesday 16:00 to 23:00; Thursday, Friday and public holidays 09:00 to midnight.

Al Sahwa Park
Nr Burj Al Sahwa R/A
omanet.com
Map **2 A3**
Al Sahwa Park is located next to the Al Sahwa clock tower and it is a great park for the whole family to enjoy. Both expat and Omani families enjoy the beautifully manicured grounds, which contain play areas for the kids, picnic spots, gazebos and a long track for those who enjoy keeping fit – the track is ideal for walking or jogging. The park covers an area of 300,000 square metres and the main attractions are the six colourful Islamic gardens. The park is open from 09:00 to midnight every day.

Kalbooh Park
Kalbooh Mutrah
omanet.com
Map **2 L2**
Situated along the coast by the village of Kalbooh, this small park is a picturesque spot for an evening stroll. It features paved walkways and a grassed amphitheatre. A selection of kiosks and a small Pizza Hut sell snacks and drinks. The views are amazing, with the sea to one side and sheer, rocky hills to the other. In the daytime there is a beautiful view along the coast of Mutrah.

Naseem Park
Nr Seeb Airport As Seeb
Map **1 G4**
This large park, opened in 1985, is located on the highway leading to the Batinah area, about 30km from Seeb International Airport. There is a train ride that goes round the park, a mini falaj system, a jasmine maze and well-tended Arabic and Japanese gardens, built to commemorate the strong ties between Japan and Oman. A cafeteria selling drinks, ice-creams and snacks is situated in the centre of the park.

Kalbooh Park

Qurm Heights Park
Nr Crowne Plaza Muscat Qurm Heights
Map **2 H2**
This small park is perched high on the cliffs in Qurm, next to the Crown Plaza Hotel. Its grassy lawn is surrounded by shady trees and plenty of plants and shrubs. At one end of the park is a collection of stone benches on a small paved area – the perfect spot for a few minutes of contemplation at the end of the day. This tranquil park is very popular in the evenings with people living in the area.

Riyam Park
Mutrah Corniche Mutrah
omanet.com
Map **2 K2**
Located on Mutrah Corniche and offering pretty views of the harbour, you can't miss this local landmark – it's the park with a gigantic white model of an incense burner perched on top of a hill! It is possible to climb up to the top of the incense burner; it's a steep climb but worth it for the views of the harbour, sea and cliffs. Riyam Park is great for kids, with lots of playground equipment and a small funfair (usually open from 16:00, depending on the season). There is plenty of shade and a pond.

A peaceful walk along the coastline

BEACHES

With over 1,700km of coastline it is hardly surprising that Oman offers some wonderful stretches of sandy beach. Many of them are unspoilt areas where you'll find peace and isolation. The following are some of the main beaches near Muscat that are popular with visitors and residents.

Al Sawadi Beach

Barka

Map **1 F4**

Al Sawadi Beach is found out near Barka, which is roughly a 45 minute drive from Muscat, making it ideal for leaving the city behind for just the morning or the afternoon. There are some beautiful beaches here, as well as the Al Sawadi Beach Resort and Spa (alsawadibeach. com) which has a kite centre and a range of recreational activities. It also has a dive school and dive centre – a reminder that Al Sawadi is the main access point to one of the best dive sites in Oman (and the Middle East) in the form of the Daymaniyat Islands. These nine islands lie some 15km out to sea and are a protected nature reserve incredibly rich in marine life.

Azaiba Beach

Nr Civil Aviation Recreation Ctr As Seeb

Map **1 G4**

Also known as Aviation, Strabag or Shell beach, this long stretch of beach is backed by dense bushes that act as a good windbreak. It's a popular camping spot. Access is mainly by 4WD, although if you don't mind a short walk you can get there

in a normal car. It is not the best beach for snorkelling, as there is no coral, but it is a good windsurfing site. Because it is a quiet beach, it is suitable for taking your dogs for a run – just make sure you don't disturb the fishermen, as this is still a working beach and they can get a bit grumpy if you get in their way. But on the other hand they are usually more than happy to sell you some fish, show you how their nets work and teach you how to cast sardine nets.

Because of construction on The Wave, access to the beach changes frequently. Make your way to the Civil Aviation Recreation Centre (map 2 B2) and the most recent tracks in the sand will guide you onto the beach.

Bandar Al Jissah

Nr Oman Dive Center Al Jissah

Map **1 G4**

While this beautiful (although quite short) stretch of beach can be very busy on Fridays and public holidays, its attraction is twofold – firstly it is accessible by two-wheel drive car, and secondly it is the best place to catch a sea taxi. Sea taxis are the small fishing boats you see loaded up with fresh fish during the week, and at weekends they go for much bigger fish – tourists. For a very small fee they will transport you and all your gear to one of the secluded beaches such as Khayran, and leave you there until a specified time when they will come and pick you up. It is widely understood that you need not pay the fee until you have been picked up. Snorkelling gear is recommended as the marine life here is stunning. A new market has opened up for them since the opening of the Shangri-La Barr Al Jissah Resort – they are offering half-hour or one-hour trips around the bay to get a glimpse of this luxurious trio of hotels from a completely different perspective. With a bit of hard bargaining you should be able to get yourself a half-hour trip for around RO 3 to 5.

To get to the beach, head towards the Al Bustan Palace, A Ritz-Carlton Hotel from Wadil Kabir – you will see the village of Qantab signposted to the right as you reach the top of the hill. Take this right turn and follow the road until you see a signpost for Oman Dive Center – Bandar Jassah is at the end of this road.

Beach Promenade
Nr Grand Hyatt Muscat Shati Al Qurm
Map **2 G2**
In the hour or two before sunset, Beach Promenade (or Qurum Beach as it is most commonly known) and shoreline stretching from the Hyatt Regency Muscat to the InterContinental Hotel becomes a lively promenade. People come here to walk, jog, jetski, play football and barbecue, and it is a pleasant spot to relax and watch the world go by as the sun goes down. Don't be confused by the concrete wall that you'll see about half way down – while this appears to be the end of the beach it is possible to walk out onto a concrete ledge and continue further. During low tide it is possible to cross the small inlet and walk all the way to the cliffs near the Crowne Plaza.

Marjan Beach
Nr Petroleum Development Oman (PDO) Recreation Centre Ras Al Hamra
Map **2 H1**
This small and quiet beach, which is easily accessible, is ideal for snorkellers as it has superb coral reefs. On good days you can see parrot fish, rays and turtles. The beach is equipped with man-made sunshades and barbecue pits.To get there, go past the Ras Al Hamra Recreation Club, keeping it on your right, and continue over the slight rise for another 150 metres. Parking for the beach is on the opposite side of the road.

Ras Al Hadd Beach
60km from Sur, Nr Turtle Beach Resort Ras Al Hadd
Map **1 H5**
The beaches around Ras Al Hadd are famous for nesting turtles especially during June and July. They are also popular with visitors who like the relaxing atmosphere and tropical surroundings. The Turtle Beach Resort (99 007 709 or 25 543 400, tbroman.com), located at the end of a beautiful turquoise bay, is a good choice for those who like to combine simplicity with a little bit of luxury. The resort has an outdoor dhow-shaped restaurant where you can have a drink overlooking the bay. Lunch and dinner are also served. You don't need to pack your tent, since the resort offers 32 sleeping cottages (RO 42 for two people which includes dinner and breakfast), each one supplied with two beds and an air ventilator.

You should definitely take your snorkelling or diving gear; this is a prime spot to see turtles, rays, moray eels and a colourful range of fish. The resort has a small motorboat and on request they will take you out to see the turtles in the summer season.

The drive from Muscat will take you between four and five hours, so many people make a weekend trip of it. To get there from Sur, follow the signs to Ras Al Hadd. After about 60km you'll reach a T-junction, where you should turn left. Turn left again after about three kilometres, following the sign for Turtle Beach Resort.

Yiti Beach
25 km from Muscat Yiti
Map **1 G4**
You need to drive through some hilly terrain to get to this beach but it is well worth it. With vast expanses of sand, there is ample room for relaxing, beach activities and camping on the beach here. The most popular place to park up for the day is near the edge of the lagoon next to the Al Moosa Beach Resthouse in the village of Hansheft, before the going gets too soft in the sand. Jabal Shaik Sam'um – a large photogenic rocky outcrop – is a favourite to check out, and adult adventurers may like clambering up to the top.

Although currently fine, be aware that the massive Salam Yiti development project is pencilled in which will take over the whole of the Yiti Beach area; in fact, there's already a bit more construction traffic around. If you head a little further out of town in this direction, you'll get to As Sifah beach, which is also stunning and possibly a little quieter.

WILDLIFE CENTRES

There is significant emphasis on the care and protection of the Omani environment, such as conserving biodiversity and promoting ecotourism. Nature reserves have been established to prevent damage to the natural habitat of many different species, including leopards, oryx and various birds and fish.

Al Hoota Cave > *p.175*
Al Hamra **24 498 258**
alhootacave.com
Map **2 F4**
The five kilometre-long cave complex is located near the base of Jebel Shams and has attracted thousands of visitors since officially opening to the public back in 2006. Extensive development projects have installed raised paths for guided tours, a dedicated visitors' centre, a restaurant, a gift shop and a cafe. This tantalising glimpse into the earth's subterranean depths also contains an underground lake, where shoals of blind fish can be seen swimming about.

Arabian Oryx Sanctuary
Al Ajaiz, Central Region Ad Duqm
24 693 537
omanet.om
Map **1 F8**
This reserve is located in the isolated area of Jiddat Al Harasis, the home of Arabia's last true nomads. The environmental resources in this area (flat plains, sand dunes, high hills and rocky slopes) support a unique desert ecosystem that benefits diverse species of flora and fauna. The Arabian Oryx is a medium-sized antelope that is well adapted to its desert existence, particularly because it has the capacity to conserve water. Unfortunately, wild Oryx died out in 1972, but thanks to the efforts of HM Sultan Qaboos, the first Oryx from a captive herd was successfully released into the wild. An entry permit for the sanctuary is available from the Office of the Adviser for Conservation of the Environment, Diwan of Royal Court (24 693 537). To get there from Muscat, follow the main Salalah highway about 500km to Hayma, and then follow the Duqm graded road to the Habab Junction. Head north on a secondary graded road for a further 23km, and then head due east following a desert track for another 23km. It is recommended that you travel in a convoy with at least two 4WD vehicles.

As Saleel Natural Park
Al Kamil Wa Al Wafi
Map **2 H5**
The As Saleel Natural Park in Al Kamil Al Wafi, approximately 55km south-west of Sur, is divided into three vegetation areas; alluvial plain covered with acacia woodland, wadis in the higher mountains, and sparsely vegetated hills and rocky outcrops forming the northern boundaries. These zones provide good habitat for some of the medium-sized wildlife species in Oman, such as gazelles, wild cats, wolves and foxes. The park has been designated for the future development of wildlife education and tourism, protecting the wildlife in its own habitat. Unfortunately unrestricted access in the past has made the animals quite shy, so a visit to this park is no guarantee of a sighting.

Daymaniyat Islands Nature Reserve
18 km off Batinah Coast Al Khaburah
Map **1 F4**
The Damaniyat Islands are a cluster of nine islands along the coast of Seeb and Barka. They are surrounded by rocks and shallow seas, and can only be reached by boat. The islands are of great environmental importance, as they are home to some endangered species and the nesting sites for several species of migratory birds. The islands themselves are off limits to visitors. You can anchor just off the islands and dive or snorkel in the surrounding waters, although you need to get permission to do this. The waters feature an abundance of marine life and the greatest diversity of corals in the region. Each year, 250 to 300 hawksbill turtles nest on the islands – this species is the most endangered of all marine turtles, and they usually nest in small numbers over a large geographical area. Therefore, this congregation of such a large group on such a small cluster of islands is of global importance.

Jebel Samhan Nature Reserve
66km past Tawi Atayr, Btwn Marbat & Sadah Sadah
Map **1 C11**
The immense Jebel Samhan Nature Reserve is in Dhofar and stretches from Marbat in the south to Shuwimiya in the northeast. The limestone highlands, scalloped mountain peaks, wadis and canyons, and the 1,500m high escarpment overlooking foothills and the coastal plain

between Marbat and Sadh, provide ideal habitat for the last-known wild population of Arabian leopard. Other wildlife present in the area includes nubian ibex, Arabian gazelle, striped hyenas, caracal, wild cats, foxes and wolves. Whales can sometimes be seen along the coast between Hadbin and Shuwaymiya. Green and loggerhead turtles also nest on the sandy beaches, and the adjacent cliffs provide a resting place for migrating birds. To get there, turn left at the signpost marked Tawi Atayr (32km before you reach Taqah). In Tawi Atayr, turn left following the signpost for Khis Adeen. Turn right after one kilometre, and then drive along the graded road for about 66km, at which point you will reach the plateau on top of Jebel Samhan.

Khors Of The Dhofar Coast
Nr Taqah Village Dhofar
Map **1 C9**
The Dhofar coast khors are valuable resources with an abundance of wildlife. One of the most important reasons for protecting the khors is their use by large numbers of migratory birds for food and rest during their annual migration – over 200 species of birds have been recorded in this area. The khors were traditionally used by the local people to water and graze their livestock, while the marine life provided rich fishing territory. With the increase in population and the expansion of the Salalah area, some of the khors' resources became threatened by over-

utilisation. Hence, the Oman government has proclaimed these valuable resources as protected areas. To witness some of the khors' beauty go to KhorRouri Beach, a few kilometres east of Taqah Village (east of Salalah).

Ras Al Jinz Sea Turtle & Natural Reserve
Sur **96 550 606**
rasaljinz-turtlereserve.com
Map **1 H5**
Turtle nesting sites on the coast of Oman have been recorded on over 275 beaches along the coast, from the Musandam in the north to near the border with Yemen in the south. Five out of the seven recognised species of marine turtle are found in Oman's waters, while the green turtle, the loggerhead, hawksbill and olive ridley are known to come ashore and nest. The giant leatherback turtle, which can weigh up to a ton, feeds in the waters off Oman's coast, but does not regularly nest here. Turtles face many threats to their survival, not least being caught in fishing nets and having their nesting sites destroyed by man. Green turtles are estimated to lay up to 60,000 egg clutches each year in Oman; the effort of about 20,000 female turtles. While they nest all along the coast, the majority of nest sites are along a 45km stretch of coastline around Ras Al Hadd (the most eastern point of the Arabian Peninsula). Here, the government has set up a reserve to allow the public to view the amazing spectacle of nesting females and newborn hatchlings. The area has been limited to the beaches at Ras Al Jinz, with access to the other beaches being prohibited. To visit the turtle reserve at Ras Al Jinz you must get a permit. However, you no longer have to apply to the Directorate General of Nature Protectorates, because you can now get one directly from the Ras Al Jinz gate. Places are limited to about 60 people and it is advisable to book well in advance if you can. A fee of RO 1 is charged for adults and 100 baisas for children. You will need to supply names and nationalities of all visitors, plus a contact phone number, visit date and your car registration number. The permit allows you to stay on the government campsite at Ras Al Jinz and to have access to the beach. When you receive the permit you will also get an information pack on using the campsite and watching the turtles.

A hatchling

Tawi Atayr & Wadi Darbat
Dhofar
Map **1 C10**
The Wadi Darbat Natural Park in the Dhofar region has stunning views of waterfalls, lakes, mountains and lush vegetation. There are also caves to explore (rich in stalactites and stalagmites) and a wide range of wildlife. During the khareef season (in summer), there is a monsoon waterfall that is 100 metres high. To get there from Taqah, drive towards Marbat and after 32km you'll find the turn-off for Tawi Atayr (famous for its 'Well of Birds' – a natural sinkhole that is over 100 metres wide and 211 metres deep, and which is home to many species of birds, particularly during the khareef). From the TawiAtayr turn-off, turn left after a few hundred metres to get onto the track that will lead you down into Wadi Darbat.

AMUSEMENT CENTRES

Foton World Fantasia
Markaz Al Bahja Al Mawalih Ash Shamaliyah **24 537 061**
Map **2 A2**
Foton specialises in 'edutainment' for children, and this fun area is a hit with kids of all ages. It has a climbing wall, arcade machine and games, bumper boats and also plays host to Oman's first rollercoaster. Although perhaps a little timid in comparison to the more famous rides in Blackpool, Coney Island or Ferrari World, the rollercoaster's status as the first of its kind in Oman makes it well worth the effort in a historical context.

Magic Planet
Muscat City Centre Al Mawalih
Al Janubiyah **2484 558 766**
magicplanet.ae
Map **2 A3**
One of ten dotted about the region, the amusement centre is popular with kids of all ages. It has a small carousel, a mini train and bumper cars as the main attractions, with an adventure playground catering for the more active youngsters. It is located next to the foodcourt in Muscat City Centre (p.297). RO 30 gets you an unlimited ride pass. Magic Planet has a party zone area that can be booked for private parties.

Marah Land (Land Of Joy)
Nr Al Qurm Natural Park Al Qurm
24 562 215
Map **2 H2**
Marah Land contains a boating lake and a fountain, as well as thrilling rides including the Space Gun, Flume Ride, Ferris wheel, bumper cars, the Giant Wheel, Horror Ride and rollercoaster. This place was designed with complete family entertainment in mind, and includes a variety of food outlets offering both Arab and international munchies. Entry fee: Adults and children over 5 pay 300 baisas to get in, but children under 4 get in for free. You can buy a RO 1 package that includes 11 free games. The park itself also plays host to a variety of international craft stalls and events during the Muscat Festival, which takes place in December/January.

Sindbad's Wonder Centre
Al Harthy Complex Al Qurm
24 794 677
Map **2 H2**
There are a host of fairground rides to amuse children, and because there are rides for all age groups, there is no age limitation. They also have computer and video games. You can bring your own food or get Sindbad's to cater in the separate dining area. Children will love the carousel, bumper cars, magic carpet train ride and spinning teacups. Parents can relax while the kids wear themselves out. There are other Sindbad Parks in Al Khuwayr (opposite SABCO supermarket), Al Masa Mall, Wadi Kabir and in Seeb (near Al Khud Roundabout).

SPECTATOR SPORTS

BULLFIGHTING
Unlike Spanish bullfighting, the Oman version is bloodless and the animals suffer little or no injury during fighting. This is not a gory sport, but rather a contest of strength between two powerful animals. The Brahmin bulls used in fighting are often pampered family pets.

At the beginning of a fight, two bulls of similar size are led into the centre of the ring to lock horns for battle. The fight is over when the weaker of the two either gives up and runs away, or is forced out of the ring. Each fight lasts just a few minutes, and usually the worst injury suffered is a bruised ego on the part of both the losing bull and its owner! There is no prize money, although sometimes the owner of the winning bull receives a token amount.

This historical form of entertainment is loved and treasured by Omanis, and you'll find that half the fun is watching the locals cheering for their favourite bull, and trying to recapture it at the end of the fight. Bullfights are held in several places along the Batinah coastline; usually on Friday afternoons at around 16:30. Barka and Seeb are the two main bullfighting sites, and a smaller ring is located in Al Sawadi. There is also a well-known bullfighting ring in Sohar.

Entrance is free, and visitors are welcome, although it can be quite difficult to know when a bullfight will take place as they tend to spring up without rhyme nor reason; public holidays and celebrations would be your best bet. Fights are not held during the hottest summer months and Ramadan.

CAMEL RACING

Camel racing is a popular traditional sport and you shouldn't miss the chance to see it up close. The camels are bred specially for the track, and it is still Bedouin families who raise and train them. The racing season runs from August to April, and races are held mainly at weekends, and on Saturdays and public holidays during the winter months. Races start at around 06:00 and continue until 09:00, so you may have to forsake your lie-in.

Announcements for camel races appear mostly in the Arabic newspapers, but if you are keen to go you can find out details from one of the tour operators. Race tracks can be found all around the country, including Seeb (the main location) in the north and Salalah in the south. In the interior you'll find many other racing

YOU CALL THE SHOTS

While the main tour activities are listed here, Oman's tour operators are a friendly bunch who are happy to cater to your needs when setting an itinerary. If you think fort is a four-letter word and museums belong in the past, your tour operator will be able to arrange a tour that is more up your street – how about a shopping tour which guides you through the souks, malls, and even gives you a crash course in bargaining? For more information, just call your tour operator (see a list on p.185) for a chat about possibilities.

tracks, sometimes clearly signposted, along the main roads. A visit to any of these might give you the opportunity to see the camels being trained, although only usually before 08:00. For a list of camel race locations and dates, plus information on events and festivals visit omantourism.gov.om.

Oman Camel Racing Association
18 November St, Nr The Chedi Muscat
Al Ghubrah Ash Shamaliyyah **26 893 805**
Map **2 E3**
Another good source for discovering venues, upcoming fixtures and previous results, pop into the office or call for a schedule. Again, you might be best getting an Arab friend to do this if you don't understand Arabic, as the grasp of English isn't great.

Oman Camel Racing Federation
Al Azaiba **24 490 494**
sportsoman.com
Map **2 F3**
The primary aim of this organisation is to hold various camel races throughout the year in different areas of Oman. However, they also hold show jumping events, although these tend to take place only during the cooler months. Keep your eyes on the local papers, as this is where you'll find details of upcoming events. Alternatively you can contact the federation for a schedule, although a good understanding of Arabic is needed as they don't speak much English.

CRICKET

There are currently 60 teams registered with the Oman Cricket Association, but many organisations have their own teams that compete in inter-company leagues and the sport is also becoming increasingly popular in schools. The Oman national team is regionally successful, winning a number of GCC tournaments.

The Oman Cricket Association also organises league matches for girls and schools on Thursdays and the men's league runs on Fridays. Matches are played on major cricket grounds throughout Oman, namely the PDO, Oman Automobile Grounds 3 and 4 and Sultan Qaboos University grounds. For details and fixtures, contact 24 787 085 or check on omanicricket.com. Entrance is free for spectators.

CYCLING

The first Tour of Oman took place in 2010 and it is part of the ongoing attempt to globalise cycling. The teams taking part include some of the best in the world, with most using the race as a precursor to the bigger Europan events that follow later in the year, such as the Tour de France. In 2012, for example, Team Sky unveiled its new rider, world champion Mark Cavendish, at the Tour of Oman.

Taking place each February, previous routes have taken riders on a loop of the historic city of Sur, up steep mountain climbs in Jebal Al Akhdar, with time trial stages running from Bander Al Jissah to the Al Bustan roundabout and back.

Spectators have also been able to watch the event at several of Oman's most famous landmarks, including Sultan Qaboos University, Al Sawadi, Al Seeb and at the finish line on Mutrah Corniche. Check out the official website (tourofoman.om) for routes; newspapers will also publish route maps on the day of each stage. There is no charge for spectators.

FOOTBALL

As in most places in the world, you don't have to travel far to see a game of football in Oman. Rural villages usually have a group knocking a ball around on the local sand and rock pitch – and you could probably join in if you wanted.

The Oman Football Association is the biggest sports association in the Sultanate, and 43 semi-professional clubs represent various states. These teams compete in various leagues and tournaments, including the Omantel League and His Majesty's Cup. Spectators are welcome. See omanfa.net for fixtures.

The Oman national team has never qualified for the World Cup but has reached the Gulf Cup of Nations final three times, winning it once. Most home games are played at Sultan Qaboos Stadium and, once again, you'll find fixtures and venues at omanfa.net.

HORSE RACING

Horse racing is not on the social agenda as it is in nearby Dubai, but it is nonetheless an enjoyable experience. Horse races are held annually and are organised by the royal stables. Check out the Royal Cavalry Club website for upcoming races rca.gov.

om. The Oman Equestrian Federation organises a national show jumping competition each winter which attracts entries from the royal stables, the Royal Oman Police, the Royal Guard of Oman and a number of private stables. The event takes place at Enam Equestrian Showgrounds at Al Seeb.

Oman Equestrian Federation
As Seeb **24 490 424**
sportsoman.com
Map **1 G4**
Organises a variety of equestrian races and show jumping, although there seem to be less events than previously. Details on competitions are published in newspapers, or you can get more information by calling the federation.

MOTORSPORTS

The Oman Automobile Association (omanauto.org) was founded in 1979 and is located in Seeb, where there is a track and spectator stadium. The association organises numerous local and international events that include the Oman National Rally Championships, karting championships, sand dune challenges and motocross races. Off-road rallies are also held once a month.

RUGBY

Muscat Rugby Football Club (muscatrugby.com) has more than 100 members and has teams that take part in the Arabian Gulf Rugby League and several other tournaments, including the Bahrain 10s and the Dubai 7s. The season runs from September to April, and there is a big social scene connected to the rugby club. Matches are played on the grass pitch in Al Khuwair and spectators are welcome.

Dhofar Nomads Rugby Club (email dhofarnomadsrfc@yahoo.co.uk), based in Salalah, also enters a team into the Dubai 7s every year, in addition to hosting other competitions and matches that spectators are welcome to attend.

TENNIS

The Oman Tennis Association oversees the national Omani team in tournaments at home and abroad. The association also organises a variety of annual local tournaments. These are mainly held at hotels and, although they are usually for a mixture of standards, there are a few that attract the professionals.

WATERSPORTS

Sailing regattas are held regularly and the staff at Marina Bander Al Rowdha (24 737 288) and Capital Area Yacht Club (24 737 712) will be able to provide you with more information on these.

Since the government set up Oman Sail (omansail.com), the profile of sailing in Oman has certainly increased. Check out the website for all races, regattas and venues; events that can be watched include the Muscat leg of the extreme sailing series, Sailing Arabia – The Tour, and the Mussanah Race Week (dinghy racing).

There is also the Oman Laser Association which organises around 10 competitions annually. The races are competitive yet friendly affairs, where the more experienced sailors readily share tips and techniques with others. Most races are held at the RAH Recreation Club, with occasional events in Sawadi Resort or the Marina Bander Al Rowdha. Marina Bander Al Rowdha has a fairly active programme with plenty of social gatherings too.

There is no dhow racing, like you'll find in Dubai and Abu Dhabi, but the Muscat Regatta and the Dubai to Muscat President's Cup take place annually in November and/or December. Spectators can head to Marina Bander Al Rowdha.

TOURS & SIGHTSEEING

As you might expect from a country with such breathtaking scenery and rich history, Oman has numerous tour operators offering an exciting range of city, desert and mountain trips. The following are descriptions of the most popular (and most general) tour itineraries available, but remember that if you have something specific in mind, many operators can tailor-make a tour for you.

When booking your tour, it is useful to book three or four days in advance if possible. Some operators will request a 50% deposit. Tours usually depart from set pick-up points, such as major hotels. As a general guideline, wear cool, comfortable clothing, and don't forget your hat and sunglasses. Desert and mountain tours require strong, flat-soled shoes, and if you're going into the desert in the cooler months, take a jacket as the temperature can drop after sunset. And don't forget your camera!

One last word on desert and mountain tours: these trips often involve some pretty extreme driving over sand dunes or through wadis. If you are pregnant, elderly, sick, are travelling with young children or you suffer from motion sickness, inform your tour company and they will arrange a gentler route for you.

BOAT TOURS & CHARTERS

Al Khayran
Marina Bandar Al Rowdha Haramil
24 737 288
alkhayran.com
Map **2 L2**
A recent addition to the Oman exploring scene, Al Khayran is a semi-submersible boat to take you beneath the ocean without getting wet. Trips leave four times a day, seven days a week, from Marina Bandar Al Rowdha where a speedy passenger boat zips you along the coastline past the Al Bustan and Shangri-La to the waiting vessel. Venture down the stairs and you'll find yourself in a submarine boasting windows onto the underwater world. Informative posters help you spot species of fish and even turtles if you're lucky. The two-hour trip includes soft drinks and costs RO 25 for tourists and expats or RO 6 for Omanis.

Marina Bandar Al Rowdha
Haramil **24 737 288**
marinaoman.net
Map **2 L2**
Marina Bandar Al Rowdha is located on the western coast of Oman, and is one of the best launch spots for fishing, diving and sailing. It has a total of 400 berths, and is fully equipped for launch, recovery, service and marine control. The marina can organise tours for whale watching, watersports, diving and fishing. For a more relaxing excursion, you can go for a cruise on a traditional dhow, or be transported to a secluded beach for an afternoon's sunbathing. The marina has its own restaurant, the Blue Marlin (p.311), which does a great alfresco breakfast.

Moon Light Dive Centre
Nr Grand Hyatt Muscat Hay As Saruj
99 317 700
moonlightdive.com
Map **2 G2**
The Moonlight Dive Centre can deliver a
customised cruise package to meet your
requirements. It offers trips for groups
(from four people to 10) in one of its three
boats, which are based on the beach in
Shati Al Qurm, next to the Hyatt Regency
Muscat. A typical cruise heads south
along Muscat's spectacular coast, visiting
rocky islands out at sea, secluded beaches
or even marina cafes for breakfast or
refreshments. Time can be allocated for
other activities as per your requirements,
such as fishing, snorkelling, sunbathing or
watersports. For a three-hour trip, expect
to pay around RO 25 per person with
discounts for groups.

Oman Charter
Marina Bandar Al Rowdha Haramil
95 044 136
omancharter.com
Map **2 L2**
Oman Charter offers all sorts of
opportunities for setting sail, from
simple day trips (island hopping, dolphin
watching, sunset cruises) and basic daily
and weekly charter packages, to part-

ownership schemes that may interest the
more serious sailor.

DHOW CHARTERS

Al Marsa Travel & Tourism
Musandam Daba **26 836 550**
almarsamusandam.com
Map **1 E2**
Al Marsa has four purpose-built dhows
that are suitable both for divers and
tourists. You can relax on the sundeck for
a day trip and discover fishing villages or
you can go on anything up to a seven-
night voyage and explore Oman's fjords.
The dhows are equipped for diving and
other watersports. Prices start at OR 38 for
divers and OR 31.500 for non-divers. Based
in Sharjah, they operate along the eastern
coastline of the UAE and Oman.

Hormuz Line Tours & Cruises
Nr Al Maha Petrol Station Khasab
050 543 2717
Map **1 E1**
Hormuz Line offers excursions and
accommodation packages tailored to your
needs. The dhow cruise options range from
one-day trips exploring the Khasab on a
traditional wooden dhow, to an overnight
tour that includes a dhow cruise. It also

Marina Bandar Al Rowdha

181

offers the opportunity for you to sail with them into the Strait of Hormuz, to swim with dolphins, snorkel around islands and to explore laidback, sleepy coastal villages.

Ibn Qais & Partners
Marina Bandar Al Rowdha Haramil
24 487 103
Map **2 L2**
Ibn Qais own the Lubna, a traditional dhow that's available for charter to any of the islands in Oman. The company provides everything you need while onboard, and even tailor-make packages for special occasions. So, if you want a birthday or anniversary celebration with a difference, you can set sail on the Lubna for an evening of good food and entertainment. Sunset cruises set sail every Thursday and Sunday from 16:00 to 18:00.

Khasab Travel & Tours
Nr Khasab Airport, Musandam Khasab
26 730 464
khasabtours.com
Map **1 E1**
Khasab Travel & Tours have a traditionally decorated Omani dhow on which to take you exploring in the fjords. It's decked out with cushions and carpets for you to lounge on while enjoying the passing scenery. The dhow will also stop and allow you to explore the villages of the Strait of Hormuz, and a session of swimming or snorkelling around Telegraph Island. Refreshments and a buffet lunch are also included.

Musandam Sea Adventure Travel & Tourism
Musandam Khasab **26 730 424**
msaoman.com
Map **1 E1**
With its dramatic fjords, Musandam is often referred to as 'the Norway of the Middle East'. Take a dhow cruise and experience the area's rocky topography where mountains jut up out of pristine waters. Land and explore remote Omani villages, and then stop at Telegraph Island for a leisurely picnic. Cruises vary in length from half-day to three-day options, and prices range from RO 15–150 per person, with children under 3 free and under 10s half price. Musandam Sea Adventure takes care of transportation, food, and lodging and creates comfortable, but adventurous, tours.

DOLPHIN AND WHALE WATCHING TOURS
There are more than 20 species of whales and dolphins either living in or passing through the seas off the coast of Oman. Although no tour operator can guarantee a sighting of these beautiful sea creatures, the odds are definitely high that you will get to see a school of dolphins swimming alongside your boat and playing in its wake. Many tour operators will tentatively rate your chances of seeing dolphins at 85% to 90%.

Whales are not so frequently seen – these gentle giants travel in smaller groups and stay under the surface for a lot longer, so you have to be a little bit more patient. Early mornings and evenings, when the seas are at their calmest, are the best times for whale sightings. It is possible to see them from the shore (usually in cliff areas, such as Musandam) but it is better to be out at sea in a boat, where the experience is closer and infinitely more exciting.

Working hard to monitor and protect these magnificent mammals is the Whale & Dolphin Research Group, part of the Environment Society of Oman (ESO). This is a group of volunteer scientists and other interested parties who work together to collect and disseminate knowledge about Oman's cetaceans (whales & dolphins). The group's activities include emergency rescue services for whales and dolphins, a collection of cetacean bones, skulls and tissue samples, maintenance of a database of cetacean sightings and strandings, cooperation with local tour operators to promote responsible whale and dolphin watching activities, and dissemination of information through articles in local and international publications to promote awareness of Oman's cetaceans and the need to protect their environment.

For further information, see arabianwildlife.com or contact the main office (24 696 912).

Marina Bandar Al Rowdha
Haramil **24 737 288**
marinaoman.net
Map **2 L2**
The Marina Bandar Al Rowdha offers dolphin tours a short distance off the coast of Muscat and is the leaving point for the Al Khayran semi-submersible boat (p.180). For more information on the marina, see p.180.

SAFARI SAVVY

Off-road driving is exhilarating but extreme, and people who suffer from motion sickness may not enjoy the experience very much. You may rest assured that your driver is a skilled professional and knows exactly what he is doing; however, remember that you are the client and have the right to request him to slow down or tackle less challenging routes if you feel the ride is too bumpy. Most drivers will take an easier route if you are with children, elderly people or people with special circumstances. Note that it may not be safe for pregnant women to go on an off-road tour.

Muscat Diving & Adventure Centre

As Seeb **24 543 002**
holiday-in-oman.com
Map **1 G4**

This upbeat tour operator can take you out to sea to spot dolphins, and they estimate the chance of a sighting at around 80%. The most common species seen are common, spinner and bottlenose. There are two boats which seat up to 15 and 20 people. Daily departures are at 07:00 and 10:00. The cruises last for three to four hours, and the cost per person is RO 20 (which includes soft drinks).

Oman Dive Center

Nr Qantab & Barr Al Jissah, Bandar Jussa
Al Amrat **24 824 240**
extradivers-worldwide.com
Map **1 G4**

Every morning, the Oman Dive Center organises a boat trip to go and spot dolphins off the coast of Muscat. Your chances of seeing dolphins (usually common, spinner, bottlenose or Indo-Pacific species) are high at any time of year and estimated at around 95%. Your chances of seeing whales are not as high, although they have been spotted from time to time (usually from October to May). The boat trip includes breakfast, served onboard.

SAFARI TOURS

Dune Dinner

There are a range of dune dinners on offer, but on a typical tour you will be collected in the mid-afternoon, when you will be driven inland towards the Hajar mountains and then off-road through the lush green scenery and freshwater pools of Wadi Abyad. Then you'll head for the undulating dunes of the nearby Abyad desert for some exciting dune driving, before stopping to watch the sun set over the sands. After a sumptuous barbecue, you'll head back to Muscat.

Full-Day Safari

This trip combines a visit to one of Oman's most spectacular wadis, Wadi Bani Khalid, with the breathtaking expanse of the Wahiba Desert. Different tour operators have different itineraries, but on the way from Muscat you will visit places such as the ruined fort of Mudairib, Shab Village and the town of Sur. Some of the unforgettable sights you may see on the way are traditional mud-brick homes clinging to steep valley walls, clear streams carrying fresh water into deep pools, and manmade irrigation systems called 'falaj'. As you leave the mountains you'll head for the Wahiba desert for an exhilarating ride over the dunes, some of which are 200 metres high.

Mountain Safari

The height and extent of Oman's mountain ranges surprise many visitors. Mountain safaris either head into the highest range, Jebel Akhdar, or up to Jebel Shams, which is Oman's highest peak at over 3,000m. On the way, you'll pass through towns (such as Nizwa) and remote villages set on terraces cut into the mountains. Ancient irrigation channels bring water to the villages to feed the crops. The top of Jebel Shams feels like the top of the world, with the entire mountain range and the awe-inspiring 'Grand Canyon' of Oman (a rocky canyon dropping thousands of metres from the plateau), way below.

Overnight Turtle Watching

Many tour operators offer trips to the famous Ras Al Jinz Turtle Sanctuary, where you can watch the rare sight of turtles coming onto the beach to lay their eggs. On your way to Ras Al Jinz you'll pass Quriyat, Wadi Shab, and the town of Sur, home to the most skilled dhow builders in Oman. After arriving at the Turtle Sanctuary, you'll be served a beach barbecue before night falls and the turtles come lumbering onto the beach to lay their eggs and bury them in the sand. After a few hours' sleep, you'll return to the beach and watch the mass of tiny hatchlings struggle out of their eggs and make their journey into the sea. On your return journey to Muscat you will get to see more of the countryside and historical settlements.

Wadi Drive

An off-road tour through the wadis can either be half-day, full-day or overnight, camping in the peaceful surroundings of the rocky wilderness. You'll get to see falaj irrigation channels, in place for centuries, bringing water from underground springs to irrigate palm plantations and vegetable terraces. Natural streams run all year round in several wadis, transforming the dry, rocky landscape into fertile areas of lush greenery and clear rock pools that are often home to fish, frogs and other wildlife. Hidden villages in the mountains, seemingly trapped in time, illustrate how people used to subsist in times gone by.

Wahiba Desert

The Wahiba Desert stretches all the way from the coast to the mountains. This tour travels into the middle of seemingly endless dunes of red and white sand. Dune driving is a must-do; a ride up and down the steep slopes, courtesy of a very skilled driver, is like a natural rollercoaster. A visit to a traditional Bedouin homestead for Arabic coffee and dates usually follows, as well as the chance to try camel riding, the oldest form of desert transport.

Overnight Desert Safari

Leave the noise of the city behind you and experience the peace of the desert for a night. After an exhilarating drive through the dunes you will set up camp in a remote area of Wahiba, where Bedouin tribes have lived traditionally for thousands of years. At sunset, enjoy a camel ride while a barbecue is prepared and then relax in comfortable surroundings under the starlit sky. In the morning, after a leisurely start, visit the flowing wadis to see the greenery and rugged mountain landscape, which form a complete contrast to the desert sights of the previous day.

CAMEL RIDES

A visit to this part of the world is hardly complete unless you've been up close and personal with a 'ship of the desert'. A ride on a camel is hard to forget – you will generally mount the camel when it is lying down, and then you need to hang on for dear life when your humped steed unfolds its gangly legs to stand up. Once you're up though, it's fairly smooth riding and you can lose yourself in your 'Lawrence of Arabia' fantasies. Don't forget to take a photo!

Many tour operators incorporate a short camel ride on their desert safaris. Alternatively, for a unique adventure, you could try a camel ride into the spectacular sand dunes. Your guide will lead you to a Bedouin camp, where you can enjoy a well-deserved rest and some refreshments. Don't forget to take your camera, so you can remember this unique experience long after the aches subside.

Desert Nights Camp
Nr Sand Coloured Mosque, 11 km from Al Wasil Bidiyyah **92 818 388**
desertnightscamp.com
Map **1 G5**
Desert Nights Camp offers a variety of desert activities, including camel rides or desert cycles for kids. Based 220km from Muscat, you can augment your camel adventure with dune bashing, sand surfing and trips to nearby encampments at Wadi Bani Khalid and Ras Al Jinz (p.203) on the coast, where you may even get to watch turtles coming ashore.

Muscat Diving & Adventure Centre
As Seeb **24 543 002**
holiday-in-oman.com
Map **1 G4**
The centre offers two main tours by camel, which are operated along eco-tourism lines. They work with Bedouin families of the Northern Region Sands (Wahiba) in the Sharqiya, and run expeditions in the Rub Al Khali in Dhofar. Camel trips or 'safaris' can vary in length from a short day ride

to a 14-day trek across the sands. This is one of Oman's most authentic tours and it allows you the opportunity to see and engage in the Bedouin way of life with an overnight stop at a Bedu campsite.

FARM & STABLE TOURS

Ostrich Farm
Nr Majan Water Factory Barka
Map **1 F4**
The Ostrich Breeding Farm in Barka is surprisingly interesting. Visitors can see the 100 adult birds or the eggs being incubated and also chicks between February and June. The farm started in 1993 when the eggs were imported from South Africa. They were the first ostriches to have been hatched in Oman since early last century when the birds became extinct in this region. The ostrich is farmed for a variety of reasons and the aim of the farm is to sustain a 300-bird breeding group to meet the ever-increasing demands for healthy meat, fine leather and exquisite feathers. Ostrich meat is considered an excellent alternative to beef, since it is low in cholesterol, but has a very similar consistency and texture. The farm is also home to about 30 crocodiles. Entrance to the farm costs 500 baisas per adult and 300 baisas per child. The timings are 07:00 to 12:00 and 15:00 to 18:00, seven days a week. To get there, turn on to Nakhal Road from the Barka Roundabout, and after four kilometres you'll see the Majan Water Factory on the right. Turn right into the private road just before the factory, and the ostrich farm is the first farm on your left.

PLACES OF WORSHIP TOURS

Sultan Qaboos Grand Mosque
As Sultan Qaboos St, Wilayat District
Al Udhaybah Al Janubiyyah
omantourism.gov.om
Map **2 E3**
This beautiful example of Islamic architecture provides a wonderful insight into the cultural heritage of Oman. It is also one of the few mosques that allow entry for non-Muslims. Apart from being a place of worship, this huge mosque is a centre for scholars and houses an Islamic reference library containing over 20,000 sources of information on Islamic sciences

and culture. The mosque is lavishly decorated, and features a 263m prayer carpet, 35 crystal chandeliers (the central one is 14 metres high and eight metres wide), and a floor entirely paved with marble. The tour takes you into the men's and women's prayer halls, where you are even allowed to take pictures. There are strict rules governing entry of non-Muslims into the mosque – you have to take your shoes off before entering, and both men and women should wear conservative clothing (women should be covered up, including their hair), and children under 10 are not permitted. The hours for the tour are strictly between 08:30 and 11:00 from Saturday to Thursday.

MAIN TOUR OPERATORS

When booking a tour it is normal practise to do so three or four days in advance. In some cases bookings can be made on shorter notice. You usually pay a 50% deposit when you make the booking, with the remainder payable when you are picked up at the start of the tour. Cancellation policies differ from company to company; cancelling your tour without an appropriate notice period may result in the loss of your deposit. Tours are often priced per vehicle rather than per person, although some tours offer fixed individual rates for tours and do not stipulate minimum numbers. On the day of your tour you will be picked up either from your hotel, residence or an agreed meeting point. Tours usually leave on time, and no-shows do not get a refund. At most times of year it is advisable to wear cool, comfortable clothing such as shorts and T-shirts. Hats and sunglasses are also recommended. If you are going on a desert or mountain tour, you should wear strong, flat-soled shoes as there is usually walking involved. You might want to take sun protection, a camera and money (in case there's a chance to buy souvenirs).

Al Azure Tours Hay As Saruj,
99 856 888, *alazuretours.com*
Al Nimer Tourism Shati Al Qurm,
24 713 270, *alnimertourism.com*
Bahwan Travel Agencies Ruwi,
24 704 455, *bahwantravels.com*
Desert Discovery Tours Al Azaiba,
24 493 232, *desertdiscovery.com*
Eihab Travels Various Locations,
24 683 900, *ohigroup.com*

Empty Quarter Tours Madinat As Sultan Qaboos, *emptyquartertours.com*
Golden Oryx Tours Ruwi, 24 489 853, *goldenoryx.com*
Grand Canyon Of Oman Tours Shati Al Qurm, 92 605 102
Gulf Ventures Oman Al Ghubrah Al Janubiyyah, 24 490 733, *gulfventures.com*
Hormuz Line Tours & Cruises Khasab, 050 543 2717
Hud Hud Travels Madinat As Sultan Qaboos, 92 920 670, *hudhudtravels.com*
Khasab Travel & Tours Khasab, 26 730 464, *khasabtours.com*
Mark Tours Ruwi, 24 782 727, *marktoursoman.com*
Muscat Diving & Adventure Centre As Seeb, 24 543 002, *holiday-in-oman.com*
Sunny Day Tours, Travel & Adventures As Seeb, 24 490 055, *sunnydayoman.com*
Turtle Beach Resorts Sur, 25 540 068, *tbroman.com*

TOURS OUTSIDE THE CITY

East Salalah Tour
Leaving from Salalah and travelling east, this tour visits many historical sites and places of interest along the picturesque coast including the fishing village of Taqa with its watchtowers and castle. Further on is Khor Rouri, a freshwater creek now separated from the sea. It is the site of the ancient city of Samharam, known for its frankincense and for being the former capital of the Dhofar region. Also on the tour is Mohammed Bin Ali's Tomb, the Ayn Razat ornamental gardens, the Hamran Water Springs and the historical trading centre of Mirbat.

West Salalah Tour
Venture inland from Salalah to the northern part of the Qara Mountains, where the road winds up hairpin bends and eventually leads to the border with Yemen. The tour goes to the Tomb of the Prophet Job, a place visited by many Islamic pilgrims, and the wadis and green pastures where they grow the finest frankincense in the world. Returning from the mountains, you will head to the spectacular Mughsail Beach where, at high tide, seawater gushes through natural blowholes in the limestone,

reaching dizzying heights. On the way back to Salalah, common stops are the bird sanctuary and Mina Raysut.

Nizwa
Nizwa is the largest city in Oman's interior, and this full-day tour explores the fascinating sights and heritage of this historically significant place. After driving deep into the Hajar mountains, you'll come to the oasis city of Nizwa, home to the Nizwa Fort (which dates back to the 17th century) and the magnificent Jabrin Fort, notable for its wall and ceiling decorations and secret passageways. Many ancient ruins, such as Bahla Fort (currently undergoing extensive renovation) and various mud-brick villages, can be seen among the date palm plantations and wadis. See also p.198.

Rustaq
Batinah, the north-west region of Oman, has always been an important area for its abundant agriculture and strategic position as the trading centre between the mountains and the coast. It is home to many forts including the oldest and largest in the country, Al Kersa Fort. En route you will also visit the ancient souks, hot springs and sandy beaches, all amid spectacular mountain scenery. See also Batinah Region, p.196.

Ubar
The discovery of the 'Lost City of Ubar' in the early 1990s caused great excitement in the archaeological world. This full-day tour takes you through some stunning scenery as you drive through the Qara mountains to the site of Ubar. This ancient city was at the crossroads of significant trade routes, making it a place of unrivalled wealth and splendour – when Marco Polo visited Ubar, he called it 'paradise'. However, at the height of its glory it sank into the desert sands, leaving no trace of its existence. Legend had it that to punish the residents of Ubar for their greed and lavish lifestyle, God caused the sand to swallow the city. When the lost city was uncovered, less than 20 years ago, it was discovered that a huge limestone cavern underneath Ubar had collapsed, causing the city to sink into the sand.

After leaving Ubar you'll continue off-road as the tour ventures into the famous sands of Rub al Khali (the Empty Quarter), for some dune driving. See also p.260.

LOCAL TRIPS

It's easy to make a great escape from the city, with plenty to enjoy just an hour or two from Muscat.

From Muscat there are a large number of places worthy of visiting that are close at hand. If it is a day trip you are after, then consider visiting a wadi or a beach. For the best of both, take a trip to Wadi Tiwi where you could try a 4WD trip up the wadi – careful, it gets very narrow and steep in places – before having a picnic at the top of the wadi and heading back down to the white sand at Fins for a well-deserved dip in the sea.

If you are more into the idea of walking in a wadi, then combining Wadi Shab with a dip in the sea at Fins would make for a great day out. It is important to stress that, in both cases, if you want to combine the two activities, you should set off fairly early in the morning or else camp the night before (or after) on the white sands in and around Fins beach.

Another popular beach, frequented by expats and locals alike, is Yiti Beach and it makes for a good day trip, as well as a thrilling overnight adventure.

If the beach doesn't appeal, then the mountains are an attractive alternative for a day trip. If you set off early on a Friday morning, it is possible to drive to Nizwa in time to make the goat market, then take a drive up Jebel Akhdar. The numerous viewing points along the winding drive to the top make for great photo ops, or even good locations to stop and enjoy a spot of alfresco brunch. Like most of the other day trips around Muscat, this itinerary could easily be split into an overnight trip by going up to the top of Jebel Akhdar and spending the night camping at one of the convenient sites up top – or even at the Jebel Akhdar Hotel (p.66) if you prefer a proper bed and running water. Then, in the morning, head back down and make an early stop at the atmospheric Nizwa market before returning to Muscat.

Jebel Shams can likewise be done as a day trip, if you're content with just doing 'the rim walk' which offers some incredible views; you can then drive to the top, get to the village and do the four hour hike, before descending to Wadi Ghule for a picnic lunch. Better still is to do an overnight or weekend getaway, giving you time to do the challenging but rewarding hike to the top and back. Be under no illusions; this is a big day of hiking and it is best to start before sunrise as, even in the winter, temperatures can really climb.

Perhaps you're after some water-based fun instead; in which case, there are plenty of diving and snorkelling adventures to be had within a 40 minute drive of the greater Muscat area. Once again, they're all easy day trips but the real magic and spirit of adventure that Oman is famous for is perhaps best enjoyed by teaming one of these active trips with an overnight stay. Bander Kharan, which lies southeast of Muscat, is a great place for both snorkelling and diving, while you can also tackle a wide range of other marine sports, such as sailing, fishing and jetskiing. It's just a 40 minute 4WD trip from the greater Muscat area. To make a good day great, take the boat to Bander Kharan – it leaves from Bandar Al Rowdha in Muscat and also takes around 40 minutes, with the added benefit of rugged cliffs, sugarcube villages and the Al Bustan Palace resort. If you're lucky, you may even get playful dolphins following the boat.

OUT OF THE CITY

BEYOND THE CITY

Oman isn't all about Muscat. Step outside the capital and there are mountains, wadis, deserts, islands and ancient cities waiting to be discovered.

Beyond Muscat, Oman boasts stunning scenery, lost cities, towering forts and unexpected lush greenery. Travelling north will bring you to the cities of Barka, Nakhal and Sohar. If time allows, the Musandam peninsula (p.192) to the north-west is highly recommended, with its main cities of Khasab and Bukha, and with scenery totally different from the rest of Oman. It features beautiful fjords and lagoons and has become a popular tourist destination.

The southern province of Dhofar, with its capital Salalah, provides a welcome change in climate in the hot summer months. While the rest of Oman is paralysed by heat, the monsoon (khareef) blowing off the Indian Ocean ensures a high percentage of rainfall in this area, resulting in cool weather and beautiful greenery. Salalah attracts international as well as local visitors for its peace and tranquility. Apart from the major regions to visit in Oman, this section also includes its largest island, Masirah, which is off the south-east coast.

MUSANDAM

The Musandam peninsula is an Oman enclave to the north, which is divided from the rest of Oman by the United Arab Emirates. It is a beautiful, largely unspoiled area. The capital is Khasab, a quaint fishing port mostly unchanged by the modern world. The Strait of Hormuz lies to the north, with Iran just across the water, the Arabian Gulf is to the west and the Gulf of Oman lies to the east; hence the area is one of great strategic importance.

Musandam is dominated by the Hajar Mountains, which also run through the UAE and into the main part of Oman. It is sometimes referred to as the Norway of the Middle East, since the jagged mountain cliffs plunge directly into the sea, and the coastline features many inlets and fjords. The views along the coastal

roads are stunning. Just a few metres off the coast you'll find beautiful and fertile coral beds, with an amazing variety of sea life including tropical fish, turtles, dolphins (a common sight) and, occasionally, sharks. Inland, the scenery is equally breathtaking, although you will need a 4WD and a good head for heights to explore it properly.

You can reach Musandam from Muscat by air, sea (via ferry) or by road. The flight takes around 90 minutes. Oman Air (24 531 111) offers internal flights and holiday packages from Muscat to Musandam; a return flight costs RO 48 and flights leave daily from Saturday to Wednesday. The National Ferries Company (800 72 000) offers deals including accommodation at the Golden Tulip Resort Khasab starting from RO 85 per person for ferry tickets, two nights in the hotel and breakfast based on two people sharing. Visitors travelling in Oman do not need an additional visa.

To drive to Musandam from Oman you need to travel through the UAE. GCC nationals and Omanis are free to travel this route without needing any travel documents, but non-GCC residents of Oman need to apply for a road permit. Travelling from Muscat by road, you leave Oman by the border checkpoint at Khatmet Melaha. You then enter Fujairah (part of the UAE) and travel to the Al Dara border checkpoint in Ras Al Khaimah (also part of UAE). Here, you leave the United Arab Emirates and reenter Omani territory at the border checkpoint. Khasab is 38km from this border.

Visitors to Oman carrying a single-entry visa may not be allowed back into Oman once they have left. Check with your nearest Oman embassy for updated information.

Bukha

Bukha is located on the western side of the Musandam peninsula, with a coastline on the Arabian Gulf. The area borders the UAE emirate of Ras Al Khaimah and is 27km north of Khasab. This small town is overlooked by the ruin of an old fort, but there is little to see other than the remains of one watchtower. The Bukha Fort is more impressive, however, and is by the side of the main road just metres from the sea. It was built in the 17th century, restored in 1990, and it is certainly the town's biggest landmark. Traditionally, fishing and boat building have been the occupations of Bukha's residents, and the town has a harbour for a small number of vessels. There is also a pleasant strip of sandy beach with a number of shelters. The village of Al Jadi, about three kilometres north of Bukha, is picturesque and has a couple of fortifications, two of which are restored watchtowers.

Dibba

At the southern end of Musandam, straddling the border with the UAE, Dibba is a small town made up of three fishing villages. Unusually, each part comes under a different jurisdiction: Dibba Bayah is in Oman, Dibba Al Hisn belongs to Sharjah, and Dibba Muhallab is part of Fujairah. The three villages share an attractive bay, fishing communities, and excellent diving locations – from here you can arrange dhow trips to take you to unspoilt dive sites along the remote eastern coast of the Musandam peninsula. The Hajar Mountains provide a wonderful backdrop, rising in places to over 1,800 metres. There is a good public beach too, where seashell collectors may find a few treasures. Dibba is also a good starting point for some stunning off-road driving into the mountains.

The Omani part of Dibba is also home to Dibba Castle, a strongly fortified, double-walled castle built by the Al Shuhah tribe over 180 years ago. You can access the rooms, and provided you don't mind pigeons you can climb all the towers for some great views over the surrounding area and out to sea.

Khasab

Khasab, the capital of the Musandam region, is surrounded by imposing and dramatic mountains that dominate the entire area, with some peaks above

Lush plantation

Waterfall and pool

Activities

This is not a place to come if you want a weekend of shopping or eating out, so be prepared to make do with the comforts of the hotel and the fulfilling experience of being among some wonderful scenery. This does make it a good place to escape the daily grind, particularly with the wide range of outdoor activities.

Boat Trips

An essential activity on any trip to Musandam, a dhow cruise around the fjords is a truly memorable experience. You can hire a dhow or a speedboat from the harbour at Khasab (remember to negotiate the rate before you leave, but expect to pay about RO 10 per hour for a speedboat and RO 25 per hour for dhows). Leisurely dhows are more stable and spacious – large enough for 20 to 25 people. Allow a minimum of three hours to explore the inlet closest to Khasab; tours usually include Telegraph Island and Hidden Cove. Alternatively, try the longer trip out to Kumzar – an ancient village set in an isolated inlet on the northernmost end of the peninsula.

On a full-day trip you'll see remote coastal villages, get a chance to swim and snorkel in the calm waters, and you are almost guaranteed to see dolphins. Khasab Travel & Tours (khasabtours.com) operates a number of dhows, or you can just turn up at the harbour and bargain hard with the independent boat owners to arrange your own private cruise. You can also just hire a small boat to take you out and drop you off on your own private beach, only 10 to 20 minutes from Khasab, then pick you up at an agreed time. It's common to pay only when you have returned to port, otherwise you might get left there for longer than you planned.

Off-Roading

To see the other side of Musandam, you can also drive up to the plateau beneath Jebel As Sayh (Jebel Harim), the highest peak in the area at 2,087 metres. This is an excellent area for camping, hiking, views across the mountain tops, and as a base for further exploration. Most of the year you can get to the top in a saloon car. If you have a 4WD, there are a number of tracks worth exploring that head over the mountains to more secluded places such as Khawr Najd, the only beach accessible by car in the fjords, or the acacia forest

2,000m. The town of Khasab is relatively spread out and has numerous date palm plantations. There is a small souk and a beach, but the port is the main area of interest.

The town relies on fishing, trade (mostly with ports in Iran) and agriculture for subsistence, and produces a range of fruit and vegetables. In fact khasab is the Arabic word for 'fertile'. At one end of the bay is the restored Khasab Fort which is open to the public. There's not that much to see inside, but its setting against the mountainous background is spectacular. Kumzan Fort is just outside Khasab. It was built in about 1600AD by the Imam but little is left of it today, apart from the two watchtowers. About 10km west of Khasab is the village of Tawi where there are prehistoric rock carvings of warriors, boats and animals.

One of Khasab's biggest draws is the diving opportunities. These waters are not recommended for beginners, but experienced divers can enjoy spectacular underwater cliffs and an abundance of marine life at sites just a short boat ride away.

near Sal Al A'la. For more detailed routes see the **UAE Off-Road Explorer**.

Hiking

This is a great area to get outside, stretch your legs and admire the scenery. There are hikes to suit all levels, including some challenging routes for the serious hiker, and the mountainous backdrop provides some fantastic views. If you like the idea of a hike without the hassle, try Khasab Travel & Tours in Khasab, or Absolute Adventure (adventure.ae) in Dibba, who will organise the hike, so all you have to do is turn up.

Diving & Snorkelling

Natural attractions abound underwater. Just off the shore are coral beds with an amazing variety of sea life, including tropical fish, turtles, dolphins, sharks, and even whales. Some of the best dive sites in the Middle East are found here, and the area is becoming increasingly popular with divers as a result. The lagoons offer a little more protection from the elements, and are great spots for snorkelling. There are more than 20 separate dive sites along the east coast for experienced divers. You can book dive trips from your hotel, or through companies such as Al Boom Diving (971 4 342 2993, alboomdiving.com) and Al Marsa Travel & Tourism (26 836 550, almarsamusandam.com).

AL DHAHIRA

With a name meaning 'the back', the Al Dhahirah region lies in Oman's interior, to the west of the Hajar mountains and bordering the UAE and Saudi Arabia. Due to the harsh environment, characterised by huge sandy plains, Al Dhahirah is sparsely populated and there is not much in the way of modern-day comforts. Water is transported from the mountains to the towns using the age-old falaj system, which is deceptively sophisticated.

This is an area where you will get to see Omanis living their lives as they have done for centuries, and if you are fortunate you may get to see displays of traditional dances and crafts. It is also a great place for exploring old forts, ancient tombs and caves. In fact, it is home to the famous beehive tombs in Ibri (also called the Bat tombs), which have been listed as a Unesco World Heritage site. While there is some debate as to whether these were actually used as tombs or whether they

were rudimentary homes for small families, it is widely accepted that the tombs date back to early civilisations that lived in the region over 5,000 years ago. Ibri was historically a critical stopping point on the overland trading route.

Buraimi

The Buraimi governance is the part of the Buraimi Oasis that falls on the Oman side of the border; the part of the oasis that falls on the UAE side is called Al Ain. Although it spans what is in effect an international border, there are no checkpoints within the town itself and the official Oman-UAE border is located about 50km east of Buraimi. Non-GCC residents travelling from Oman will need a road permit. Like Ibri, Buraimi can trace its history back to its strategic position at the intersection of various caravan routes to and from Oman. There is an extensive falaj system that keeps the region fertile. Buraimi is an oasis and therefore is pleasantly green with plenty of date palm plantations. It also benefits from a cooler, less humid climate than coastal regions, making it a popular destination during the summer months.

It is home to a famous mud fort, Hisn Al Khandaq, which has been extensively restored and is open to visitors. There is also a must-see camel souk where the merchants will happily explain the differences between one camel and another, and may even make a serious attempt at convincing you to buy one. Watching the camels being loaded onto their new owners' pick-up trucks is a show in itself. You might find there is more to do in neighbouring Al Ain, although hotels are generally cheaper in Buraimi itself. A word of warning: UAE taxi drivers will cruise for passengers in Buraimi although they may refuse to use the meter, so it is up to you to negotiate a price before you get in the cab.

Ibri

Ibri lies 300km to the west of Muscat, between the foothills of the Hajar Mountains and the vast Rub Al Khali desert. With its central location, it was a historically important stopover for merchants travelling between the different regions of the Arabian Peninsula and trading remains active today. The bustling souk sells a range of merchandise including locally produced woven palm goods. The most fascinating sight though is the auction which takes place every morning, where residents, farmers and traders from the town and surrounding villages come together to haggle over dates, fruit and vegetables, livestock, camels and honey. The souk is situated near Ibri's impressive fort, which is notable for the large mosque set within its walls.

BATINAH

With a coastline stretching north-west from Muscat to the UAE border, Batinah has a collection of beautiful coastal towns and villages that are worth visiting. The most populated area after Muscat, Batinah has 12 wilayats: Awabi, Barka, Khabura, Liwa, Musanaa, Nakhal, Rustaq, Saham, Shinas, Sohar, Swaiq and Wadi Mawail. Inland, towards the Western Hajars, there are dramatic peaks and wadis, and numerous areas of historical interest.

Barka

Barka is a small coastal town west of Muscat. It makes for an interesting daytrip or as a stop off on a visit to Sohar, further along the coast. Famous for its fortnightly bullfights and large central fort, Barka is located only a few hundred metres from the shore of the Gulf of Oman. The place is still home to craftsmen practising traditional trades including weaving. The historical fort, Bait Naa'man, and the Ostrich Breeding Farm are both attractions worth your time.

Nakhal

Only 30 kilometres inland from Barka and 100 kilometres from Muscat, with its restored fort set on a hill, Nakhal is definitely worth a quick trip. If you have the energy, climb to the top of the watchtowers to be rewarded with magnificent views of the surrounding countryside and town. Inside the fort, visitors can see the prison, kitchen, living quarters of the Wali (leader) and the male and female majlis. The area is also well known for the Al Thowarah hot springs. The natural spring water is channelled into the falaj system to irrigate the surrounding date plantations, and you can dip your toe or have a paddle in the run-off water.

Rustaq

In the middle ages, Rustaq (or Rostaq) was the capital of Oman. However, today it is best known for its large and dramatic fort, which has been extended over the years.

Rustaq is located in the Western Hajar Mountains about 170km south-west of Muscat. The fort has been restored and the main watchtower is believed to be of Sassanid origin. It was well placed to withstand long sieges since it has its own water supplies. Apparently, at one time there was a tunnel connecting this fort to the nearby fort in Al Hazm.

There is a small souk near the fort, selling a variety of items. Not far from there you'll find the hot springs that Rustaq is most famous for. The water in these springs is believed to have healing powers – it has a high sulphur content, which is supposed to provide relief for sufferers of arthritis and rheumatism.

About 20km north of Rustaq is the village of Al Hazm, which has an interesting fort. It was built in around 1700AD and the original falaj system is still in working order today. There is also an excellent view of the countryside from the watchtower.

DAKHILIYA

Despite being isolated from the sea, Dhakhiliya was historically important as many trade routes between the coast and the interior passed through the region. While you are in this part of the Sultanate, be sure to take your time and check out the various forts and ruins, namely the Bahla fort on Balhool Mountain and Jabrin fort, where it is believed the Imam Bilarab (who built the place in the 1600s) is buried. Al Hoota Cave is nearby and seeing as you're here you may as well nip to the Batand Al Ayn tombs that date back to the third millennium BC.

Bahla

The ancient walled city of Bahla is only two hours' drive away from Muscat, and just 40km from Nizwa. It has a small population of around 60,000, and contains 46 separate villages. While it is not yet on the mainstream tourist map (although efforts are being made to attract more tourists to the area), archaeology buffs and history enthusiasts will find that it is well worth a visit. It is believed to be one of the oldest inhabited regions in Oman, and archaeologists have found artefacts here dating back to the third century BC. It was historically a strategic stopover on the old trading route from Muscat to other parts of the Arabian Peninsula. Apart from the historical buildings and the traditional way of life, Bahla also has a rich and diverse ecology – a balanced mixture of fertile land, mountains, wadis and desert. The productive soil, fed by a continuous supply of water from Jabal Akhdar, has in the past yielded crops of wheat, barley, cotton and sugar cane, and today it is still home to many viable date plantations.

The town is characterised by its many winding roads, some so narrow that you have to pull over to let an oncoming car pass. Whether you explore the town of Bahla on foot or by car, you will find an eclectic balance of the new, functioning town, the ancient, fascinating ruins, and the many date plantations that are perfect picnic spots. Bahla is enclosed by a protective, fortified wall that stretches for 12km around the town. Although large sections of the wall are still standing, parts of it are in ruins and earmarked for eventual reconstruction.

Forts & Ruins

The Bahla Fort, situated on Balhool Mountain, is one of the main attractions in Bahla. It is included on Unesco's list of World Heritage sites, and has undergone careful and extensive renovation under Unesco's sponsorship and supervision. The ruins of the fort tower 50m above the village, and although its famous windtowers have been almost totally destroyed over time, they were once thought to be the tallest structures in Oman. At the time of this guide going to print, Bahla Fort was still under renovation and not open to the public, but there were plans to reopen at some point during 2012. Contact the Ministry of Tourism hotline (800 777 99) to check if it is open before you travel. In the area around the fort you can wander through deserted mud-brick villages, the largest of which is Al Aqar. You can explore the ancient houses at your leisure, and in some houses you can even go up to higher storeys and look through the old window frames for a unique perspective. It is a fascinating glimpse into the past, showing you what life was like in Oman's olden times. The ruins of the mosque are particularly interesting.

Located about 12 kilometres south of Bahla is the fascinating three-storey Jabrin Fort, which has been extensively restored and redecorated. The Imam Bilarab

originally built it in the 1600s as a grand country residence. His tomb is still located within the fort, to the left of the main entrance. It is believed that Jabrin Fort was home to one of the first schools in Oman, way back in the 17th century. Interesting for its wall and ceiling decorations and the water channels running through the kitchens, kids especially will love finding secret passageways and staircases, and climbing up the towers, which offer views out over the surrounding barren countryside. For more information on this and other forts in Oman, visit the website of the Ministry of Heritage and Culture (mhc.gov.om).

The Souk

There is no better place to rub shoulders with the friendly people of Bahla than at the traditional market or 'souk'. Locals gather here to trade in livestock and socialise under the shade of a huge central tree. Goats are tethered to this tree before being bought or sold. In the alleyways leading away from this central livestock trading area, you'll find many small shops that sell traditional crafts, Omani antiques (a particularly good spot to hunt for a genuine antique khanjar), rugs, spices and nuts. You can watch the local silversmith at work, repairing khanjars and jewellery in the same way it has been done for generations. The souk also has sections for fruit and vegetables, all of which are locally produced, and the locally grown dates are delicious.

You can't visit the area without buying some distinctive Bahla pottery to take home with you. Bahla is a good source of high quality clay, and there are many skilled potters in the area (all male – it is only in the southern regions of Oman that you will find female potters). You can see them working at the traditional pottery site, which is located just past the souk. There is also a pottery factory, built by the government in the late 1980s, and the Alladawi clay pots workshop that boasts four industrial kilns, each of which is able to produce around a hundred pots each month. While you will probably buy a piece of pottery for ornamental purposes (plant pots, vases, incense burners or candle holders), clay pots are still used for practical purposes in Bahla, such as carrying and cooling water, and storing food and dates.

Fanja

The picturesque village of Fanja is situated next to an extensive palm grove that runs alongside Wadi Fanja. It is around 70km from Muscat, and the approach is one of the most scenic views that Oman has to offer. The village has a dramatic tower perched on top of a hill offering spectacular views of the surrounding scenery and the wadi below. Fanja is renowned for its pottery and visitors can wander round the market bargaining for locally produced pots, local fruits and vegetables, honey and woven goods made from palm leaves.

Nizwa

About 140km from Muscat, Nizwa is a popular destination for tourists and residents of Oman alike. In the sixth and seventh centuries, Nizwa was the capital of Oman and the centre for trade between the coastal and interior regions. It is still the largest and most important town in this area of the interior. Historically, the town enjoyed a reputation as a haven for poets, writers, intellectuals and religious leaders, and for centuries it was considered the cultural and political capital of the country. Positioned as it is alongside two wadis, Nizwa is a fertile sea of green with an oasis of date plantations stretching eight kilometres from the town.

Its two notable attractions include Nizwa's 17th century fort and the magnificent Jabrin Fort (see p.197), renowned for its wall and ceiling decorations and its secret passageways and staircases, but many ancient ruins and mud brick villages can be seen among the date palm plantations and the wadis.

The 17th century Nizwa Fort (omantourism.gov.om) is surprisingly large, and although not quite as visually impressive as some others, it is one of the most interesting forts to visit. You can wander through the maze of passageways and up to the battlements, where the views out over Nizwa in all directions show the sheer size of the oasis, with palm trees extending as far as the eye can see. High-tech displays and areas with extensive exhibits are recent additions, transforming it into a top-class attraction where you could easily spend a few hours.

Nizwa Souk

In the centre of Nizwa, close to the fort and mosque, the souk lies hidden behind imposing sand-coloured walls. Enter

Nizwa Souk

through one of the enormous carved wooden doors and you'll find a small village of traditionally designed buildings, each labelled to indicate the products they sell – Silver Souk, Fish Souk, Meat Souk. etc. Although these buildings are all clean, well lit and renovated, the place remains full of atmosphere and traders conduct business as they have done for centuries. The souks are well laid out and vibrant with local colour, especially in the early morning. The shop owners are an unobtrusive bunch and are happy to sit and drink coffee while you browse.

In the silver and craft souk, you'll find a mixture of old and new items made locally, such as Bahla pottery, old wooden chests, silverwork from the different regions of Oman, antique rifles and frankincense, as well as modern imports from India. You can watch silversmiths hammering intricate patterns into the hilts of khanjars and join the many antique silver dealers who come here from Muscat in search of treasure for their stores. Although prices

THE KHAREEF
The coastal region is subject to weather conditions quite different from the rest of the country, and as such the scenery is completely different to that in many areas further north. From June to September the monsoon rains (or khareef), transforms the countryside around the southern Dhofar area into a beautiful green expanse, featuring lush fields, swollen rivers and stunning waterfalls. The foothills of the mountains, a few kilometres inland, are often covered with a thick blanket of fog during this time. The rain and fog cause a significant temperature drop, making Salalah a popular destination for residents of other Gulf countries trying to escape the summer heat.

are rising as tourism increases, with hard bargaining you can sometimes get a better price than in Muscat.

The Goat Souk is the scene of a lively animal market early on Friday mornings from 07:00 where cows, goats and sheep are auctioned. It's an open-air market located close to the entrance on the left, and worth visiting, especially just before the religious holidays when farmers sell their livestock for the festivities.

Sumail

The town of Sumail (or Samail) sits in the Sumail Gap, a natural valley that divides the Hajar Mountain chain into the Eastern and Western Hajars. As the most direct path between the coastal regions and the interior of the country, this route has always been an important artery. Irrigated by countless wadis and man-made falaj systems, the area is green and fertile, and the dates produced here are highly rated.

Dakhiliya Activities

Camping

The Western Hajars offer many places to set up camp in wadis or along hiking routes. Don't miss out on the magnificent views and photo opportunities to be had on Jebel Shams or the Sayq Plateau. You'll find that the higher areas are a lot cooler – temperatures average around 10 to 15 degrees cooler than down below, so it can therefore be more appealing than camping at lower altitudes. It is even possible to camp high up in the middle of summer.

On the Sayq Plateau, a popular place to camp is Diana's Viewpoint (named after Princess Diana, who visited in 1990). It is on the edge of a promontory with spectacular views, and there is plenty of space. As

with camping anywhere in the wilderness, minimise your impact and leave no trace of your stay behind.

On Jebel Shams there is a good campsite at the start of the W4 hike, at around 1,950 metres. Also in the area, the off-road route to Qiyut off the Nizwa-Bahla road gets you quickly up high to masses of camping spots and great views.

On the northern side of the mountains you can camp in Wadi Al Abyad next to the pools, perfect for a dip to cool off in warmer weather, or try one of the campsites set spectacularly beneath the awesome north face of Jebel Shams in the 'treasure chest' of Oman, Wadi As Sahtan, which has almost endless possibilities for exploring.

Hiking

Oman has plenty to offer hikers, and the best area of all is the Western Hajar Mountains. There are many excellent routes to be enjoyed, ranging from short easy walks to spectacular viewpoints, to longer and more arduous treks up high peaks. Jebel Shams has numerous impressive hikes. One of the shorter ones is the four-hour Balcony Walk along Jebel Shams Plateau, which has incredible canyon views. Be sure that on any hike, short or long, you consider the weather conditions. Always carry plenty of water and food, check your routes before setting out, notify someone as to your itinerary, and wear appropriate clothing. Be warned: no mountain rescue services exist, so anyone venturing out into mountains should be experienced, or be with someone who is.

Recently, the Ministry of Tourism has sponsored the installation of via ferrata routes in the Hajars, including on Jebal Shams. These are mountainous routes with fixed wire cables, metal rungs and ladders which allow adventurous walkers and climbers to ascend steep rocks and mountains in relative safety. Check out the ministry of tourism website (omantourism. gov.om) for a full list of routes.

Wadi Al Abyad
Just over an hour west of Muscat, the pools of Wadi Al Abyad are great to visit throughout the year. From the end of the track, a short stroll will get you to increasingly larger pools where you can easily spend the whole day. Alternatively, you can take the easy two-hour hike through the wadi to the town of Al Abyad.

Jebel Shams, Jebel Akhdar and Wadi An Nakhur are definite must-sees. Jebel Shams, the 'Mountain of the Sun', has rugged terrain and is actually a fairly easy trek with several good camping locations. Below the summit, Wadi An Nakhur has some of the most stupendous views in the country, offering ample photo opportunities as you drive through the 'Grand Canyon of Oman'. The Sayq Plateau on top of Jebel Akhdar has spectacular scenery and beautiful little mountain villages.

Snake Canyon
Adventurers wishing to complete this spectacular, challenging hike should know that it involves some daring jumps into rock pools and a fair bit of swimming through ravines, although the addition of via ferrata routes makes some sections easier and faster, with several parts made even more thrilling – there's an exciting series of traverses and zip line crossings some 100m above the canyon floor. It takes around three to four hours, and is something you'll remember forever. Keep a close eye on the weather, as rains from miles away could cause flash floods in a matter of minutes.

Misfat Al Abryyin
This ancient village, with terraced palm plantations built unusually on a steeply sloping hillside, is just a short distance from Al Hamra. Rich red soil, ancient houses and the ruins of a watchtower perched on the mountain add to the character of Misfat Al Abryyin. The falaj network is one of the most intricate in Oman and snakes its way around banana, lemon and date trees.

DHOFAR
Dhofar is the southernmost region of Oman, bordering Saudi Arabia and the Republic of Yemen. Dhofar frankincense is regarded as the finest in the world and once made this area immensely wealthy and important. Visitors still flock to the coast to enjoy the lush greenery and cool weather.

Salalah
Salalah is the capital of Dhofar, the southernmost region of Oman, and is over 1,000 kilometres from Muscat. It is possible to get there by road, but the drive is long and boring, with little of interest to see or do along the way. You may therefore prefer to fly, and Oman Air operates up to five flights a day from Muscat.

The landscape features plenty of trees, mainly at the border of the desert at the lower reaches of the jebels. You'll also find an impressive grouping of trees in Wadi Qahshan that runs through the mountainous backdrop of the Mughsayl-Sarfait road which links Salalah with the Yemen border. This is where frankincense trees grow and are farmed by local villagers. They cut into the trunks and allow the sap to seep out and harden into lumps that are then scraped off and traded in bulk.

Salalah has a museum, and the souks are worthy of a visit. Al Husn Souk is the place to head if you're after silver jewellery or traditional souvenirs. It's also an excellent place to pick up some fine Dhofar frankincense. At Al Hafah Souk, south of Salalah, you'll find plenty of perfume and locally prepared food. Al Sinaw Souk is where Bedouin tribes used to conduct their business, and is famous for authentic Bedouin jewellery.

If you are camping and need to get supplies, you'll find a branch of Lulu's Hypermarket in Salalah, which offers a wide range of goods.

The restaurants and bars within Salalah's hotels are your best bet for a night out. Both the Hilton and the Crowne Plaza have various outlets, which are popular with locals and tourists.

Souk Al Hafah
Al Hafah, Salalah
Map **1 F3**
Set in the coconut groves of the Al Hafah area, three kilometres from Salalah, this is the best place in Oman to buy frankincense and incense powders. There are dozens of buckets sitting around with

DHOFAR MUST-DOS

Frankincense Trail

Wadi Dawkah, with its resident frankincense trees, is a Unesco World Heritage Site. After a short drive along a graded road, you will reach an outcrop overlooking several trees. The main areas of trees have been fenced off for protection, but if you want to get closer there are a few trees just near the parking area.

Mountain Drive

Head off road and you'll be rewarded with spectacular views over Salalah and out to sea. A short drive takes you past attractions such as a small lake in a stunning wadi, a large sinkhole and even some massive baobab trees. In good weather, the viewpoints and campsites are unparalleled.

Salalah Museum

Get a feel for what life was really like for the small, yet growing, population of Salalah from as early as the 11th century. See ancient writings and manuscripts, traditional equipment, old pottery and the earliest forms of currency. Contact the museum on 23 294 549 for current opening hours.

Blowholes

If you visit during khareef, drive along the coastline at Al Mughsayl to find one of the most spectacular natural sights in Oman – the Al Mughsayl blowholes. Thundering waves have eroded caverns underfoot and the only way out is up through small openings below the metal grates. Stand well back; the force generated is quite astonishing.

Nabi Ayoub's Tomb

Nabi Ayoub (also known as the prophet Job) was a respected religious figure who is said to have used this area to conduct his daily prayers. He dedicated his life to God and was put to rest in the same spot – facing Jerusalem – where he chose to worship. Located 40km from Salalah, this shrine is a popular tourist attraction.

Camping

Just 20km past the turnoff to the Tawi Atayr sinkhole, you'll find several sidetracks to the edge of the escarpment overlooking the east coast and the sleepy town of Mirbat. In winter the views are consistently spectacular and it is a highly recommended camping spot. In Khor Ruwi, you'll find some great campsites near the mouth of the lagoon, on the low, flat rocks just up from the beach. Just over 15km from the main road running along Jabal al Qamar, there's a stunning bird's-eye view of the secluded beaches on Oman's south coast. There are several spots perfect for camping just before and just after this viewpoint; however, please remember not to disturb the locals, and if you camp here during the khareef be prepared for mud.

different qualities and compositions of perfumes and you can either ask a local to explain the differences to you, or just buy the one you like best. The scents are generally quite potent and a little goes a long way. Frankincense is poured into a bag and weighed, while incense comes in little silver or copper pots. Remember to buy some charcoal for burning the incense and some brightly painted clay Dhofari burners to put them in. You can also buy textiles, gold and silver, Indian and Arabic dresses and some traditional souvenirs. Local coffee shops serve snacks such as hummus and mishkak (Omani style barbecued meat).

Out Of The City

Salalah is relatively small and, depending on the length of time you are there, you may wish to explore further afield. Wadi Darbat is within easy driving distance from Salalah, and features some great attractions. The Travertine Curtain, which looks like a huge pitted wall and is over 150m high, turns into a spectacular waterfall during the khareef as the entire contents of Wadi Darbat flow over this escarpment – it's Arabia's answer to Niagara Falls. There are several paths taking you towards the base of the cliff, with the going getting easier as you move past the trees towards the open grassland. Enjoy the spectacular views, and don't forget the camera. On a safety note, there are no guard rails, and the edge drops off steeply, so keep children well back.

Wadi Darbat itself is misty, moody and muddy during the khareef, but in winter it is a verdant oasis. As you approach the wadi, just two kilometres from the Darbat turnoff, look out for the natural arch up to your right – this interesting feature can be reached with a short hike, and offers superb views over the surrounding valley, as well as a collection of small caves with stalactites and stalagmites. As inviting as it may seem, the water in Wadi Darbat is not for swimming in, due to the risk of picking up a bilharzia infection.

Khor Ruwi, which is near the coastline in the Wadi Darbat area, used to be a bustling seaport, although it's hard to believe now. It is also home to an important archaeological site that was once the palace of the famed Queen of Sheba, and is where the waters of Wadi Darbat flow before finally reaching the ocean. The area is great for birdwatching, and flamingos are common from autumn to spring. From Khawr Ruwi you can hike up to the headlands above the eastern entrance to the lagoon – a large, flat plateau eventually leads to an abrupt edge with a 30m drop to the ocean.

Ubar

At the crossroads of ancient trade routes, the Lost City of Ubar (referred to as Iram in the Quran) thrived as merchants came from far and wide to buy much sought-after incense. Traders converged to sell pottery, spices and fabric from India and China in return for the unique silver frankincense of Oman. The commerce made Ubar a city of unrivalled wealth and splendour and those who visited it referred to it as 'paradise'. According to the Quran, the wickedness of the inhabitants led Allah to destroy the city and all roads leading to it, causing it to sink into the sand. For a thousand years the city's location remained unknown, until British explorer Sir Ranulph Fiennes, in a 20-year search using modern satellite technology, discovered the city beneath the shifting sands of the Omani desert near Shisr, north of Salalah. Excavations have revealed the thick outer walls of a vast octagonal fortress with eight towers or pillars at its corners, and numerous pots and artefacts dating back thousands of years. Debate continues as to whether this is indeed Ubar, but the site is fascinating nonetheless and it was clearly an important desert settlement at one point. Tours of the city will take you through the Qara Mountains where you can enjoy the stunning landscape (see p.186).

AL WUSTA

In contrast to Oman's other regions, Al Wusta has few sites of historical interest, and is often only seen from a car window as people make the long drive between Muscat and Salalah. However, the region does boast areas of natural beauty, a mild summer climate and an abundance of wildlife. Al Wusta also has around 170km of coastline, which includes some rocky beaches but also some amazing long stretches of white sandy beaches.

The Jiddat Al Harasis region in Al Wusta is where Arabian oryx were last recorded in the wild, and a sanctuary for these magnificent desert creatures has been established there. The sanctuary has been supported by the World Wildlife Fund, and it has been remarkably successful – thanks to some careful breeding programmes, the first herd of Arabian oryx was released back into the wild in 1992.

SHARQIYA

Sharqiya is a region of contrasts. The coastline features numerous fishing villages and ports, and the area's beaches are home to some of the most important turtle breeding grounds in the world. Inland, you'll find a combination of breathtaking wadis and dramatic expanses of sand dunes.

Masirah Island

Masirah Island lies 20km off the south-east coast of Oman and is the Sultanate's largest island. It is about 80km long and 18km wide, with hills in the centre and a circumference of picturesque isolated beaches. The island is off the coast of the Barr Al Hikman area, and can be accessed by taking a ferry from Shana'a – but only during high tide. The ferry leaves regularly but there are no set times and it seems to set off when full or when the ferry from the other side arrives. You can cross with your car, and the crossing takes around 90 minutes. There is a military base on the island, and the main town of Hilf, with its 8,000 residents, has some shops, and a couple of restaurants, but otherwise the island is relatively undeveloped.

There are, however, now four hotels on the island: the two star Masirah Hotel (RO 21 for a double room, 25 504 4 01); the two-star Serabis Hotel (RO 25 for a double room, 25 504 6 99), the two-star Danat Al-Khaleej Hotel (RO 25 for a double room, 25 504 533) and the four-star Masirah Iisland Resort (RO 75 for a double room, 25 504 274).

The highest point of the island is Jebel Hamra at 275m, and a network of graded roads connects parts of the island. Masirah's beaches are internationally recognised for their importance as turtle breeding grounds. Four species of turtle come ashore to lay their eggs here – green turtles, hawksbill, olive ridley and loggerheads. Masirah is thought to be home to the world's largest nesting population of loggerhead turtles, estimated at 30,000 females.

Over the past few years, Masirah has also become a hotspot for watersports enthusiasts: the beaches of the east coast offer some of the best surfing in the region, with waves of seven or eight feet on a good day. The summer months – far cooler here than in most the rest of the Gulf – are also a good time for windsurfing, but the strong winds that lash the island during this time can be unpleasant and make camping on the beach quite uncomfortable.

Usually, however, the beaches are ideal for camping, and you'll find yourself sharing your habitat with the donkeys, camels, goats and gazelles that roam the island. Conchologists will be in their element here as the beaches are home to a vast range of shells, some of which are quite rare.

Ras Al Jinz

If you've come here to see turtles, then you're in the right place. Some people think that winter is the best time to see the turtles, but you'll only see a few dozen per night. Summer is the peak season, with several hundred turtles nesting every night. Summer is also a good time to visit Ras al Jinz, because the ever-present winds and eastern exposure towards the Arabian Sea help keep the area a good 10-15°C cooler than Muscat. Take note that this area is windy all year round, so pitching tents can be difficult, and you will constantly be seeking shelter from the wind.

Along with an interactive visitor centre and research station, new accommodation huts have been opened for those seeking a little style (96 550 606, rasaljinz-turtlereserve.com). For others, there are simple shelters and facilities to make use of (for a fee of RO 4) when camping in the area. A less windy (and more expensive) option is to stay at Al Naseem Tourist Camp (99 328 858, desertdiscovery.com), located shortly after you take the left turn towards Ras al Jinz.

When you arrive at the turtle beach, check in and pay the small entrance fee. You might see some young turtle hatchlings on display. Information about the nature talks and turtle viewing sessions (which happen every night) can be obtained here. Thanks to the new visitor centre and facilities, the nightly tours, which were once a little unorganised, are more structured, and the rush of tourists is better contained. On long weekends, Ras Al Jinz often sees more than a hundred visitors, all wanting to watch the turtles nesting at night.

Obey the directions given by the rangers (of which there are rarely more than two or three) and resist the urge to crowd forward when viewing the turtles. It should go without saying that you should not disturb nesting turtles, but observing people at Ras al Jinz shows that a constant reminder is still necessary.

Sur

Sur is an old fishing and trading port 300km south-east of Muscat. For centuries, the town was famed for its boatbuilding and became quite prosperous as a result. Its fortunes did decline somewhat with the advent of more modern vessels and construction techniques, but Sur is enjoying something of a revival; with its pretty cornice and forts, the town is definitely worth a visit, as is the Sineslah Fort which overlooks Sur, offering breathtaking views of the area and its coastline. Sur is home to an interesting Marine Museum which is located on the premises of the Al-Aruba sports club near the main entrance to Sineslah Fort. It was established in 1987 to showcase Sur's matitime heritage and, inside, you can view equipment and tools of maritime navigation as well as photographs of Sur taken over a century ago.

The Arabic word Sur means a walled fortified area and there is evidence of the ancient defences throughout the town. As the first port of call in Arabia for traders from the Far East, it is believed that trading with the African coast dates back to as early as the 6th century AD.

From Muscat there are two roads to Sur. The Sur highway (Route 23) is the best option if you're looking for a smoother ride. The 300km single tarmac road, leading through the mountains and crossing some wadis, will take you to Sur in between three and four hours. Alternatively, you can take the coastal road (direction Quriyat-Sur). In terms of distance this route is much shorter (only about 150km), but it takes at least four hours to navigate. In Quriyat turn right to Sur at the roundabout, then follow the asphalt road and keep following the signposts to Sur (not Tiwi). Before long the tarmac changes to gravel.

There are a few highlights along this route: Bimmah Sinkhole is located six kilometres after Dibab Village, just 500 metres off the road on your right. Tiwi Beach (also known as White Sand Beach) makes a perfect stop for some snorkelling or relaxing (just don't go on public holidays, especially if you don't like crowds). Wadi Shab, one of the most stunning wadis in Oman, is just past Tiwi Village. The end of the coastal road is marked by an oasis and the ancient city of Qalhat, which is famous for its dry stone walls, the remains of ancient water cisterns and the scattered headstones of a cemetery. There is also a shrine to a saintly woman known as Bibi Miriam, although it is in poor repair. From here you progress into the mountains, where you will encounter some steep slopes and hair-raising descents.

You will eventually reach the enormous LNG (liquefied natural gas) plant. Head south for around 15km to get into Sur. If you came along the Muscat-Sur highway, you will first pass Sur Bilad, a suburb of Sur. This is where you can visit the very impressive Bilad Fort.

Tiwi

Tiwi is a small fishing village up the coast from Sur, situated in a little cove between two of the most stunning wadis in the area – Wadi Tiwi and Wadi Shab. These verdant green oases are a must-see for anyone visiting the area, for their crystal clear pools and lush vegetation including palm and banana plantations. The residents of Tiwi are spread across nine small villages and there are endless opportunities for walking and exploring. In Wadi Shab you can start your tour with a trip across the water, courtesy of a small boat operated by locals. Further along the wadi you can swim through pools and access a cave with a waterfall inside. Tiwi Beach, also known as the White Sands Beach, is a nice, tranquil spot to stop off at.

PERFECT POINT OF VIEW

In its 2011 book, *Secret Journeys of a Lifetime,* National Geographic named the view from Sur across the creek to Aija as being among the world's top ten ocean views. Certainly, witnessing the drama of rough ocean waters meeting rough, craggy mountains is something not to be missed. Just make sure you pack your camera.

TURTLE POWER

Turtles are one of the ancient wonders of the seas and, evolutionarily speaking, have remained unchanged for approximately 90 million years. Of the seven recognised species of marine turtle, five are found in the seas of the Sultanate of Oman and are known to nest on its beaches. These are the green, hawksbill, olive ridley, leatherback, and loggerhead. Most prevalent are the green turtle, with an estimated 20,000 females laying eggs from June to November on more than 275 beaches along Oman's coastline.

Once every two to four years, females typically lay two or three clutches (at two-week intervals), each of 100–120 eggs. The survival rate for turtles is abysmal: only two or three turtles per 10,000 reach adulthood. Like salmon, turtles return to lay eggs at the exact location of their birth. Although the eggs may hatch at different times, all baby turtles (five centimetres long on average) emerge from the sand at the same time and are guided by moonlight to the sea. Interestingly, the temperature of the sand determines the sex of turtles during their eight-week incubation. Temperatures in the range of 26–28°c are favourable for males while 30–34°c is ideal for females. Global warming provides further evidence that females are going to take over the world!

Adult turtles feed mainly on sea grass and sea weed and reach sexual maturity at around 20 years of age. Females travel as far as Somalia and India in search of food – a distance upwards of 3,000km. This is especially surprising given that a fully-grown turtle weighs 140–160kg and the shell is often greater than one metre in length.

If you visit any turtle beaches, keep your distance and do not disturb the nesting females. It's best to avoid using any lights (including flash photography) — they disorient hatchlings and scare away adults. The best time for photography is at daybreak as the last of the females return to the sea.

THE GREAT OUTDOORS

With a burgeoning reputation as an adventuring hotspot, the call of nature in Oman is loud and intrepid.

Desert

In the desert, there are various places to stay, all offering much the same experience. If you have a 4WD, then you'll be able to make your own way; if not, then the main desert camps all have a pick-up point from where you'll be collected and transported to the camp.

Most offer some kind of dune bashing experience, either in your own car or in one of their cars with a driver provided, while some have extras such as swimming pools and quad bikes. The latter are perhaps the best option for families with children. All of the camps are booked on a dinner, bed and breakfast basis and some will even see Bedouin women come into the camp in the morning to sell their wares or offer camel rides.

The Al Areesh Camp (p.78) is fairly close to the main road and most cars can make it to the gate. The camp can accommodate up to 150 guests in small huts and tents, some with 'en-suite' bathrooms, while others digs have ablution facilities. The Al Raha Camp (p.78) is further into the desert and definitely requires transport (which comes at an extra cost) to get to the camp. Facilities here take a barasti beach hut or tent style, and the large camp can accommodate up to 200 guests.

The 1000 Nights Camp (p.76) is deep into the Wahiba Sands and the campsite feels more genuine, although with a swimming pool, terrace and dining area, this is far from 'roughing it'. Accommodation is in Bedouin tents, Arabic tents and Sheikh tents, with roofless toilets and showers.

The Desert Nights Camp (p.78) is at the most luxurious end of the scale. The camp offers 24 double tented 'suites', two deluxe family tents and four 'attached units', accommodating a maximum of 64 people. There's an onsite restaurant and bar, as well as all manner of sports and excursions.

Mountains

If the mountain experience is for you, then there are two main mountains people tend to visit, namely Jebel Shams and Jebel Akhdar. Jebel Shams is the highest and the great thing about this mountain is the abundance of hiking trails. Jebel Akhdar is the green mountain and has an amazing scenic drive to get to the top, but there is a police road block at the bottom and only 4WDs are allowed to go up the mountain as there have been many accidents (and deaths) due to brakes failing on the way down the mountain.

To get to the top of Jebel Akhdar, it is black top road all the way, with many twists and turns and a fairly steep gradient. To reach the top of Jebel Shams, the road is a little more difficult as it is black top only a part of the way and then changes to a dirt road. Jabal Shams Resort (99 382 639) offers various different chalets to choose from, as well as providing the full Bedouin tent experience. There is a restaurant onsite, although this is somewhere you visit for the amazing views and experiences, rather than creature comforts. Jabel Shams Base Camp (p.78), offering 15 bungalows and 15 Bedouin tents, is a stop for dedicated hikers as the rooms and services are basic but clean.

Al Jebel Al Akhdar Hotel (25 429 009) is a simple but clean and not unpleasant hotel that has good but basic facilities including a restaurant and room service. Sahab Hotel (25 429 288, sahab-hotel. com) is a new and luxurious boutique-style hotel and resort with double rooms that have great views out over the mountains, private gardens and an infinity pool.

Turtles

If you are looking for a unique and natural experience, then a night with the turtles is a must. When it comes to nature conservation, Oman still has much to learn and the turtle watching experience can be a bit overcrowded at certain times of the year, but that is just testament to it being an amazing draw.

The leatherback turtles come up onto the beach to nest and lay their eggs, the greatest numbers doing so between June and October, but they can be seen all year round. It is a real treat to see the egg laying process in the late evening (about 23:00) but then, in the early hours of the morning (04:00-05:00), you might be lucky enough to see the babies making their way back down to the ocean. The two main areas to see the turtles at are Ras Al Jinz and Ras Al Hadd. Places to stay in both Ras Al Hadd and Ras al Jinz are limited.

Turtle Beach Resort (p.186) has been around for about 10 years. It is a traditional and basic venue, but offers 22 barasti style huts. Ras Al Hadd Hotel is a nuts and bolts hotel offering clean rooms and a modest breakfast. It is located 15km from the Ras Al Jinz beach where the turtles can be seen. Al Naseem Camp is a basic hutted camp with an ablution facility providing toilets, cold water showers and basins. The accommodation is on a dinner, bed and breakfast basis.

Along with an interactive visitors' centre, a research station, a small restaurant and a 40 seater restaurant, the Ras Al Jinz Turtle Reserve (rasaljinz-turtlereserve. com) recently opened some new, clean and relatively luxurious accommodation with prices including bed, breakfast and a guided turtle viewing. The air-conditioned rooms have TVs and Wi-Fi throughout, and make for an attractive alternative to camping on the beach if you're in search of a bit more comfort.

THE UNITED ARAB EMIRATES

Visiting Oman's northern neighbour is relatively easy and certainly worthwhile, offering an altogether different Gulf experience.

ABU DHABI

Dubai may be the UAE's brashest member, but Abu Dhabi remains both the nation's capital and the richest of all the emirates, with a blossoming, burgeoning city to prove it. Recently, there has been a greater commitment to tourism, and projects such as Yas Island with its Grand Prix racetrack (p.28) and Ferrari World themepark (p.295), and the development of the Desert Islands, are proof of that. While there isn't much you can get in Abu Dhabi that you can't find in Dubai, its slightly slower pace makes for a refreshing change. The city lies on an island and is connected to the mainland by bridges. It is home to numerous internationally renowned hotels, a few shiny shopping malls, and culture in the form of heritage sites and souks. Abu Dhabi is marketed as the cultural capital of the UAE and is home to an annual jazz festival, a film festival, and a music and arts festival; it also hosts numerous exhibitions throughout the year. Once complete, Saadiyat Island will become the focus for much of the cultural activity. Find out more from the Authority for Culture & Heritage (adach.ae).

In the cooler months, the extended corniche is a lovely spot for a stroll, and on weekend evenings the area comes alive with families meeting up to enjoy a barbecue and shisha.

The many islands to the west of the city are popular with boating and watersports enthusiasts, and driving west past the city reveals kilometre upon kilometre of gorgeous, untouched sea and a few open beaches. The coast between Dubai and Abu Dhabi is also home to a few beaches that are popular with watersports enthusiasts, jetskiers in particular, and provide a good, quick getaway from Dubai.

The emirate is also home to a large part of the Empty Quarter (Rub Al Khali), the largest sand desert in the world. The large Liwa Oasis crescent acts as a gateway to the endless dunes and is a popular weekend destination for adventure-hungry residents from Dubai.

For further information, check out the Abu Mini Visitors' Guide, Al Gharbia Visitors' Guide or the Abu Dhabi Explorer – see askexplorer.com.

ABU DHABI ATTRACTIONS

Al Bateen
Abu Dhabi
This is one of Abu Dhabi's oldest districts and home to a dhow building yard, the Al Bateen Marina, a few historically accurate buildings and the future Al Bateen Wharf. It's a nice area to walk around, with plenty of open green spaces.

The Corniche
Off Corniche Rd, Central Abu Dhabi
Abu Dhabi
Corniche Road boasts six kilometres of parks that include children's play areas, separate cycle and pedestrian paths, cafes and restaurants, and a lifeguarded beach park. There is plenty of parking on the city side of Corniche Road, and underpasses at all the major intersections connect to the waterfront side. Bikes can also be rented from outside the Hiltonia Club for Dhs.20 per day.

Ferrari World Abu Dhabi
Yas Island Abu Dhabi **+971 2 496 8001**
ferrariworldabudhabi.com
Billed as the world's largest indoor theme park, Ferrari World is part F1 amusement

park and part museum dedicated to the Italian supercar marque. There's plenty to keep little ones entertained and high adrenaline rides (including the world's fastest rollercoaster) for teens and adults. The whole park sits under a giant, sweeping roof and the comfort of air conditioning makes it great for a family day out during those stifling summer months. General admission: Dhs.225 for adults and Dhs.165 for kids.

Heritage Village
Nr Marina Mall Abu Dhabi
+971 2 681 4455
torath.ae
Located near Marina Mall, this educational village offers a glimpse into the country's past. Traditional aspects of Bedouin life are explained and craftsmen demonstrate traditional skills.

Manarat Al Saadiyat
Saadiyat Cultural District Abu Dhabi
+971 2 406 1400
saadiyat.ae
This visitors' centre is a taster of the cultural offerings to come on Saadiyat. Along with a presentation on the island's future development, there are exhibition spaces that have welcomed some impressive displays.

Qasr Al Hosn
Al Nasr St Abu Dhabi **+971 2 621 5300**
adach.ae
Also known as the Old or White Fort, this is the oldest building in Abu Dhabi and dates back to 1793. Located in central Abu Dhabi, the fort has undergone a series of renovations over the years and, at the time of writing, it was closed for a major renovation that will see it become one of the UAE's foremost cultural visitor attractions.

Sheikh Zayed Grand Mosque
Shk Rashid Bin Saeed Al Maktoum St Abu Dhabi **+971 2 441 6444**
szgmc.ae
One of the largest mosques in the world, this architectural masterpiece can accommodate 40,000 worshippers. It features 82 domes and the world's largest hand-woven Persian carpet. It is open to non-Muslims every day except Friday, and complimentary tours run at 10:00 from Sunday to Thursday.

Sir Bani Yas Island
Abu Dhabi **+971 2 406 1400**
desertislands.com
One part nature reserve, the other part luxury resort and spa, Sir Bani Yas Island is the centrepiece of Abu Dhabi's Desert Islands development plan. Home to the Arabian Wildlife Park, and Desert Island Resort & Spa, the island has thousands of free-roaming animals. Hiking, mountain biking and 4WD safaris, as well as snorkelling and kayaking trips, are available and you can reach the island by a private seaplane.

The Souk At Central Market
Nr Hamdan St Abu Dhabi
+971 2 810 7810
centralmarket.ae
The capital's latest shopping offering, The Souk at Central Market is rapidly becoming one of Abu Dhabi's major hubs and attractions, offering a mix of high fashion, traditional goods and great eating and drinking options. The Marriott Renaissance and Marriott Courtyard onsite offer further F&B options.

The Souk At Qaryat Al Beri
Qaryat Al Beri Complex Abu Dhabi
+971 2 558 1670
soukqaryatalberi.com
A recreation of a traditional Arabian souk, with small canals which weave their way between boutiques, cafes and some excellent restaurants, many of which have spectacular views over the creek. The Shangri-La and Traders hotels make up part of the complex and you can float from one end to the other on a tourist abra ride.

Yas Island
Abu Dhabi
yasisland.ae
Yas has emerged as Abu Dhabi's latest tourism hotspot; in addition to hosting the annual Formula 1 Grand Prix at the Yas Marina Circuit, the island boasts several resorts with luxurious spas and restaurants, a world-class golf course, and Ferrari World, which houses the world's fastest rollercoaster. Yas Arena and Flash Forum stadiums also stage regular concerts by internationally acclaimed musicians. Most recently, the largest IKEA in the UAE opened its doors to eager shoppers in 2011 and, looking ahead, more hotels and a waterpark are set to open within the year.

ABU DHABI HOTELS

Al Raha Beach Hotel
Nr Al Raha Mall Abu Dhabi
+971 2 508 0555
danathotels.com
Excellent service, a gorgeous spa and superb levels of comfort in an idyllic boutique beach setting just outside Abu Dhabi city.

Aloft Abu Dhabi
Abu Dhabi National Exhibition Centre (ADNEC) Abu Dhabi **+971 2 654 5000**
aloftabudhabi.com
A real designer offering at the National Exhibition Centre, Aloft is a modern, trendy 408-bedroom affair. The pool bar is a popular spot for residents and visitors.

Beach Rotana Abu Dhabi
Nr Abu Dhabi Mall, Tourist Club St Abu Dhabi **+971 2 697 9000**
rotana.com
Offering loads of popular dining options, as well as a private beach, sports courts and the Zen spa.

Crowne Plaza Yas Island
Yas Island Abu Dhabi **+971 2 656 3000**
ichotelsgroup.com
Sitting right next to Yas Links, this well-equipped hotel is just five minutes from Yas Marina and Ferrari World.

Danat Jebel Dhanna Resort
Jebel Dhanna Abu Dhabi
+971 2 801 2222
danathotels.com
Located 240 kilometres west of Abu Dhabi city, close to Sir Bani Yas Island, this resort features plenty of watersports, a private beach and sand golf.

Emirates Palace
Corniche Road West Abu Dhabi
+971 2 690 9000
kempinski.com
The ultimate in ostentatious luxury, with 14 bars and restaurants, 394 rooms and suites with butler service, an amazing collection of pools and a private beach. Be warned, without a reservation you won't be getting anywhere near this exclusive property. Large, open-air concerts are held in the 200-acre palace gardens in the cooler months. Check the website for details of what's on.

Fairmont Bab Al Bahr
Nr Al Maqta & Mussafa Bridges
Abu Dhabi **+971 2 654 3333**
fairmont.com
This luxury hotel overlooks the creek between the mainland and the city's island, next door to the Qaryat Al Beri complex. It is also home to some of the city's best restaurants and bars, like the offerings from Frankie Dettori and Marco Pierre White.

Golden Tulip Al Jazira Hotel & Resort
Nr Racing & Polo Club, Dubai – Abu Dhabi Rd Abu Dhabi **+971 2 562 9100**
goldentulipaljazira.com
Less than an hour's drive from Dubai, this hotel in Abu Dhabi emirate offers luxury beach bungalows which are great for a weekend getaway.

Hilton Abu Dhabi
Corniche Rd West Abu Dhabi
+971 2 681 1900
hilton.com
This 10-storey luxury hotel on Corniche Road has three swimming pools and a private beach club where there's a wide range of watersports on offer. Each room boasts enviable views, and the hotel houses some of the best restaurants in the city, including BiCE.

InterContinental Abu Dhabi
Bainunah St Abu Dhabi **+971 2 666 6888**
ichotelsgroup.com
Adjacent to the marina, the hotel is surrounded by lush parks and gardens. With five restaurants, four bars and 330 deluxe rooms offering views of the city and the Arabian Gulf, the hotel is popular with business travellers. Following the hotel's recent renovation, many of the restaurants and bars are worth a visit.

Jumeirah At Etihad Towers
Nr Emirates Palace, West Corniche
Abu Dhabi **+971 2 811 5555**
jumeirah.com
The first property that the famed Dubai brand has opened in the capital, the Jumeirah At Etihad Towers certainly makes quite an impression. Located in a soaring tower, almost 400 rooms overlook Emirates Palace, the breakwater and the Corniche; in fact, the views are so good that a dedicated viewing platform is set to open

Some of Abu Dhabi's luxurious hotels

soon. The elegant, giant glass windowed lobby makes quite an impression and it's a sense of luxury that is reflected throughout the hotel, its rooms and the excellent gym and spa. As a Jumeirah property, the F&B outlets are, of course, excellent – especially the spectacular Quest restaurant.

Le Meridien Abu Dhabi
Nr Old Abu Dhabi Co-op Society, Tourist Club St, Abu Dhabi **+971 2 644 6666**
lemeridienabudhabi.com
Famous for its health club and spa, private beach and Culinary Village, there is a children's swimming pool and activities including tennis, squash and volleyball.

Liwa Hotel
Nr Mezzaira Village, Mezaira Abu Dhabi **+971 2 882 2000**
almarfapearlhotels.com
The majestic Liwa Hotel overlooks the Rub Al Khali desert, one of the most stunning panoramas in the world. Facilities include a beautiful pool, a sauna, Jacuzzi and steam room, tennis and volleyball courts.

One To One Hotel – The Village
Off Al Salam St Abu Dhabi
+971 2 495 2000
onetoonehotels.com
Resembling a boutique European hotel, the One To One offers a personal experience with stylish rooms.

Qasr Al Sarab Desert Resort By Anantara
1 Qasr Al Sarab Rd Abu Dhabi
+971 2 886 2088
anantara.com
This hotel has a stunning and truly unique location amid the giant dunes outside Liwa, not far from the Saudi border. Designed to resemble an Arabic fort, guests can enjoy a wide range of desert activities before relaxing in oversized bathtubs, dining on gourmet dishes and being pampered in the spa.

Rocco Forte Hotel Abu Dhabi
Shk Rashid Bin Saeed Al Maktoum Rd Abu Dhabi **+971 2 617 0000**
roccofortehotelabudhabi.com
The Rocco Forte name is synonymous with luxury and the Abu Dhabi hotel is no different. The stunning wave-like glass building is home to almost 300 rooms and suites that share state-of-the-art facilities. The Sports City location (restaurants look back out towards Sheikh Zayed Grand Mosque) makes this predominantly a business hotel, but with one of Abu Dhabi's largest spas and fitness centres, a delightful pool area and several excellent outlets, it also has plenty to offer the leisure visitor.

Shangri-La Hotel Qaryat Al Beri
Qaryat Al Beri Complex Abu Dhabi
+971 2 509 8888
shangri-la.com
Overlooking the creek that separates Abu Dhabi island from the mainland, the rooms all have private terraces. The adjoining Souk Qaryat Al Beri houses a variety of restaurants connected by waterways.

The St Regis Saadiyat Island Resort
Saadiyat Beach Abu Dhabi
+971 2 498 8888
stregissaadiyatisland.com
Quite unlike any other hotel in Abu Dhabi – or the UAE for that matter – the St Regis looks more like a California beach retreat, with the vastly proportioned public spaces and stunning colonial style rooms all offering views over the beautiful central pools, restaurant and private windswept, sandy beach (and one hole of the neighbouring Saadiyat Beach links course). A true beach resort, with leisure facilities and dining (55 and 5th The Grill is particularly recommended) worth travelling for, the St Regis feels like it's a million miles from the city.

Yas Island Rotana
Golf Plaza Abu Dhabi **+971 2 656 4000**
rotana.com
Another superb Yas hotel, with sports, fitness and spa facilities which are modern and top notch in terms of quality. The rooms and restaurants are equally well-considered affairs.

Yas Viceroy Abu Dhabi
Nr Yas Marina Abu Dhabi
+971 2 656 0000
viceroyhotelsandresorts.com
Another in the UAE's long list of iconic hotels, this space-age architectural wonder straddles the F1 circuit with a bridge that offers the best views come race day – the cars speed past below. The hotel has 499 state-of-the-art rooms and the hotel is home to some of the capital's best restaurants and bars.

DUBAI

Cliches tend to trip off the tongue when describing Abu Dhabi's little brother – the city of gold, sleepy fishing village transformed into modern metropolis, the Vegas of the Middle East, and so on. The truth is that, while the emirate boasts an incredible number of attractions claiming to be the tallest, biggest or longest, it's not all bright lights – the atmospheric old town around the Creek, and the restored Bastakiya area are musts for any visitor wanting to scratch Dubai's cultural surface, and the beautiful Jumeirah Mosque (p.214) is one of the few mosques in the region open to non-Muslims, offering a rare chance to learn about the impact of Islam on the local people.

Dubai is also a great place for families and, from amusement parks and aquariums to child-friendly hotels and restaurants, you'll find plenty of ways to keep the kids busy while in town.

Beyond the city, the desert opens up further possibilities and many visitors choose to combine a city break with a couple of nights' camping with a tour group, or relaxing at a luxury desert resort such as Al Maha (+971 4 832 9900) or Bab Al Shams (+971 4 809 6100).

That said, if it's bright lights you're after, Dubai outshines the rest of the region. The emirate has been successful in its quest for economic diversification, and its focus on tourism revenues has resulted in a fantastic array of superlative-laden attractions for tourists and residents alike.

From skiing on real snow at Ski Dubai (p.215) and plunging through shark-infested waters at Aquaventure (+971 4 426 0000), to shopping till you drop at The Dubai Mall (p.214) and surveying the entire city from the world's tallest building, Burj Khalifa (see opposite), a weekend trip to Dubai promises an action-packed break.

Its selection of five-star hotels, restaurants, bars and clubs will ensure a well fed and watered stay, and luxury spas and clean beaches provide ample opportunities to relax.

For more help on planning a trip to Dubai, log on to **askexplorer.com** where you can find listings of upcoming events and loads more information about Dubai's hotels, restaurants and attractions. While you're there, you can order a copy of **Dubai Mini Visitors' Guide** or **Dubai Top Ten** – both are essential guides for your weekend breaks in the city of gold.

Dubai Aquarium

DUBAI ATTRACTIONS

Adventure HQ
Times Square Dubai **+971 4 346 6824**
adventurehq.ae
In addition to stocking up on active wear and outdoors goods, adrenalin addicts will find a couple of top-notch indoors thrills, the Cable Climb and the Chill Chamber.

At The Top
Burj Khalifa Dubai **+971 4 888 8124**
burjkhalifa.ae
In less than 60 seconds, a high-speed lift whisks visitors up to the 124th floor of the world's tallest tower. From the Burj Khalifa observation deck, you can survey a 360 degree view of the city. Advance bookings are Dhs.100 for adults and Dhs.75 for children; tickets bought on the day cost Dhs.400.

Dubai Aquarium & Underwater Zoo
The Dubai Mall Dubai **+971 4 448 5200**
thedubaiaquarium.com
Located, somewhat bizarrely, in the middle of The Dubai Mall, this aquarium displays over 33,000 tropical fish to passing shoppers free of charge. For a

closer view of the main tank's inhabitants, however (which include fearsome looking but generally friendly sand tiger sharks) you can pay to walk through the 270° viewing tunnel. Also well worth a look is the Underwater Zoo, which includes residents such as penguins, piranhas and an octopus. If you're feeling really adventurous, you can even go for a scuba dive in the tank (call ahead to book), ride a glass-bottomed boat or feed the sharks.

The Dubai Mall
Nr Interchange 1, Financial Centre Rd Dubai **+971 4 800 38224 6255**
thedubaimall.com
One of the world's largest shopping malls, The Dubai Mall is a shopper's paradise housing some 1,200 stores, including the famous New York department store, Bloomingdale's. Even if you're not in town to shop, you should make a trip to the mall anyway to view the many attractions within. There is an Olympic sized ice rink, an indoor waterfall, a 22-screen cinema, Sega World indoor theme park, KidZania edutainment centre, the Dubai Aquarium & Underwater Zoo and some great alfresco dining venues with views of the spectacular musical displays of the Dubai Fountain.

Dubai Museum
Al Fahidi Fort Dubai **+971 4 353 1862**
definitelydubai.com
Located in Al Fahidi Fort, this museum is creative, well thought-out and interesting for all the family. The fort was originally built in 1787 as the residence of the ruler of Dubai and for sea defence, and then renovated in 1970 to house the museum. All aspects of Dubai's past are represented. You can walk through a souk from the 1950s, stroll through an oasis, see into a traditional house, get up close to local wildlife, learn about the archaeological finds or go 'underwater' to discover the pearl diving and fishing industries. There are some entertaining mannequins to pose with too. Entry costs Dhs.3 for adults and Dhs.1 for children under 6 years old. Open daily 08:30 to 20:30 (14:30 to 20:30 on Fridays).

Heritage & Diving Village
Nr Shk Saeed Al Maktoum House Dubai **+971 4 393 7139**
definitelydubai.com
Located near the mouth of Dubai Creek, the Heritage & Diving Village focuses on Dubai's maritime past, its pearl diving traditions and local architecture. Visitors can observe traditional potters and weavers practising their craft the way it has been done for centuries. Local women, meanwhile, serve traditionally cooked snacks – one of the rare opportunities you'll have to sample genuine Emirati cuisine. It is particularly lively during the Dubai Shopping Festival and Eid celebrations, with performances including traditional sword dancing. Open daily 08:30 to 22:00 (Fridays 15:30-22:00). The village is very close to Sheikh Saeed Al Maktoum's House, the home of the much-loved former ruler of Dubai, and is a good example of a traditional home and houses a number of interesting photographic exhibits.

Jumeirah Mosque
Jumeira Rd Dubai **+971 4 353 6666**
cultures.ae
This is the best known mosque in the city and, arguably, its most beautiful too, as its image features on the Dhs.500 banknote. The Sheikh Mohammed Centre for Cultural Understanding (cultures.ae) organises mosque tours for non-Muslims on Saturday, Sunday, Tuesday and Thursday mornings at 10:00. Visitors are guided around the mosque and told all about the building, and then the hosts give a talk on Islam and prayer rituals. The tour offers a fascinating insight into the culture and beliefs of the local population, and is thoroughly recommended. You must dress conservatively – no shorts and no sleeveless tops. Women must also cover their hair with a head scarf or shawl, and all visitors will be asked to remove their shoes. Cameras are allowed, pre-booking is essential and there is a registration fee of Dhs.10 per person.

KidZania
The Dubai Mall Dubai **+971 4 448 5222**
kidzania.ae
This is fast becoming one of The Dubai Mall's main attractions, offering kids the opportunity to become adults for the day. Billed as a 'real-life city' for children, youngsters can dress up and act out more than 75 different roles, from policeman to pilot and doctor to designer. The KidZania city even has its own currency, which children can earn and spend. It's intended to be both fun and educational. Dhs.95 to 130 entry.

The Lost Chambers
Atlantis The Palm Dubai
+971 4 426 0000
atlantisthepalm.com
The ruins of the mysterious lost city provide the theme for the aquarium at Atlantis. The maze of underwater tunnels give visitors ample opportunity to get up close to the aquarium's 65,000 inhabitants, which range from sharks and eels to rays and piranhas, as well as multitudes of exotic fish. The entrance fee is Dhs.100 for adults and Dhs. 70 for 7 to 11 year olds.

SEGA Republic
The Dubai Mall Dubai
+971 4 448 8484
segarepublic.com
This indoor theme park located in Dubai Mall offers a range of thrills, courtesy of the nine main attractions and the 150 arcade games. A Power Pass (Dhs.150) gets you all-day access to the big attractions, which include stomach-flipping rides like the Sonic Hopper, the SpinGear and the Halfpipe Canyon. Unlike many other shopping mall amusement centres, SEGA Republic is for all ages.

Ski Dubai
Mall Of The Emirates Dubai
+971 4 800 386
theplaymania.com
Ski Dubai is the Middle East's first indoor ski resort, with more than 22,500 square metres of real snow. The temperature hovers around – 3 celcius, even when it's closer to +50 outside, to make for a cooling excursion from city life. Competent skiers and boarders can choose between five runs and a freestyle area, skiing and snowboarding lessons are available for beginners, and there is a huge snowpark for the little ones. Slope pass and lesson prices include the hire charge for jackets, trousers, boots, socks, helmets and either skis and poles or a snowboard, but it's worth bringing your own gloves as these are charged extra on top of everything else. Freestyle nights are held every other week on Mondays from 20:00 to 23:00.

Souk Al Bahar
Dubai **+971 4 362 7011**
soukalbahar.ae
With atmospheric passageways, Souk Al Bahar is designed to resemble a traditional souk. It houses a host of designer

Ski Dubai

boutiques and shops selling Arab wares such as carpets, paintings, jewellery, clothes and perfumes, but its main attractions are the restaurants and bars, many of which have terraces with views of the Dubai Fountain and Burj Khalifa.

Souk Madinat Jumeirah
Al Sufouh Rd Dubai **+971 4 366 8888**
jumeirah.com
This modern shopping mall is a recreation of a traditional souk with confusingly winding passageways, authentic architecture and interconnecting waterways traversed by motorised abras (traditional boats). It houses a collection of boutique shops, galleries, cafes and bars and the alfresco dining venues are always buzzing during the evenings of the cooler months.

Stargate
Zabeel Park Dubai **+971 4 325 9988**
stargatedubai.com
Kids will love Stargate; this massive complex, located in Zabeel Park, is free to enter, with access to the five giant play domes paid for by a rechargeable card. Each area contains a different adventure; there's a multistorey soft-play area, two go-kart tracks, an ice rink, an indoor rollercoaster and a 3D fun zone. The walkways connecting the play domes house plenty of food venues and retail outlets, and there are enough arcade games dotted throughout to keep everyone happy.

DUBAI HOTELS

The Address Downtown Dubai
Emaar Blvd Dubai **+971 4 436 8888**
theaddress.com
Even at over 300 metres in height, The Address is dwarfed by its neighbour, the Burj Khalifa – but breathtaking views, beautiful interiors and eight dining outlets (including Neos, the panoramic bar on the 63rd floor) make this one of the most popular spots in town. There are also two more The Address hotels, located at Dubai Mall and Dubai Marina, while The Address brand runs the small boutique hotel at The Montgomerie golf course.

Atlantis The Palm
Crescent Rd Dubai **+971 4 4260 000**
atlantisthepalm.com
With a staggering 1,539 rooms and suites, all of which boast views of either the Arabian Gulf or the Palm Jumeirah, Atlantis is without doubt one of Dubai's grandest and most famous hotels. It has no less than four fancy restaurants featuring the cuisine of Michelin-starred chefs, including a branch of the world-famous chain Nobu. It is also home to Aquaventure, the biggest water park in the Middle East, and the Lost Chambers aquarium.

Bonnington Jumeirah Lakes Towers
Nr Almas Tower Dubai **+971 4 356 0000**
bonningtontower.com
This British five-star institution made its Dubai debut in Jumeirah Lakes Towers. Containing both hotel suites and serviced apartments, as well as six restaurants and bars, and a leisure deck with infinity pool, it has great connections to Dubai Marina, as well as the rest of the city via the nearby Metro stop.

Burj Al Arab
Nr Wild Wadi, Jumeira Rd Dubai **+971 4 301 7777**
jumeirah.com
Standing on its own man-made island, this dramatic Dubai icon's unique architecture is today recognised around the world. Each suite covers two floors and is serviced by a private team of butlers. You can't just wander in to check it out or snap photos; to get into the hotel as a non-guest, you will need a restaurant reservation.

Desert Palm Dubai
Al Awir Rd Dubai **+971 4 323 8888**
desertpalm.peraquum.com
Located outside the bustle of the city, Desert Palm is so tranquil you'll never want to leave. Overlooking polo fields, guests can choose from suites, or private villas with a pool. The extensive spa menu features massage and holistic therapies including reiki. Signature restaurant Rare is a must for meat lovers, while Epicure is a gourmet deli and a great breakfast venue.

Dubai Festival City
Al Rebat St Dubai **+971 4 80 0332**
dubaifestivalcity.com
DFC has two hotels to choose from. The InterContinental (+971 4 701 1111) has extensive spa facilities, a swanky cocktail bar and great views from all its rooms and suites; next door is the Crowne Plaza (+971 4 701 2222) with the ever-popular Belgian Beer Café.

Hilton Dubai Creek

Baniyas Rd Dubai +**971 4 227 1111**
hilton.com
With very flash yet understated elegance, this ultra-minimalist hotel features interiors of wood, glass and chrome. Centrally located and overlooking the Dubai Creek, with splendid views of the Arabian dhow trading posts, the hotel has two renowned restaurants in Glasshouse Brasserie and new Dubai gastronomic darling Table 9 by Nick and Scott.

Jumeirah Beach Hotel

Nr Wild Wadi, Jumeira Rd Dubai
+**971 4 348 0000**
jumeirah.com
Shaped like an ocean wave, with a fun and colourful interior, the hotel has 598 rooms and suites and 19 private villas, all with a sea view. It is also home to some excellent food and beverage outlets, including Uptown for happy hour cocktails and La Parrilla for some of the best steaks in the city. The hotel enjoys a great view of the Burj Al Arab. This hotel is particularly popular with kids and families who love Wild Wadi Water Park, which is located on the site.

Kempinski Hotel Mall Of The Emirates

Mall Of The Emirates, Dubai,
+**971 4 341 0000**
kempinski.com
Located in Mall Of The Emirates, this chic hotel's 400 deluxe rooms enjoy direct access to the shopping extravaganza of the iconic mall and Ski Dubai, the indoor ski slope. Check into one of the 15 exclusive ski chalet rooms, remove your boots, put your feet up to the (fake) fire and tuck into an apres-ski afternoon tea while watching the world slide by.

Madinat Jumeirah

Nr Burj Al Arab, Jumeira Rd Dubai
+**971 4 366 8888**
jumeirah.com
This extravagant resort has two hotels, Al Qasr and Mina A'Salam, with no fewer than 940 luxurious rooms and suites, and the exclusive Dar Al Masyaf summer houses, all linked by man-made waterways navigated by wooden abra boats which whisk guests around the resort. Nestled between the two hotels is Souk Madinat, with over 95 shops and 44 bars and restaurants to choose from.

One&Only Royal Mirage

Al Sufouh Rd Dubai +**971 4 399 9999**
oneandonlyresorts.com
This stunningly beautiful resort is home to three different properties: The Palace, Arabian Court and Residence & Spa. The service and dining (opt for the Beach, Bar & Grill for a romantic evening out; try delectable Moroccan cuisine in the opulent Tagine; or enjoy cocktails with a view in the Rooftop and Sports Lounge) are renowned, and a luxury spa treatment here is the ultimate indulgence.

The Palace – The Old Town

Dubai +**971 4 428 7888**
theaddress.com
Palatial indeed, The Palace faces the mighty Burj Khalifa and the spectacular Dubai Fountain. Styled with traditional Arabic architecture, this opulent hotel boasts 242 luxurious rooms and suites, a beautiful spa and some excellent restaurants, including Argentinean steakhouse Asado, and majlis-style shisha tents arranged around the stunning pool.

Park Hyatt Dubai

Nr Dubai Creek Golf & Yacht Club Dubai
+**971 4 602 1234**
hyatt.com
Enjoying a prime waterfront location within the grounds of Dubai Creek Golf & Yacht Club, the Park Hyatt is Mediterranean in style with low-rise buildings, natural colours and stylish decor. The hotel's 225 rooms and suites all boast beautiful views, as do some great dining outlets; try The Thai Kitchen. The hotel also houses one of the city's best spas, which features a luxury couples' massage option.

Raffles Dubai

Wafi Dubai +**971 4 324 8888**
raffles.com
With 248 stunning suites, the renowned Raffles Amrita Spa and unique Botanical Sky Garden, this is one of Dubai's most noteworthy city hotels. Nine food and beverage outlets offer a mix of international and far eastern cuisine.

The Ritz-Carlton, Dubai

The Walk, Jumeirah Beach Residence
Dubai +**971 4 399 4000**
ritzcarlton.com
Even though it is the only low-rise building amid the sea of Marina towers behind it, all 138 rooms have beautiful views of the

Gulf – the Ritz-Carlton was, after all, here years before the rest of the marina was built. Afternoon tea in the Lobby Lounge is a must, and there are several other excellent restaurants and a very good spa onsite. Ritz-Carlton has also added another property to its offerings, with a new 341-room hotel in the DIFC area.

The Westin Dubai Mina Seyahi Beach Resort & Marina
Al Sufouh Rd Dubai **+971 4 399 4141**
westinminaseyahi.com
Set on 1,200 metres of private beach, The Westin has 294 spacious rooms and suites with all the luxury amenities you would expect of a five-star hotel, including the aptly named Heavenly Spa. There are plenty of dining venues, including perennially popular Italian Bussola, Senyar for cocktails and tapas, and wine and cheese bar Oeno.

AL AIN

Al Ain is Abu Dhabi emirate's second city and of great historical significance in the UAE. Its location, on ancient trading routes between Oman and the Arabian Gulf, rendered the oasis strategically important.

Commonly known as 'The Garden City', Al Ain features many oases and lovely patches of greenery for the public to enjoy. After a greening programme instigated by

the late Sheikh Zayed, the seven natural oases are now set amid tree-lined streets and beautiful urban parks.

Its unique history means that Al Ain is home to a variety of interesting sights and attractions, including the Hili Archaeological Garden and the Al Ain Museum.

Just outside the city sits one of the largest mountains in the UAE, Jebel Hafeet. The rolling, grass-covered hills of Green Mubazzarah Park (+971 3 783 9555) at the bottom of the mountain are great for picnics and mid afternoon naps.

Al Ain's archaeological and historical legacy is of such significance that the city was recently placed on the list of World Heritage Sites by Unesco.

AL AIN ATTRACTIONS

Al Ain Camel & Livestock Souk
Nr Bawadi Mall, Zayed Bin Sultan St
Al Ain
adach.ae
Conditions at the souk have improved dramatically, with spacious pens for the animals and ample parking for visitors. A visit to the market is a fantastic way to mingle with locals and witness camel and goat trading as it's taken place for centuries. Arrive early, preferably before 09:00, to soak up the atmosphere.

Al Ain National Museum

Al Ain National Museum

Nr Sultan Fort, Zayed Bin Sultan St Al Ain
+971 3 764 1595
adach.ae
Divided into three main sections –
archaeology, ethnography and gifts – the
presentations include photographs,
Bedouin jewellery, musical instruments,
weapons and a traditional majlis.

Al Ain Oasis

Nr Al Ain National Museum Al Ain
adach.ae
This impressive oasis in the heart of
the city is filled with palm plantations,
many of which are still working farms.
The cool, shady walkways transport you
from the heat and noise of the city to
an otherworldly, tranquil haven. You
are welcome to wander through the
plantations, but it's best to stick to the
paved areas. The farms have plenty of
working examples of falaj, the traditional
irrigation system which has been used for
centuries to tap into underground wells.
There are eight different entrances, some
of which have arched gates, and there is
no entry fee.

Al Ain Zoo

Nhayyan First St Al Ain **+971 3 800 2977**
alainzoo.ae
Stretching over 900 hectares, this is
arguably the largest and best zoo in the
Gulf region. With ample greenery, a casual
stroll through the paths that criss-cross the
park makes for a wonderful family day out.
As well as seeing large mammals, reptiles
and big cats, you can get up close to some
rare and common local species such as
the Arabian Oryx and sand gazelle, or pay
a visit to the fantastic birdhouse. Since its
founding, the zoo has been a centre for
endangered species' conservation and
visitors can look forward to spotting true
rarities. Nearly 30% of the 180 species
are endangered and the park is even
home to a stunning pair of white tigers
and white lions which are some of the
zoo's biggest draws. Family nights, with
activities from sports games to cartoon
screenings, take place on Wednesdays.
A park train regularly departs from the
central concourse, providing a whirlwind
tour of the zoo. The park is open daily from
09:00 to 20:00 in winter and from 16:00 to
22:00 during summer. Entrance is Dhs.15
for adults, Dhs.5 for children and it's free
for those under 2 years.

Al Jahili Fort

Nr Central Public Gardens Al Ain
+971 3 784 3996
adach.ae
Celebrated as the birthplace of the late
Sheikh Zayed bin Sultan Al Nahyan, the
picturesque fort was erected in 1891 to
defend Al Ain's precious palm groves. It
is set in beautifully landscaped gardens
and visitors are encouraged to explore the
exterior. It's also the stunning venue for
a number of concerts in the Abu Dhabi
Classics series.

Hili Archaeological Park

Al Ain adach.ae
Located 10 kilometres outside Al Ain on
the Dubai-Al Ain highway, the gardens
are home to a Bronze Age settlement
(2,500–2,000BC), which was excavated and
restored in 1995. Many of the artefacts
found during the excavation are now on
display in the Al Ain National Museum
(p.220).

Hili Fun City

Mohammed Bin Khalifa St,
Off Emirates St Al Ain **+971 3 784 5542**
hilifuncity.ae
The recently renovated 22 hectare park
may not compete with the world's greatest
theme parks in terms of the rides on offer,
but the spacious, leafy grounds make Hili
Fun City a perfect destination for family
outings. There are plenty of arcade games
and refreshment stands, or you could bring
your own picnic. Located on the eastern
side of the park is a mammoth 60 by 30
metre ice rink. The park is open 16:00 to
22:00 (Monday to Thursday), 12:00 to 22:00
(Friday and Saturday), with Wednesdays
reserved for ladies and children only.
The park is closed on Sundays and for
Ramadan (when annual maintenance takes
place). Special opening hours apply for the
June-August period. Entrance costs Dhs.45
(Mondays and Tuesdays, Dhs.40); free for
kids up to 89cm tall. The Dhs.25 admission
fee to the ice rink includes the rental of
skates for one hour.

Wadi Adventure

Nr Green Mubazzarah, Off Al Ain Fayda
Rd Al Ain **+971 3 781 8422**
wadiadventure.ae
Located at the bottom of Jebel Hafeet and
beside Green Mubazzarah, Wadi Adventure
is a man-made water adventure park.
The impressive whitewater rafting and

kayaking runs – with a combined length of more than 1.1km – are among the major draws, but you'll also find a gigantic surf pool complete with a man-made beach and 3-metre waves. The other facilities include regular swimming pools for adults and kids, a rope course, a white-knuckle timber swing and a climbing wall, as well as several food and beverage outlets. The centre opened in January 2012.

AL AIN HOTELS

Al Ain Rotana
Zayed Bin Sultan Rd Al Ain
+971 3 754 5111
rotana.com
Located in the centre of the city, the hotel's rooms, suites and chalets are extremely spacious and modern. The other facilities include a beautiful garden pool and good fitness facilities. In addition, the hotel is also a nightlife hub with six dining venues, including the ever-popular Trader Vic's and a highly recommended Lebanese restaurant.

Al Massa Hotel
Nr Hamdan Bin Mohd & Al Baladiah Sts Al Ain **+971 3 762 8884**
almasahotels.com
This city centre establishment has 50 rooms and 12 suites, along with a cafe and Lebanese-style restaurant. It is a little dated but clean and welcoming if you're simply looking for a place to stay in the centre of town.

Asfar Resort
Nr Safeer Mall, Al Masoody Rd Al Ain
+971 3 762 8882
asfarhotels.com
Located near Safeer Mall, around 4km from the Omani border, this relaxed resort offers 53 well-equipped rooms ranging from studios to two-bedroom suites. In addition to a sunny swimming pool and a palm tree lined lounging area, the facilities include a gym, while the resort's onsite restaurant, Rendezvouz, serves up a wide range of international dishes.

Ayla Hotel
Khalifa Bin Zayed Al Awwal St Al Ain
+971 3 761 0111
aylahotels.com
A new hotel near the town centre, the rooms are practical and tasteful, while

there's a modern gym, indoor pool, sauna, Jacuzzi and basic spa offerings. Dining options are simple but adequate, although Ayla is aimed mainly at an Arab market (and a business one at that) and outlets are therefore not licensed. Western tourists shouldn't be put off – the hotel has a local flavour that creates a welcoming, relaxed atmosphere.

City Seasons Hotel Al Ain
Khalifa Bin Zayed St Al Ain
+971 3 755 0220
cityseasonsgroup.com
This hotel has 89 lovely rooms and suites with excellent facilities. Executive suites have a separate living room and kitchen facilities. The hotel has a fitness centre, swimming pool and sun deck.

Danat Al Ain Resort
Nr Khalid Bin Sultan & Al Salam Sts Al Ain **+971 3 704 6000**
danathotels.com
One of the most enjoyable inland resorts in the UAE, this hotel has beautifully landscaped gardens, fun swimming pools, luxurious guestrooms, deluxe villas and a Royal Villa with a private Jacuzzi. It also has great facilities for families to enjoy, and a delightful spa.

Hilton Al Ain
Nr Khalid Bin Sultan & Zayed Bin Sultan Sts Al Ain **+971 3 768 6666**
hilton.com
Located near the heart of Al Ain, this ageing hotel is a key landmark and sits in lush, landscaped gardens that contain a nine hole golf course, tennis and squash courts, a health club and a nice pool area. It is particularly convenient for visiting the wildlife park and Jebel Hafeet. The Hiltonia Sports Bar and Paco's Bar are both popular haunts.

Mercure Grand Jebel Hafeet Al Ain
Al Ain **+971 3 783 8888**
mercure.com
Situated in a spectacular location near the top of Jebel Hafeet, the Mercure offers incredible views of Al Ain from all of its simply but adequately decorated rooms and terraced restaurants. There are also three swimming pools, and a water slide. There is a pub, buffet restaurant and poolside cafe serving excellent evening barbecues and shisha.

SHARJAH

Despite being eclipsed by Dubai in the international spotlight, Sharjah has substantially more culture and heritage to offer. So much so, that it was named the cultural capital of the Arab world by Unesco in 1998, thanks to its eclectic mix of museums, heritage preservation and traditional souks. The border between Dubai and Sharjah cities is barely noticeable when driving from one to the other. This means it's easy to visit and explore Sharjah without having to check into a hotel.

Sharjah is built around Khalid Lagoon, also known as the creek, and the surrounding Buheirah Corniche is a popular spot for an evening stroll. From various points around the lagoon, small dhows can be hired to take you out on the water to see the city lights. Joining Khalid Lagoon to Al Khan Lagoon, Al Qasba (p.222) is home to a variety of cultural events, exhibitions, theatre and music – all held on the canal-side walkways or at dedicated venues. The city's main cultural centres, The Heritage Area (p.223) and The Arts Area, are two of the most impressive collections of museums and heritage sites in the region. The ruling Al Qassimi family are renowned collectors of historical artefacts and art, and in an emirate known for its conservatism, many of the works held within the Arts Area are surprising in their modernity. Sharjah's cultural worth is so great that visitors should avoid trying to absorb it all in one trip.

Shoppers will have a blast too, searching for gifts in Sharjah's souks. Souk Al Arsah (p.224) is the oldest souk in the emirate, while the Central Souk is known for its well-respected upstairs carpet shops. There's also high-street shopping at Sharjah Mega Mall (sharjahmegamall.com, 06 574 2574) for days when culture and curiosities aren't on the agenda.

For further information on Sharjah, check out the Sharjah Mini Visitors' Guide, available in bookstores and at askexplorer.com.

SHARJAH ATTRACTIONS

Al Mahatta Museum
Nr Dept of Immigration Sharjah
+971 6 573 3079
sharjahmuseums.ae
Home to the first airfield in the Gulf, opened in 1932, Sharjah played an important role as a primary stop-off point for the first commercial flights from Britain to India, and the museum looks at the impact this had on the traditional way of life in Sharjah and this part of the world overall. Four of the original propeller planes have been fully restored and are on display. Located behind Al Estiqlal Street, entry is Dhs.5 for adults and Dhs.10 for families.

Al Qasba
Nr Al Khan Lagoon Sharjah
+971 6 556 0777
alqasba.ae
With an ever-changing events calendar that includes Arabic poetry readings, film viewings and musical events, the emphasis at Al Qasba is clearly on culture, but there's more on offer. The complex's shops, event spaces and restaurants are laid out between Sharjah's two lagoons and are packed on cooler evenings with window shoppers, diners and families. Motorised abras provide tours up and down the canal, but the biggest and most visible draw is the Eye of the Emirates – a 60 metre high observation wheel with air-conditioned pods offering amazing views over Sharjah and across to Dubai.

Sharjah Aquarium
Nr Sharjah Martime Museum Sharjah
+971 6 528 5288
sharjahaquarium.ae
Although eclipsed by the two aquariums that opened in Dubai in 2008, Sharjah Aquarium is the city's newest attraction and draws big crowds, especially at the weekends. Situated next door to Sharjah Maritime Museum at the mouth of Al Khan Lagoon, its location allows visitors to view the Gulf's natural underwater life. There are over 250 species in the aquarium, as well as many interactive displays to educate visitors. Opening hours are 08:00 to 20:00 Monday to Thursday, 16:00 to 21:00 on Fridays and 08:00 to 21:00 on Saturdays; closed Sundays. Admission is Dhs.20 for adults, Dhs.10 for children and Dhs.50 for families.

Sharjah Archaeology Museum
Shk Rashid Bin Saqr Al Qassimi St Sharjah **+971 6 566 5466**
archaeologymuseum.ae
This hi-tech museum offers an interesting display of antiquities from the region. Using well-designed displays and documentary film, the museum traces man's first steps and progress across the

Arabian Peninsula through the ages, and one area features the latest discoveries from excavation sites in the UAE. The museum is closed on Sundays, and for part of the afternoon on other days, so it is best to call before you visit to check times.

Sharjah Art Museum
Sharjah Arts Area Sharjah
+971 6 568 8222
sharjahmuseums.ae
The Arts Area centrepiece, the Art Museum was originally built to house the personal collection of over 300 paintings and maps belonging to the ruler, HH Dr Sheikh Sultan bin Mohammed Al Qassimi. Permanent displays include the work of 18th century artists, with oil paintings and watercolours depicting life in the Arab world, while other exhibits change frequently. There's an art reference library, bookshop and coffee shop, and the museum hosts various cultural activities. The museum is closed on Friday mornings, while Wednesday afternoons are for ladies only.

Sharjah Desert Park
Interchange 9, Al Dhaid Rd, Al Sajaá
Sharjah **+971 6 531 1999**
Located 25 kilometres outside the city, the Sharjah Desert Park complex comprises the Natural History Museum, the Arabian Wildlife Centre, the Children's Farm and the recently opened Sharjah Botanical Museum. The Natural History and Botanical Museums feature interactive displays on the relationships between man and the

natural world in the UAE and beyond, while at the Arabian Wildlife Centre you get the chance to see many reptiles, birds, creepy crawlies, and mammals, including the rare Arabian leopard. The facilities are excellent and the animals are treated well. There is also a Children's Farm with animals that can be fed and petted. Picnic areas are available, plus cafes and shops. Closed on Tuesdays, entry costs Dhs.5 for children, Dhs.15 for adults and includes access to everything.

Sharjah Discovery Centre
Nr Interchange 4, Al Dhaid Rd Sharjah
+971 6 558 6577
sharjahmuseums.ae
The Discovery Centre is a great family day out and children of all ages, including toddlers, can explore the many themed areas and experiment and interact with the exhibits. The underlying aim is to teach youngsters about the biological, physical and technological worlds in a practical, and interesting, way. There is good pushchair access, an in-house cafe for light bites, and ample parking. Entrance is Dhs.5 for children and Dhs.10 for adults. The centre is open from 08:00 to 14:00 Sunday to Thursday, and 16:00 to 20:00 Friday and Saturday. Be aware it can get busy at weekends.

Sharjah Heritage Area
Nr Sharjah Arts Area, Al Merraija Sharjah
+971 6 569 3999
sharjahtourism.ae
The beautifully restored heritage area is a cultural treasure trove that includes a

number of old buildings, such as Al Hisn Fort (Sharjah Fort), Sharjah Islamic Museum, Sharjah Heritage Museum (Bait Al Naboodah), the Maritime Museum, the Majlis of Ibrahim Mohammed Al Midfa and the Old Souk (Souk Al Arsah). Traditional local architecture and life from the past 150 years is described, depicted and displayed throughout this extensive area. Toilets can be found at each venue and, when the time comes for a rest, there's an Arabic coffee shop in the shaded courtyard of Souk Al Arsah.

Sharjah Maritime Museum
Nr Sharjah Aquarium Sharjah **+971 6 522 2002**
sharjahmuseums.ae
With the goal of documenting the development of seafaring in the Middle East, the museum's displays feature fishing, trading, pearl diving and boat construction methods native to the UAE. Each room in the museum informs visitors about a different aspect of the marine industry. The museum also houses several real examples of traditional seafaring boats.

Sharjah Museum Of Islamic Civilization
Nr Sharjah Creek, Corniche St Sharjah **+971 6 565 5455**
islamicmuseum.ae
With vaulted rooms, and impressive galleries and halls, the architecture of this recently opened museum alone makes a visit worthwhile, but with over 5,000 Islamic artefacts, and reams of information, this is one of the best places to learn about Islam and Islamic culture. The museum is organised according to five themes: the Islamic religion, Islamic art, artefacts, craftsmen and weaponry, each in its own gallery; the Temporary Exhibition Gallery hosts a programme of visiting exhibitions. Entry for adults is Dhs.5; children are free.

Sharjah Science Museum
Nr Sharjah TV station Sharjah **+971 6 566 8777**
sharjahmuseums.ae
The interactive museum's exhibits and demonstrations cover subjects such as aerodynamics, cryogenics, electricity and colour. There's also a planetarium and children's area where the under 5s and their parents can learn together. The Learning Centre offers more in-depth

programmes on many of the subjects covered in the museum. Entry costs Dhs.5 for children aged 3 to 17 years; and Dhs.10 for adults.

SHARJAH HOTELS

Corniche Al Buhaira Hotel
Corniche Rd Sharjah **+971 6 519 2222**
A beautiful new resort which is located right on the Corniche and boasts some of the best facilities in the emirate.

Lou' Lou'a Beach Resort
Al Meena St Sharjah **+971 6 528 5000**
loulouabeach.com
Beach resort situated on the Sharjah coast. Offers watersports and spa facilities.

Radisson Blu Resort Sharjah
Corniche Rd Sharjah **+971 6 565 7777**
radissonblu.com
Located on the Sharjah Corniche, close to the city's main cultural attractions, the hotel has its own beach.

Sharjah Rotana
Al Arouba St Sharjah **+971 6 563 7777**
rotana.com
Located in the centre of the city, the Rotana caters mostly to business travellers.

AJMAN

The smallest of the emirates, Ajman's centre is just 10 kilometres from Sharjah city centre, and the two cities pretty much merge along the coast. Ajman has a nice stretch of beach and a pleasant corniche to walk along, while the Ajman Kempinksi Hotel & Resort is a grand offering for those wanting a luxurious stay. If you're on a tighter budget, there are several cheaper options along the beach. Ajman Museum (p.225) houses a variety of interesting displays in a restored fort that is well worth visiting, as much for the building as for its contents. The tiny emirate is known for being one of the largest boat-building centres in the region. While mainly modern boats emerge from the yards these days, you may still catch a glimpse of a traditionally built wooden dhow sailing out to sea. The emirate's main souk is a reminder of a slower pace of life and of days gone by, while the modern Ajman City Centre (+971 6 743 2888) houses shops and a cinema.

AJMAN ATTRACTIONS

Ajman Museum
Nr Clock Tower R/A, Al Bustan Ajman
+971 6 742 3824
acm.gov.ae
Ajman Museum's interesting and well-arranged displays have descriptions in both English and Arabic. The museum has a variety of exhibits, including a collection of Ajman-issued passports and dioramas of ancient life, but it's the building itself that will most impress visitors. Housed in a fortress dating back to around 1775, the museum is a fascinating example of traditional architecture, with imposing watchtowers and traditional windtowers. Entry is Dhs.5 for adults. Morning opening times are 09:00 to 13:00 then 16:00 to 19:00 in the evening. Closed on Fridays.

AJMAN HOTELS

Kempinski Hotel Ajman
Sheikh Humaid Bin Rashid Al Nuaimi St Ajman **+971 6 714 5555**
kempinski.com
Visitors to Ajman can relax on half a kilometre of the Kempinski's private beach or around its superb pool facilities. The hotel has 185 seaview rooms and a diverse range of international restaurants, cafes and bars, as well as a grand ballroom. The Laguna Spa offers a comprehensive spa menu, including an outdoor Balinese massage.

UMM AL QUWAIN

Nestled between Ajman and Ras Al Khaimah, not much has changed in Umm Al Quwain over the years. The main industries are still fishing and date cultivation. The emirate has six forts, and a few old watchtowers surround the town. With plenty of mangroves and birdlife, the emirate's lagoon is a popular weekend spot for boat trips, windsurfing and other watersports. Another popular family activity is crab hunting at Flamingo Beach Resort. At nightfall, groups of hunters set off into the shallow mangrove waters with a guide, where they spear crabs which are barbecued and served on return to the resort.

The area north of the lagoon is a regional activity centre. Emirates Motorplex (motorplex.ae) hosts motorsport events, including the Emirates Motocross Championship, and Dreamland Aqua

Park is one of the emirate's most popular attractions. Barracuda Beach Resort is a favoured destination for Dubai residents thanks to its well-stocked duty-free liquor store.

The emirate has not escaped the attention of the developers and a project currently underway will see over 9,000 homes and a marina emerge on the shore of the Khor Al Beidah wildlife area.

UMM AL QUWAIN ATTRACTIONS

Dreamland Aqua Park
El Itihad Rd, RAK Highway
Umm Al Quwain **+971 6 768 1888**
dreamlanduae.com
With over 25 water rides, including four 'twisting dragons', Dreamland Aqua Park is massive. If extreme slides aren't your thing, there's the lazy river, a wave pool, an aqua play area, and a high-salinity floating pool. Overnight accommodation in provided tents or huts is also available. Admission is Dhs.135 for adults and Dhs.85 for children under 1.2m, while children under 2 go free. The park is open all-year-round; Fridays, Saturdays and holidays are for families only.

UMM AL QUWAIN HOTELS

Barracuda Beach Resort
Nr Dreamland Aqua Park, Khor Al Baida
Umm Al Quwain **+971 6 768 1555**
barracuda.ae
Known throughout the UAE for its popular tax-free booze emporium, Barracuda is also a pleasant resort for quick weekend getaways. Aside from the main hotel, the resort offers several lagoon-side one-bedroom chalets that can each accommodate up to five people. The chalets come with kitchenettes and barbecues – perfect for private overnight parties. There's also a large pool and Jacuzzi.

Flamingo Beach Resort
Nr Horsehead R/A Umm Al Quwain
+971 6 765 0000
flamingoresort.ae
Cheap and cheerful, this resort is surrounded by a shallow lagoon dotted with green islands that attract birdlife including migrating flamingos. Evening crab hunts are available for non-guests.

Imar Spa

Nr Palma Beach Hotel Umm Al Quwain
+971 6 766 4440
imarspa.com
This five-star ladies-only spa haven is in the heart of Umm Al Quwain, in a peaceful, seaside setting. The hotel has a small private beach and terrace, a fabulous temperature-controlled pool and a saltwater aqua therapy pool. There are only two twin rooms and three singles so booking in advance is advised.

RAS AL KHAIMAH

With the Hajar Mountains rising just behind the city, the Arabian Gulf stretching out from the shore and the desert starting in the south near the farms and ghaf forests of Digdagga, Ras Al Khaimah (RAK) has possibly the best scenery of any emirate. The most northerly emirate, a creek divides the main city into the old town and the newer Al Nakheel district.

The past couple of years have witnessed RAK's transformation into a prominent weekend destination, and several new resorts have opened for the overworked residents of Dubai and Abu Dhabi. The Tower Links Golf Course (+971 7 227 9939, towerlinks.com) is laid out among the mangroves around the creek and is popular at weekends, as is Al Hamra Golf Club (alhamragolf.com).

Ras Al Khaimah contains several archaeological sites, some dating back all the way to 3000BC. Take the Al Ram road out of the Al Nakheel district and towards the Hajar Mountains to discover some of the area's history, including the Dhayah Fort, Shimal Archaeological Site and Sheba's Palace.

The bare ruins of the Dhayah Fort can be spotted from the road, but you might need a 4WD to access them. Further inland are the Shimal archaeological site and Sheba's Palace. Both are a little obscure, but worth the difficulty of finding them. Shimal includes a tomb from the Umm An Nar period, roughly 5,000 years ago. Built as a communal burial place, the remains of more than 400 bodies have now been found there.

Further down the same road is another tomb – this one dates back to the Wadi Suq period (2000BC). Many of the artefacts discovered in these locations can now be found at the National Museum at Ras Al Khaimah (p.226), while the Pearl Excursion and Pearl Museum (rakpearls.com) are reminders of Ras Al Khaimah's more recent heritage and trade.

At the other end of the spectrum, Manar Mall (manarmall.com) is a large shopping and leisure facility, housing a cinema complex, family entertainment centre and dining options overlooking the creek and mangroves; Al Hamra Mall (alhamramall. com) and Safeer Mall (mysafeer.com) are also popular.

The town is quiet, relaxing and a good starting point for exploring the surrounding mountains, visiting the ancient sites of Ghalilah and Shimal, the hot springs at Khatt and the camel racetrack at Digdagga. There are also several chances to get into the mountains north of the city, as well as south of RAK in places like Jebel Yibir – the tallest mountain in the country, where a new track takes you nearly to the top for spectacular views.

RAS AL KHAIMAH ATTRACTIONS

Ice Land Water Park

Al Jazeera Ras Al Khaimah
+971 7 206 7888
icelandwaterpark.com
The UAE's latest water park is the first major attraction to open in the giant WOW RAK tourist destination. The polar-themed Iceland has more than 50 rides and attractions, including Penguin Falls, Snow River and Mount Cyclone. Open from 10:00 every day; adult entry costs Dhs.150 while entry for children under 1.2m tall is Dhs.100.

National Museum Of Ras Al Khaimah

Nr Police HQ Ras Al Khaimah
+971 7 233 3411
rasalkhaimahtourism.com
Housed in an impressive fort that was once the home of the present ruler of Ras Al Khaimah, this museum focuses on local natural history and archaeological displays, including a variety of paraphernalia from pre-oil, Bedouin life. Look out for fossils set in the rock strata of the walls of the fort – these date back 190 million years. Entrance is only Dhs.2 for adults and Dhs.1 for children; directions can be found on the museum website. Open every day except Tuesday and public holidays.

RAS AL KHAIMAH HOTELS

Al Hamra Fort Hotel & Beach Resort
Off Sheikh Mohd Bin Salem Rd
Ras Al Khaimah **+971 7 244 6666**
alhamrafort.com
A building of traditional Arab architecture, set among acres of lush gardens and along a delightful strip of sandy beach, this hotel offers a peaceful getaway and slower pace of life. A range of watersports and activities, including two floodlit golf courses and an onsite dive centre, will keep you entertained, and the eight themed eateries offer a wide variety of international cuisines and atmosphere.

Al Hamra Palace Beach Resort
Ras Al Khaimah **+971 7 206 7222**
casahotelsandresorts.com
Located on a private beach in the Arabian Gulf, this five-star resort offers luxurious suites with fully equipped kitchenettes. The Sea Breeze restaurant serves traditional Arab food, while guests can have a refreshing swim in the outdoor pool or enjoy the tennis court and fitness centre. The resort is just a five minute drive from Al Hamra Golf Club.

Banyan Tree Al Wadi
Al Mazraa Ras Al Khaimah
+971 7 206 7777
banyantree.com
Banyan Tree Al Wadi combines superior luxury with exclusive spa facilities, desert activities and a wildlife conservation area. Set within Wadi Khadeja, the villas are designed for optimum relaxation with private pools and views of the desert. Not cheap, but extremely opulent.

The Cove Rotana Resort
Off Shk Mohd Bin Salem Rd, Arcoob
Ras Al Khaimah **+971 7 206 6000**
rotana.com
Built into the hills overlooking the Arabian Gulf, The Cove's sprawling layout of 204 rooms, 72 private villas and winding pathways is reminiscent of an old Mediterranean hill town. The resort revolves around an immaculate lagoon, protected from the sea by 600 metres of pristine beach. A Bodylines spa and several impressive restaurants round out the package.

Golden Tulip Khatt Springs Resort & Spa
Nr Hajjar Mountains, Khatt
Ras Al Khaimah **+971 7 244 8777**
goldentulipkhattsprings.com
Simple and subdued, Golden Tulip Khatt Springs Resort & Spa relies on mountain views, uninterrupted tranquillity and incredible spa packages to attract weekend visitors. Next to the hotel, you can take a dip in the public Khatt Hot Springs – piping hot water which, it is claimed, has curative powers. Men and women have separate pools and a variety of massages is also available. It's a good idea to visit the hot springs in the morning and avoid Fridays as it can get very busy with families.

Hilton Ras Al Khaimah Resort & Spa
Al Maareedh St, Al Mairid Ras Al Khaimah **+971 7 228 8844**
hilton.com
Tucked away on an exclusive bay, out of sight of the city, the resort's many guest rooms and villas are perfect for a beach break. The pool bar, spa and laid-back dining options make this one of the most relaxing destinations in the region. Guests of the older Hilton Ras Al Khaimah (+971 7 228 8888, hilton.com), located in the city, can use the facilities.

FUJAIRAH
A trip to the East Coast is a must – made up of the emirate of Fujairah and several enclaves belonging to Sharjah, the villages along the East Coast sit between the rugged Hajar Mountains and the gorgeous Gulf of Oman. Fujairah city has seen little development compared to cities on the west coast, but the real draw here is the landscape.

The mountains and wadis that stretch west of the coast contain some of the country's best and most accessible camping spots and the beaches, reefs and villages that line the coast attract visitors from Dubai throughout the year.

Previously, the journey to the East Coast involved a two-hour drive that took in some of the country's most scenic mountain passes. If you're happy to sacrifice some of those views for time, however, the new Sheikh Khalifa Highway cuts the journey time between Dubai and Fujairah to just 30 minutes.

Bidiyah

The site of the oldest mosque in the UAE, Bidiyah is one of the oldest settlements on the East Coast and is believed to have been inhabited since 3000BC. The mosque is made from gypsum, stone and mud bricks finished off with plaster, and its original design of four domes supported by a central pillar was considered unique, but the shape was changed to stepped domes during renovations. It is believed to date back to the middle of the 15th century. The mosque is still used for prayer, so non-Muslim visitors can't enter. Built next to a low hillside with several watchtowers on the ridge behind, the area is now colourfully lit up at night.

Dibba

Located at the northern-most point of the East Coast, on the border with Musandam (p.192), Dibba is made up of three fishing villages. Unusually, each part comes under a different jurisdiction: Dibba Al Hisn is part of Sharjah, Dibba Muhallab is Fujairah and Dibba Bayah is Oman. The three Dibbas share an attractive bay, fishing communities, and excellent diving locations – from here you can arrange dhow trips to take you to unspoilt dive locations in Musandam (see Tour Operators, p.185). The Hajar Mountains provide a wonderful backdrop, rising in places to over 1,800 metres. There are some good public beaches too, where your only company will be crabs and seagulls, and where seashell collectors may find a few treasures.

Fujairah

Fujairah town is a mix of old and new. Its hillsides are dotted with ancient forts and watchtowers, which add an air of mystery and charm; most are undergoing restoration work. Fujairah is also a busy trading centre, with its modern container port and thriving free zone attracting major companies from around the world.

Off the coast, the seas and coral reefs are great for fishing, diving and watersports. It is a good place for birdwatching during the spring and autumn migrations as it is on the route from Africa to Central Asia. Since Fujairah is close to the mountains and many areas of natural beauty, it makes an excellent base from which to explore the countryside and discover wadis, forts, waterfalls and even natural hot springs.

Kalba

Just to the south of Fujairah, Kalba is renowned for its mangrove forest and golden beaches. It's a pretty fishing village that has retained much of its historical charm. The mountain road linking Kalba to Hatta makes for an interesting alternative for returning to Dubai.

Khor Kalba

Set in a beautiful tidal estuary, Khor Kalba is one of the oldest mangrove forests in Arabia and is home to a variety of plant, marine and birdlife not found anywhere else in the UAE. The mangroves in the estuary flourish thanks to a mix of seawater and freshwater from the mountains, but they are now receding due to the excessive use of water from inland wells.

For birdwatchers, the area is especially good during the spring and autumn migrations when special species of bird include Sykes's warbler. It is also home to a rare subspecies of white collared kingfisher, which breeds here and in Oman, and nowhere else in the world. A canoe tour by Desert Rangers (+971 4 357 2200) is ideal for reaching the heart of the reserve. You may also bump into one of the region's endangered turtles.

Al Hisn Kalba

Nr Bait Sheikh Saeed Bin Hamed Al Qasimi Kalba
sdci.gov.ae

This complex consists of the restored residence of Sheikh Sayed Al Qassimi and Al Hisn Fort. It houses the town's museum and contains a limited display of weapons. It doesn't take long to get round but there's also a collection of rides for children. Entrance is Dhs.3 for individuals and Dhs.6 for families.

FUJAIRAH ATTRACTIONS

Dibba Castle

Dibba

Hidden away in the Omani part of Dibba (aka Daba), next to vast farms and plantations, Dibba Castle is an interesting place to have a poke around. Built over 180 years ago, it has been restored and, while there aren't a lot of artefacts on show, you can access all the rooms and climb up the towers, where you'll get views over the castle and its surroundings. It is signposted off the road past the UAE border check post.

Fujairah Fort
Nr Fujairah Heritage Village, Al Sharia
Fujairah Fort has recently undergone a major renovation programme. Although you cannot enter the fort itself, the surrounding heritage buildings are open for viewing. Carbon dating estimates the main part of the fort to be over 500 years old.

Fujairah Heritage Village
Nr Fujairah Fort, Al Sharia
Situated just outside the city, this collection of fishing boats, simple dhows and tools depicts life in the UAE before oil was discovered. There are two spring-fed swimming pools for men and women and chalets can be hired by the day.

Fujairah Museum
Nr Fujairah Heritage Village, Al Sharia
+971 9 222 9085
Offers permanent exhibitions on traditional ways of life including the not-so-distant nomadic Bedouin culture. There are also several artefacts on display that were found during archaeological excavations of the emirate. Some of the items include weapons from the bronze and iron ages, finely painted pottery, carved soapstone vessels and silver coins. The museum is open from 07:30 to 18:00 from Saturday to Thursday and from 14:00 to 18:00 on Friday. Entry fee is Dhs.5.

FUJAIRAH HOTELS

Fujairah Rotana Resort & Spa Al Aqah Beach
Al Aqah Beach Fujairah **+971 9 244 9888**
rotana.com
Each guest room has its own balcony and view over the sea. The hotel offers some of the best dining options on the east coast, as well as a spa, private beach and pool.

Golden Tulip Resort Dibba
Mina Rd Dibba **26 836 654**
goldentulipdibba.com
Simple, clean rooms and a great beach make this a good option for an affordable getaway. You can take a dhow cruise and it is also in a great location for snorkelling.

Hilton Fujairah Resort
Al Ghourfa Rd Fujairah **+971 9 222 2411**
hilton.com
Set at the north end of Fujairah's corniche, just a stone's throw from the foothills of

the Hajars, this relaxing resort has all the facilities needed for a wonderful weekend away. If you get tired of lounging by the swimming pool, or activities like tennis, snooker, basketball or even watersports on the private beach, you could always explore the surrounding mountains.

Iberotel Miramar Al Aqah Beach Resort
Fujairah **+971 9 244 9994**
iberotel.com
A lovely low-rise Moroccan style resort with luxurious rooms spread around a huge pool area, the hotel has onsite shops, a spa, a gym and several good restaurants. Also boasts a watersports centre.

Le Meridien Al Aqah Beach Resort
Dibba – Khor Fakkan Rd Fujairah
+971 9 244 9000
lemeridien-alaqah.com
All of the rooms at Le Meridien Al Aqa have views over the Indian Ocean, and the grounds are covered by lush foliage. It is particularly geared up for families, with a kids' pool and outdoor and indoor play areas. There's an extensive spa, a dive centre, and entertainment options include a cinema, bars and restaurants serving a range of Thai, Indian and European cuisine.

Radisson Blu Resort Fujairah
Al Faqeet, Dibba Fujairah
+971 9 244 9700
radissonblu.com
Its pastel exterior might be an acquired taste, but the modern, business-like interior and wonderful restaurants that lie within make this hotel a bit of a treat for the senses. The whole place is reminiscent of a spa, with clean lines and wholesome colours. There is, in fact, a wonderful Japanese spa and plenty of private beach.

Sandy Beach Hotel & Resort
Dibba – Khorfakkan Rd Fujairah
+971 9 244 5555
sandybm.com
Snoopy Island, one of the best diving spots in the country, is right off the coast from the Sandy Beach Hotel, making it a firm favourite with UAE residents. Day trippers can purchase a day-pass to access the pool, and watersports and beach bar services. There is also a Five-Star PADI Dive Centre within the hotel that rents diving and snorkelling gear for exploring the reefs around Snoopy Island.

FURTHER AFIELD

GCC

Over the past decade, the countries that make up the Gulf Cooperation Council (Kuwait, Bahrain, Qatar, Oman and Saudi Arabia) have been busily building their own tourism industries in an effort to diversify their oil-based economies.

Several well-known international brands have opened hotels and governments have made a real effort to promote heritage and culture. To learn more about the region's history, see the UAE chapter on p.208.

BAHRAIN

Just an hour's flight away, Bahrain is small enough to be explored in a weekend away. With traditional architecture, miles of souks, excellent shopping and some truly outstanding bars and restaurants, you can choose from a cultural escape or a fun-packed break. Formula 1 fans will not want to miss the Grand Prix that usually takes place in April – see the *Bahrain Mini Visitors' Guide* for more on what to do on this action-packed island.

BAHRAIN ATTRACTIONS

Bahrain Fort
Nr Karbabad Village, Karbabad Manama
This impressive 16th century Portuguese fort is built on the remains of several previous settlements, dating back to the Dilmun era of around 2800BC. There are several large, informative notices dotted around the area, and some information booklets are available in English. Entry is free and the fort is open from 08:00 to 20:00 every day including Friday. The village that lies near to the entrance to the fort is worth a visit on its own. Nearly every square inch of the place, from walls to satellite dishes, is covered in brightly coloured murals.

Bahrain National Museum
Nr Al Fatih Highway, East Corniche Manama
Situated right on the corniche, this museum documents Bahraini life from before the introduction of oil. Children will love the Hall of Graves and the museum often hosts impressive international exhibits from other museums.

Beit Al Qur'an
Nr Diplomat Radisson Blu Hotel Manama **+973 1729 0101**
The building may not look like much from afar, but a closer inspection reveals walls covered in beautiful Arabic calligraphy. The museum displays examples of historical calligraphy and Islamic manuscripts. Entrance is free, but donations are welcome.

The Burial Mounds
South of Saar Village & West of A'ali Village Manama
One of the most remarkable sights in Bahrain is the vast area of burial mounds at Saar, near A'ali Village, at Hamad Town and at Sakhir. The mounds were built during the Dilmun, Tylos and Helenistic periods and are anything from 2,000 to 4,000 years old. The largest burial mounds, which are known as the Royal Tombs, are found in and around A'ali Village.

La Fontaine Centre Of Contemporary Art
92 Hoora Ave Manama **+973 1723 0123**
lafontaineartcentre.net
This place is a true architectural gem. There are wind towers, cool corridors, a Pilates studio that has to be seen to be believed, a world-class restaurant, an extensive spa, regular film screenings and art exhibitions. These make La Fontaine a unique jewel in Bahrain's crown. The enormous fountain in the courtyard is worth a visit.

BAHRAIN HOTELS

Al Bander Hotel & Resort
Nr Bahrain Yacht Club, Maámeer Sitra **+973 1770 1201**
albander.com
Located at the southern end of Sitra, this resort has a wide range of facilities, including sprawling swimming pools and watersports on the resort's private stretch of beach. Accommodation takes either cabana style or the form of chalets, and there are activities for kids and a variety of food and dining options.

Novotel Al Dana Resort Bahrain
121 Sheikh Hamad Causeway, Al Muharraq Manama **+973 1729 8008**
novotel.com
Conveniently located on the causeway just minutes from the airport and close to the city, yet with its own beach, this hotel is a great choice for families. There's also a large pool, an indoor and outdoor play area, as well as good watersports facilities.

The Ritz-Carlton, Bahrain Hotel & Spa
Off King Abdulla The Second Ave Manama **+973 1758 0000**
ritzcarlton.com
The hotel has one of the best beaches in Bahrain, in a man-made lagoon surrounded by lush gardens. The 600 metre private beach sweeps round the lagoon with its own island and private marina. Along with the nine quality dining venues and comprehensive business facilities, hotel residents have access to all of the club facilities, including the racquet sport courts, the luxurious spa and watersport activities.

KUWAIT
Kuwait may be one of the world's smallest countries but its 500 kilometre coastline has endless golden beaches that remain refreshingly tranquil. From the Grand Mosque to the Kuwait Towers there are many architectural splendours to explore, while Al Qurain House, which still shows the scars of war with its immortal bullet holes, gives you a fascinating insight into the troubled times of the Iraqi invasion. There is also Green Island, an artificial island home to restaurants, a children's play area and a great alternative view of Kuwait's shoreline. For accommodation options, try the Four Points by Sheraton (+965 2242 2055, fourpointskuwait.com), Courtyard Kuwait City (+965 229 97000, marriott.com) or Radisson Blu (+965 2567 3000, radissonblu.com).

QATAR
Qatar once had a sleepy reputation, but things are changing fast. Development and investment in the country means it is becoming increasingly popular with visitors – and even more money is set to pour in following the announcement that Qatar will host the 2022 World Cup, the first major global sporting event to be held in the Middle East. With an attractive corniche, world-class museums (the architecturally-stunning Arab Museum of Modern Art opened to much fanfare in 2011) and cultural centres, and plenty of hotels with leisure and entertainment facilities, the capital Doha makes a perfect weekend retreat. Away from the city, the inland sea (Khor Al Udaid) in the south of the country makes a great day trip. The *Qatar Mini Visitors' Guide* has details of all these activities and includes a pull-out map.

QATAR ATTRACTIONS

Education City
Al Luqta St Doha **+974 4454 0400**
myeducationcity.com
This massive complex contains some of the most tasteful contemporary architecture in the Middle East. Education City is home to a number of the world's best universities and is a clear example of Qatar's plans for the future. A drive through the campuses will no doubt impress any architecture buffs.

Katara Cultural Village
Off Lusail St Doha **+974 4408 0000**
katara.net
Designed as a recreation of a large Qatari village, this is a unique space where musicians, dancers, actors, photographers and artists can meet to collaborate on projects. Open to the public too, there are two concert halls for opera, ballet and theatrical productions, an outdoor amphitheatre, galleries, workshops, cafes, restaurants and souks.

Mathaf – Arab Museum Of Modern Art
Education City Doha **+974 4402 8855**
mathaf.org.qa
Housed in a former school, redesigned by the French architect Jean-François Bodin, Mathaf holds its own, impressive permanent collection and regularly welcomes other exhibitions. Education is central to the museum, and there's a great library full of resources, as well as a museum shop and relaxed, contemporary cafe space.

Museum Of Islamic Art
The Corniche Doha **+974 4422 4444**
qma.org.qa
Architect IM Pei has created an elegant home for this impressive collection. The building is beautifully subtle, with details

drawn from a wide range of Islamic influences. The collection is showcased as a journey through time, countries and cultures, and the oldest pieces date from the ninth century.

Souk Waqif
Off Grand Hamad St Doha
The city's oldest market, Souk Waqif, was renovated in 2004 using traditional building methods and materials. The resulting complex is now one of the most beautiful and authentic modern souks in the Gulf. The most refreshing aspect of the souk area is its dual purpose – tourists can easily stroll the narrow alleys in search of souvenirs while locals can purchase everything from fishing nets to pots and pans. Aside from the many shops and restaurants, there is the Waqif Art Center, which houses several small galleries and craft shops.

QATAR HOTELS

Four Seasons Hotel
Corniche St Doha +**974 4494 8888**
fourseasons.com
One of the finest hotels in the city, the Four Seasons has an exclusive beach and marina, first-class service and excellent restaurants, including the classy Italian eatery Il Teatro.

La Cigale Hotel
60 Suhaim Bin Hamad St Doha
+**974 4428 8888**
lacigalehotel.com
La Cigale has a reputation for first-class hospitality and is an exclusive nightlife destination.

Movenpick Hotel Doha
Corniche Rd Doha +**974 4429 1111**
moevenpick-hotels.com
This modern hotel boasts breathtaking views of the corniche. Popular with business travellers, this boutique-style hotel also attracts tourists with its excellent restaurants and leisure facilities which include a swimming pool, whirlpool and steam bath.

Ramada Plaza Doha
Salwa Rd Doha +**974 4428 1428**
ramadaplazadoha.com
With a new wing now open and plenty of restaurants, bars and lounges to enjoy, the Ramada is a staple of Doha's nightlife.

The Ritz-Carlton, Doha
West Bay Lagoon Doha +**974 4484 8000**
ritzcarlton.com
The opulent Ritz-Carlton is a perfect stop-off if you're sailing in the region, with its 235 berth marina and clubhouse. You can expect 5 star touches as standard at this resort. All of the 374 rooms and suites have breathtaking views over the sea or marina. The beach club has a great selection of watersports and there's a lavish spa. You'll be spoilt for choice with nine international and local restaurants, and can finish the night with either a cigar at Habanos or a cocktail at the Admiral Club.

Sharq Village & Spa
Ras Abu Abboud St Doha
+**974 4425 6666**
sharqvillage.com
Reminiscent of a traditional Qatari town, Sharq Village & Spa is another example of Qatar's insistence on spectacular architecture. The Six Senses Spa was constructed using traditional building techniques and the resort's restaurants are some of the finest in Doha.

W Doha Hotel & Residences
West Bay Doha +**974 4453 5000**
whoteldoha.com
Adding a touch of fun to Doha's rather conservative luxury hotel scene, the W Hotel chain is known for its funky design and an fabulous level and quality of individualised service. Every inch of the hotel is an exercise in architectural minimalism, and its central location makes exploring Doha easy.

SAUDI ARABIA
The Kingdom of Saudi Arabia has some incredible scenery, fascinating heritage sites, and diving locations that are among the best in the world.

Sadly, due to the difficulty in obtaining tourist visas, few expats are likely to experience this diverse and intriguing country. Limited transit visas, available through agents, allow visitors a three day stay in the kingdom en route to another country, such as the UAE or Bahrain. Recent press reports suggest that the Kingdom will issue more tourist visas in order to boost tourism, and give better access to business travellers now that it is part of the WTO. Until then, take a look at sauditourism.com.sa to see what you're missing.

Clockwise from top left: Kuwait sky at night, Qatar's Souq Waqif, Bahrain Fort

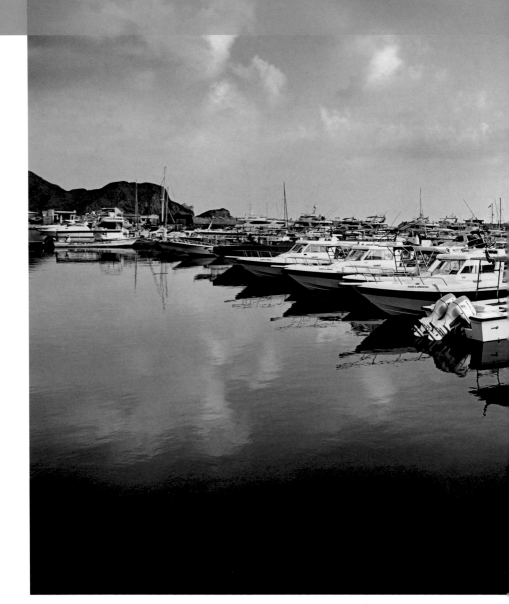

RELAX & **RE-ENERGISE**

ACTIVITIES & HOBBIES **236**
DIVING **246**

ACTIVITIES & HOBBIES

From aerobics and art classes to volleyball and yoga, there's something for everyone in and around Muscat.

AEROBICS & FITNESS CLASSES

Aerobics is an excellent way to keep fit throughout the year, no matter what the temperature is like outside. Classes are available in most of the hotels and you can choose from different disciplines and timings to suit you. Most health clubs around Muscat offer classes in aerobics, with costs per class ranging from RO 1.500-2.500 for members and RO 2.500-3.500 for non-members.

Aqua aerobics is an excellent way to combine aerobic activity with the chance to splash about in water. It's great for people of all ages, body shapes and with various medical conditions, as the water provides protection for the joints. Many of the local health clubs offer aqua aerobics; see the Health Club table (p.148) for more information.

ART CLASSES

Classic Music & Arts Institute
Nr Al Qurum Natural Park Al Qurm
24 560 025
Map **2 H2**
The institute offers an array of art classes for children and adults. Take your pick

BEACH CLUBS

Beach clubs offer a similar range of facilities to health clubs (p.148) but with the added bonus of beach access. They are very popular with families on weekends, and offer a peaceful environment in which you can swim, play sports or just lounge in the sun. Most include some excellent food and beverage outlets, so people tend to stay for the day. Generally beach clubs require you to be a member before you can use their facilities, although many also have day guest rates.

from silk painting, mosaic work, glass painting and pottery. Instruction is given in English and each course requires at least four members to sign up. Sessions are sociable and coffee and tea is served during the class. A 30 minute class costs RO 10 for children or adults, with an hour-long lesson costing RO 20. Discounts are available for morning classes.

The Omani Society For Fine Arts
Hay As Saruj **24 692 090**
osfa.gov.om
Map **2 G2**
The Omani Society for Fine Arts was established in 1993 to encourage fine art and photography in the country. The group organises a number of activities and initiatives to support artists in Oman, and participates in various international exhibitions and events. One of the group's aims is also to encourage and support youngsters and hobbyists.

BIRDWATCHING

Oman is an extremely interesting country for the birdwatcher. Because of its location at the junction of three bio-geographical areas, the keen observer can see Palaearctic and African bird species, as well as others from further east. It doesn't require much to take yourself on a birding expedition – as long as you follow the usual rules of not heading off-road without a guide and all the necessary equipment. But to find out more about birding in Oman and what books are available, log on to birdsoman.com which is updated on regular basis.

Some tour companies offer birdwatching trips and the Muscat Diving & Adventure Centre (see details opposite) is among these. Birdwatchers in Oman are fortunate to be able to take advantage of the fact that the sultanate lies on the migration path for thousands of exotic birds doing the long haul flight between Asia and Africa.

The beaches and lagoons along the coastline are good places to spot a rich variety of marine birdlife, from storks and herons to flamingos and ducks. For a detailed introduction to the birdlife in Oman, the *Birdwatching Guide to Oman* (Hanne & Jens Eriksen and Panadda& Dave E. Sargeant) is invaluable. You'll find other publications and recent photographs on birdsoman.com. You can also contact the Oman Bird Group via the Natural History Museum, and the Muscat Diving & Adventure Center (see below).

Some tour operators (see the list of main tour operators on p.185) also offer birdwatching trips for as little as RO 30 per person.

Muscat Diving & Adventure Centre
As Seeb 24 543 002
holiday-in-oman.com
Map **1 G4**
This company does birdwatching tours throughout the week (upon request). You'll be collected from your hotel and accompanied by an experienced birder who will help you to identify your sightings and fill you in on all the details about Oman's birdlife, from the little green bee-eater to the huge lappet faced vulture. A half-day tour costs RO 55 per person and you need to book a place on a tour 24 hours in advance.

BOWLING

Oman Bowling Centre
Nr Holiday Inn Al Khuwayr Al Janubiyyah
24 480 747
Map **2 F3**
This large bowling centre has 10 computerised lanes and a good set-up that includes a coffee shop where you can get refreshments while relaxing and watching everyone working on their game. It is open 10:00 to 02:00 Sunday to Tuesday, Thursday to Friday and 11:30 to 02:00 Saturday & Wednesday, and the very reasonable price of RO 1.500 (RO 1 before 18:00 Saturday to Tuesday) per game includes shoe hire.

BRIDGE

Muscat Bridge League
PDO RAH Club Ras Al Hamra
99 354 467
Map **2 H1**
Dedicated bridge players in Oman have been organising weekly bridge sessions every Saturday evenings for over 20 years. Attendance ranges from five to seven tables and the game is played over 22 to 24 boards. There is a nominal table charge. Full-day sessions are occasionally held here. The game is friendly, with varying degrees of competence, and visiting players are always welcome. In an effort to popularise the game further, Muscat Bridge League is planning to hold sessions to teach the game to those interested.

CAMPING

Typically, residents of Oman spend their winter weekends camping on the beach, swimming, or tackling the dunes of the Wahiba Sands in a 4WD and trying out sand-skiing. Even the heat of the summer doesn't stop some hardy sports enthusiasts from spending their leisure hours sailing the Gulf or hitting the greens. Alternatively, if you stay in Oman during the summer, you can always retreat to the mountains, where you can enjoy cooler weather.

For more information on where to camp, and some slightly more luxurious destinations to try your hand at a spot of 'glamping', see Places To Stay, p.64.

CANOEING & KAYAKING

There may not be any rivers or lakes in Oman, but its coastline is fantastic for canoeing and kayaking enthusiasts. The coast is full of inlets and sheltered bays, many of which have isolated beaches that make for excellent picnic spots. Paddling allows you access to otherwise hidden places of natural beauty and it's a good way to appreciate the country's abundant bird and marine life. Adventurous canoeists with sea-going canoes can tour the stunning waterways of the Musandam (p.192), where you'll see some spectacularly rocky coastlines with fjord-like inlets and towering cliffs – some of which reach heights of 1,000m. Many hotels and adventure centres hire out sea kayaks, or you can bring your own.

Muscat Diving & Adventure Centre
As Seeb **24 543 002**
holiday-in-oman.com
Map **1 G4**
If you are going to take to the waters, a good way to do so is in a kayak and with a guide. You've got over 1,700km of rugged coastline to explore and you can stop at any of the small fishing villages in between. Muscat Diving & Adventure Centre hires out single and double sea-kayaks. Renting a kayak (with or without a guide) costs from RO 20 per person. You'll need to put down a credit card deposit – presumably to prevent you from sailing off into the sunset.

CANYONING
Oman's interesting topography makes canyoning a popular activity here. It's not for the timid though, as it's often challenging and treacherous and involves using various methods, such as abseiling, scrambling and swimming, to ascend or descend a canyon. There are some awesome treks in the country including Wadi Shab, Snake Canyon, Wadi Hajir, Wadi Haylayn and Wadi Qashah, each with its own individual challenge and beauty and each with opportunities for canyoning.

There are risks associated with scrambling or abseiling down uneven and slippery surfaces so it's really advisable that you go as part of a group and ensure that you have at least basic knowledge of first aid. Dress lightly, take sun protection along and always expect to get wet.

Although canyoning is an activity more commonly enjoyed by experienced groups, some tour companies do offer adventurous treks.

CAVING
The caving network in the Hajar Mountains of Oman is extensive, and much of it has yet to be explored and mapped. The area includes what's believed to be the second largest cave system in the world. The most famous cave in Oman, and the most stunning in terms of size, is the Majlis Al Jinn. Entering it is not for the fainthearted as it starts with a 180m abseil from the entrance in the roof. Caving here ranges from the fairly safe to the extremely dangerous. Even with an experienced leader, it's not for the casual tourist or

the poorly equipped. It's important to understand the dangers. Make sure you take plenty of water and basic first aid equipment. Some of the cave exploration here is among the most hair-raising in the world and should only be attempted by experienced, fit cavers, preferably accompanied by someone who has traversed the caves before.

The Al Hoota Cave (also seen as Al Hotti or Hoti Cave) can be found at the foot of Jabal Shams in Tanuf Valley. At over five kilometres long, Al Hoota was previously one of the most challenging caves in Oman, with its one entrance being strictly for experienced cavers equipped with ropes, safety equipment, and a guide familiar with the cave. However, the Oman Ministry of Tourism has recently completed an overhaul of the caves, making them safer and transforming them from an adventurous location reserved only for experience cavers, into a fascinating ecotourism attraction. The first entrance to the cave can be found near the village of Al Hotta (about 1,000m above sea level), and the other is near the town of Al Hamra (about 800m above sea level). Inside the cave, you can see an amazing collection of crystals, stalactites and stalagmites, but perhaps the most interesting sight is the underground lake in the main cave. The lake is inhabited by thousands of blind, transparent fish, who rely on floods to carry in nourishment from the outside world.

The lower cave can only be reached in a train that transports visitors through a tunnel near the main entrance. You will be able to see the underground lake from a special viewing balcony (monitors are provided so that you can get a more close-up view). After you have toured the caves, spend some time in the visitor centre (this, by the way, is where you will get your ticket for the cave tour). A natural history museum was still under construction at time of going to print, but the visitor centre has a couple of restaurants and some heritage shops where you can buy locally made pottery, silver and carpets. To get to the caves, head for Nizwa, and when you reach Nizwa old town take the road for Al Hamra. When you get to Wadi Tanuf, turn right and head for Al Hotta. The cave is approximately a 20 minute drive from Nizwa. Please note that the main cave is closed during July and August. See alhootacave.com for more information. One of the largest sinkholes in the world,

THE LOST WORLD

In spite of winding down for kilometres under Jabal Shams and being, according to estimates, some two million years old, Al Hoota Cave was actually only discovered just over 50 years ago when a local villager went in search of a goat that had fallen through the cave's opening. Today, the cave welcomes thousands of visitors a year.

Teyq Cave, is located between Taqa and Mirbat. The two wadis in the sinkhole keep it topped up with water when it rains. Sultan Qaboos University houses an active Earth Sciences Department, and this is a good source of information on the sinkhole (squ.edu.om).

Muscat Diving & Adventure Centre
As Seeb **24 543 002**
holiday-in-oman.com
Map **1 G4**
Try caving with the skilled guides and instructors of the Muscat Diving and Adventure Centre. Among their hottest destinations is the 7th Hole. – the company offers a two-day expedition through the cave. It includes a compulsory half-day training session before the trip to ensure that you're familiar with the skills, techniques and equipment you will need, and the guides will assess your confidence and skill levels at the same time. The breathtaking abseil in and out of the 120-metre deep chamber is not to be missed. Prices start at RO 130 per person (self-drive) which includes equipment, training sessions and a two-day trip.

CLIMBING
First-time climbers in Oman need to get used to the nature of the rock – most climbs are on fairly soft and brittle limestone that's not always reliable. Rock that looks strong can easily flake and become detached when pulled too hard, so climbing in Oman is often more subtle than athletic, requiring balance and patience. The friction though is superb, and invites delicate moves using pressure and counter pressure.

Apart from the quality of the rock, Oman's hot climate is another limiting factor and during the summer months of May to September the temperatures can reach 50°C. For the dedicated climber it is possible to climb through the summer, if you pick your crag carefully. North-facing crags are usually in the shade in the afternoon. The usual climbing equipment will be sufficient, but you'll have to bring your own gear as there are no dedicated shops in Oman selling it.

The Muscat Diving and Adventure Centre (listed opposite) can supply you with equipment and also guide you to the best climbs.

Muscat Diving & Adventure Centre
As Seeb **24 543 002**
holiday-in-oman.com
Map **1 G4**
MDAC have qualified instructors who will show you the ropes of climbing and help you discover a more adventurous side of Oman. Their routes include some good, large walls and they've been busy bolting more sports routes. The instructors offer tuition on an individual or group basis. Apart from climbing, the centre also offers activities such as abseiling, canyoning, caving, kayaking and trekking. All equipment is provided, and prices start at RO 8 per person.

COOKERY CLASSES
Several of the premier hotels in Muscat offer gourmet nights. These special evenings provide food lovers the opportunity to create the works of a renowned chef. Naturally, tasting and sampling is absolutely unavoidable in the course of the class, but the real treat comes right at the end when the feast is laid out for all to enjoy.

Most of the chefs allow you to walk away with their recipes in hand, so you're all set to create your own in-home fine dining. Contact the food and beverage departments of the major hotels to find out if they hold gourmet nights.

CRICKET
With the numbers of expats from cricket loving nations living in Oman, as well as an increasing number of Omanis entering the sport, there is plenty of opportunity to get yourself in a team here.

There are currently 60 teams registered with the Oman Cricket Association (omanicricket.com), but many organisations have their own teams for inter company competitions and the sport is also becoming more popular in schools. The Oman national team won the Gulf Cup in 2009 and recently finished third in the 2011 Asian Cricket Council T20 championship after defeating hosts Nepal in a playoff.

If you want to start your own team and play in the various leagues and regional competitions, you can register with the Oman Cricket Association. The only conditions are that you have at least one

Omani in your team, and that he bats in the top five. If you don't have an Omani on your team, you have to play with only 10 men.

Oman Cricket Association
Ruwi **24 787 085**
omanicricket.com
Map **2 J3**
The Oman Cricket Association has been organising league tournaments since 1979. There are currently 60 teams, playing in eight divisions. Every team must register with the association to play in these league. The cricket season begins in September and lasts until March, with tournaments beginning sometime in April. If you're interested in playing please contact Madhu Sampat or Jesrani.

CYCLING
Oman has tremendous scope for cycling, with many routes that run both along the beautiful coastline and through the rugged hills and mountains. Cycling is a great way to get to know Muscat too – you can ride along the corniche at Mutrah, weave through old Muscat, and scale the roads through the spectacularly rocky mountains to Al Bustan and Qantab. However, it currently remains a fairly niche pastime.

While riding in traffic requires caution in any country, it requires particular attention in the Middle East. Drivers are not very sympathetic towards cyclists and don't allow them much space or time. You need to be particularly careful in the busy parts of town, especially at junctions and roundabouts. On the plus side, road surfaces are decent and punctures are a rarity. Joining a cycling club will quickly introduce you to the routes and safety issues of cycling in and around Muscat.

Most of the main roads in the city have a hard shoulder that provides a fairly safe lane for cyclists. Although bikes are not allowed in most of Muscat's parks, there are some nice rides through the quieter, residential, and pleasantly green areas of the city.

Muscat Cycling Club
Various Locations **99 324 594**
new5.muscatcyclingclub.com
The Muscat Cycling Club welcomes both road and off-road cyclists, so whether you prefer speeding down the big Omani highways or bumping your way over rocks and through wadis, the group will happily accommodate you. This fast growing group currently has more than 80 riders and meets regularly for weekend rides, with off-roaders heading out on Thursdays and road cycling groups going out on Fridays. They have an active social schedule and always welcome new members. Contact Michel le Fur for further information.

DANCE CLASSES

Club Olympus Gym & Fitness Centre
Grand Hyatt Muscat Hay As Saruj
24 641 234
muscat.hyatt.com
Map **2 G2**
Proving that getting fit isn't all about gym apparatus and endless reps, the Grand Hyatt's health club also offers a variety of enjoyable and social dance classes. Children aged 8 and older can sign up for modern dance classes, while adults can choose from salsa, belly dancing and various Latin dance. Some of these classes are mixed. Call the hotel to find out about timings and when the next course will begin.

Peter Emery Langille
Various Locations **92 605 102**
Feel like trying something completely different? Peter Emery Langille offers English and Scottish country dancing, as well as traditional Sri Lankan Sinhalese dancing. He welcomes everyone to his classes, whether you're an accomplished dancer or not – all you need is plenty of energy and the willingness to try something new. All the dances are taught to the appropriate music, which often provides half of the evening's fun. They are also usually quite social affairs. He will teach a class or dance workshop wherever there are eight or more people who want to learn, and his regular classes are held at various venues in the Al Batinah region, Muscat and Barka. You don't need to bring along a partner, but couples are welcome. For the latest venues and times, or to enquire about demonstrations or a specific class, email him on freeman@squ.edu.om.

DESERT DRIVING COURSES

National Training Institute
Al Khuwayr Al Janubiyah
24 472 121
ntioman.com
Map **2 F3**
If you would like to learn how to put your 4WD through its paces off-road, or to pick up some expert advice on desert, wadi or mountain driving, sign up for one of NTI's courses. You will first learn the theoretical side of driving off-road, followed by plenty of hands-on practice in the vehicles. Topics covered include how to control skids, braking safely on sandy or rocky surfaces, and learning how to drive in the desert. Instructors also offer advice on safety precautions, emergency procedures and what to do when things go wrong. The NTI also runs a two-day defensive driving course; if you're struggling to get used to Omani driving, this could help you learn to cope with the roads and other drivers.

DIVING

Blu Zone Water Sports
Marina Bander Al Rowdha Sidab
24 737 293
bluzonediving.com
Map **2 L3**
Blu Zone is a family-run PADI Gold Palm IDC five star dive centre with experienced instructors and guides. They offer daily dive trips as well as courses from beginner to instructor level and, for those wanting to hone specific skills, they offer wreck, deep, navigation, search and recovery, peak performance and night diving speciality courses too. The Bubblemaker course is available for children aged 8 to 10 and there's a Junior Open Water Diver course available for children aged 10 years and older who are keen to get underwater. Non-divers can go on dolphin watching cruises and snorkelling trips. The centre also has a swimming pool, kids' pool, restaurant and a Jacuzzi for you to relax in after a dive.

Capital Area Yacht Centre
Haramil **24 737 712**
caycoman.com
Map **2 L3**
CAYC Divers offer a variety of activities including diving, snorkelling and wreck dives. They also offer PADI courses for those who want to learn how to dive, and for divers who want to specialise or advance their skills. CAYC is a members-only club but members are welcome to bring guests along. Dive boats go out every day of the week.

Extra Divers Leisure
Al Sawadi Beach Resort & Spa Barka
97 259 099
alsawadibeach.com
Map **1 F4**
With a recently refurbished dive centre, Extra Divers offer good facilities for people to take dive courses in, as well as trips to the famous islands the company is named after. The dive centre has new equipment for 15 divers and 50 snorkellers, a classroom with space for four students, and a library full of the latest PADI videos and DVDs. They offer a range of PADI courses from Bubblemaker and Discover Scuba for kids, all the way to Dive Master for adults. Their dive excursions go out to 17 distinctly different sites around the Dimaniyat Islands.

Extra Divers Musandam
Golden Tulip Khasab Hotel Resort
Khasab **26 730 501**
musandam-diving.com
Map **1 E1**
Extra Divers Musandam has a dive centre in Khasab on the Musandam Peninsula. A relatively new operation, the facilities include equipment hire, a compressor, tanks, dive shop and a dry room. Staff offer instruction for SSI and courses in German, English and French. The company runs daily two-tank dives for RO 47 from 09:00 to 15:00. This charge includes equipment, soft drinks, fruit and biscuits.

Global Scuba
Civil Aviation Club Al Udhaybah Ash Shamaliyyah **99 317 518**
global-scuba.com
Map **2 D2**
Global Scuba's dive centre is conveniently located just 25 to 30 minutes away from the Daymaniyat Islands by boat, and they also offer dive trips to Fahal Island. They run a range of PADI courses, from beginner to advanced and in a whole lot of specialities. They also do dolphin watching and snorkelling trips for those who prefer to keep their heads above water.

Explore Oman from the sea

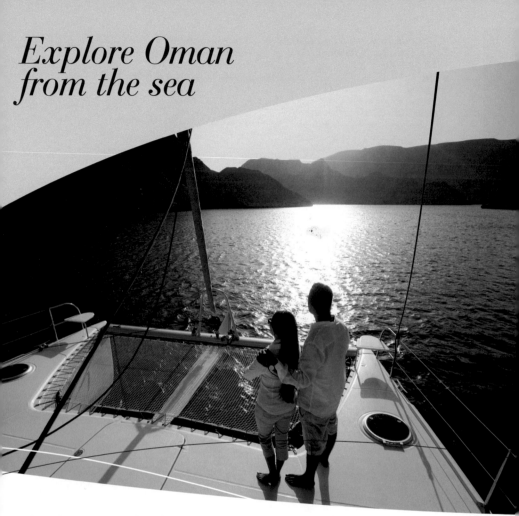

23°37'55"N 58°16'03"E

Natural beauty extends way beyond Oman's stunning coastline. Its sea is home to some of the most colourful life on the planet. Equidistant between two of the capital's most adored maritime destinations, the jaw dropping Damaniyat Islands and Bandar Khayran, Almouj Marina is the perfect base to explore these diverse environments.

For berthing enquiries please contact the Almouj Marina team on **+968 2453 4400** or at **info@almoujmarina.com**

Hormuz Line Tours & Cruises
Nr Al Maha Petrol Station Khasab
050 543 2717
Map **1 E1**
Among the range of activity tours that Hormuz Line offer, are also plenty of options for avid divers. You can book yourself on a single day or even an overnight cruise on a dhow and spend your time snorkelling. You can also try scuba diving off the beaches and islands of Khasab for RO 50. Speak to the company if you have specific needs and requests and they will organise an expedition according to your needs and wants.

Khasab Travel & Tours
Nr Khasab Airport, Khasab **26 730 464**
khasabtours.com
Map **1 E1**
With diving in the UAE and surrounding areas being fairly limited, a dive trip off the Musandam peninsula is a welcome addition to your log book. Diving here has been described as being an 'experienced diver's dive' because of strong currents. That said, the area offers a variety of sites, some more sheltered and shallow, Sidab which are perfect for beginners. Khasab Travel & Tours will take out groups with a

minimum of two adults to enjoy the good visibility and the excellent marine life.

Muscat Diving & Adventure Centre
As Seeb **24 543 002**
holiday-in-oman.com
Map **1 G4**
Catering to all of your water sporting needs, the Muscat Diving and Adventure Centre makes the most of the abundance of fascinating sea life that Oman has to offer. Experienced and proficient instructors are on hand to do Discover Scuba courses, or to organise trips for snorkellers and divers. A two-dive trip with full equipment costs RO 55.

Nomad Ocean Adventures
Nr The Harbour, Al Biah Dibba
050 885 3238
discovernomad.com
Map **1 E2**
Nomad Ocean Adventures can organise excursions to your specifications. In addition to offering diving and snorkelling, they can also arrange for you to go on a dhow cruise, to go deep sea fishing, trekking or stay overnight in a traditional Arabian campsite. For qualified divers

Diving in Oman

a single dive, with all equipment, starts at RO 20, while a weekend package at a guesthouse with two dives and full equipment costs around RO 70. For more details, call Christophe on his UAE mobile (+971 50 885 3238) or email him on chris@discovernomad.com.

Oman Dive Center
Nr Qantab & Barr Al Jissah, Bandar Jussa
Al Amrat **24 824 240**
extradivers-worldwide.com
Map **1 G4**
Popularly known as ODC, this centre is set in the picturesque and sheltered bay of Bandar Al Jissah. The bay is perfect for snorkellers and for novices to practise their new skills in before venturing out to the ocean. The training facilities here have been awarded five-star PADI status, and they run the full range of courses, including a first aid one. Activities include day and night diving, snorkelling, underwater photography and wreck diving. Day trips to the Daymaniyat Islands, the Quriyat wreck and a new wreck dive at Al Munnassir can be arranged for divers and snorkellers, and ODC provide accommodation in their luxury barasti-style huts on the beach.

Omanta Scuba Diving Academy
Boat House, InterContinental Muscat
Hay As Saruj **97 700 564**
omantascuba.com
Map **2 G2**
Located in the grounds of the InterContinental Hotel, this dive centre (known as OSDA) is one of the newest and most advanced dive centres in Oman. Offering a full range of courses (OSDA is a 5 star instructor development centre), as well as daily trips to some top-notch dive sites, the centre is something of a diving hub, with a multi-media classroom, a compressor room and a well-stocked dive store selling brands like Scubapro and Dive System. Plus, for those not diving, there are all the hotel facilities to enjoy. Popular trips include Junn Island, Doc's Wall and Clive Rock.

Scuba Oman
Khasab **99 558 488**
scubaoman.com
Map **1 E1**
Scuba Oman offers diving and snorkelling trips, PADI courses, dolphin watching and more. The company can take underwater

fans to the depths of over 100 dive sites, with all levels of experience catered for. A range of courses are available, including discovery dives and specialities like rescue and open water sessions.

DRAMA GROUPS

Muscat Amateur Theatre
Various Locations **24 514 144**
muscatamateurtheatre.com
The Muscat Amateur Theatre group was formed in 1980, and to date it has put on over 50 plays by a wide variety of playwrights. Their repertoire ranges from Neil Simon to Shakespeare, so you're sure to find a play to suit your theatrical tastes. The group performs at various venues in Muscat's hotels, including the Hotel InterContinental.

ENVIRONMENTAL GROUPS
Oman is fortunate to have some beautiful natural assets together with a government that is interested and active in environmental issues, always making them a high priority. There are currently three nature reserves where there is a facility for controlled tourism – the Damaniyat Islands, the Ras Al Jinz turtle reserve and the Arabian Oryx Sanctuary. You may need a permit to visit these fascinating reserves and to find out more information about them, refer to their entries in the Exploring chapter (Damaniyat Islands Nature Reserve, p.174, Ras Al Jinz Turtle Reserve, p.176 and Arabian Oryx Sanctuary, p.174).

In addition to the government's efforts to promote protection of the environment, there are also several interest groups and environmental organisations in Oman. The Sultanate is a member of the International Whaling Commission, and although it is not yet a signatory to CITES (Convention on International Trade in Endangered Species), it follows the guidelines laid down by CITES, such as stopping trade in endangered species.

On an everyday level, there are increasing numbers of bottle/can recycling points around Muscat. These are sponsored by various local companies, and are mainly located near shopping centres.

DIVING

With more than 2,000 kilometres of coastline and all manner of underwater treasures to discover, diving in Oman is a real treat.

If you are fortunate enough to live in Oman, year-round diving is one of its most breathtaking pleasures. Oman has a long coastline and a variety of underwater treasures – coral reefs and shipwrecks provide a multitude of dwellings for an array of marine life. The quantity and variety of sea life in what is still a quiet diving destination will keep even the most jaded diver enthralled. While you're underwater, it won't be other divers you bump into, but turtles, cuttlefish, stingrays, moray eels… the list is endless.

While Oman's waters suit novice and advanced divers alike, experienced divers with a penchant for more adventure will find cave diving a unique experience. Please be aware that all divers must have a diving permit from the ROP to dive in the waters off Oman, and most obtain their permits through the club or dive centre they are diving with (it is usually included in the dive price).

Night dives are very popular, and provide the opportunity to see many nocturnal marine creatures that you wouldn't normally see. The phosphorescence in Oman's waters is more visible after dark and this green-blue substance, released by plankton as a result of chemical reactions from their vigorous movements, makes for an amazing underwater display.

If all this sounds wonderful but you've never dived, don't worry – there are plenty of centres that provide training in PADI or BSAC, depending on your preference. PADI's Open Water Certification is ideal if you're on holiday here or want to get into the sea without too much delay, and your skill levels are easily added to with a variety of Advanced and Specialist courses. BSAC training courses are of a longer duration and especially good for the novice diver who wants to take it slowly and thoroughly.

Below is a list of a few of the most popular dive sites in Oman, but keep in mind that each site is extensive and you could spend years exploring every nook and cranny.

Fahal Island

Located in Muscat's Qurm region. This island has around 10 dive sites and is good in a variety of weather conditions, so even if you head out on a particularly windy day, there's usually at least one area of the island that will offer perfect diving conditions. Diving depth is from three to 42 metres. Around Fahal Island are isolated reefs, a swim-through cave, and artificial reef balls. The most notable fish in the area are angelfish, trigger fish and large broom-tail. Also, look out for diamond-shaped stingrays (who enjoy backflipping out of the water), honeycomb eels and a few friendly sharks. The islands also sport a large variety of corals. Non-divers will find good snorkelling on the western side of the island.

Bander Khayran

Located near Muscat, 20 to 30 minutes by boat or 40 minutes by 4WD. This area consists of a small fjord system littered with inlets. The diving depth here ranges between one and 30 metres. It's known for diverse and beautiful corals – table, bush, boulder, brain, hedgehog, cauliflower, and pore corals, often all intermixed and always in a variety of colours. Of course, all that coral means a wide variety of marine life is attracted to the area too.

Al-Munassir Naval Shipwreck

Located near Bander Khayran. In April 2003, the Royal Navy of Oman sank this naval ship to create an artificial reef in

Omani waters. It lies at a depth of about 30 metres and spans a length of 84 metres. All the ship's canons and guns were removed before it was sunk, and the rooms in the ship have been opened up for divers to penetrate them easily. Making your way through the ship's engine, dining and other rooms is an excellent opportunity for divers to learn orientation. It's also a great site to watch marine life go about its daily business within and around the vessel.

Daymaniyat Islands

The Daymaniyat Islands span approximately 20 kilometres from Seeb to Barka and consist of nine islands, named numerically from D1 to D9. The Oman government has designated the islands and their surrounding reefs a national nature reserve, and access to the islands is controlled. This has allowed for the growth of an extensive coral reef and abundant sea life, and the islands are well known for the magnificent diving. The diving depth of the islands ranges from one to 30 metres.

Oman Dive Center

Finally, Oman Dive Center is a popular destination, not just for learning to dive but also for a fun weekend away from the city. There are two organised daily dives. A two-dive package, including all the equipment and transport at dive spots, costs around RO 35, although that figure will be a little higher still if you'd like to dive the Dayminiyat Islands.

For RO 5 (less on weekdays), you can get a day pass to the Oman Dive Center and make use of its facilities. The centre has a dive pool, which you can use when there are no lessons in progress, as well as a special kids' pool. Both pools are shaded. You can also use the private beach. The dive centre has an excellent in-house restaurant and, if it isn't too hot, you can sit on the shaded terrace and enjoy a delicious lunch.

There are also a number of barasti style wood and straw chalets on the beach that are available for hire if you want accommodation with a difference. To get there, when following the road from Ruwi and Wadil Kabir to Al Bustan, you will see the village of Qantab signposted to the right just past the top of the hill. Take this right turn and follow the road until you reach the roundabout, where you can turn left for Oman Dive Center or go straight for the Barr Al Jissah Resort at the end of the road.

Bays are ideal for diving and snorkelling

ESO Whale & Dolphin Research Group

Various Locations **92 497 536**
eso.org.om

Part of the Environment Society of Oman (ESO), this is a group of volunteer scientists and other interested parties who collect and disseminate knowledge about Oman's dolphins and whales. They are independent researchers whose work is recognised and approved by local Ministries. They work closely with the Oman Natural History Museum, the Ministry of Agriculture and Fisheries, and the Raysut Marine Laboratory. The group's primary activities include emergency rescue services for whales and dolphins, maintenance of a database of sightings and strandings, and cooperation with local tour operators to promote responsible whale and dolphin-watching activities. If you are interested in volunteering or just want to find out more about local whales and dolphins, check out the website or call Howard Gray on 92 497 536.

The Historical Association Of Oman

Various Locations **24 563 074**
hao.org.om

The Historical Association of Oman is a non profit-making organisation, established in 1972, with the aims of documenting and distributing information about Oman's history, whether natural, national, linguistic or cultural, and to encourage research. In addition to the usual activities including lectures, trips and publishing, the HAO conducts research and assists, researchers from within and outside the country. The most recent projects embarked upon are two documentation projects of old settlements in Bawshar and Manah, funded by the US Ambassadors Fund for Cultural Preservation. Meetings are held twice a month on Monday evenings from 20:00, with venues varying so call for more details.

PDO Planetarium

Nr Oil & Gas Exhibition Centre, Seeh Al Maleh St Mina Al Fahl **24 675 542**
pdo.co.om
Map **2 H2**

Astronomers of all ages can gaze up at the twinkly dome of the PDO Planetarium, which opened in 2000. Since then, seven different shows have been presented, three of which have been locally produced. On Wednesdays at 19:00 and Thursdays at 10:00 shows are held in English, and on Wednesdays at 16:00 and Thursdays at 11:30 shows are held in Arabic. All last about an hour and are free of charge. The planetarium also hosts guest lecturers, conferences and workshops and can arrange special social gatherings when astronomical events occur. Booking is required in advance. For more info see the website.

FIRST AID

KTS Group

Various Locations **99 470 104**
ktsgroup.org

Kibara Technical Services is an international organisation that provides first aid training in 82 different countries, including Oman. Instruction is given in English and Arabic and the course teaches practical skills. Courses include emergency first aid, basic first aid and advanced trauma and life support. Courses can be carried out in a convenient location with timings to suit you. The National Training institute (p.242) also offers first aid courses.

Oman Dive Center

Nr Qantab & Barr Al Jissah, Bandar Jussa Al Amrat **24 824 240**
extradivers-worldwide.com
Map **1 G4**

While first aid will be covered briefly in some of the dive training it does, the Oman Dive Center also offers a general introductory first aid course aptly called the Emergency First Responder. This course is suitable for everyone, not just divers, and can be taught either at the dive centre, or at a location of your choice.

FISHING

Coastal Fishing

The Sultanate of Oman boasts some of the best surf fishing in the world. The coastline from Al Khaluf down to Salalah is home to a variety of species belonging to the warm waters of the Indian Ocean. Depending on where you've chosen to cast your line, the species you're likely to catch include blue fish, trevally, shark, black bream, rays, grouper and spotted grunter. Blue fish will range from five pounds upwards, and ray and shark anywhere between 10 and 200.

Light and heavy tackle combos are a must for fishing these waters. All the various species tend to take turns in feeding during the day and night. Ensure your secondary tackle supplies are plentiful as you will often experience toothy beasts taking your bait. Fishing along these coastal coves is seasonal due to the severe weather conditions caused by the monsoon.

The coastline of Oman beyond Al Khaluf can be taxing on both vehicles and supplies. This is not the place for a jaunt down to the beach with rod in hand and, in fact, most people choose not to travel the roads with their boats in tow, but rather to sail from one harbour to the next. The villagers along the coastline of Oman are very friendly and always happy to help, but do remember that you're in a Muslim country and have respect for their traditions and religious beliefs. Maps of the Oman coastline are available and it will be very helpful to have one on your first few trips at least.

Big Game Fishing

The season from October to April is best for big game fishing. The rest of the year tends to be slow, as the fish move further south to avoid the higher waters in summer. The true Indian Ocean meets the Gulf of Oman off Ras Al Hadd and you'll clearly see the difference between the colours and surface textures of these two bodies of water. The most common big game fish during the high season is yellowfin tuna. A tricky fish to hook by nature, successful fishermen sometimes land them in weights exceeding 100 pounds. Although much larger specimens are available to offshore anglers, these are usually only caught south of Muscat or much further out than the average fisherman cares to venture. On rare occasions yellowfin tuna close to the 250lb mark have been caught within 10km of Muscat's coast.

Sailfish dominate the waters off Muscat during September and October, and it's thought that they migrate through the region on their way to the Arabian Gulf for breeding. They're often caught close to shore and vary in weight from 60 to 110 pounds. Mai mai or dolphin fish are found in abundance from the end of July to September. Travelling in schools, these fish make for some fast, light-tackle action. They average about 15lb, but you might occasionally land

something in the 35-45lb range. Black marlin sometimes travel into the coastal waters off Muscat but there's only been one confirmed capture to date – and that one weighed in at a whopping 400lb. Reports that marlin can be found in greater abundance off the coastal area of Ra's Al Hadd have been confirmed by the local commercial fisheries who estimate that an average of 10 marlin a day are brought in by their boats. The season is typically from November to April. The length of the Oman coastline is met by underwater mountain ranges and drop-offs that go down to 300m and more in some areas. Due to the deep water ridges rising up into the warm coastal shallows, an abundance of game species are found feeding on the bait fish, that in turn thrive on the nutrients brought up from the depths – an excellent example of the natural food chain.

Hormuz Line Tours & Cruises
Nr Al Maha Petrol Station Khasab
050 543 2717
Map **1 E1**
With their main office in Khasab on the Musandam Peninsula, Hormuz Line are happy to organise excursions to your specifications. If your interest in fishing is more leisurely you can get a good insight into the traditional lifestyle of Omani fishermen and the Bedouin from their dhow cruise fishing tours. You'll share the early morning hustle and bustle of life in the fishing harbour and visit a number of different villages for a glimpse of a way of life that hasn't changed much over the years. If you want to actively fish while you're out on one of their dhow charters, have a chat to them about what they can organise for you.

Sidab Sea Tours
Nr Marina Bander Al Rowdha Haramil
99 461 834
sidabseatours.com
Map **2 L3**
While there will always be tales of the one that got away, and some days when all of them do, you're almost guaranteed an end to the tall stories when you've got a local skipper who knows the waters like the back of his hand. Sidab Sea Tours organises four-hour professional game fishing excursions for RO 180 per boat (maximum six people), with barracuda, tuna, marlin and sailfish as the intended

targets. For a more relaxed experience you can try traditional handline fishing 'Omani style'. Whatever you choose as your bait, all tackle and equipment is provided and soft drinks are available on board. A longer all day excursion can be arranged, which includes a beach lunch, for around RO 300.

FOOTBALL

As in most places in the world, you don't have to travel far to see a game of football in Oman. Rural villages usually have a group knocking a ball around on the local sand and rock pitch – and you could probably join in if you wanted. There are also often teams kicking about on the beaches, particularly at the InterContinental beach strip.

There's a semi-professional football league in Oman that teams such as the Oman Club, Sidab and Quriyat participate in. A maximum of two expatriate players are allowed to join each of these clubs, so the majority of expat football fans play in the weekly social soccer games at the grounds of the Oman Club. The main teams include Loan Service, Deuch PDO, Aerworks, British PDO, Royal Flight and the Sultan Qaboos University Squad. Unfortunately, all of the above teams only accept players from within their own organisations, making it difficult for newcomers to get into the game. So you could always start a team of your own, either via your company or group of friends.

The schools have taken charge of the footie scene for children. The PSSL schools soccer league has five age categories, ranging from under 9s to under 19s. The students play from September to December, with the Irishman's cup for the under-13s a fitting climax to the season. The Al Sahwa school and PDO Elementary usually fare well in the youngest age group, while the ABA School and Indian School Wadi Kabir tend to dominate the under 11s. The ABA and the Indian School Muscat are strong in the under 13 sector, while Muscat Private School, British School and ISM are the main rivals in the under 15s category.

In the older age groups, Royal Guard and Sultan School tend to be the dominant forces. Touch football is also played at the PDO Elementary playing field Sunday and Tuesday evenings from 17:30 till 19:00 – you simply need to turn up.

GOLF

Golf in Oman is a growing sport, both in popularity and the number of courses on which to play. Traditional 'brown' courses are gradually being replaced with a range of green courses, such as the 18-hole Muscat Hills Golf and Country Club (designed by top golf course designer David Thomas) in the hills behind the Golden Tulip Hotel in Seeb. The completion of Oman's first green golf course is hoped to boost the country's tourism sector, and put the Sultanate on the golfing world map.

Another 18-hole links course, designed by Greg Norman, was formally opened at The Wave in 2011. There are several golf tournaments on Oman's annual calendar, such as the Oman Ladies' Open Championship, the Men's Oman National Championship and the Ras al Ghala Trophy.

Those who have never played golf in the Middle East should be warned that the game here can be more physically demanding than elsewhere in the world – even acclimatised golfers avoid playing in the heat of the day during the summer months. It's always wise to carry plenty of drinking water and wear a sun hat.

Almouj Golf > p.251
The Wave, Muscat Al Mawalih Ash Shamaliyah **22 005 990**
almoujgolf.com
Map **2 B2**
Following the opening of the first nine holes of the course in 2011, the rest of the course is expected to open fully at some point in 2012. A country club is currently being designed too so weary golfers can take a load off their feet and relax into the stunning sea-side vista. Other plans include an academy, flood lit practice holes and driving range.

Ghallah Wentworth Golf Club
Nr Dolphin Residential Complex Bawshar **24 591 248**
Map **2 E4**
This is a really decent challenge for any level of player. The club has a driving range built on concrete tee boxes and a few sets of clubs for hire. Players should bring their own Astroturf mats for teeing off. There are two separate golf seasons; an 18 hole season in winter, and a nine hole season in summer, while competitions for both of these two categories are organised accordingly. Lessons are also available upon request.

ALMOUJ GOLF
THE WAVE MUSCAT · OMAN

Oman. Stunning beaches, incredible deserts, breathtaking mountains and tricky bunkers.

إلهام عماني. تصميم جريج نورمان.
Inspired by Oman. Designed by Greg Norman.

Marco Polo Golf Course
Crowne Plaza Resort Salalah Salalah
23 238 000 crowneplaza.com
Map **4 K8**
A relative newcomer on the Oman golfing scene, this is a grass course that includes a driving range, putting green and a nice training area. The course itself is an unusual nine hole, par three that is actually set in a coconut grove. You can hire golf clubs if you wish, and even benefit from the assistance of a professional golf instructor on request.

Muscat Hills Golf & Country Club
Nr Muscat International Airport
Muscat Hills **24 510 065**
muscathills.com
Map **2 C4**
The Muscat Hills Golf & Country Club has been carefully carved into the jebels, with great care taken to maintain the natural beauty of the surrounding landscape and wadis. It opened in March 2009 and is the first 18 hole par 72 championship grass course in the Sultanate of Oman. In addition to the golf course, the Muscat Hills Golf & Country Club offers members and residents tennis and squash facilities, a large swimming pool, a gymnasium and a fairly lavish spa. Although not yet

completed, the smart clubhouse boasts some F&B offerings, with restaurants, a conference room, a pro shop and lounges all on their way.

HASHING
Sometimes described as 'drinking clubs with a running problem', the Hash House Harriers form a worldwide family of social running clubs. The aim of running in this setup is not to win, but to merely be there and to take part. The first hash club was formed in Kuala Lumpur in 1938, and it's now the largest running organisation in the world, with members in over 1,600 chapters in 180 countries.

Hashing consists of running, jogging or walking around varied courses, often cross-country, laid out by a couple of hares. It's a fun way to keep fit and meet new people, as clubs are very sociable and the running is generally not competitive.

Jebel Hash House Harriers
Various Locations **99 506 454**
jebelhashoman.com
Founded in 1985, the Jebel Hash is a social, non-competitive running club that forms part of the worldwide Hash House Harriers family. There are always two trails to follow

Almouj Golf

– one for those who prefer to walk, and a longer one for the more energetic joggers or runners. A social gathering follows every run, so be prepared; running fitness may not be the only kind of endurance that you need. The Jebel Hash runs take can place anywhere within Muscat and its surroundings. Apart from meeting new and interesting people, it's a great way of seeing some places you might have otherwise missed.

Muscat Hash House Harriers
Various Locations **99 329 630**
muscath3.org
More familiarly known as the Muscat Hash, this group meets every Saturday evening at various locations around the Omani capital, depending on where the hare has set the run. Meeting times also vary in accordance with the changing times of dusk and there is a RO 1 fee for each meeting you attend. The celebrations laid on for various international holidays are always lively.

HIKING
There are many documented treks in Oman that are rated according to difficulty. But, whatever your hiking skills or fitness, Muscat is full of easily accessible local walks that you can do on your own or as part of a group. If you prefer to venture further afield, Jabal Shams has numerous hikes. Check out the *Oman Trekking Explorer* for 12 hiking routes printed on handy cards.

The land's ancient geological history has created inspiring gorges, wadis, peaks, ridges and plateaus. The terrain is heavily eroded and shattered due to the harsh climate, but there are many excellent routes to be enjoyed. These range from short easy walks leading to spectacular viewpoints, to longer, more arduous treks up high peaks. Many of the paths follow ancient Bedouin and Shihuh trails through the mountains. Some of these are still used today as the only means of access to remote settlements.

The main mountainous area, shared in part with the United Arab Emirates, is the Al Hajar Range, which splits into the Northern, Eastern and Western Hajars. The highest peak in this range, at just over 3,000m, is Jabal Shams in the west (in Arabic 'jabal' means mountain and 'shams' means sun). The spectacular 'Grand Canyon of Oman' is also found in this area. One of the shorter, less rigorous hikes, at just four hours, is the Balcony Walk (or Rim Walk) along the Jabal Shams Plateau. Incredible canyon views and a trek through an abandoned village will delight everyone who summons up the energy to try it out.

Adventure trekkers looking for a more challenging experience will be inspired by the Al Hawb to Jabal Shams summit route. This hike requires good climbing abilities and an overnight camp. It may take up to 12 hours to reach the summit and the trek can be a 20 hour round trip, depending on the descent path you choose, but the views at the top are the ultimate reward for all that hard work.

In the south, near Salalah, are the Dhofar Mountains, whose highest point is Jebel Samhan. Many of the mountains here are over 2,000m, providing excellent walking and fabulous views.

Be sure that on any hike, short or long, you consider the weather conditions. Always carry plenty of water and snacks, check your routes before setting out, notify a friend as to your whereabouts and your itinerary, and wear light boots and appropriate clothing. Take a compass or GPS and check the customs and conditions of the area before taking on any long trips.

Be warned: no mountain rescue services exist, and anyone venturing out into mountains should be reasonably experienced, or be with someone who knows the area. As long as you are properly prepared, your trek will be an outstanding experience leaving you with nothing but fond memories… and possibly a sore pair of feet.

Donkey Trekking
Various Locations **99 348 440**
Donkey Trekking offers trips along Oman's fairly new hiking trails in the spectacular Hajar Mountains. Donkeys carry your luggage, freeing you up to enjoy the views. The trails take you into remote areas of the mountains, near the village of Misfat Al A'briyeen, where you can sleep under the stars, eat traditional food and get into the local culture. Trips can be custom designed, depending on your requirements, to include trekking without donkeys and desert camping. Call Ahmed for more details or email thestars200@gmail.com.

Khasab Travel & Tours
Nr Khasab Airport Khasab **26 730 464**
khasabtours.com
Map **1 E1**
One of the most peaceful ways to visit the mountains of Musandam is to trek through them. Khasab Travels & Tours offers a number of routes, their favourite being one that takes you on a crossing from Sham Fjord to Kumzar. Your trail winds past an abandoned village with old pottery and derelict houses, and includes an overnight stop in the mountains. The views over the Gulf of Arabia and Gulf of Oman are amazing and have to be experienced. Groups must consist of at least 10 adults.

Muscat Diving & Adventure Centre
As Seeb **24 543 002**
holiday-in-oman.com
Map **1 G4**
Thanks to Oman's varied terrain, your trekking adventure can be as easy or as difficult as you want it to be. Whether you decide on little more than a brisk walk through a pleasant wadi, or a challenging hike through harsh rocky desert, the Muscat Diving and Adventure Centre has a number of different routes for you. Each tour has a minimum group size of four.

HORSE RIDING

Al Fursan Stable
Al Qurum Natural Park Al Qurm
99 386 978
Map **2 H2**
Al Fursan Stable (also known as Shah Mohammed Khalili's stables) caters for riders of all ages and levels; from beginners through to competent riders. In addition to riding and show-jumping lessons

given by their qualified trainers, it also offers pleasure trips to Qurm Garden, Qurm Nature Reserve, the Creek, and the breathtaking beach in Shati Al Qurm, all accompanied by a guide for RO 15 per hour.

Qurm Equestrian School
Al Qurm Natural Park Al Qurm
99 339 222
Map **2 H2**
Located in the beautiful Qurm Park, the Qurm Equestrian School is open 16:00 to 18:00 every day and teaches everyone from beginners to advanced riders. The school offers beach rides, carriage rides and carriage rental for weddings or special events. There are instructors who provide one-hour lessons in riding and show jumping, for those who just want to ride for enjoyment or those who want to ride competitively. The school has donkeys for small children to ride, and it has introduced a Pony Club for kids. Call the number above, or call Astrid on 99 422 401.

ICE HOCKEY

Oman Ice Hockey
Al Khuwayr Al Janubiyyah
omanicehockey.com
Map **2 F3**
The Omani National Ice Hockey team currently consists of 20 players, a coach, a team coordinator and a team manager, and that team was invited by the Kuwait Committee of Ice Hockey to compete in the first GCC Hockey Cup, which was held in Kuwait in May 2010. There are currently efforts to register Oman Ice Hockey as an Omani Association and, if that happens, it will become the governing body for ice hockey in Oman, organising teams and competitions for both junior and senior level ice hockey. Check out the website for upcoming fixtures and tournaments.

SPORTS & LEISURE FACILITIES
Muscat's health and beach clubs are one-stop fitness and leisure shops. They are mainly located in hotels and include access to the beach facilities, the hotel health club and various activities. You can expect to find specialised instructors for everything from aerobics to salsa, and swimming to tennis. Many health clubs have separate facilities for men and women, as well as 'ladies only' times. Shop around to see which clubs offer timings and facilities that are best suited to you.

ICE SKATING

Fun Zone
Al Qurum Natural Park Al Qurm
24 701 495
funzoneoman.com
Map **2 H2**
Opened in December 2011, the Fun Zone ice rink is open all day from 09:00 right through to midnight. Skate sessions cost RO 3 per person, including skate hire,

and sessions are 90 minutes long – visit the website for accurate session times. Mondays are ladies-only between 09:00 and 18:00.

JETSKIING

Much of Oman's coastline is open and accessible and jetskiing is becoming a more popular pastime here, especially along the coast of Muscat. Be wary of fishermen and swimmers and it's a good idea to remain 500m from the shore. In the past jet skiers have been prosecuted for accidents involving jetskis. Most hotels and resorts hire out jetskis for about RO 7 to 10 for half an hour. Make sure you get a life jacket and a helmet with the jetski.

KIDS ACTIVITIES

Finding activities to keep your kids busy could keep you very busy. Fortunately there are a few options available. Avid skateboarders who have PDO membership can go to the PDO skate park. Kids here are usually aged from 5 to 14, and they meet a few times during the week to skate together, show off new tricks and swap tips. The park has a specially constructed half-pipe, ramps and rails. Unfortunately, skaters without membership to PDO will have to stick to skating on the streets.

The British School Muscat also runs a few kids' activities and is the venue for meets for the 1st Cubs and Beavers and the 4th Muscat Brownies. You can contact the school on 24 600 842 to find out more details. Al Sawadi Beach Resort (p.67) has some excellent facilities for children throughout the year, including a kids' pool and a huge playground. During the summer the resort has a special kids' festival, where children can take part in arts and crafts, sports and games, while you relax around the pool.

Little Town, an indoor playground in Bareeq Al Shatti mall (p.296), opened in early 2009 to provide a space for kids to burn off energy while parents browse the shops or enjoy a coffee in one of the nearby cafes. It is open from 09:00 to 22:00.

Kids' Rest

Al Qurum Complex Al Qurm **92 358 583**
Map **2 H2**
Kids' Rest is a children's play area situated on the first floor of Al Qurum Complex

(p.300). It's very popular with mothers of young children who can leave them here while they go off and do their shopping. Apart from a huge range of colourful, clean and safe toys, Kids' Rest also has a soft-play area for tiny tots.

Little Town

Bareeq Al Shatti Hay As Saruj
99 426 636
littletownoman.com
Map **2 G2**
This play area in shopping mall Bareeq Al Shatti (p.296) is a welcome addition to the area. If offers an indoor play area for kids aged up to 7, has a coffee shop for parents and is open from 09:00 to 21:00 from Saturday to Tuesday, 10:00 to 22:00 from Wednesday to Thursday and 16:00 to 21:00 on Friday.

KITE SURFING

Kite surfing is one of the fastest growing and most extreme water sports, not only in Oman, but in the region as a whole. But, with plenty of uncrowded beaches and superb wind conditions, kite surfing is definitely on the rise in Oman too.

The sport involves you surfing the waves on a wakeboard while holding on to and steering a large kite that powers you along. You'll find a small group of kite surf enthusiasts who gather on Thursday and Friday afternoons at Azaiba Beach. This is a relatively quiet and sandy spot that offers perfect kite surfing conditions when winds exceed 10 knots. Be careful of the occasional car or group of people wandering across the beach, especially in the early evenings – you wouldn't want to become entangled in them.

During summer, hardcore kite surfers escape the relatively light conditions of Muscat and head for the east coast, where the winds can often get up to 15 to 30 knots.

In fact, Masirah Island, just off the east coast, is becoming one of the region's must-visit kite surfing spots; in summer, kiters from all over the GCC flock there for the high winds and temperatures that are far lower than in Dubai, Abu Dhabi and even Muscat. At present there is no kite surf school or kite surf shop in Oman, but if you have a chat with any one of the regulars they will be able to offer advice about where to buy equipment and how to get started.

LIBRARIES

Biblioteque Francaise

Omani-French Centre Madinat As Sultan Qaboos **246 975 79**
ambafrance-om.org
Map **2 G2**
This is a lending library and information resource for French books and videos. Bibliotheque Francaise carries a wide selection of fiction and non-fiction literature by French and foreign authors, as well as magazines, French videos and children's books. Books are lent for a two-week period. The library is open from 16:00 to 20:30 Saturday to Sunday, 09:30 to 12:30 and 16:00 to 20:30 Monday to Tuesday, 17:00 to 20:00 Wednesday and 09:00 to 12:00 Thursday.

Information Resource Centre (IRC)

American Embassy Madinat As Sultan Qaboos **24 643 400**
http://oman.usembassy.gov
Map **2 G3**
This highly informative reference library specialises in US policy, legislation, trade data and social and cultural issues. In addition, the IRC offers students and researchers access to the internet and computer databases. There is also a reading section – the IRC carries around 20 periodicals in hard copy, including *Time, Newsweek, Business Week, National Geographic, Fortune and the Harvard Business Review* so you can keep updated without paying the high cover prices of imported titles. Full text versions of more than 200 online journals and magazines are available. There are many books on American states, literature, art, social history and science as well as information on Oman.

Oman Chamber Of Commerce & Industry

CBD Area Ruwi **24 763 700**
chamberoman.com
Map **2 K3**
This small but well-stocked library has a range of reference books, periodicals, newspapers, trade and industrial catalogues and directories. Most are in Arabic, but there is a small collection of English books on business or trade-related subjects, such as economics, accounting, management and finance. An internet facility is available at a nominal charge and there are a number of CD-ROMS and business related videos. You may borrow books from the library but you must pay a bond of value of the book plus 100% of the value, plus 500 baisa per book. The library is open from 07:30 to 14:00 from Saturday to Wednesday and from 08:00 to 12:00 on Thursday.

Public Knowledge Library

Nr PDO main gates Mina Al Fahl **24 673 111**
publiclibrary.gov.om
Map **2 J2**
This library contains over 14,500 volumes, with a balanced split between Arabic and English. The subjects covered are mainly in the areas of science and technology, but there are also materials covering topics in the humanities and social sciences, such as environmental issues and Omani history. You'll also find general encyclopaedias, language resources, dictionaries and atlases here, and a video collection has been added to the library's resources.

MARTIAL ARTS

Black Stallion Martial Arts

Al Falaj Hotel Bayt Al Falaj **24 702 311**
Map **2 J2**
Black Stallion offers a variety of martial arts classes for children and adults. Options include karate, taekwondo kicks, aikido, judo, nun-chacko, kick-boxing, Philippine arnis and gymnastics. Classes range in cost from RO 20 for children and RO 25 for adults per month or RO 3 per session. Timings are from 17:00 to 21:00, Sunday to Thursday. Whatever your skill or fitness levels to begin with, these classes can help increase both your physical prowess and mental well-being.

Fit & Tough

Hammer Gym, Al Khuwayr 33 Al Khuwayr Al Janubiyyah **99 629 490**
Map **2 F3**
Fit & Tough holds classes at the Hammer Gym. They teach students at all levels and provide one-on-one coaching with street combat expert Jess Beltran. The classes will help you to gain confidence, develop strength (of the mental and physical sort) and improve your physique.

MOTOCROSS

Oman Automobile Association
Nr Golden Tulip Hotel Hay Al Urfan
24 510 239
omanauto.org
Map **2 C3**
The Oman Automobile Association operates under the umbrella of the Oman Automobile Association (OAA) and offers many activities, one of which is motocross. The OAC has an excellent one-kilometre sandy motocross track complete with hills, jumps, twists and turns. It's terrific for learning on or sharpening your skills. Membership of the club is required and you need to provide your own bikes and equipment although there is an area where you can store your bike for a fee. The OAC hosts a number of local and international rallies throughout the year with off-road rallies held once a month.

MOTORCYCLING

Bikers Oman
Nr Golden Oryx Rest Ruwi
24 789 680
http://sjsoman.com/bikersoman
Map **2 J3**
If you're a biker or a bike enthusiast looking to indulge your passion, or at least share it with other petrol heads, check out bikersoman.com. By joining this online biking fellowship you'll be one of the first to know about what's new in town, any planned bike rides, who's selling their lean mean machine, and you'll even score special discounts at outlets that sell biking gear, parts, accessories and souvenirs. New bikers can find out more about the tests involved and are able to hire a bike through the website for RO 5. Email contactus@bikersoman.com for more information.

Harley Owners' Group – Muscat Chapter
Nr Zakher Mall Al Khuwayr Al Janubiyyah
24 489 428
hog-muscat.com
Map **2 G3**
When the Harley Davidson showroom opened in 1998, the Muscat chapter of the Harley Owners Group commenced its activities. The Harley Owners' Group (HOG), which includes both expat and Omani riders, meets at the 'HOG Pen' (coffee

Mountain biking

shop) in the Harley Davidson showroom regularly and arranges activities, rides and events for Harley Davidson enthusiasts and their families. Rides are usually held on Tuesday evenings and Friday mornings, while an overnight ride is organised at least once a month (in the cooler months). For more information visit the Harley Davidson showroom or visit the HOG Muscat website.

MOUNTAIN BIKING
Muscat and its surrounding areas have some great mountain biking routes – due to its location amid the rocky mountains along the coast, the city offers rides virtually from your door. There are many off-road tracks that wind their way through the quieter neighbourhoods, wadis and along the coast. The Bawshar dunes are close to the city and also offer some great rides, as do Sayh Ad Dhabi or the route from the InterContinental to the desalination plant.

Riding in the mountains is adventurous and generally rocky, technical and challenging. There are many tracks to follow and the terrain is on a par with the classic trail areas of Utah and Arizona in the USA. Those who are just getting into mountain biking should start on the tracks in the gentler hilly areas. For hardcore mountain bikers there is a good range of topography, from highly technical rocky trails to mountain routes that can take hours to climb and minutes to descend! Be prepared and sensible – the sun is strong, you'll need far more water than you think and it's very easy to get lost or to have an accident.

Muscat Diving & Adventure Centre (holiday-in-oman.com) now offers mountain biking trips. For more information on biking in Oman, or to get together with other mountain bikers contact Muscat Cycling Club (see p.179 in Cycling).

MUSIC LESSONS

Associated Board Of The Royal Schools Of Music
As Seeb **99 440 441**
abrsm.org
Map **1 G4**
The Associated Board of the Royal Schools of Music was established in 1889, as part of an agreement between the Royal Academy of Music and the Royal College of Music. The board acts as an examining body for local music examinations and aims to improve the standard of musical education across the Sultanate. It offers a scheme of examinations suitable for candidates at different stages of ability in all the main orchestral instruments, as well as in singing and music theory. It also maintains a database of suitably-qualified music teachers in Oman.

Classic Music & Arts Institute
Nr Al Qurm Natural Park Al Qurm
24 560 025
Map **2 H2**
The institute's team of fully trained musicians offers a wide range of lessons in piano, vocals, cello, Arabic violin and beginner oud, and classical and acoustic guitar. They often have other visiting musicians and they are happy to connect musicians with teachers in the area. Costs are kept reasonable and children are encouraged to use their skills in ensemble work. Lessons are available for children aged 7 and above. Each child receives a report from their teacher and regular

concerts are arranged for the institute's aspiring musicians.

Melody Music Centre
Way 1952 Darsayt **24 782 834**
Map **2 J2**
The Melody Music Centre opened in the mid '90s. Since then, it has obtained recognition from the UK's Associated Board of the Royal Schools of Music to teach both a theoretical and practical syllabus. Examinations take place for different grades, ranging from Preparatory Grade One to Grade Eight levels. It also offers classes in piano, keyboard, guitar, drums, conga drums, violin, arnatic vocal and classical dance (Bharatanatyam). The centre has other branches in Al Khuwayr (24 486 647) and in Wadi Kabir (24 811 482).

PILATES

Palm Beach Club
InterContinental Muscat Hay As Saruj
24 680 000
ichotelsgroup.com
Map **2 G2**
Pilates is a method of exercising that works on building your core stability and strength. It involves the use of exercise apparatus or work on mats. The Palm Beach Club at the Hotel InterContinental offers Pilates classes every Wednesday. The classes are an hour long and start at 09:30. They cost RO 3 for members and RO 5 for non-members and booking is essential.

QUAD BIKES

The rough terrain and dunes of Oman's remote areas attract all kinds of motor sports enthusiasts. If you're into motorbikes, quads or dune buggies, and you have your own, it's easy to take yourself and a few friends for a fun day out – you don't run the risk of bumping into anyone else and you can explore at will. The Bausher Sands, just outside Muscat, are very popular and a great place to fly your bike or quad off a dune. If you don't have your own quad, you can rent one at many of the hotels and beach resorts. Unlike dune buggies, quad bikes have no roll cages and therefore extra care should be taken. Where possible get training and wear protective gear to make the most of your thrills-and-spills adventure.

Clockwise from top left: Climbing, motocross, quad biking

Off-Roading

With vast areas of virtually untouched wilderness in Oman, wadi and dune bashing are activities many residents enjoy immensely. Most off-road journeys are on existing tracks to protect the environment from any damage – the sandy dunes and rocky wadis support a surprising variety of flora and fauna that exist in a delicate balance.

Dune bashing, or desert driving, is one of the toughest challenges for both car and driver – it's also a great deal of fun once you've mastered it. The golden rule is never to go alone. If you're new to this activity it's essential to go with an experienced off-roader. Driving on sand requires very different skills to road driving. Useful equipment to take with you includes shovels, strong tow ropes, a pressure gauge, foot pump or compressor, matting or planks of wood, a full tool kit for the car, a spare tyre in good condition, a car jack (with an extra piece of wood to prevent it from sinking in the sand), extra petrol and plenty of water for both cars and passengers.

If you don't think your driving skills are up to scratch, you could try dune bashing through any of the major tour companies (see Tour Operators, p.185). All offer a range of desert and mountain safaris.

Driving in the wadis is usually more straightforward. Wadis are (usually dry) gullies, carved through the rock by rushing floodwaters, following the course of seasonal rivers. The main safety precaution to take when wadi bashing is to keep your eyes open for developing thunder storms – the wadis can fill up quickly and you will need to make your way to higher ground smartly to avoid flash floods.

It is always advisable to go off road with at least two vehicles. If anything goes wrong, you'll be glad of an extra pair of hands and a tow. Although it requires marginally less skill than in the desert, when you drive in the mountains and wadis you still need to use your common sense and forward planning (you need to think ahead about choice of gears for the hills and river crossings).

Close to Muscat are the Bawshar dunes. Although this is a small area, it has numerous criss-cross tracks through the sand that provide you with an easy introduction to this challenging sport. When you're ready for more serious stuff, head for the Wahiba Sands, just over two hours from Muscat, for endless stretches of undulating desert. Or try The Empty Quarter (Rub Al Khali), which is spectacular in its seclusion, remoteness and the impressive size of the dunes.

The Hajar Mountains offer amazing drives through rugged mountain scenery. You'll pass remote mountain villages and freshwater rock pools as the rough tracks take you to incredible views up to 3,000m above sea level.

The better-known wadis are often over-visited, especially by tour companies. This is not necessarily because they're the best but because they are the easiest to get to. If you are more adventurous and are prepared to travel further, you can find some amazing, almost untouched places.

For further information and tips for driving off road, check out the *Oman Off-Road Explorer*. This fabulous book features 26 detailed routes (along with detailed maps and GPS points), stunning satellite imagery, information on outdoor activities, striking photos and a useful off-road directory.

REIKI

Reiki (pronounced ray-key) is a hands-on healing art developed in the early 1900s by Mikao Usui in Japan. The word Reiki comes from the Japanese words Rei and Ki, meaning universal life energy, and is used to describe both the energy and the Usui system of using it. The technique is based on the belief that energy can be channelled into a patient by means of touch and converted into 'universal life force energy', which has a healing effect.

Like meditation, Reiki can emotionally cleanse, physically invigorate and leave you more focused. You can learn the art of Reiki to practice on yourself or others, directly or remotely. Reiki master Peter Emery Langille does all levels of attunements and is available for individual appointments, classes, group sessions and distant healing work as well. You can call him on 92 605 102 for information or to make an appointment, or email him on freeman@squ.edu.om.

RUGBY

Muscat Rugby Club
Nr American British Academy
Al Khuwayr Al Janubiyyah
muscatrugby.com
Map **2 G3**
Located next to the American British
Academy, the Muscat Rugby Club is both
a sporting facility and a social centre. The
club currently has more than 100 members
and they all enjoy free use of the facilities
and free flights to away games (for playing
members). The club takes part in the
Arabian Gulf Rugby League and several
other tournaments, including the Bahrain
10s and the Dubai 7s. The rugby season
runs from September to April; adults
play on Sunday and Wednesday at 18:00,
children aged 7 to 16 play on Mondays
from 17:00. There is also a big social scene
connected to the rugby club with regular
events for all ages. Check the website for
further information.

RUNNING

Muscat Road Runners
Various Locations
muscatroadrunners.com
The Road Runners meet twice a week
and run competitively on Tuesdays, with
a designated race organiser responsible
for timekeeping and results. Social runs
take place every Sunday, where a member
of the group hosts a run and provides
refreshments afterwards. Summer runs
tend to be short due to temperatures.
Winter runs are longer, culminating in the
half marathon in late February.

Oman Athletics Association
Musandam Bldg Ruwi
omanathletic.org
Map **2 J3**
The OAA's main role is to train the
national Omani team in track and field
events, preparing them for national
and international competitions.
The organisation also arranges local
competitions – in activities from running to
marathons – which are open to everyone.
There are categories for adults and children
and medals are awarded for first, second
and third positions. The OAA maintains a
list of contacts for all sporting activities, so
if you would like details about a particular
event or interest, email oma@mf.iaaf.org.

SAILING

Sailing off the coast of Muscat is a
wonderful experience, both in winter
when temperatures are perfect for
watersports, and in the summer
when it offers a great escape from the
scorching heat inland. Unfortunately,
much of the club sailing in and around
Muscat is closed to outsiders and the
facilities are limited to employees of
particular companies. That said, sailing
regattas are held regularly and the
people at Marina Bander Al Rowdha
(2473 7288), Capital Area Yacht Centre
(2473 7712) and Almouj Marina (2453
4400) can give you more information
on these. There is also the Oman Laser
Association (p.261). This is definitely a
sport where word of mouth is the best
way to get information.

Many companies will take you out for
a pleasure or fishing cruise, either for a
couple of hours or for a full day. Muscat
Diving and Adventure Centre (24 543
002) offer a wide range of activities so
call them and find out what they can
offer you. There are also companies, like
Oman Charter (p.181), from whom you
can charter your own boat – whether
you take it for a single day or several
weeks is up to you.

Oman Laser Association
Various Locations **97 718 393**
rahbc.pdorc.com
The Laser is a popular one-man
sailing boat and in Oman Laser sailing
is represented by the Oman Laser
Association. The OLA have been
promoting the interests of laser sailing
and small boat sailing in general here
for over 20 years. They organise around
10 competitions annually. The races
are competitive yet friendly affairs,
where the more experienced sailors
readily share tips and techniques with
others. Most races are held at the RAH
Recreation Club, with occasional events
in Sawadi Resort or the Marina Bandar
Al-Rowdha. There are occasionally co-
organised events aimed at expanding
the Omani Laser fleet, that include
instruction for beginners and organised
races. Races are organised at places like
Al Sawadi Beach Resort, Civil Aviation
Beach Club, Capital Area Yacht Club and
Marina Bander Al-Rowdha. Find out
more on http://rahbc.pdorc.com/Sailing/
laser/laser-home.htm.

Oman Sail

The Wave, Muscat Al Mawalih Ash Shamaliyah **95 153 789**
omansail.com
Map **2 B2**

A relatively recent addition to the sailing schools, Oman Sail has grown out of the successful national programme to reinvigorate the skills of sailing that served in times gone by. Very popular with schools and other associations, the lessons are taught by professional instructors and even sometimes the superstar sailors themselves, who take a very hands-on method of education. Sailing packages consisting of theory and practical aspects start from around RO 40 and are available from a number of locations around Oman.

SANDBOARDING & SKIING

Head out to any stretch of the desert in the interior of Oman, find yourself some big dunes and feel the rush of the wind as you take a fast ride down the sandy slopes. It's an easy sport to learn, it doesn't hurt when you fall, and you'll feel a real sense of achievement when you master it and glide to the bottom. Most people tend to use old snowboards, but you'll even find the odd skier taking to the sandy slopes. Standard snowboards or skis can be used. The best places for sandboarding and skiing are where you'll find the biggest dunes – the Wahiba Sands area or the massive dunes of the Empty Quarter in the south-west of the country. Many tour companies and camps

Sailing

provide equipment and direction. One of these is the Desert Camp at Wahiba Sands, which offers sandskiing or surfing from their permanent campsite. Call 99 311 338 for more information.

SCOUTS & GUIDES

1st Muscat Guides
Various Locations bgifc.org.uk
British Guides in Foreign Countries is a division of the United Kingdom Guide Association, which caters for girls wishing to continue their Guiding while living overseas. The groups are open to all nationalities, but there is sometimes a waiting list and priority is given to girls who have been members in their own country. All of the packs base their programme on the British system to provide continuity.

1st Oman Scout Group
Various Locations **99 242 078**
omanbga.org
The Scout Association started in Oman in 1975 and acts under the auspices of the United Kingdom British Groups Abroad. There are different groups for different ages: Beavers (ages 6 to 8), Cubs (ages 8 to 10), Scouts (ages 10 to 14) and Explorers (ages 14 to 18). The association focuses on outdoor activities such as camping, map reading, astronomy, cycling, first aid and conservation, and members can earn a variety of challenge badges. For more information, contact Sonia on the number above.

SINGING

Muscat Singers
The British School – Muscat Madinat As Sultan Qaboos
muscatsingers.org
Map **2 G2**
One of the longest established choirs in Muscat, this group welcomes new singers from all backgrounds and nationalities. The choir covers a broad spectrum of music, ranging from classical and light opera through to folk and jazz. Much of the singing is in parts and there is always a need for new members of all singing styles. The ability to read music is not essential but previous experience of choral singing is an advantage. The minimum age is 15 years, but there is no

Snorkelling

upper limit. The choir meets on Saturday evenings (starting from 19:30) at the British School Muscat.

SNORKELLING
The number and variety of sea creatures are incredible and the seas are pristine. You don't need much to get into this activity: a mask, snorkel, a pair of fins to motor you along and plenty of sun protection (a rash vest is a very good investment). Most hotels or dive centres will rent out equipment, and you can buy good gear at dive shops. Costs vary greatly so shop around.

SOCIAL GROUPS

American Women's Group Oman
Various Locations
awgoman.com
An international organisation that has been serving the women of Muscat for more than 30 years, AWG boasts almost 1,000 members representing over 45 nationalities. Meetings are held in local

hotels and each meeting features a short programme, announcements of interest, sign-up sheets for various activities, and the opportunity to meet and talk with other women. See the website for meeting times. For membership details, contact the Membership Chair by email.

Caledonian Society Of Oman
Various Locations
caledoniansocietyofoman.com
One of the oldest expatriate societies in Oman, having been founded back in the early 1970s. It is the only British society that's officially registered with the British Embassy here, but it is also possibly one of the least known – maybe because it doesn't hold regular monthly meetings, unlike the American Women's Group and the Women's Guild of Oman. The society, however, does arrange annual events, some of which are purely for fun and others are fundraisers (although also fun). For more information, visit the website.

The National Association For Cancer Awareness
Various Locations **24 498 716**
ocancer.org.om
Cancer survivor Ms Yuthar Al-Rawahy promised herself while she was under active treatment that, if she were to survive her third bout of cancer, she would develop a patient advocacy group in Oman. The association's aims are to create awareness, teach self-examination in order that early diagnosis can be made, and help people to accept their diagnosis and work towards successful treatment. The association has met with much support from cancer patients, friends and relatives and it is the first patient advocacy group in the country.

Royal Omani Amateur Radio Society
Madinat Al Ilam **24 600 407**
roars.org.om
Map **2 G2**
ROARS was founded in 1972 and its membership currently stands at 188. The Society offers courses to Omanis who want to obtain amateur radio licences, with classes held on Sunday and Tuesday evenings. But anyone of any nationality may join, as long as they have a current amateur radio licence from their home country. Membership costs RO 15 per year and the society holds seminars, expeditions, trips and social gatherings several times a year.

Women's Guild In Oman
Mina Al Fahl
womensguildoman.com
Map **2 J2**
The guild has an excellent reputation in Oman for distributing funds to charities in the country. While fundraising is an important part of the guild's aims, it also sets out to provide an opportunity for women to meet and enjoy a varied programme of speakers and events (including weekly coffee mornings and the popular Crystal Ball annual fundraiser) and to offer its members fellowship. Membership is open to women of all ages and nationalities and it currently boasts over 1,000 members. The regular newsletter is an invaluable resource for events around Muscat and classified ads.

SQUASH

Grand Hyatt Muscat
Way 3032 Hay As Saruj **24 641 234**
muscat.grand.hyatt.com
Map **2 G2**
The Club Olympus Gym & Fitness Centre has squash courts that are available for both games and coaching. If it's lessons you're interested in, call Mr Fathi on 99 416 391 for more details – he will happily arrange coaching for players of all ages and skill levels. Lessons cost RO 13 for 45 minutes.

SURFING
The idea of surfing in Oman may not inspire images of Hawaii style waves, but you'd be surprised by how popular the sport is here. And really, you generally have all the ingredients you need for a good day's surfing. Although it might not be one of the world's great surf spots, Oman is certainly one of the better places to catch a wave in the Gulf because part of its coast lies on the Indian Ocean. So surfers in other Gulf countries, like the UAE, often make regular trips to Oman to get their fix. While there are currently no major surf clubs in Oman, the Dubai surfers' group has an excellent website that gives information on surfing in the UAE, the Arabian Gulf and in Oman (surfersofdubai.com).

The eastern side of Masirah Island is one of the better surfing spots. It's easily reached by ferry from Sana on the mainland, followed by a short drive to the other side of the island. Ferry times depend on the tide. It obviously depends on the season but the waves here average four to six feet.

SWIMMING

Most hotels have swimming pools that are open for public use. Day charges range from RO 2.500 (at Al Falaj) to RO 10 (at the five-star hotels), but expect to pay a bit more at the weekends and keep in mind that the beach clubs tend to be more expensive. You can also swim off the beaches, whether at a public beach or hotel beach club. Remember to be modest in your choice of swimwear and to wear it only on the beach. The tides and currents here can be surprisingly strong, so do not underestimate them. With this in mind, take due care when swimming on quiet beaches. For your own safety it's better to choose somewhere with a few people around.

In summer, jellyfish can be a problem, both in the water and when washed up on the beach. All varieties are somewhat poisonous but one particular variety, the box jellyfish, can be lethal. Stone fish and sea snakes are also not creatures you want to tangle with, but they're shy, retiring types and do tend to keep well away from the more populated areas. Swimming lessons are widely available and prices of these will vary.

TENNIS

Tennis is popular in Oman and you'll find courts available for public use at hotels, or courts belonging to private organisations that are only open to members. Many hotels have floodlit courts to allow play in the evenings, when temperatures are a bit lower. Prices for hiring courts vary between about RO 3 and RO 6. The Oman Tennis Association oversees the national Omani team in tournaments at home and abroad. The association also organises a variety of annual local tournaments. These are mainly held at hotels and are usually for a mixture of standards, but some are for professionals only. Coaching is available at the hotels by a variety of freelance coaches and again prices vary. Expect to pay between RO 11 and RO 20 for an hour-long private lesson. Fathi provides coaching for groups, individuals and kids at the Grand Hyatt (24 641 155).

Cliff Club
Crowne Plaza Muscat Al Qurm **24 660 660**
ichotelsgroup.com
Map **2 H2**
Resident tennis professional Vafu (92 352 204) offers tennis coaching at reasonable rates. A one-hour private lesson costs RO 13 for members and RO 15 for non-members, or you can buy a package: five lessons for RO 60 (RO 70 for non-members); 10 lessons for RO 115; 20 hours for RO 230 (RO 260 for non-members). Group lessons are also available for groups of two to seven people.

TRIATHLON

Surprisingly, considering the extreme heat, training for and participating in triathlons is popular here. Clearly, enthusiasts of this sport enjoy a good challenge and Oman certainly provides one. Check out the Oman Triathlon page on Facebook for information on training, as well as the numerous annual events. Hash House Harriers clubs (p.252) are also good sources of information regarding triathlon schedules. Events are also usually well advertised at hotels and in local newspapers.

VOLLEYBALL

The Bawshar Club leads the way for sport-loving women in Oman. It was the first Omani Club to start a woman's football team and now has organised a women's volleyball tournament, in conjunction with the Oman Women Sports Development Committee (OWSDC). The tournament covered football, volleyball and basketball and was open to girls between 12 and 19. Call the Oman Volleyball Association for more information (24 121 140).

YOGA

Exercise for body and mind. A class usually consists of a series of postures and ends with a meditation session, leaving you feeling stretched and relaxed. In Oman, you can sign up for classes at some of the hotel health clubs and one or two other organisations. At the Palm Beach Club (24 680 660) at the InterContinental Muscat, you can attend classes on Saturdays and Mondays from 09:30 to 10:30, on Sundays from 18:45 to 20:00 and on Tuesdays from 17:30 to 18:45. Members pay RO 3 and non-members are charged RO 5.

SHOPPING

SHOPPING **268**   WHERE TO GO FOR... **270**
WHAT & WHERE TO BUY **272**   PLACES TO SHOP **290**

SHOPPING

From traditional garb and local designs to the latest high street stores and global brands, you'll find them all in Muscat's malls and markets.

Muscat is the shopping capital of Oman and offers a cosmopolitan range of shops and goods. From expensive boutiques to handicraft stalls and everything in between, shoppers are never far away from finding what they want. The fact that goods are tax-free means items like carpets, textiles and gold are often cheaper than they are in other countries, while many imported goods fetch prices similar to what they do elsewhere. The key to shopping like a pro in Muscat is to bargain where possible or to wait for the sales when prices can be cut up by up to 70%.

Oman has some of the liveliest, most authentic and colourful traditional markets (souks) in the region. Distinguished old men in their dishdashas sit behind the counters in small shops, while bejeweled women in their abayas haggle with authority. Modern shopping centres, replete with global brands and ample parking, are pivotal social settings. They provide air-conditioned entertainment for a mix of nationalities that are there to see and be seen, shop or just pass the time.

Wednesday, Thursday and Friday nights are the busiest shopping times and it can get a little too crowded, even for the serious shopper. During Ramadan, some shops are open until midnight, supermarkets are packed to the brim with unbelievable amounts of food, and the queues are long, especially in the evenings. Many shops have sales during the annual Muscat Festival in January and in the months around the two Eid holidays, and there are invariably numerous promotions and raffles up for grabs.

REFUNDS, EXCHANGES & CONSUMER RIGHTS

In general, you'll have no problem in trying to exchange goods that are faulty or that you've changed your mind about as long as they are unworn, unused, still in their original packaging if possible, and you have the receipt. However, most retailers will only either exchange the item or give store credit; very few will refund you. Shop assistants are always willing to help and exchanging goods is generally easy enough. However, if you insist on a refund it's best to ask to see the manager or to leave your number and ask the assistant to call you once they've discussed your case with their supervisor. It's likely to require some chasing up but with a bit of persistence you can sometimes get your money back. Getting angry rarely works; it's better to remain unfailingly polite. If you really feel you've been unfairly treated read about consumer rights below.

Consumer Rights

Taking a retailer to court in Oman is likely to be a very lengthy and costly procedure and will probably cause you a great deal more stress than the original problem did. Instead, try to sort things out with a compromise. Perhaps you can have an item exchanged, or a service upgraded?

The souks of Ruwi

The key is to remain calm and, if you're not getting anywhere, you could try to involve an Omani friend in your negotiations. If the problem cannot be resolved, try the Oman Association for Consumer Protection. Its offices are at the Al Harthy Complex in Al Qurm or you could try calling 24 817 013. You might struggle to get through, but once you do they may be able to help you sort out your problem.

Refund Policies

Some of the larger shops display their refund policies clearly (for example, underwear is non-returnable) and only allow exchanges for a limited period (usually seven days from date of purchase). Many international department stores are more proactive with their customer service policies, so it may be best to stick with the big name shops when you're looking to buy larger, more expensive items.

HOW TO PAY

International credit cards like Visa, MasterCard, Diner's Club and American Express are widely accepted by established retailers in Muscat and Salalah. Small traders in the souks and local convenience stores only take cash, but some jewellery shops in the Mutrah Souk will accept credit cards. You might be able to pay with post-dated local cheques when buying expensive items like cars, but this depends on your credentials and the vendor's reputation. There seems to be a fairly relaxed attitude to accepting foreign currency and in many places you can pay with dollars, sterling or one of the GCC currencies (the UAE dirham is accepted almost everywhere). However, it's always good to carry some local currency with you, and there are plenty of money exchanges (see p.124).

BARGAINING

Although bargaining can feel alien and uncomfortable for many visitors, it's a time-honoured tradition in this part of

SHOP & SHIP

If you want to get goods shipped from overseas to Oman, check out the 'shop & ship' service offered by Aramex (aramex.com). It gives you a UK or US mailbox, and then ships the contents of your mailbox to you at competitive rate.

the world, one that both parties invariably get enjoyment from. Outside of the souks or the stores in Ruwi, bargaining is less common and involves more subtle hinting than overt haggling.

You can politely enquire if the price is 'before discount', or mention that you're paying cash. Sometimes even if you don't ask for a discount, the assistant will pass it on to you anyway, which can be a welcome surprise. In the souk though you're expected to haggle and if you're paying cash you'll find vendors will often drop the price substantially. In contrast to other countries in the region where you may be badgered into buying something after accepting a glass of mint tea, bargaining in Oman is less stressful and it can be fun if you relax and take your time. Sellers remain polite and don't normally push for a sale. The key is to decide on how much you want to pay for the item (scout out other shops to get an idea) and to be prepared to walk away if you don't get it for that.

Be A Discount Diva

Something is always on sale in Oman: if it's not slashed prices during the Muscat Festival or discounts over Eid, it's buy-two-get-one-free banded packs in Carrefour or 25% off everything in Marks & Spencer for one day only.

SHIPPING

Sending purchases abroad can be a tedious business but there are many shipping and cargo agencies that make it easier. Items can be sent by sea freight (the least expensive option), air freight or courier. You'll find companies that offer this service under 'Courier Services', 'Cargo Services' or 'Shipping Companies' in the Omantel telephone directory or in the newspapers' classified ads. Most airlines also have a cargo service division, but your chosen destination may not necessarily be on their list of routes. When buying carpets or furniture, some shops may arrange shipping for you. You should always ask what this will cost first – that antique wooden chest may not seem like such a bargain after adding in the shipping costs. Shops will sometimes issue a certificate stating that the item is worth less than it is to save you money on import duty. This is highly illegal, of course, but they seem to have no qualms about doing it.

WHERE TO GO FOR...

After a special something with a bit of local flavour? Try one of these goods – they all make for great gifts.

Silver

The bling factor of the country is massively heightened by its reputation and popularity for high quality silverware. Not just used for jewellery, silver is popular in decorating weapons as well as making everyday objects like coffee pots and pipes. Each region in the Sultanate has its own distinctive design.

Don't be put off by the blackened and dusty bits of beauty; there is nothing that a bit of polish can't fix. Seek and ye shall find some real treasures.

Textiles

Oman is a haven for textile lovers with an array of fabric, textures, prices, colours and prints. Even the smallest towns will have fabric stores so shop to your heart's (and wallet's) desire. Surprisingly, cotton isn't very big in the Arab world but silk and linen are plentiful. Look out for beautiful Indian printed cushion covers and bed spreads that are bound to bring a touch of the exotic to your daily life.

Perfume

Strong heady smells tend to dominate much of Oman and pure frankincense, jasmine and musk actually originated from this very region. The souks are a fabulous place to find the perfect scent with hundreds of fragrances vying for your attention. Be careful; some of the purer stuff is super strong and a drop or two on your scarf can last for a few days.

Oudh is highly valued in the Middle East and can fetch astonishing prices.

Made from the resin of Aloeswood trees and imported from India, Cambodia and Malaysia, Oudh is worn on clothes and skin and usually only on important occasions. Amouage is said to be 'the world's most valuable perfume' and is made here in Oman. You can visit the Amouage factory in Rusayl, past Seeb, to see just how the perfume is made (Sunday to Thursday, 08:30-16:30, amouage.com).

Carpets

Camel or goat hair, sheep wool or cotton, dyed, weaved, patterned or still in their natural states, weaving is one of Oman's major handicrafts and the skill is still passed down through generations.

Carpet shopping can be an absolute minefield but also an incredible pleasure with so much to look through and choose from. The best thing to do is have a set budget and know how big or small you want it to be. The carpet's origin, intricacy of design, its material and whether it is machine made or hand-woven will all dictate its value.

Hand-woven products tend to have more imperfections but this actually increases their value. Shop around and you are bound to find something to please your sensibilities and your pocket. And don't forget to haggle!

Souvenirs

Shopping for presents in Oman is really hard because it's so good you'll want one of everything for yourself! Traditional Arabic gear makes for the best presents and a lot of the souks sell all the Arabic goodies you can imagine, although knick knacks can usually be found in supermarkets and malls too.

Some 'typical' purchases

WHAT & WHERE TO BUY

You can get most of the things you need in Muscat although the shopping areas are rather scattered across the city and you'll need a car or taxi to move from one to another. The following pages cover the main categories of items to be found in Oman, and where you can find them.

ALCOHOL

Anyone over 21 can buy alcohol at licensed bars, restaurants and some clubs, for consumption on the premises. However, to buy alcohol for home consumption you need a liquor licence. You have to have your employer request a licence, which looks like a mini passport, on your behalf, and not all companies will assist with this – it depends what kind of business it is and their attitudes towards alcohol. Muslims are not allowed to apply for a liquor licence. For more information on how to get your licence, see p.85 in the Living in Oman section.

Alcohol is not sold in supermarkets but there are a number of bottle stores in Muscat. These are usually hidden away and there's no indication on the outside that these shops sell alcohol. Look for names like Onas, African & Eastern LLC, Gulf Supply Services, and Oman United Agency, or ask around. You can buy alcohol on the black market but it's a dodgy move and not recommended and besides, the cheaper the tipple, the worse the hangover. It's illegal to transport alcohol unless you're taking it from the shop or the airport duty free to your house (even then you should make sure you have a receipt in case you are stopped by the police).

African & Eastern Madinat As Sultan Qaboos, 24 602 121, *africaneastern.com*
Gulf Supply Services Al Wadi Al Kabir, 24 810 709, *gulfsupplyoman.com*
Oman United Agencies Madinat As Sultan Qaboos, 24 603 892

ART

Muscat has a reasonable selection of galleries. These sell paintings, mainly, and a few selected pieces of sculpture, jewellery and pottery, often created by local or expatriate artists. Foreign artists and photographers with an interest in Omani culture and landscapes often hold exhibitions in museums and galleries; check the local papers or *The Week* for details of upcoming events.

The Mutrah Souk, Qurum City Centre and Al Harthy Complex, the Omani Fine Arts Society, and the Bait Muzna Gallery are treasure troves of local and Arabian art. For more information, see Art Galleries (p.166).

Al Madina Art Gallery Madinat As Sultan Qaboos, 24 691 380
Bait Muzna Gallery 24 739 204, *baitmuznagallery.com*
The Omani Society For Fine Arts Hay As Saruj, 24 692 090, *osfa.gov.om*

ART & CRAFT SUPPLIES

Shah Nagardas Manji carries basic art supplies like oil paints, acrylics, pastels, brushes and drawing paper, and you'll find stores in Al Qurm, Madinate Sultan Qaboos and Ruwi. Serious artists are better off bringing their materials from home or ordering on the internet as specialised supplies are hard to come by. When you're ready to display your work, the many framing shops in Ruwi High Street provide quick, professional and inexpensive service.

Office Supplies Co Al Qurm, 24 563 033, *omzest.com*
The Omani Society For Fine Arts Hay As Saruj, 24 692 090, *osfa.gov.om*
Shah Nagardas Manji & Co Al Qurm, 24 562 655, *shahnagardas.com*

BICYCLES

It's probably not wise to pedal down the Sultan Qaboos Highway, but there are plenty of quieter roads that are safe for cyclists. Mountain biking (p.257) is popular and a ride around the steep hills of the Qantab area will certainly give your legs a workout.

Al Muianee Trading Wadi Hattat, 24 878 887
Babyshop 96 473 101, *babyshopstores.com*
Sun & Sand Sports Al Mawalih Al Janubiyah, 24 558 355, *sunandsandsports.com*
Toys 'R' Us Al Mawalih Ash Shamaliyah, 24 540 360, *toysrusinc.com*

BOOKS

Due to the laws of supply and demand, the range of imported books and magazines available in Muscat is relatively limited. To bring a title into the country, it must first be checked for its content. Books that are deemed to be against the religious, cultural, political or moral sensitivities of the country will be banned. Of course, books can be ordered from amazon.com but packages are often opened and examined first.

Foreign newspapers and magazines are flown in regularly but are expensive. Magazines that contain illicit material are censored with the aid of a black marker pen, as opposed to being banned completely. Subscription magazines may take longer to reach you, as someone has to go through all the racy pictures of scantily clad women and dress them up with black ink.

Latest releases aside, there are some beautiful coffee table books full of inspired photographs of Oman and its people. These are really good for taking home to show people you don't live in a country filled with nothing but sand. Prices for paperbacks are almost the same as in other countries. The large branches of Borders are very popular for their new releases, great non-fiction sections plus magazines and stationery. The Family Bookshop, Al Manahil and Turtle's cater primarily for English speakers, but also stock Arabic titles, and they both have a good selection of children's books. Al Batra Bookshop stocks mostly reference books, hobby books, some children's books and older fiction titles. Most of the larger hotels have small bookshops that stock a limited range of fiction, travel books and books on Oman. Supermarkets like Carrefour, Al Fair and The Sultan Center also carry a reasonable selection of books and magazines. If you can't find what you're looking for, you can order books online, although make sure you take into account the extra fee – the cost of postage may double the price of the book.

One particularly interesting bookshop is House of Prose in Al Qurm. A second-hand bookshop that stocks mainly fiction, travel and biographical titles, they have a buyback policy that refunds half the price you originally paid for any of their books if you return it in good condition and can show the receipt.

Their 'look-out list' is useful if you have a request for a particular title. They stock about 20,000 books in Muscat and another 20,000 at their shops in Dubai, and books can be sold back to either store. Alternatively, the American Women's Group holds periodic second-hand book sales and exchanges.

Stationery

Whether you're looking for a pencil sharpener or professional standard plotting paper, there are stationery shops all over the city. Hypermarkets like Carrefour and Lulu carry all the basics, including huge ranges of back-to-school supplies. While they may be cheap, you might find that to get the best deals you have to buy a pack of 20 identical pencil sharpeners or banded packs of pencils. Of course if you're looking for quality not quantity, head for Mont Blanc where you can offload hundreds of rials on a single pen.

Al Batra Bookshop Al Qurm, 24 563 662, *albatra.com*
Al Fair Madinat As Sultan Qaboos, 24 561 905
Al Wadi Commercial Centre Al Qurm, 24 564 782
Carrefour Muscat City Centre, 800 732 32 *carrefouroman.com*
Borders Madinat Al Ilam, 24 470 489
Lulu Hypermarket Al Khuwayr, 24 504 504, *luluhypermarket.com*
Montblanc Muscat City Centre, 24 558 079, *rivoligroup.com*
Office Supplies Co Al Qurm, 24 563 033, *omzest.com*
Qurum City Centre Madinat Al Ilam, 24 470 700, *qurumcitycentre.com*
SABCO Commercial Centre Al Qurm, 24 566 701, *sabcogroup.com*
Sultan Center Al Qurm, 24 567 666, *sultan-center.com*

CAMERA EQUIPMENT

Those who enjoy photography, whether amateur or pro, will find a reasonable selection of cameras in Muscat. You may not find all of a brand's models in the range, but you'll have a fair bit of choice and prices are comparable to what you pay in duty free stores. For the average holiday snapper there are plenty of choices. Most electronics shops sell a variety of film and digital point-and-shoot cameras. Sales staff are generally helpful and patient with even the greatest of technophobes. There is never any harm in trying to haggle over the price a little – you never know, it might just work, and you could get a reduced price or an extra or two thrown in for good measure. Most department stores also usually have some kind of photography section, with cameras from the likes of Nikon, Pentax, Olympus and Samsung.

Professional photographers or serious hobbyists should check out Salam Stores in Al Qurm. They carry medium format cameras (Bronica and Sigma), lenses and camera accessories, like Manfrotto tripods. They will also help you set up your darkroom, supply you with a Durst enlarger and train you in its use. Foto Magic is a reliable outlet for buying and developing film and downloading images from digital cameras, and has a branch in most shopping areas. You can also ask them to print pictures on greeting cards, mugs or T-shirts if you're looking for a personalised gift for someone.

Capital Store Al Qurm, 99 811 050, *csoman.om*
Centrepoint Madinat As Sultan Qaboos, 96 473 101, *landmarkgroupme.com*
Khimji's Luxury & Lifestyle Various Locations, 24 560 419, *khimji.com*
Markaz Al Bahja >*p.87* Al Mawalih Ash Shamaliyyah, 24 540 200, *albahja.com*
OHI Electronics Al Qurm, 24 565 490, *ohielec.com*
Photocentre Al Qurm, 24 565 305, *photocent.com*
SABCO Commercial Centre Al Qurm, 24 566 701, *sabcogroup.com*
Shah Nagardas Manji & Co Ruwi, 24 702 772, *shahnagardas.com*
Zakher Shopping Mall Al Khuwayr Al Janubiyyah, 24 489 884, *zakhermall.com*

CAR ACCESSORIES

Cars are one of the best buys in Oman, with prices usually much lower than in your home country. This could be your only chance to drive a really luxurious petrol guzzler, rather than something more practical. It is almost de rigeur to own a four-wheel drive, even if the closest you get to off-roading is parking on the pavement. See the lists of new and used car dealers on p.112.

Wherever there are cars, there will be accessories for them. Hypermarkets like Carrefour sell ranges including steering wheel covers, rubber mats, sheep skin seat covers and even little vacuum cleaners that you can plug into the cigarette lighter. The other outlets listed in the table are the places to go if you need tyres, spare parts, or if you want to transform your car to look like something from MTV's Pimp My Ride.

Car Care Centre Al Hayl Ash Shamaliyyah, 99 337 786
Carrefour Al Mawalih Al Janubiyah, 800 732 32, *carrefouroman.com*
Hisin Majees Trading Wadi Kabir, 24 811 442
Ibrahim Essa Al Sheti Al Udhaybah Ash Shamaliyyah, 26 840 720
Opal Marketing & Industry As Seeb, 24 453 044, *precisiontunegcc.com*
Sadween Trading Al Wadi Al Kabir, 24 837 570

CARPETS

Weaving is one of Oman's major handicrafts and the skills have been passed down through the generations. Camel and goat hair, sheep wool and cotton are all used in weaving, either in their natural state or coloured with plant dyes or murex shells. Designs are usually simple stripes and occasionally geometric figures. Traditional spinning and weaving in the Sultanate of Oman is worth reading if you want to learn more about this art.

Carpet shopping can be a minefield for those who know little about it, so it's a good idea to read up about it first and to browse around a number of shops before committing yourself to buying so that you can get an idea of designs and cost. The price reflects the quality of the carpet, with silk being more expensive than wool or cotton. There's also a significant difference between hand-made and machine-made carpets – hand-made carpets will have some imperfections in the design and weaving, and are usually more expensive. The more knots per square inch, the better the quality of the carpet and the higher the price.

Carpets from Turkey, Iran, Pakistan, Central Asia and China are easy to find in Muscat. All of the shopping centres have at least one carpet shop, which is good news for those people who like to shop in an air-conditioned environment, and many of them sell authentic antique carpets from Iran or Afghanistan and will provide you with a certificate stating its age and value. It's not that easy to find good imported carpets in other areas of Oman, although Salalah and Nizwa may have a few stores.

You can find local carpets in the Omani National Heritage Gallery in Shati Al Qurm, or you can buy them directly from the weavers on the long, winding road to Jabel Shams. A 1.5m x 2.5m rug of sheep wool will cost around RO 30. Bargaining is expected and you'll disappoint the seller if you don't even try (see a guide to bargaining on p.269). The seller will elaborately roll out countless carpets for you to view, but don't let this make you feel obliged to buy. Once you reach an agreed price though, you're committed. Some shops will let their regular customers take a carpet home for a few days to 'try it out' with your furniture.

Traditional carpets

Carpet Bazaar Hay As Saruj, 24 696 142
Gulf Shell Trading Al Qurm, 24 571 630
Oriental Carpets & Handicrafts Al Qurm, 24 564 786
Persian Carpets Al Qurm, 24 562 139

COMPUTERS

You'll find plenty of computer shops with stock up to the ceilings and knowledgeable staff in Muscat. The best of these are in Al Wadi Centre in Al Qurm, Computer Street in Ruwi and Carrefour in Qurum City Centre (p.298) which often has good deals on laptops. You'll also find E-Max at Muscat City Centre (p.297) which is fairly cheap and there are authorised dealers for Apple in Al Harthy Complex, and Dell Computers on the Al Khuwayr slip road.

Prices aren't bad, but you must bargain before agreeing on a price. You can also strike a deal where a vendor will get you a PC, printer, scanner, desk and chair (depending of course on what you want), bring it all round and install it for you. Getting computers fixed is easy and usually cheap, but you may get frustrated at deadlines that aren't met.

Outside Muscat you won't find much in terms of technology and may have to wait a long time for anything you've ordered. The Omani government has been clamping down on the sale of pirated software since it became a member of the World Trade Organisation. However, you can still find copies of PC and Playstation games in small shops in Ruwi and Al Qurm for as little as RO 1 if you're happy to turn a blind eye.

Carrefour Al Mawalih Al Janubiyah, 800 732 32, *carrefouroman.com*
Computer Xpress Ruwi, 24 835 631
Faisal Al Alawi Trading Ruwi, 24 702 812
Modern Electronic House Al Qurm, 24 565 848

EYEWEAR

Life in Oman is definitely easier with a pair of sunglasses. The strength of the sun, the days at the beach and the long drives mean you're going to want to protect your eyes. All kinds of sunglasses are available in the malls, in Ruwi and in the souk, from designer eyewear to rip-offs and everything in between. Prices range from a few rials to many hundreds but as competition is fierce you can often find a good bargain in designer shades. Make sure they offer 100% UVA and UVB protection and are large and dark enough to protect your eyes from the sun's glare. Polarised lenses are particularly good if you spend a lot of time on the water. Shopping centres have opticians that will make prescription eyeglasses, prescription sunglasses and contact lenses (hard, soft, gas permeable and thoric).They usually offer free eye tests if you order from them. Disposable contact lenses and coloured contact lenses are also available. You'll find lens cleaning solutions at opticians and pharmacies.

Al Ghazal Opticians Al Qurm,
24 563 546
Al Said Optics Al Qurm, 24 566 272
Grand Optics Al Mawalih Al Janubiyah,
24 558 890, *grandoptics.com*
Hassan Opticals Co Al Qurm,
24 565 499
Oman Opticals Salalah, 23 293 714
Ridwan Al Qurm, 24 564 027
Yateem Optician Al Qurm,
24 563 716, *yateemgroup.com*

FASHION

Your fashion options in Muscat have
expanded substantially over the last few
years. This is largely thanks to the new
Qurum City Centre (p.298) home of H&M,
Monsoon and Next, and Muscat City
Centre (p.297). This large mall is located
quite far out of town past the Seeb Airport
but with its array of shops that you may
well recognise from home – Mango, Fat
Face, Gap, Promod, Forever 21, Splash
and Zara – it's worth the trip. Stores here
receive new stock every four to six months.

Markaz al Bahja, past City Centre, has
a Marks & Spencer and a few smaller
shops where you can pick up some
good bargains. Some of the places will
do alterations if items don't quite fit.
The Sultan Center has a small range of
sportswear and hypermarkets like Lulu
and Carrefour also have clothing sections
where you can pick up a few bargains.

The Al Qurm shopping area contains
five shopping centres and numerous shops
within walking distance of each other. The
Centrepoint stocks fashions for all ages
and sizes and has a reasonably-priced
accessories department. They also run
frequent sales.

There isn't yet a range of designer
boutiques for women although men
have been able to shop for designer suits,
jackets and casuals at places like Tahani,
Cerutti, Jazz and Moustache in SABCO
for some time. Moustach sells a variety
of men's designer gear including Armani
Jeans, Damat, Dolce & Gabbana, Ferre,
Trussardi, Tween and Iceberg. Jazz has
begun to cater for ladies and now stocks
Miss Sixty, Cerutti and Indian Rose. Capital
Store carries men's suits by Loewe and
you'll find Hugo Boss at Salam Stores.

Sana Stores and Ruwi High Street
are good places to pick up textiles, saris
and salwarkameez, but for something
different call Taalali in Mutrah Souk for an

appointment. Florence Rusconi, a French
designer, reworks traditional Omani clothes
into tops. Accessories are also available.
You could also enlist the services of a tailor.

Workmanship can vary but generally
the quality is very high for the amount
you pay. If you take along your fabric
and a photo, drawing or sample of what
you want, a tailor will copy it. Good sales
are generally held during Ramadan and
the Eid holidays, but also in January
and September/October when shops
are clearing old stock. Discounts of 70%
are not uncommon, but be prepared to
sort through a rack of odd sizes and last
season's styles.

Fashion – Shoes

From knee-high boots to plastic flip-flops,
you'll be able to find the shoes you need
in Muscat, although the range is not quite
as good in other parts of Oman. Most sizes
are available; just be sure to specify to the
sales assistant whether you mean the UK or
US size. Sports stores are best for trainers
and running shoes, as staff will be able to
advise you on fit and support. Shoe City,
which has branches in the Centrepoint and
Muscat City Centre, has a wide range of
shoes for the whole family. You'll find good
quality leather shoes in various outlets in
Muscat and Qurum City Centres and in
World of Shoes in the Al Khamis Plaza.

The Athlete's Foot Al Qurm,
24 567 438, *theathletesfoot.com*
Bench Al Mawalih Al Janubiyah,
24 558 048, *benchtm.com*
Bhs Al Qurm, 24 562 456,
alshaya.com
Centrepoint Madinat As Sultan Qaboos,
96 473 101, *landmarkgroupme.com*
Charles & Keith Al Mawalih Al Janubiyah,
24 558 011, *charleskeith.com*
Clarks Al Qurm, 24 560 992
Giordano Al Mawalih Al Janubiyah,
24 558 139
Hang Ten Al Mawalih Al Janubiyah,
24 558 870
Jazz Hay As Saruj, 24 695 965
Khimji Ramdas Ruwi, 24 795 901,
khimji.com
Mango Al Mawalih Al Janubiyah,
24 558 244
Marks & Spencer Al Mawalih Al
Janubiyah, 98 24 558 455,
marksandspencerme.com
Milano Al Mawalih Al Janubiyah,
24 558 834, *alshaya.com*

Monsoon Al Mawalih Al Janubiyah, 98 24 558 902
Moustache Shati Al Qurm, 24 693 392
Next Al Mawalih Al Janubiyah, 24 558 801
Nine West Al Qurm, 24 561 872
Promod Al Mawalih Al Janubiyah, 24 558 240
Sana Fashions Al Wadi Al Kabir, 24 810 289
Shoe Mart Al Mawalih Al Janubiyah, 964 731 15
Splash Madinat As Sultan Qaboos, 96 473 101, *splashfashions.com*
Spring Al Mawalih Al Janubiyah, 24 558 049
World of Shoes Al Qurm, 24 565 259

Bhs Al Qurm, 24 562 456, *alshaya.com*
Carrefour Al Mawalih Al Janubiyah, 800 732 32, *carrefouroman.com*
Inner Lines Al Mawalih Al Janubiyah, 24 558 228
Mango Al Mawalih Al Janubiyah, 24 558 244
Marks & Spencer Al Mawalih Al Janubiyah, 24 558 455, *marksandspencerme.com*
Next Al Mawalih Al Janubiyah, 24 558 801
Sana Fashions Al Wadi Al Kabir, 24 810 289
Splash Al Mawalih Al Janubiyah, 96 473 114, *splashfashions.com*

Fashion – Lingerie

Lingerie is big business in the Middle East and you might be surprised by what's lurking under some of those conservative clothes. A browse around a specialist lingerie shop, like Triumph and Inner Lines (both in City Centre) and High Lady in Al Wadi Centre, can be eye opening.

If you're looking for something a bit more everyday and functional, you can try old favourites Next, Marks & Spencer or Bhs, all of which have a good cotton range to suit the climate. Prices can be inflated compared to in the UK, but you could always wait for the sales and stock up then. Carrefour and Lulu Hypermarkets have good lingerie sections, as do Woolworths Lingerie, Splash, Next, Calvin Klein (all in Muscat City Centre) and Sana Fashions in Wadi Kabir. You'll find plenty of affordable underwear and nightwear at the Mutrah Souk and Ruwi High Street, if you're not particular about colours or cotton content.

SHOES & CLOTHING SIZES

Figuring out your size isn't rocket science – it just helps to do a bit of pre-planning. Firstly, check the label in an item; you'll often find international sizes printed on them. Secondly, check with the store; it will usually have a conversion chart either on display or available to use. Otherwise, you can remember that a UK size is always two sizes higher than a US size (so a UK 10 is a US 6). To convert European sizes into US sizes, subtract 32 (so a European 38 is actually a US 6). Therefore, you obviously subtract 28 to convert roughly from European sizes to UK sizes.

Shoes can be trickier; for example, a woman's UK 6 is a European 39 and a US 8.5. A man's UK 10 is a European 44 and a US 10.5. If in doubt, ask an assistant for help, but you'll soon start remembering your vital numbers across all their various international incarnations.

FOOD

Oman has a good range of supermarkets and grocery shops that cater to its multinational population's culinary needs. Although there are some speciality items that you won't find, most things are available somewhere if you look hard enough or ask your friends. Prices vary considerably, even among supermarkets. Imported items are sometimes double what they would cost in their country of origin, and locally made equivalents are much cheaper and just as good. Carrefour (Qurm and Muscat City Centres), the Sultan Center, Lulu Hypermarket and Al Fair are the biggest and most popular supermarkets. The smaller ones, like Pic n Save and Family Supermarket, might not be as well laid out, but they do carry a wide range of goods that's sometimes even cheaper than you'll find in the hypermarkets.

During Ramadan, mountains of food, both fresh and tinned, are on sale. They seem to specialise in feeding large families; products are bundled up with sticky tape and sold for a rial so it's a good time to stock up on non-perishables. Carrefour, the well-known French hypermarket, sells everything from laptops and French cheeses to shoes and stationery. It has an excellent selection of fresh fruits, vegetables, meats and seafood and a good bakery where croissants, baguettes, European style breads, cakes, and Arabic and Indian sweets are made on the premises. It also stocks a small section of Filipino and Indian foods.

Al Fair supermarket, with branches in Al Qurm, Madinat Sultan Qaboos, and

The fish market

fruit and vegetable markets in Wadi Kabir in Ruwi, Mutrah and Al Mawaleh on the road to Nizwa.

Fish
If you get to the Mutrah fish souk early in the morning you'll find the freshest catches straight off the boat. A browse among the stalls reveals an amazing variety of fish and seafood, some still squirming or struggling to get out of the baskets. Fishermen in the Azaiba beach area may also sell their daily catch to you. The larger supermarkets carry fresh seafood and fish (whole, filleted or in steaks), in slightly less-smelly surroundings.

Vegetarians
Vegetarians shouldn't have too much difficulty finding suitable products in Oman. Fresh and imported fruits and vegetables are widely available and cheap, especially in open-air markets. Spices and nuts imported from all over the world are sold by the scoop in large supermarkets. Al Fair also carries some soya based products, but the choice is limited.

Carrefour Al Mawalih Al Janubiyah, 800 732 32, *carrefouroman.com*
Godiva Chocolates Al Qurm, 24 562 367
Lulu Hypermarket Al Ghubrah Al Janubiyyah, 24 504 504, *luluhypermarket.com*
Markaz Al Bahja > *p.87* Al Mawalih Ash Shamaliyah, 24 540 200, *albahja.com*
Patchi Al Mawalih Al Janubiyah, 24 558 032, *patchi.com*
Safeer Supermarket Al Khuwayr Al Janubiyyah, 24 479 211
Spinneys Shati Al Qurm, 24 607 075, *spinneys.com*
Sultan Center Al Qurm, 24 567 666, *sultan-center.com*

Al Sarooj, is favoured by expats for its British, European and Asian foods. It's the only supermarket that sells frozen pork and pork products like paté, proscuitto, salami and ham. Al Fair also has a 'Monday Market' when special items are on sale. The Lulu Hypermarket in Al Ghubbrah has a good fresh produce section selling fresh Thai herbs and grated coconut.

There are plenty of local convenience stores in residential areas, some of which have a small produce section with onions, garlic, ginger and a small range of vegetables. Petrol stations have also entered the market with their own forecourt shops – these little shops sell necessities from quick, hot snacks to washing powder, and some are open 24 hours a day. Look out for Select shops at Shell stations, and Souk shops at Al Maha.

Fruit & Vegetables
A lot of fresh fruits, vegetables and herbs are used in Middle Eastern cuisine, and produce coming from this region can be amazingly cheap. A box of Jordanian oranges, for example, costs as little as one rial – a bonus for people who love freshly squeezed orange juice. Excluding imported fresh produce, fruits and vegetables are, in general, very affordable, especially if bought from places like the

FURNITURE
It is possible to furnish a house quite cheaply in Oman although you may have trouble finding what you want if your tastes run to the minimalist or modern. A great new addition is Gecko in Jawaharat A'Shati mall, where you'll find pieces imported from Bali, in addition to gorgeous fabrics from Designer's Guild and the ever-popular Fatboy beanbags in a range of sizes and styles.

On the Al Khuwayr service road, parallel to Sultan Qaboos Street, you'll find vast stores selling what Europeans call 'Arabic style' furniture (confusingly, Arabs call it 'European style'). Think statuesque horses and mirrors looming over you on your headboard and bright sofas with silver lions'-claw legs. You can dilute the gaudiness by ordering them in different colours or sizes to those on display in the showroom. These shops also stock curtains and orthopaedic mattresses. Home Centre, Centrepoint and a Danish shop, ID Design, in Markaz al Bahja that sells Scandinavian furniture are all popular. These large stores generally have good sales during Ramadan and around September.

While Muscat doesn't have its own IKEA yet, there is a huge store in Dubai and you'll be amazed at how much flat-pack furniture you can fit into one carload. There are also some excellent shops selling wooden furniture but don't be taken in by the 'antiques' label; most of the items here are mass-produced in India and artificially aged. There are a few furniture stores in Al Qurm around Al-Araimi and SABCO. Marina in Al-Araimi and Bombay in Markaz al Bahja have lovely Anglo-Indian colonial pieces, and prices are fixed so you don't have to worry about haggling.

The many excellent wood and metal working shops in Wadi Kabir in Ruwi will make any piece of furniture you want for a reasonable price. Ruwi is also a good place to find readymade furniture and home furnishing shops – try Al Baladiyah Street and Ruwi High Street up to the Al Hamriyah Roundabout. You can reduce prices by bargaining. Stock isn't always unlimited though and things can disappear if you don't buy it there and then, so if you see something you love grab it you can. Every area has shops that make curtains and blinds. You'll probably have to wade through books and books of fabric samples, but the end result (custom made curtains that fit your windows perfectly) will be worth it. While these places will be able to offer advice on styles, it will make it easier and quicker if you go with something specific in mind, and even a picture if possible.

Al Batna Commercial Centre (Antiques) Al Qurm, 24 560 284
Furniture Village Al Mawalih Ash Shamaliyah, 24 481 701, *furniturevillage.net*

Home Centre Al Mawalih Al Janubiyah, 24 558 063, *landmarkgroupme.com*
Hyat Furniture Al Khuwayr Al Janubiyyah, 24 478 664
ID Design Markaz Al Bahja, 24 545 658, *iddesignoman.com*
International Golden Furniture (IGF) Madinat As Sultan Qaboos, 24 600 335, *igfoman.com*
Lifestyle Al Mawalih Al Janubiyah, 96 473 113, *lifestylegulf.com*
Maathir Al Qurm, 24 562 585
Marina Gulf Trading Co. Al Qurm, 24 562 221, *marinagulf.com*
Najeeb Alla Baksh (Antiques) Al Qurm, 24 564 415
The Shuram Group Hay As Saruj, 24 600 919, *shuramgroup.com*
Tahani Antiques Hay As Saruj, 24 601 866
Tavola Madinat As Sultan Qaboos, 24 605 630
Teejan Furnishing Al Khuwayr Al Janubiyyah, 24 489 490
United Furniture Co Madinat As Sultan Qaboos, 24 603 416

GIFTS

Larger supermarkets like Carrefour, Sultan Center and Al Fair carry English greeting cards, wrapping paper and stationery, while specialist shops can be found in the Al Harthy Complex, SABCO, Zaher Mall and City Centre. Birthdays and most holidays (Christmas, Easter, Mothers' Day) are catered for and you can surprise friends back home with special Eid cards. The offerings here may be a little soppy or sentimental so, if you're after a wider range or a humorous card, try Carlt on Cards or the Sultan Center. For some witty cards imported from New York, check out the stand outside Totemin Jawharat A'Shati Complex. Cards with Omani themes, created by local artists, can be found in museum gift shops and at Murtada AK Trading in Mutrah Souk. Apart from costing less, they are good quality and make original alternatives to standard greeting cards. While postcards can cost as little as 100 baisas, greeting cards and wrapping paper are more expensive.

Al Fair Madinat As Sultan Qaboos, 24 561 905
Carlton Cards Al Qurm, 24 562 799
Carrefour Al Mawalih Al Janubiyah, 800 732 32, *carrefouroman.com*

Marks & Spencer Al Mawalih Al
Janubiyah, 24 558 455,
marksandspencerme.com
Murtada AK Trading Mutrah,
24 711 632
Sultan Center Al Qurm, 24 567 666,
sultan-center.com

HOME APPLIANCES

Muscat's shops stock a reasonable
selection of electronics and home
appliances, from well-known brands to
knock-offs. Prices are competitive and
can be brought down even further by
bargaining. Widescreen televisions and
home theatres are bargains compared
to back home, although it's still smart to
shop around. The branches of Carrefour
in Muscat City Centre and Qurum City
Centre have a wide range of inexpensive
items, which is great for people furnishing
a house without a company allowance,
but prices here are fixed. Larger appliances
such as washing machines and fridges
are delivered and installed free of charge
and a 12 month warranty is given on
most items. Ruwi High Street is good for
browsing and comparing prices as all the
showrooms are here. If you don't see what
you're looking for, ask, as it may be hidden
in the back room.

If you live in Salalah you can usually
find good deals on appliances in town, so
there's no need to go all the way to Muscat.
Warranties, after-sales service, delivery
and installation should all be discussed
before you buy. If you're intending to
take anything overseas with you, confirm
its compatibility with the power supply.
Check notice boards or classifieds for
second-hand items. Expats who are
leaving often sell things at reasonable
prices in order to clear them quickly. This is
especially good if you're looking for large
appliances or air conditioners.

Capital Store 99 811 969,
csoman.com
Carrefour 800 732 32,
carrefouroman.com
Lulu Hypermarket 24 504 504,
luluhypermarket.com
Muscat Electronics Co 24 796 591,
muscatelectronics.com
OHI Electronics 24 565 490,
ohielec.com
Sony 24 564 485, *sony-mea.com*

HANDBAGS

Local ladies love their accessories – the
humble handbag has become a major
status symbol, especially since it is often
the only item visible when dressed in
the long black abaya. As a result, you
can get some amazing creations (both
in terms of craftsmanship and price)
at various exclusive boutiques around
town plus stores like Zara, Forever 21 and
Accessorize. For the less label conscious,
handbags are sold in most fashion,
luggage and accessories shops, and even
in supermarkets like Carrefour – so keep
your eyes peeled for fab bags next time
you're doing your grocery shopping.
Capital Store sells a range of Givenchy
handbags.

Al Araimi Complex Al Qurm,
24 566 557, *alaraimicomplex.com*
Capital Store Salalah, 23 297 910,
csoman.om
Carrefour Al Mawalih Al Janubiyah,
800 732 32, *carrefouroman.com*
Centrepoint Madinat As Sultan Qaboos,
96 473 101, *landmarkgroupme.com*
Lifestyle Al Mawalih Al Janubiyah,
473 113, *lifestylegulf.com*
Mango Al Mawalih Al Janubiyah,
24 558 244
Markaz Al Bahja > *p.87* Al Mawalih Ash
Shamaliyah, 24 540 200,
albahja.com
Marks & Spencer Al Mawalih Al
Janubiyah, 24 558 455,
marksandspencerme.com
Monsoon Al Mawalih Al Janubiyah,
24 558 902
Next Al Mawalih Al Janubiyah,
24 558 801
Qurum City Centre Madinat Al Ilam,
24 470 700, *qurumcitycentre.com*
SABCO Commercial Centre Al Qurm,
24 566 701, *sabcogroup.com*
Salman Stores Various Locations,
24 796 925, *salmancorporation.com*
Splash Al Mawalih Al Janubiyah,
96 473 114, *splashfashions.com*

HARDWARE & DIY

DIY enthusiasts will find Honda Street
in Ruwi a veritable paradise. It's one
long street of nothing but hardware,
tools, paints and construction materials,
from washers to entire bathroom suites
in marble. Parking can be a problem,
particularly on Thursdays. Carrefour, Sultan

WATCH THIS SPACE

Those who love the finer things in life will be delighted to discover that Muscat is home to arguably the Middle East's most upmarket watch and jewellery emporium – the recently-opened Khimji's Watches (khimji.com) showroom in Shati Al Qurm. The showroom's brands reads like a who's who of luxury, with Cartier, IWC, Bell & Ross, Piaget, Vertu, Mikimoto and Oris just a few of the marques on offer; in fact, there are even dedicated zones for the likes of Rolex and Chopard, where even the decor matches the brands' identities. Prices won't be in reach for everyone, but this showroom is well worth a visit – like a museum or art gallery dedicated to fine living.

Center, Safeer and Lulu Hypermarket also have some good DIY equipment, but the smaller shops are sometimes better because you can negotiate the price. The shops have counters directly inside the door, so you have to ask for what you want rather than browse around for it. If you are not inclined to put up your own shelves, enquire at the shops and someone will come round and do it for a couple of rials. DIY furniture bought in Home Centre is assembled in your home for free.

Carrefour Al Mawalih Al Janubiyah, 800 732 32, *carrefouroman.com*
Lulu Hypermarket Salalah, 23 218 400, *luluhypermarket.com*
Safeer Hypermarket Al Badi, 24 496 019
Souk Al Khuwayr Al Khuwayr Al Janubiyyah
Sultan Center Al Qurm, 24 567 666, *sultan-center.com*

HEALTH FOOD & SPECIAL DIETARY REQUIREMENTS

While you won't find quite the same range of organic, bio and health foods that you'll find in your home country, things are improving in Oman. Al Fair has some non-dairy, low fat, low calorie products but these are usually mixed in with the regular items. The Sultan Center also has a very limited range in its dietetic section. GNC in Muscat City Centre stocks a comprehensive range of nutritional supplements and alternative remedies – it also offers a membership option where for just RO 3, you'll get a card which gives you 20% discount on all purchases during the first week of every month. Muscat Pharmacy, and The Health Store in the Al Qurum Complex, also

stock nutritional supplements, and gym enthusiasts who swear by protein and food supplements should check out Sport One. The supermarkets have a limited selection of multivitamins for kids and adults, but it's good to check the sell-by dates.

Al Fair Al Qurm, 24 561 912
General Nutrician Centre (GNC) Al Mawalih Al Janubiyah, 24 558 222, *gnc.com.sa*
Muscat Pharmacy & Stores Al Wadi Al Kabir, 24 814 501, *muscatpharmacy.net*

JEWELLERY & WATCHES

Silver

Omani silverwork has been held in such high regard in Gulf countries that many 'antique' pieces of silver today are labelled Omani to enhance their value and reputation. Silver was used not only to make necklaces, anklets, rings, bracelets and other forms of wedding jewellery, but also to decorate weapons and create everyday objects such as coffee pots, pipes, thorn-picks and ear-cleaners. Each region in Oman has its distinctive designs. If you are a serious collector of Omani silver, the books *Silver, the Traditional Art of Oman* and *The Craft Heritage of Oman* are indispensable.

A short walk around the souks of Muscat and the interior will reveal a variety of dusty, black looking silver that will look great with a bit of polish. There are small boxes used to hold kohl, and huge earrings which might terrify you on first sight but that are actually hooked over the top of the ears and not for pierced ears. A lot of this is wedding jewellery and although it might look ancient, it's unlikely to be very old. Traditionally, a woman's wedding

The Khimji's Watches showroom

jewellery was melted down and sold or refashioned on her death, but inherited pieces are not uncommon. Bedouin women may also sell their silver jewellery as Eid approaches in order to have some cash for celebrations; the souk in Sinaw is a good source. You may also see Maria Theresa dollars (or thalers) which were the legal currency in Oman until the 1960s. Take your time to browse and you can dig up some real treasures.

Watches

As with jewellery, watches are cheaper here than in Europe. Supermarkets stock cheap to medium-priced watches, while dedicated watch showrooms stock pieces priced from average to outlandish!

SILVER CURRENCY

Maria Theresa (1717-1780) was a Hapsburg by birth and the wife and Empress of the Holy Roman Emperor Francis I. The Maria Theresa thaler made its debut in 1751 at a time when Omani traders were desperately in need of an internationally acceptable and reliable currency. They liked the texture of the coin and its consistent silver content so they adopted it. Craftsmen used the thalers to make intricate pieces of silver jewellery. When Oman's own currency was introduced in 1970 the need for thalers died out.

Al Asala Jewellery Al Wadi Commercial Centre, 24 560 654
Al Felaiij Jewellers Muscat City Centre, 24 558 518
Al Qurum Jewellers SABCO Commercial Centre, 24 562 558
Alukkas Jewellery Muscat City Centre, 24 558 034, *alukkas.com*
Damas 24 788 946, *damasjewel.com*
Future Jewellery SABCO Commercial Centre, 24 565 637
Hamdam Hasan Swaid Al Jimi SABCO Commercial Centre, 24 565 167
Himat Jewellers Muscat City Centre, 24 558 088, *himatjewellers.com*
Jewellery Corner SABCO Commercial Centre, 24 563 946
Khimji's Watches >*p.viii* Shatti Al Qurum/ Hay As Saruj, 24 699 173, *khimji.com*
Mouawad Al Khamis Plaza, 24 560 945, *mouawad.com*
Muscat Watch Centre SABCO Commercial Centre, 24 562 459
Ruwi Jewellers Al Khamis Plaza, 24 565 977
Tiffany & Co. Salalah, 23 211 976
Watch House Muscat City Centre, 24 558 838

KIDS' ITEMS

You won't have any trouble shopping for children's clothes in Muscat. From the moment your baby is born right up until they are too cool for kids' clothes, there is a huge range available. The presence of some popular stores from your home country will be comforting, such as Marks & Spencer, Mexx, H&M, Pumpkin Patch and Next, and you'll be able to kit your kids out in exactly the same clothes their friends back home are wearing (although maybe with a slight time delay). However, clothes in these outlets are often quite pricey compared to what you'd pay at home. If you're looking for cheap, cheerful clothing that you don't mind getting muddy or covered in paint, you'll find some bargains at Carrefour, Sana Fashions or Lulu Hypermarket. While some of the stock may seem a bit garish at first glance, a good rummage often yields some great results and it is not unknown to make brand-name discoveries. If you are stocking up on clothes for a new baby, head for Mothercare, Adams and the Baby Shop, where you'll find most of the things you'll need.

Muscat is a child-friendly city, and you'll find plenty of shops selling toys for your little angels. There is something for everyone, from hi-tech baby learning laptops to cheap plastic tat (which your kids will probably prefer, despite your best intentions). Remember that not all toys conform to international safety standards though. All this means is that you will need to make a judgement call and ensure your kids only play with the dodgy toys under constant supervision.

Toys R Us, Baby Shop, and The Toy Store in City Centre carry everything from dolls to computer games, perfect for one-stop shopping. The supermarkets also stock good ranges of toys and Ruwi High Street is excellent for lower priced items. Mothercare, Babyshop and Adams are where to head if you're looking for soft toys suitable for newborns and infants. If you're looking for second-hand items like prams, cots and large toys, keep an eye on supermarket notice boards. Some churches and societies lend out baby equipment too, so ask around or contact Muscat Mums (p.128).

Adams Muscat City Centre, 24 558 914, *adams.co.uk*
Babyshop Centrepoint, 96 473 101, *babyshopstores.com*
Babyshop Muscat City Centre, 964 731 13, *babyshopstores.com*
Bhs Nr Sabco Centre, 24 562 456, *alshaya.com*

Carrefour Muscat City Centre, 800 732 32, *carrefouroman.com*
Hang Ten Muscat City Centre, 24 558 870
Lulu Hypermarket, 24 504 504, *luluhypermarket.com*
Marks & Spencer Muscat City Centre, 24 558 455, *marksandspencerme.com*
Monsoon Muscat City Centre, 24 558 902
Mothercare Nr Sabco Centre, 24 562 456, *mothercare.com*
Next Muscat City Centre, 24 558 801
Pumpkin Patch Muscat City Centre, 24 558 085, *pumpkinpatch.co.uk*
Safeer Hypermarket Nr Azaiba Hotel, 24 496 019
Sana Fashions Nr Indian School, 24 810 289

LUGGAGE & LEATHER

There's nothing like a full range of Louis Vuitton luggage to show off with in airports, and since you'll probably be travelling back home once or twice a year, you may as well do it in style. Head for Capital Stores, Salam Stores, Salman Stores or Khimji's Luxury & Lifestyle for a range of luxury luggage at luxury prices. If you'd rather spend your money on holidays than hand luggage, there's a lane off Ruwi High Street that specialises in budget suitcases and bags in every colour and size. Somehow word of what you're looking for travels as you walk along the street, so by the time you reach the end traders will be offering you a 'small black air cabin bag, madam?' Lulu Hypermarket also sells some suitcases and laptop bags. Carrefour and the Sultan Center have functional bags and suitcases, similar to those you'd find in the souk. Copies of designer handbags can be found in some shops, and these make good presents, although some are of better quality than others. If you're looking for a leather jacket, try men's clothing stores in Al Qurm and City Centre. Non-branded leather jackets from Pakistan can be found in the small Qurum City Centre souk.

MATERNITY ITEMS

Fashion conscious mums-to-be won't find a huge choice of maternity clothing in Oman, a few of the big name stores do have selections for you. And if Marks & Spencer, Max and H&M don't deliver the goods in terms of flair and individual style, you could always ask a tailor to whip up something for you.

Marks & Spencer Al Mawalih Al Janubiyah, 24 558 455, *marksandspencerme.com*
Mothercare Al Qurm, 24 562 456, *mothercare.com*
Next Al Mawalih Al Janubiyah, 24 558 801

MEDICINE

A green cross, or an image of what looks like a snake wrapped around a glass, on a shop sign indicates a pharmacy (or a chemist), and you'll find pharmacies all over Oman.

Many drugs that you need a prescription for in other parts of the world can be bought over the counter without a visit to the doctor. Pharmacists are willing to listen to your symptoms and suggest a remedy, but will not prescribe antibiotics. They can also recommend a cheaper alternative of the same drug.

On your first attempt to buy a medicine that you regularly use in your home country, try taking an empty packet or the package insert with you if possible. The medicine you use may not be available here, but the pharmacist will be able to tell you of a suitable alternative. Remember to check the expiry date of the medicine before buying it.

Pharmacies also carry beauty products, sunscreen, baby care items and perfumes, usually at a set discount. Opening hours are usually from 09:00 to 13:00 and 16:00 to 20:00. The following pharmacies are open 24 hours a day: Scientific Pharmacy in Qurum (24 566 601); Muscat Pharmacy in Ruwi (24 702 542) and Al Sarooj (24 695 536).

A list of the pharmacies that are on 24 hour duty can be found in daily newspapers, as well as on 90.4 FM radio and the English Evening News on Oman TV. If you need over the counter medication for fever, a sore throat or muscle pain, try the larger supermarkets like Sultan Center and Carrefour.

See also Pharmacies, p.144.

MOBILE PHONES

A mobile phone (often known as GSM in Oman) is considered an essential accessory and most shopping areas and malls have at least one outlet selling a range of models. There are some specialist stores, while all of the major electronic stores such as Jumbo and E-Max sell mobiles, as does Carrefour.

MUSIC & DVDS

There are no megastores that sell music or movies in Oman, but there are many smaller outlets within shopping centres that stock current releases on CD and DVD. Carrefour and Sultan Center also carry a small range. The latest offerings by international musicians are available on CDs and sometimes cassettes. You can also get a reasonable range of Arabic, Bollywood and classical music. New releases tend to sell out quickly. If you can't find what you are looking for, some shop owners might be able to order certain titles for you; or you can order on the internet if you're prepared to pay the postage (try amazon.com). Censorship is alive and well and there may be some films that you can't get in Oman; or films that you can get but that have been cut. If you order online your package will usually be held at the post office until you go there in person to oversee a search. If anything in it is deemed offensive, it will be confiscated or censored. Of course there are the usual pirated DVDs and VCDs doing the rounds – just remember that the chances are high that you'll get a poor quality copy.

MUSICAL INSTRUMENTS

Musicians will find it hard to get what they want in Oman as there are a limited number of shops that sell instruments. Musiq Souq (24 562 265) in the Al Wadi Centre, Al Qurm, has the widest range and they also offer music lessons. Sheet music is not widely available and you might want to order it from the internet or buy some on your next trip abroad.

OUTDOOR GOODS

Oman is a perfect location for outdoor activities, and weekend breaks in a wadi or in the desert are popular. Mild temperatures and low humidity make the winter months of November to March the best time for camping, picnics, diving, kite surfing, climbing and trekking, or just sitting on your porch with a sundowner. Even in the summer, outdoor activities can be pleasant if you go to the mountains or south to Salalah during the 'khareef', or spend an evening on the beach (although the humidity can be taxing). Omanis enjoy a good evening of chilling out, singing and barbecuing fresh seafood. Most of the supermarkets carry basic outdoor gear such as cooler boxes, barbecue stands, folding chairs and tables, gas stoves, tents and even portable toilets and showers. You can kit yourself out cheaply at Carrefour and Sultan Center while Ruwi High Street and the Mutrah Souk are good for plastic mats. If your idea of enjoying the outdoor life is limited to your patio or garden, take a trip to Centrepoint (formerly City Plaza) or Ruwi High Street for plastic chairs and tables.

Carrefour Al Mawalih Al Janubiyah, 800 732 32, *carrefouroman.com*
Home Centre Al Mawalih Al Janubiyah, 24 558 063, *landmarkgroupme.com*
Khimji's Luxury & Lifestyle > *p.viii* Various Locations, 24 560 419, *khimji.com*
Lulu Hypermarket Al Ghubrah Al Janubiyyah, 24 504 504, *luluhypermarket.com*

PARTY ACCESSORIES
Large formal or themed parties aren't that common in Oman, where garden parties and casual barbecues are more popular. Supermarkets and stationery shops serve basic party needs and Toys R Us has a good kids' party selection. While there are no independent party organisers in Oman, the larger hotels might be able to help you plan a special event.

Fancy Dress & Costumes
There are no specialist costume shops here, so if you're going to a fancy dress party and don't sew, head straight to a tailor. Explaining your design to them

FRANKINCENSE
Oman is home to the world's finest frankincense. Luban (frankincense in resin form) is a good purchase and the fragrance lasts for a long time. Frankincense is one of the essential notes used by Amouage – the Omani perfume house that is often said to produce some of the world's finest fragrances, not to mention some of its most expensive.

could be amusing as it will be something rather different from their usual requests. Factor in time before the party to try it on and have it refitted if necessary.

Al Fair Nr Al Sarooj Plaza, 24 607 075
Carrefour Al Mawalih Al Janubiyah, 800 732 32, *carrefouroman.com*
Lulu Hypermarket Sohar, 26 805 544, *luluhypermarket.com*
Markaz Al Bahja > *p.87* Al Mawalih Ash Shamaliyah, 24 540 200, *albahja.com*
Zakher Shopping Mall Al Khuwayr Al Janubiyyah, 24 489 884, *zakhermall.com*

PERFUMES & COSMETICS
Ajmal Perfumes Al Qurm, 24 562 359, *ajmalperfume.com*
Al Bustan Fragrances Al Qurm, 24 798 241, *perfumesofoman.com*
Amouage > *p.287* Mawaleh, 24 534 800; Muscat City Centre, 24 558 581; SABCO Commercial Centre, 24 560 533 *amouage.com*
Areej Muscat Al Mawalih Al Janubiyah, 24 558 752
Capital Store Salalah, 23 297 910, *csoman.om*
MAC Al Mawalih Al Janubiyah, 24 558 842

PLANTS & FLOWERS
Given Oman's climate, flowers are a real luxury, so they make a really nice present for a special occasion or for someone you love. There's a reasonable selection of florists in Al Qurm – worth mentioning are Caravan in the Al-Harthy Complex and The Flower Shop in SABCO. Bella La Rose in Al Qurum Complex specialises in (you guessed it) roses, and a stunning arrangement of 10 roses sprinkled with gold dust is reasonably priced at around RO 9. Simple bouquets can be bought at Sultan Center, Al Fair and Carrefour, and cost between RO 2 and RO 7, depending on the number and kind of flowers included. It's usually cheaper and quicker to send flowers internationally via the internet than to use a local florist.

Al Fair Madinat As Sultan Qaboos, 24 561 905
Angel Flowers Shati Al Qurm, 24 605 158

AMOUAGE

THE GIFT OF KINGS

WWW.AMOUAGE.COM

Traditional items make great souvenirs

classified ad in one of the local newspapers.

There is a row of shops behind the Polyglot Institute at the Wadi Adai Roundabout that sell second-hand furniture. They offer a delivery and assembly service for large items. House of Prose at Al Wadi Commercial Centre buys and sells used books and if you buy one from them you can sell it back for the half the original price if it's in good condition and you have the receipt.

SOUVENIRS

Shopping for presents in Oman is really tough because you always want to buy one for yourself as well. And why shouldn't you? If you're worried about your baggage allowance, find out how to ship goods home on p.269.

Traditional Arabic items make good gifts and ornaments. Popular items include the traditional coffee pot and small decorated cups used for drinking kahwa (Arabic coffee), incense burners, wedding chests and traditional Omani khanjars (daggers). Khanjars are almost always sold encased in an elaborately wrought sheath, and are arguably the most recognisable symbol of Oman. If you do buy one though, make sure you pack it in your suitcase rather than your hand luggage.

Other souvenirs that should evoke memories of your time in Arabia are miniature dhows crafted from wood or silver, Quran holders, pottery camels, the traditional hat worn by Omani men (a 'kumah'), clay pots and jars from Bahla, woven milking baskets with leather bottoms, and even ancient rifles.

Heavy silver Omani wedding jewellery is another wonderful souvenir and occasionally you'll find a rare piece or collector's item. Many souvenir items are made in India but sold as the real thing and it's not always easy to spot the fakes. Although the souks generally offer the best buys, it may be difficult to tell how genuine and old articles are unless you're an expert in Omani crafts.

The Oman Heritage Gallery, near the InterContinental Hotel in Shati Al Qurm, is a government-run shop that sells genuine craft items. It was established to keep traditional skills such as pottery and weaving alive and the staff will be able to tell you about the various items, where they come from and how long they took to

Bella La Rose Al Qurm, 24 566 766, *bellalarose.com*
Caravans Floral Al Qurm, 24 566 795
Carrefour Al Mawalih Al Janubiyah, 800 732 32, *carrefouroman.com*
The Flower Shop Al Qurm, 24 560 043
La Bonita Al Mawalih Ash Shamaliyah, 24 535 197
Sultan Center Al Qurm, 24 567 666, *sultan-center.com*

SECOND-HAND ITEMS

Churches and charity groups will take your unwanted clothes, toys and appliances off your hands as donations for people in need. The Catholic Church in Ruwi operates a charity shop, which is worth a visit for its abundant selection of nearly new clothing and home furnishings.

For second-hand baby equipment contact Muscat Mums (p.128) who host garage sales and send out a weekly email newsletter with goods advertised. If you want to make a few rials out of the stuff you no longer need, you can put a notice upon supermarket noticeboards or book a

make. The goods are more expensive than in other places, but they are genuine – and you're helping to keep these traditions alive and providing an income for the artisans. If you want a comprehensive reminder of Omani crafts, you can pick up the hefty, highly informative and beautifully illustrated *The Craft Heritage of Oman*, a two-volume coffee table book that covers everything on the subject.

If you love humorous 'kitsch', you'll have a field day in the souks where you'll find singing camels (choose from the Macarana or Habibi for a more authentic feel), T-shirts featuring the adventures of Tintin and Snowy in Oman, or the famous mosque alarm clock that wakes you up with the call to prayer. Don't leave Oman without one.

Sabco Souk Al Qurm, 24 566 701
Silver World Mutrah, 24 714 373

SPORTS GOODS

Most shopping centres have sports shops that stock a good range of sports clothing and equipment. You'll easily find racquets, balls and exercise equipment, although prices may be a little steeper than you would like. Diving equipment is easy to track down; there are shops at the Oman Dive Center near Qantab and at ScubaTec in the Al Wadi Centre.

Adidas Al Mawalih Al Janubiyah, 24 558 900, *adidas.com*
Magic Cup Sports Ruwi, 24 786 688
Marina Bandar Al Rowdha Haramil, 24 737 288, *marinaoman.net*
Markaz Al Bahja > *p.87* Al Mawalih Ash Shamaliyah, 24 540 200, *albahja.com*
Muscat Sports Al Qurm, 24 564 364
Oman Dive Center Al Amrat, 24 824 240, *extradivers-worldwide.com*

HIGHEST BIDDER

If you fancy a bit of competition when it comes to buying (or just like to get a real bargain) then visit omanbay.com. This website allows sellers to post items as diverse as shoes and boats for buyers to bid on. There are also occasionally properties to rent listed too and it's a great site for picking up cheap books in the '1 Rial Shop' section.

Sports For All Al Qurm, 24 560 086
Sun & Sand Sports Al Mawalih Al Janubiyah, 24 558 355, *sunandsandsports.com*
Supa Sportsman Al Humriyyah, 24 833 192

TEXTILES & HABERDASHERY

Textile shops in Oman are excellent and you can buy just about any fabric in any colour, although pure cotton can be difficult to find as it's not that popular among Arab customers. Even the smallest towns have fabric shops selling material by the yard. Shop assistants can advise you on how much fabric you need for the garment you have in mind. In Muscat, you'll find textile shops in all the major malls and on Ruwi High Street. In Ruwi, you can buy cheap saris that make interesting curtains and tablecloths. The Al Khamis Plaza in Al Qurm has two stores, Reise Oman and InStyle, that stock a huge range of silk and linen, and a basement store that sells printed Indian cushions and bedspreads at reasonable prices. Abu Hani sells a range of printed cotton for making bedding and quilts.

Tailoring

In Europe, having an outfit made to order is a luxury few can afford, but in Oman it's cheap and easy. The many fabric shops sell such a vibrant range of material that you'll be spoilt for choice, but once you've made your selection you're then ready to find a tailor. There are many tailors in Oman, some good, some not so good, and word of mouth is the best way to find one of the good ones.

In Muscat, most of the tailors are located in little shops in the back streets of Ruwi, the Mutrah Souk, or in the Al Wadi Centre or Al Khuwayr Souk. The process is an interesting one and may test your patience in the beginning. The best results come from bringing a picture or an original garment for the tailor to copy, or the shop might have a few magazines for you to browse through.

Sometimes the language barrier is problematic, but that's where the power of pictures comes in useful. When trying a tailor for the first time, order just one garment so you can check the quality of the work. Confirm the price before you leave the shop, and make sure you're clear about what the price includes (such as lining, zips or buttons) – and feel free to negotiate.

Always try the garment on when you pick it up, so that you can have alterations made if necessary. In this case alterations are usually free of charge.

Ahmed Abdul Rahman Traders Ruwi, 24 787 756
Instyle Al Qurm, 24 563 242
Mehdi Store Ruwi, 24 788 728
Mutrah Tailoring House Ruwi, 24 701 960
Raymond Shop Al Qurm, 24 561 142
Reise Oman Al Qurm, 24 571 609

WEDDING ITEMS

While it is not common for expats to get married in Oman, if you decide to do so you should be able to find almost everything you need to plan the perfect wedding. See p.129 for more details regarding help with planning your wedding – if you get yourself a good banquet organiser at one of the top hotels, they will probably have an army of contacts ready to follow your instructions.

Al Azad Flower Shop Madinat As Sultan Qaboos, 24 611 689
Bella La Rose Al Qurm, 24 566 766, *bellalarose.com*
Caesar Flower & Gifts Al Khuwayr Al Janubiyyah, 24 484 899
Caravans Floral Al Qurm, 24 566 795
The Flower Shop Al Qurm, 24 560 043
Gatherings 96 053 280, *gatheringsoman.com*
Greens Flowers & Plants Al Qurm, 24 496 975, *qbgoman.com*
Hemanth BG 99 743 039, *omanfotos.com*
Little Shop Of Flowers Hay As Saruj, 24 603 383

OUDH

Oudh is highly valued in the Middle East and can fetch astonishing prices. The perfume is made from the resin of Aloeswood trees and is imported from India, Cambodia and Malaysia. It's worn on the clothes and the skin and usually only on important occasions such as Eid, weddings, funerals or to celebrate the birth of a child.

Marks & Spencer Al Mawalih Al Janubiyah, 24 558 455, *marksandspencerme.com*
Maya Parfenova Green Leaf Photography 96 049 464, *mayaparfenova-photography.com*
Monsoon Al Mawalih Al Janubiyah, 24 558 902
Proshots Madinat As Sultan Qaboos, 24 692 469, *proshots.org*
Rahwanji Cards Wadi Kabir, 24 811 465, *ir-cards.com*
Risail Photo Laboratory 24 510 014
Rose For You Al Khuwayr Al Janubiyyah, 973 337 000
Rosie Gabrielle Photography 95 219 032, *rosiegabrielle.com*
The Ruwi Centre For Wedding Cards 24 816 775
Salim Al Harthy Photography 92 091 119, *salimphoto.com*
Therese Johnson Photography 95 167 417, *theresejohnson.com*

PLACES TO SHOP

DEPARTMENT STORES

Capital Store

Various Locations **24 561 888**
csoman.com

Capital Store is the ultimate shopping destination if you like luxury, and plenty of it too. This is where to head if you're looking for a Mont Blanc watch or pen, branded luggage, Dior sunglasses, or jewellery by Misaki and Nina Ricci. Capital also stocks a fantastic range of crystal and china, tableware, appliances and homewares, as well as one of Oman's widest ranges of perfumes and cosmetics. They also stock Pentax and Samsung digital cameras, and a range of accessories.

In total, there are six Capital Store branches around Oman: SABCO Centre (99 811 969), Qurm (99 811 050), Markaz Al Bahja (99 811 303), Qurm Commercial Centre (99 860 933), Centrepoint (99 811 363), Al Bustan (92 805 488), Sohar (99 866 283), Centrepoint Salalah (92 805 488) and Salalah (23 297 910).

If you've got cash to splash, with its range of products, and a nice personal touch, Capital does offer a great shopping experience.

Khimji's Luxury & Lifestyle
Various Locations **24 796 161**
khimji.com
The word megastore, when referred
to Khimji's, doesn't so much refer to
the size of the store as to the mega,
upmost exclusivity of the brands
you'll find in these beautiful stores.
Khimji's Leisure & Lifestyle stores are
veritable who's whos of upmarket
brands, showcasing the likes of Chanel,
Benetton, Moulinex, Samsonite, Sheaffer,
Ray-Ban, Nikon and Swarovski.

Departments cover everything from
fashion, footwear and sunglasses to
household goods, electrical appliances,
gadgets, luggage, pens and perfumes.
Other brands you'll find instore include
Bvlgari, Cross, Noritake and Mora. There
are branches of Khimji's in Ruwi (24 796
161), Qurm (24 560 419), Madinat Sultan
Qaboos (24 696 678) and Salalah
(23 295 671).

Marks & Spencer
Muscat City Centre Al Mawalih Al
Janubiyah **24 558 455**
marksandspencerme.com
Map **2 A3**
M&S (as it is fondly called by British
expats) is one of Britain's best-known
and most trusted department store
brands. It sells a range of quality men's,
women's and children's clothes and
shoes, as well as a teeny-tiny range
of food items (mainly sweets and
chocolates, but it's enough to remind
you how brilliant the UK's M&S food halls
are). One thing that you should definitely
keep a look out for whenever you are
passing by is their book section: it is very
small but they often have some great
children's classic titles at surprisingly
reasonable prices.

Marks & Spencer is famous for
underwear – they have some lacy
numbers, practical cotton whites and
a lovely range of sleepwear. Ladies of
unconventional sizes will be pleased to
discover that not only do they have a
petite range, but their normal clothes
go up to size 20 and in some lines, even
larger. You'll also be able to shop here for
purses and handbags, home furnishings
(they do stock a small range of
household items like candles, cushions,
cookware and utensils),
and a fantastic selection of makeup
and toiletries.

Shopping in a mall

Salman Stores
Various Locations **24 796 925**
salmancorporation.com
Salman Stores was founded in 1953 as
a retailer of quality kitchen and home
products. Just over 50 years later, the
group has grown into a leading importer,
distributor and retailer in Oman and
their range of products has expanded
dramatically. This is the place to go if you're
looking for tableware, glass and crystal
items, porcelain and china, cutlery, and
electrical appliances. Salman also stocks a
range of luxurious linen and luggage.

Only well-known brand names are good
enough for Salman Stores, so you can
expect to find Tefal cookware, Luminarc
crystal, Singer sewing machines, Helios
flasks and Giordano watches, to name
a few. Salman Stores has branches inAl
Qurum Complex (2456 0135), Mutrah
(2479 6925), Ruwi (2479 2343) and Salalah
(2329 3146).

MARKETS & SOUKS
Souk is the Arabic word for a place where
all variety of goods are bought, sold or
exchanged. Traditionally, dhows from the
Far East, Africa, Ceylon and India would

discharge their cargo and the goods would be bargained over in the souks adjacent to the docks.

Over the years, the items on sale have changed from spices, silk and perfume, to include electronic goods and the latest consumer trends. However, the atmosphere of a bustling market with noisy bargaining and friendly rivalry for customers remains. Souks are lively, colourful and full of people from all walks of life– so they're well worth a visit, even if you're not buying.

Oman's souks are some of the most fascinating in the Arab world, having retained the traditional way of doing business that has been lost in many places elsewhere. Apart from the obvious commercial purpose they serve, they're also a focal point for social interaction. In the interior, Bedouins come in from the desert and villagers from the mountains to meet other tribes or catch up on the latest news.

Every important town in Oman has at least one souk. The biggest and most famous of these are in Mutrah, Nizwa, Sinaw and Salalah and there's a women-only souk in Ibra every Wednesday morning. In addition to the permanent souks, pre-Eid markets known as 'habta' souks spring up overnight in places like Fanja, Samayil, Suroor, Nafa'a and Nizwa.

Visiting the souk is a fascinating experience at any time, but it's best to go in the late afternoon or early morning when it is cooler. Business begins at 07:00 (except for Mutrah souk, which starts at 09:30) with a break for midday prayers from 12:30 or 13:00 until 16:30. By 21.00 everything starts to close. On Fridays the souks only open in the afternoon and Thursdays and Fridays are the busiest – the best time to see the souk at full throttle and to take an active part in it.

AL MARSA VILLAGE

Although not yet quite a fully-fledged shopping district, the Al Marsa Village community on The Wave Muscat has a small retail area that is now open, providing residents and visitors with some of the basics (Kwik Kleen, WH Smith, Al Fair supermarket) as well as a handful of F&B offerings, such as Costa Coffee, Shang Thai and Pizza Express.

Gold Souk

Salalah
Map **4 H7**
People unfamiliar with Arabic gold may think it's of a poorer quality, but the reverse is usually true. Most of the gold sold in the region is 24 carat, and often softer and better quality than gold bought elsewhere in the world. However, it is very yellow and you may find that the designs are a bit gaudy, depending on your tastes. A visit to the Salalah Gold Souk may give you an opportunity to see young Dhofari girls choosing their wedding gold. You can shop around for a traditional Dhofari design, or design your own piece and have it made. This souk shouldn't be confused with the gold souk in Souk Al Haffa – the Salalah Gold Souk is situated in the Salalah Centre (after Pizza Hut, turn right 50 metres before the traffic lights).

Mutrah Fish & Vegetable Market

Nr Sultan Qaboos Port Mutrah
Map **2 K2**
The old fish market, at the Mutrah end of the Corniche, was a real traditional gem – as smelly, muddy and bloody as it would have been for hundreds of years. Unfortunately, however, that site has now been closed and is being renovated to create a huge, state-of-the-art fish market that will have more floor space, as well as cafes and seafood restaurants – although perhaps less of the charm. In the meantime, there's a temporary fish market here near Sultan Qaboos Port and you can still witness the true hustle and bustle of an Arabic market. It's also the best place to buy fresh seafood at low prices, but you'll have to get there early to score the catch of the day. From 06:30 the small fishing boats are dragged up the beach next to the market to unload their trophies. There always seems to be at least one of everything the Indian Ocean has to offer on display: tuna, hammour, kingfish, bream, octopus and prawns. Once you've wandered round the stalls and selected your fish, you can have it cleaned and gutted. It's fascinating to watch and the service costs only a few baisas.

Mutrah Souk

Nr Mutrah Corniche Mutrah
Map **2 K2**
Also known locally as Al Dhalam Market, this is one of the most interesting souks in the Gulf. The warren-like souk is still

Traditional tailoring in Muscat

a source of many Omani families' daily household supplies, as well as a draw for souvenir-hunting tourists. The main entrance is on Mutrah Corniche but there are many small streets in the village behind the Corniche that lead into the souk. The main thoroughfare is primarily for household goods, shoes and ready-made garments. Further inside, you can enjoy the mixed scent of frankincense, perfume oils, fresh jasmine and spices. The real excitement lies in exploring the side streets. The layout is confusing, but keep walking and you'll invariably end up either at the Corniche or at the main thoroughfare. Wander down any of the side alleys and you'll discover a selection of tiny shops full of dusty Omani silver, stalls of gleaming white dishdashas and embroidered kumahs, vivid cloth, multi-coloured head scarves, Omani pots, paintings, hookah pipes, framed khanjars, leatherwork and incense. There are plenty of bargains and no price is fixed.

When you get tired, you can stop at the juice bar before tackling the next section. Most of the shops here open from 09:30 to 13:00 and 16:00 to 23:00 daily, but are closed on Friday mornings and on Eid holiday weekends. There is paid parking all along both sides of Corniche Road from the Fish Roundabout, although it does get quite congested in the evenings.

Sinaw Souk

Nr Al Mudaybi, A'Sharqiyah Sinaw
Map **1 F5**
About two hours' drive from Muscat is Sinaw (at the crossroads of Route 33 and Route 27), a surprisingly busy outpost town set between the Wahibah Sands and the edge of the Empty Quarter. Behind mud-coloured walls and through green metal doors in the middle of the town is the souk, which is where Bedouins gather to do business and to socialise. It's all go around the outside walls, where camels, goats and young cattle are auctioned off.

Loading the animals into trucks is a tricky business and the camels in particular can deliver knockout kicks and need at least six men to push them in. Despite the indignity of it all, they manage to maintain their haughty demeanour. Fruits and vegetables are sold in the central covered area. Bedouin women in their metallic face masks ('burqa') happily trade next to men – which is quite unusual – and joke with you as you try on one of their masks.

Around the covered area are small shops selling jewellery where you can watch old silver being melted down to fashion new jewellery. Sinaw is a good place to find increasingly rare Bedouin silverwork, especially in the weeks approaching Eid when many come to trade livestock or old silver for little luxuries. The souk is closed on Eid holidays.

SHOPPING MALLS

Main Shopping Malls

Al Araimi Complex

Al Qurm **24 566 557**
alaraimicomplex.com
Map **2 H2**
This bright and spacious complex boasts over 70 shops with a wide array of consumer items. There are several opticians and jewellery stores as well as three banks. The first floor is devoted mainly to reasonably priced ladies' clothes shops (Nice Lady, Urban) and textile shops (Silk Island, Lakhoos). The ground floor shops include a few perfume shops (Ajmal, Maathir), a luxury home decor store (Marina), a photo processing store (Fotomagic) and a good children's toy store (Smart Kids Toys). In addition, there are a few eating outlets with Café Ceramique being one of the most popular. In this cafe, people can enjoy good quality food in a casual setting as well as/or taking part in ceramic painting activities. The basement holds many electronic and household appliance store as well as a recently opened pet store (Animal World).

The big parking lot is nearly always full as it's one of the last free parking areas in the Al Qurm shopping area. If you can't find a parking space there, the adjacent car parks offer pay parking at reasonable rates. This is one of three main malls in the vicinity, and therefore you can expect the area to get incredibly busy at peak shopping times. However, check your watch if you go there and the car park is deserted – most shops inside Al-Araimi close down for the lunchtime shift (usually 13:00 to 16:00).

Outlets include: Abdul Samad Qureshi, Ad Dirham Trading, Advanced Watches, Ajmal, Al Emad Trading, Al Khonji, Al Felaij Watches, Al Raid Jewellery, Al Shabab, Al Yashmac, Aman Trading, Annie Opticians,

Surprise your loved ones from **6 pm** to **7 am** worldwide, from **65** Bz/min

As good as being there

- Fixed line off-peak rates from **65 Bz** per minute
- Mobile off-peak rates from **85 Bz** per minute

Now, off-peak rates start earlier and extend longer, for 13 hours every day, 24 hours on Fridays and national holidays. Call more often, share more.
Make your loved ones smile!

For details SMS country code to 90000

Arabian Oud, Asdaful Khaleej Trading, Athlete Foot, Azawi Trading, Al Zakhir Trading, Cafe Ceramique, Canon, Charles & Keith, Chrome Shoes, City Watch, Colour Plus, Dgal, Elegance, Family Jewellery, Fatima Mohsin, Fotomagic, Genetco, Giordano, Golden Pearl Jewellery, Gulf Shells, H Flow, Hadeq Al Sinaw Trading, Hang Ten, House of Aoud Amber & Perfumea, Jumbo Electronics, Khazana, Lakhoos, L'Artisan, Levis, LG Electrical, Loay Intl, Lovely Lace, Lynes, Maathir Perfumes, Marina Gulf Trading, Modern Capital Opticians, Muscat Sports, My Jewellery, National Choice, Nice Lady, Nurmajan, OHI Electronics, Pretty Girls Centre, Princessa, Pure Gold, Ovation, Queens Tailoring, Raymond Shop, Remeh Trading, Riyam Marketing, Santus Trading, Opticians, Shatoosh Formasar, Soul Sheetal, Silk IslandTrading, Smart Kids Toys, Sudasia, Syed Junaid, The Athlete's Foot, Trendz, Urban, Yateem Optician, Zahrat Al Hana, Zahrat Al Khair.

Bareeq Al Shatti

Nr Beach Hotel, As Sultan Qaboos St Hay As Saruj **24 643 898**
bareeqalshatti.com
Map **2 H2**
One of the newest shopping spots in Muscat, Bareeq Al Shatti is situated below a popular residential block opposite the Beach Hotel in Shatti. It offers some great one-off shops and restaurants in addition to essentials such as a dental clinic, mini supermarket, hair salons, optician and a pharmacy. It's also a good choice for a quick bite, with several coffee shops and a foodcourt.

Kids will be entertained at Little Town, an indoor play area, while adults can use some free time at the beauticians and even a specialized eye lash salon. Arabic fusion restaurant Ubhar (24 699 826) is particularly recommended with its stylish interior, extensive menu and tasty choices for lunch and dinner, or just a juice with friends. Meanwhile, hungry teenagers and families are flocking to B+F Roadside Diner (24 698 836) with its retro menu of burger and shakes served in a modern interior. Bareeq Al Shatti's shops are open 10:00 to 22:00 Saturday to Thursday and 14:00 to 22:00 on Fridays, with the various restaurants closing later depending on the day.

Outlets include: Aballa Cafe, Afnan Dental Clinic, Ajmal International, Al-Farsy Pharmacy, Al-Qandeel Travel & Tourism, Ammar Saloon, Automatic Restaurant, Bread Talk, Buffet Restaurant, Bugatti, Candy Bouquet, Caribou Coffee, Colombian Aroma Café, Costa Coffee, The Cream & Fudge Factory, German Eye Centre, Grand Spa, Home House, Little Beauty Center, Little Town, Oman Arab Bank, Porsche Design, Pure Gold, Second Cup, Sham Optix, Shoe Palace, Supa Sportsman, Tips & Toes, Triple Time, Xtreme Lashes.

Jawharat A'Shati & Oasis By The Sea Commercial Complex

Way 2817, Nr InterContinental Hotel, Al Kharijiyah St Hay As Saruj **24 692 113**
jascomplex.com
Map **2 G2**
These lively beachfront locations sit side-by-side and attract visitors from all over the city. Shops are arranged on either side of a carpark that's a little too small to cope with the weekend crowds. Lunchtime and weekday evenings are more relaxed. You'll find some unusual items on sale here, like hand-rolled cigars, Turkish ice cream, chocolate covered dates, Italian coffee and Omani handicrafts, to mention a few. Totem sells unique clothing and footwear (plus Havaianas) while Pomegranate boasts a great selection of witty cards. For delightful home decor head to Gecko where you'll find gorgeous Balinese pieces and Designer's Guild fabrics and wallpapers. A browse around The Oman Heritage Gallery is like spending time in a museum, and you can buy some beautiful, traditional crafts, all handmade by local artists. Nails, Muscat's only salon devoted purely to pampering your hands and feet, is hidden behind red and pink glass walls on the first floor, and a new addition is a Spa Bar for men. If you're shopping for furniture you'll find Shuram, the sole agents for IKEA in Oman here.

There's also Moustach which sells designer gear for men.

Women are taken care of by the Eye Candy boutique which sells a stunning mix of designer clothing from the likes of See by Chloe, Essa and Paul & Joe plus sunglasses by Tom Ford. It is also the only Oman stockist of popular Australian makeup brand Becca.

The main attraction, though, is food. The centre is home to several restaurants, nearly all of which have open areas where you can watch the sun set over the sea.

The Sheraton Qurm Resorts' Sushi Night buffet on Thursdays is always popular, the O Sole Mio Italian restaurant at the carpark entrance is highly regarded, and D'Arcy's Kitchen serves hearty international food from breakfast to dinner and is popular with expats. And if your life is empty without your huge cup of cappuccino, you have the choice of Starbucks or Costa Coffee. Pizza Express and nearby Motif Beach Cafe are great for lunch or dinner, while Pane Caldo's Italian dishes (and antipasti platters) are particularly recommended. On a practical level, there's a post office, a barber and a brokerage house on the top floor of the right hand building, and a car rental agency on the opposite side. An Oman Arab Bank ATM is located outside the Casa del Habano cigar shop.

Outlets include: Beach Shop, Beauty Centre, Casa del Habana Cigar Shop, Costa Coffee, Eye Candy, Foto Magic, Gecko, Golden Pearl Jewellery, Gulf Jewellery House, Jazz, Moustach, Muscat Pharmacy, Muscat Pharmacy Perfumes & Cosmetics, Nick & Friends, Persian Carpet, Pizza Express, Second Cup, Shoe Palace, Totem and Tahani Co.

Markaz Al Bahja > *p.87*
Al Seeb St Al Mawalih Ash Shamaliyah
24 540 200
albahja.com
Map **2 A2**
This pleasant, medium-sized shopping mall is located just past Muscat City Centre as you drive to Sohar. It is now fairly quiet, since the relocation of Marks & Spencer and Toys R Us to Muscat City Centre. The main attraction now is the Danish furniture store ID Design. Cafes include Mood Café, Costa and The Coffee Bean & Tea Leaf. On the first floor, you will find a foodcourt (fast food outlets) and the Fantasia amusement centre for children. This includes a mini rollercoaster, bumper boats, electronic games etc. As well as ID Design on the ground floor, there is also the well-stocked Al Fair supermarket. The ground floor has a four screen cinema and some household tile suppliers.

Outlets include: Ajmal, Al Faisal, Al Jamil Optical, Al Lubahna, Asdaf, Baqa Fashion, Bank Muscat, Black Net Abayas, Bodum, Capital Skin Care Centre, Capital Store, Computer Book Shop, Clothes & Accessories, Elle, Eyewear, Fancy World,

Film and Audio World, Fulla Fashions, Golden Pearl Jewellery, Haider Stores, Happy Saloon, Ibn al Naamani, ID Design, La Bonita, Laura, Lujaina Fashions, Mohd. Sharief Stores, Muscat Bakery Stores, Muscat Pharmacy, Muscat Sports, Muscat Watch Center, National Fanar, Perfect Woman Fashion, Rado Tissot, Shoe Palace International, Stones, Yazin Mobil, Zone.

Muscat City Centre
As Seeb St Al Mawalih Al Janubiyah
24 558 888
citycentremuscat.com
Map **2 A3**
This is currently the busiest, biggest and most modern mall in Oman. Not even its location past Seeb Airport deters people who come from far and wide to shop here. At weekends the huge parking area is heaving with cars and you'll be lucky to find an empty space.

The main shop in City Centre is the French hypermarket, Carrefour. It is a great first stop for people setting up home in Oman – here is where you can buy all the things you need for a new house such as brooms, mops, ironing boards, towels, pots and cooking utensils. On the food side, you can buy delicious French breads and pastries as well as other European products. Carrefour is open from 09:00 until midnight and is busiest at weekends and during Ramadan, when there are in-store promotions. If a mega shopping trip around this gigantic mall leaves you feeling peckish, the L-shaped foodcourt has the usual fastfood places, as well as Arabic, Indian, Italian and Chinese cuisine, Baskin Robbins and Subway.

Next to the foodcourt there is a Magic Planet amusement centre for children, and there is a coffee shop at each end of the mall – one Starbucks and one Costa – great for resting weary legs and watching the world go by.

Other shops in the mall sell fashion, shoes, jewellery and even special items such as Omani halwa, chocolate covered dates and local handicrafts. The latest additions include Marks & Spencer, Toys R Us, Victoria's Secrets and Gap. The mall is open from 10:00 (except for Carrefour, which opens an hour earlier) to 22:00. None of the shops close for lunch.

Outlets include: Adams, Adidas, Al Felaij Jewellers, Alukkas, Amouage, Anoosh, Arabian Oud, Areej, Baby Shop, Carlton

Cards, Carrefour, Claire's, Colange, Damas, Early Learning Centre, Forever 21, Foto Magic, Gap, Gasoline, Grand Opticals, Himat, Hour Choice, Lakhoos Money Exchange, MAC, Mango, Mikyojy, Milano, Millenium Games, Misako, Monsoon, Mont Blanc, Mothercare, Muscat Pharmacy, Nawras, Next, Nine West, Oman Mobile, Pretty Fit, Promod, Pumpkin Patch, Splash/Lifestyle, Sun and Sand Sports, Swatch, The Watch House, Zara.

Qurum City Centre

Nr Muscat International School Madinat Al Ilam **24 470 700**
qurumcitycentre.com
Map **2 H2**
Qurum City Centre is one of the newest malls in the capital, offering some of the same stores as its sister destination out near the airport (p.297). It is anchored by an enormous Carrefour which is a welcome addition to the area and packed at weekends.

Other shops include Jumbo Electronics, Monsoon, H&M, Next, Mango, L'Occitane, Early Learning Centre, Aldo, Bose, Borders and Adidas. In addition to these, you will also find telecom provider outlets, a pharmacy, National Bank of Oman, Foto Magic and Magrabi Opticals. The large foodcourt includes all the usual suspects such as KFC, Pizza Hut, McDonald's, Cinnabon, Magic Wok, Starbucks, Costa and Coffee Republic plus a branch of Italian restaurant Biella.

The customer service facilities include 1,000 parking bays, taxi drop-off and pick-up zones, numerous ATMs, information desks, toilets, prayer rooms and wheelchairs for the elderly or people with disabilities.

Qurum City Centre is open from 10:00 to 22:00 Saturday to Thursday, 14:00 to 22:00 on Fridays and Carrefour is open 09:00 to midnight throughout the week.

Outlets include: Accessorize, Adidas, Aldo, Bendon, Biella, Body Shop, Borders, Bose, Bossini, Carrefour, Cellucom, Cinnabon, Claire's, Coffee Republic, Cold Stone Creamery, Costa Coffee, Damas, Early Learning Centre, Fillings, Foto Magic, GeeKay, Giordano, Gulf Greetings, H&M, Hatam, Hour Choice, Inglot, Jumbo, KFC, Kipling, L'Occitane, MAC, Magic Wok, Magrabi Opticals, Mango, McDonald's, Monsoon, Mothercare, Muscat Pharmacy, National Bank of Oman, Nawras, Next,

Nokia, Oman Mobile, Osh Kosh, Pablosky, Pierre Cardin, Pizza Hut, Porsche Design, Promod, Pure Gold, Rado, Shamiana, Starbucks, Steve Madden, Sun Spot, Swatch, Tap a L'Oeil, Zahara Tours.

SABCO Commercial Centre

Al Qurm **24 566 701**
sabcogroup.com
Map **2 H2**
This was one of the first true shopping malls in Oman and, while there are some who prefer the more modern, glitzier malls, SABCO retains a loyal following of shoppers who love it because it is tried, tested and trusted, and they know where everything is. On the positive side, it is usually fairly quiet, so it's perfect if you hate the more frantic atmosphere of the busier centres. It is, however, often quite difficult to find parking here and it is one of the few areas in Muscat where you must pay for parking.

Aside from that, shopping here is a fairly relaxing experience and there are plenty of wooden benches on which to flop down after you have exhausted yourself with a marathon shopping trip. These benches are also the ideal locations for a bit of people watching.

You can buy yourself a bottle of the world-famous (and locally made) Amouage perfume in Amouage's shop, Oman Perfumery, which is near the entrance to the mall. The jewellery shop upstairs is excellent for repairing jewellery, as well as for manufacturing pieces according to your own designs. SABCO is also home to upmarket outlets like Godiva, Cerruti, Raymond Weil and Philippe Charriol and Creatures Pet.

There's a busy coffee shop in the lobby, and a nearby HSBC ATM. The main attractions for most visitors to the mall include Nine West, The Body Shop and The Flower Shop. The authentically decorated souk in the corner of the SABCO centre is an Aladdin's cave of old Omani silver, local handicrafts, souvenirs and pashminas from India. You may also find some Pakistani leather. Bargaining is allowed, making the prices competitive with Mutrah souk.

Outlets include: Abu Mehad Money Exchange, Al Batra Bookshop, Al Felaij Jewellers, Al Felaij Watches, Al Gazal Opticians, Al Khamis, Al Qurum Jewellers, Al Raid, Amouage Oman Perfumery, Capital Store, Carlton Cards, Cerruti, Elle,

Muscat City Centre

Foto Magic, Future Jewellery, Gardini, Godiva Chocolates, Jazeera Electronics, Jazz, Jewellery Corner, Le Carat, Modern Electronics, House, Moustach, Muscat Beauty Salon, Muscat Pharmacy, Perfumes, Muscat Pharmacy, Muscat Watch Centre, New Age Music, Nine West, Philippe Charriol, Rana Abdulrahim, Raymond Weil, Samsung, Shakeela Hamad Mohd, Silver Jewel Box, Snowhite Laundry, Sports For All, Tahani, The Body Shop, The Flower Shop, Video Centre.

Other Shopping Centres

Al Harthy Complex
Nr Sultan Centre Al Qurm **24 564 481**
Map **2 H2**
This stand-alone building beside the bustling Sultan Centre looks either like a giant space rocket or a futuristic mosque. Whatever your interpretation, the mall is an impressive landmark, especially at night when the lattice roof and the blue dome are lit up. One of the calmer malls in terms of shopping and parking, it's popular for its internet cafe, Muscat Pizza and Kargeen Cafe. The complex also provides a good range of services – a post office, key cutting kiosk, a barber and a few tailors. The Oman Association for

Consumer Protection has an office on one of the upper floors, and it's worth paying them a visit if you have a complaint you haven't been able to resolve. At The Gallery you'll find paintings by Omani artists, while Cards Store has a fair selection of humorous greeting cards, toys and souvenir T-shirts.

Fresh and dried flowers can be ordered from Caravans, and the Modern Technical Computer Centre sells Apple computers and accessories. The first floor is almost entirely made up of shops for women and young girls, including the biggest branch of Muscat Pharmacy Perfumes and Cosmetics.

Also within the mall is a shop run by the Association for the Welfare of Handicapped Children where you can buy cheap accessories, cosmetics and T-shirts – and shop as much as you like because it's all in the name of charity! A small amusement park in the basement will keep the kids occupied.

Outlets include: Abu Ayat, Ajmal Perfumes, Al Felaij Jewelers, Al Mira Mobil Phones, Al Sulaiman Jewellers, Aman, Gift Store, Happy Salon (for children), Health & Beauty Natural Herbs Centre, Horialbra Shoes, Italian Jewellery, Muscat Apollo

Photoshop, North Oasis Tailoring, Oman Perfumes Centre, Oman Trading, Patchi, Qurum Textiles, Rahela Trading, Steps and The Unique Corner.

Al Khamis Plaza
Al Qurm **24 562 791**
Map **2 H2**
The medium-sized Al Khamis Plaza in Qurm is spread over three floors and the top floor is a shoe shopper's heaven. There's a branch of Clarks, and a World of Shoes where you can buy brands like Sebago, Caterpillar and Dockers and Arabic-style sandals for men and women. Other draw cards are the textile shops that have an amazing range of Indian silks, men's shops with suits from Pierre Cardin and Lanvin, and the elaborate and exclusive Mouawad Jewellery. The fountain next to the pleasant Café de Lotus provides the soothing sound of running water. Parking is free, but demand is high.

Outlets include: Abu Hani Textiles, Al Fahid, Al Shaza, Anakah, Arabian Oud, Crystal Gallery, Damas, Dunya Stores, Fashion House, Hamood al Hadhramy, Indian Art Palace, Instyle Fashion Textiles, Kwik Kleen, Oman Optical, Oxygen, Risail Sports, Ruwi Jewellers, Savtalfan, Suhool Al Qurm, Tareti and Yateem Optician.

Al Masa Mall
Hay As Saruj **24 693 341**
Map **2 G2**
Al Masa Mall's location in Shati Al Qurm makes it popular and easily accessible for most of the city's residents. Al Masa Mall offers a decent shopping variety, with stores selling everything from electronic goods and cosmetics to home decor and furnishings.

Some of the newest stores to open their doors include Radio Shack, Red Earth, Sanrio and Supa Sport.

The mall's large foodcourt and entertainment areas are particularly busy at evenings and weekends; almost every type of food imaginable is available, while there are many indoor games and arcades, as well as a dedicated kids' play centre and a ten pin bowling centre.

Al Qurm Complex
Al Qurm **24 563 672**
Map **2 H2**
Looking like a sprawling Omani fort, complete with flags and enormous, carved wooden doors guarding the Al Fair supermarket, CCC is a gathering place for locals and expats of both sexes. It is also popular with families who take the kids to Kids Rest (p.255), the play area upstairs. The opening of Canadian coffee

Jewellery and textile stores

shop chain, Second Cup, over the road has resulted in a definite surge in customer traffic. They serve gourmet coffee and tea, lovely desserts and snacks in modern, comfy surroundings. To the left of the main entrance of the shopping centre is a small souk where you can pick up a wide range of leather goods, trinkets and Omani handicrafts. The Al Fair Supermarket, which sells western food products (including pork) occupies one wing of CCC. Just outside Al Fair is an Oman International Bank ATM.

The other half of Qurm Commercial Centre is a shopping centre with the usual range of jewellery, phone, carpet and perfume shops under a beautiful stained glass ceiling. Health nuts will love this centre. The Health Shop carries multivitamin protein drinks, Scholl foot products, orthopaedic cushions and pillows and blood pressure monitors. Island Natural Herbs has a wall of dried bark and herbs guarded by two old Omani men who can presumably concoct anything for what ails you, as well as 'natural' slimming products for women. Sport One is full of huge plastic jars of food supplements for those looking to increase their body mass.

There's a small amusement park for kids, a key cutter, and an internet cafe. The centre's outside walls enclose a gigantic parking lot bordered by small shops and food outlets, including Bollywood Chaat, Pizza Hut, McDonald's, Baskin Robbins and Nando's. Opening hours are 08:30 to 21:00 but individual shop hours may vary.

Outlets include: Ad'dirham, Al Basim, Al Batna, Al Felaij Watches, Al Khamis, Al-Marooji Travel & Tourism, Al Nazim, Al Raid, Al Shabiba, Ameera Oud, Bella La Rose, Capital Store Perfumes, Cards Store, Damas, Daraah, Foto Magic, Gardini, Gulf Jewellers, Hamood Textiles, Jazeera Electronics, Kids' Corner, King of Perfumes, Kwik Kleen, Le Carat, Mobile Phone City, Modern Music, Muscat Watch Centre, Nafaf, Najeeb Technical, Nine West, Philippe Charriol, Raymond Weil, Reham Beauty Centre, Ridhwan Opticals, Riyam, Roses, Salman Stores, Sony, Sports For All, Tahoos, The Body Shop, Waleed Pharmacy and Yiti Art Gallery.

Centrepoint
Nr Madinat As Sultan Qaboos Signal
Madinat As Sultan Qaboos **96 473 101**
landmarkgroupme.com
Map **2 G3**
More of a department store than a mall, this big two-storey building is a very popular

destination and home to all manner of stores catering to all tastes and budgets, from baby clothes to homeware and all that's in between.

Incorporates outlets for Home Centre, Baby Shop, Shoe Mart, Splash, and Lifestyle. On the ground floor, fashion items and toys can be found; there is also a small play area for children and a prayer room for Muslim customers. On the first floor, there is a wide variety of household items, decorative items, artificial flowers and furniture.

Souk Al Khuwayr
Al Khuwayr Al Janubiyyah
Map **2 F3**
Also known as the Al Khuwayr Commercial Centre, this is not a souk in the traditional sense, but rather a collection of small shops in one huge block in the middle of Al Khuwayr. It offers a range of goods and services including tailors, furniture makers, second-hand electrical shops, hardware shops, one-rial shops, launderettes, a bakery, a pharmacy and a few coffee shops.

Cheap household items and fabrics are without doubt two of the main draws, but you can also have film developed here (or have digital images printed), and there's a government-run fruit and vegetable market where you can get good quality fresh produce at a fraction of the price you'll find in supermarkets.

Zakher Shopping Mall
Al Khuwayr Al Janubiyyah **24 489 884**
zakhermall.com
Map **2 G3**
A small shopping centre, Zakher has the usual selection of shops found in other malls and an internet coffee shop. The shops cater mostly to an Arabic clientele, so if you're looking for dishdasha, Arabic art, or even a few traditional souvenirs, it's a good destination.

You can also buy high-end Bang & Olufsen and G Hanz audio and video equipment at Photocentre on the ground floor, and it boasts a CD and video store and a full colour copy centre. There's a National Bank of Oman ATM near the mall entrance.

Outlets include: Ajmal Perfumes, Body Shop, Emerald Jewellery, Hallmark Cards Store, Muscat Pharmacy, My Fashion, Optic Bazaar and Snow Star Sweets and Gifts.

GOING OUT

GOING OUT

It may be quieter than some of its neighbours, but Oman offers plenty to delight and entertain, from pubs and clubs to comedy nights and concerts.

Muscat is home to a wide variety of dining experiences. Aside from the usual hotel options, there are some interesting independent Arab restaurants to be found if you take the time to explore. With tourism being actively promoted in Oman, the nightlife is constantly improving.

While Muscat isn't famous for its buzzing nightlife, some hotel bars have extended their opening hours to 03:00 (thus brightening up the social scene a bit). Be aware though, that drunk and disorderly behaviour in public is frowned upon and fortunately most expats seem to respect this. If you want to buy alcohol for consumption at home, you need to apply for a liquor licence. Only non-Muslim residents with a labour card are allowed to apply. A trip to the movies is another popular pastime in Oman and film lovers who want to see the latest Bollywood, Hollywood and Arabic releases are reasonably well catered for.

NIGHTLIFE

Life in Muscat is led at a relatively sedate pace, which is good for the stress levels

INTERNET CAFES

Internet cafes or shops can be found in most areas of Oman, generally in shopping centres, but also in small shops. Not surprisingly, Muscat has more internet cafes than the rest of Oman, especially in Ruwi. Prices range from 400 to 700 baisas per hour, with different rates during the evenings and on weekends. Many places allow you to pay per quarter of an hour. You should shop around for a cafe that suits your needs – not all have broadband, printers, scanners or webcams. The best value shop is Mamoon Internet Services in Al Khuwair (24 692 369). They have the cheapest rates and the best service and equipment. First Internet Cafe in the Al Qurum Complex Shopping Centre is the most expensive at 700 baisas per hour (no broadband).

but this does also mean that there's less chance of a wild night on the town here than in other cities in region, like Dubai or Bahrain. Places tend to wind down quite early but, considering its size, Muscat has a reasonable variety of restaurants and bars.

The following section covers cafes, bars, pubs and nightclubs as well as 'cultural' entertainment such as theatre and comedy. A lot of Muscat's social scene may appear a little exclusive to a newcomer, with cliques that seem to have limited memberships. However, once you're in, you're in and the expat community is in fact very friendly and welcoming. As there isn't a huge range of places to go out to, you will start to see familiar faces out and about.

Many people socialise at home, particularly after the bars and nightclubs have closed and especially during Ramadan. In addition, much of the nightlife centres around the hotels, which generally organise events throughout the year. Special nights are arranged about a month in advance, so it is a good idea to have your name added to their mailing lists to receive information on what's happening. They will usually email, fax or mail you details of forthcoming events.

If you're after a bar scene, check out some of the places listed in the Restaurants section on p.308. Some restaurants also function as a bar, and a few even have a dancefloor so you can eat, drink and be merry. Throughout the week, some of the bars and restaurants hold special nights and promotions to attract custom. Wednesdays and Thursdays are the busiest nights out as, depending on what working week you follow, they are the start of the weekend. Most bars and nightclubs close between midnight and 01:00, especially those in hotels, while the occasional bar will stay open until 03:00.

Capri Court

Drinks

While Oman is a Muslim country, it has a relatively liberal attitude towards the consumption of alcohol by non-Muslims. Alcohol is generally available in hotel restaurants and bars that have the appropriate licence. However, drinking alcohol in these establishments can be an expensive pastime – nearly double what you are probably used to paying. Non-Muslims can apply for an alcohol permit that allows them to purchase alcohol from a liquor store. You're not likely to find a huge selection in your local off-licence, and wine can cost three times more than you usually pay, but spirits are cheaper. Local bottled water is produced either in Oman or the neighbouring Emirates and is of a high quality, even compared to premium-imported brands. So instead of paying for an international label, try the local water which should go down well at around 200 baisas for a 1.5 litre bottle.

COMEDY NIGHTS

The regular comedy scene in Muscat is unfortunately rather limited, but shows are held on an ad hoc basis. The Green Can Laughter Factory makes a regular return to Muscat (part of the Laughter Factory,

a comedy promoter based in Dubai) and is very well received. Keep an eye out in the local press and at the hotels or get your name on hotel mailout lists – regular venues include the Radisson BLU hotel (p.70) and Crowne Plaza (p.68).

CONCERTS & LIVE MUSIC

Classical music performances are held at the Royal Opera House, with the seasons changing every six months or so. Check the schedule at their website (rohmuscat. org.om) but be warned that the tickets are often sold out weeks in advance. Some of the hotels, particularly the Grand Hyatt Muscat (p.68) and the Al Bustan Palace (p.67) also arrange events where, for example, the Royal Oman Symphony Orchestra might perform. There is a fairly regular pop and rock concert scene, and you might be able to catch a few performances from big name stars: keep an eye (or ear) out for announcements in newspapers, email newsletters and on the radio.

DOOR POLICY

Some of the cooler hang outs implement a members' only policy that allows them to control the clientele frequenting the place. At quieter times though, non-members may have no problem getting in, even if unaccompanied by a member. Basically, the management uses the rule to disallow entry if they don't like the look of you or your group, in which case they will point to their sign and say 'sorry'. Large groups of men are often refused entry, so breaking up your group by recruiting some friendly ladies is a worthwhile tactic. Getting irate really won't get you anywhere, so if you're refused entry your best bet is to move on and find somewhere else that's more accommodating.

DVD & Video Rental

Because most people have satellite TV, DVD and video rental shops are not as booming as they used to be. And then of course there is the easy access to cheap and nasty DVDs – the fact that they are illegal doesn't seem to deter many people and the salesmen do a roaring trade. However, there are times when rental places still come in handy – especially when it is too hot to go outside and there is nothing good on TV. Video Club in Al Khuwayr (near Home Centre) usually has a good selection of fairly recent releases (24 600 079).

THEATRE

Theatre in Muscat is limited, but there are occasional professional performances. The amateur theatre companies always welcome new members, either on stage or behind the scenes. The Muscat Amateur Theatre (p.245) is one of these and there are regular performances at the InterContinental (p.68) which usually includes a buffet dinner. There are also the occasional murder mystery dinners where you're encouraged to display your thespian skills by being part of the performance.

CINEMAS

Al Bahja Cinema Markaz Al Bahja, As Seeb, 24 540 856, *albahjacinema.net*
City Cinema, Shati Al Qurm Bldg 195, Way 3005, Block 228, Shati Al Qurm, 24 607 360, *citycinemaoman.net*
Ruwi Cinema Nr Mansoor Ali Centre, Ruwi, 24 780 380, *movies.theemiratesnetwork.com*

EATING OUT

Oman's multicultural heritage and population is reflected in the variety of international cuisine you'll find here. From Arabic to Mediterranean to Polynesian and everything in between, you'll have a fine time exploring. Eating out is a time-honoured Arabic pastime; it's seen as an opportunity for friends and family to exchange news, gossip and argue the merits of anything from a foreign leader to the latest mobile phone.

Most restaurants open early in the evening, around 19:00, but generally don't get busy until about 21:00. Lunchtimes can vary between 12:00 and 15:00 so check before you arrive. Many of the places we've covered here are very popular, so if you want to dine out at the weekend, particularly if there's a group of you, it's best to book a table.

A large number of Oman's restaurants are situated in hotels, especially in Muscat, but there are also many independent restaurants throughout the town, some of which are licensed. (If you want to have a tipple with your meal, check for the Alcohol Available icon in individual reviews). While the licensed restaurants are popular for obvious reasons, there are a vast number of excellent independent restaurants around town that shouldn't be ignored just because they are 'dry'.

The more upmarket restaurants tend to specialise in one or two types of cuisine, while the smaller outlets will often entice you with a variety, so it's not uncommon to find an Indian restaurant that also offers Thai and Chinese dishes. Many also have theme nights featuring different types of cuisine, such as seafood, Italian or sushi. Some have weekly buffet nights when you can eat, and sometimes drink, as much as you like for a good value, all-inclusive price. Easy on the purse strings but hard on the waist band...

Delivery & Takeaways

Most fastfood outlets, including Burger King and Pizza Hut, offer free home delivery, but you can also order dishes from your favourite local eatery and have them deliver too. So you can get shawarmas, sweet and sour noodles or butter chicken delivered to your doorstep and enjoy all the comfort of eating in – without the washing up that usually goes with it.

Street food

to satisfy even the most ravenous veggie diner. Also, due to the large number of Indians and Pakistanis, who are often vegetarian by religion, you'll find a large number of restaurants – many small but incredibly cheap – that offer vegetarian dishes in a range of cooking styles.

A word of warning: if you are a strict vegetarian, always confirm that your meal is completely meat-free when ordering. Some of the restaurants cook their 'vegetarian' selection with animal fat, or on the same grill as their meat dishes. Also, in some places you may need to check all the ingredients as seemingly vegetarian dishes may contain unwelcome extras.

STREET FOOD

Sidewalk stands throughout the city sell shawarma, rolled pita bread filled with lamb or chicken carved from a rotating spit, and plenty of salad. Costing about 300 baisas each, these are inexpensive, well worth trying, and offer an excellent alternative fast food to the usual burger. The stands generally also sell other dishes, such as falafel, ta'amiya, (small savoury balls of deep-fried beans) or foul (a paste made from fava beans).

While most shawarma stands offer virtually the same thing, there are some that stand out from the rest, and sometimes, surprisingly, it's the smallest, most low-key place that you only happen on by chance.

You'll find that regulars are often adamant that their particular favourite serves the best falafel in town. You'll find your favourite too – often the very first place you eat at when you come to Oman. Even if it's superb though, you should make the effort to look around as every restaurant has its own way of doing things.

Special Deals & Theme Nights

Some places, usually hotels, hold occasional promotions with various themes – the InterCon (p.68) and Al Bustan Palace (p.67), for example, come particularly highly recommended.

These offers also run alongside special nights, such as ladies' nights, which are usually held weekly, and happy hours. The weekly and monthly what's on/entertainment publications and the venue itself will be able to update you on the latest promotions.

Events like quiz nights tend to be hosted by most popular bars and pubs and many attract quite a following, with Rock Bottom (p.24 564 443) holding an especially popular quiz. As a bonus, the (liquid) prizes are often quite good.

VEGETARIAN

Vegetarians will probably be pleasantly surprised by the range and variety of vegetarian cuisine that is offered in Muscat's restaurants. Arabic food, although dominated by meat in the main course, actually offers a staggering range of mostly vegetarian mezze, and the general affection for fresh vegetables, chick peas and aubergines provides enough variety

BRUNCH & OTHER DEALS

Friday brunch is perfect for a lazy (or, sometimes, start and end!) to the weekend, especially once the really hot weather arrives. Popular with all sections of the community, it provides Thursday night revellers with a gentle awakening, while, for families and groups of friends, it's a pleasant way to spend the day together.

Many of the venues put on a variety of fun activities for the kids, allowing parents to relax and concentrate on the fine food and drinks. Different brunches appeal to different crowds; some have fantastic buffets, others are in spectacular surroundings, and some offer amazing prices for all you can eat.

A number of the four and five-star hotels offer an incredibly enticing spread as well as use of their pool, gardens or beach as part of the deal. Ask around and find out who does what, where and for how much, and make a day of it.

HYGIENE

Don't be fooled by the appearance of some of the outlets you come across in Oman. Many are probably not as bad as they might look. Then again, some of them are, so use your judgment. The local authorities are clamping down on hygiene so many places have bucked up their ideas and started to follow procedures and guidelines as laid out by the municipality.

TIPPING

Tipping is up to you. The service charge is not generally passed on to the waiting staff and it applies regardless of whether the service was excellent or lousy. So if you would like to reward the waiting staff directly, a 10% tip will be much appreciated.

Try to hand it directly to the person you'd like to thank, as at some establishments tips go straight into the till. Most people tend to leave their change as a tip, particularly in cafes.

CATERERS

A popular and easy way to put on a party, special occasion or business lunch, in-house catering allows you to relax and enjoy yourself, without worrying about the cooking.

A number of companies offer this service, so decide on the type of food you want, be it Indian, Chinese, Lebanese or finger food, and ask your favourite restaurant or cafe whether they do outside catering. Most of the larger hotels have a catering department that's usually capable of servicing extravagant five-star functions. You're not confined to the house – how about throwing a party in the desert or on a dhow? Depending on requirements, they will provide anything from the meal to crockery, waiters, furniture and even a clearing up service. Costs vary according to the number of people and food. Check the Yellow Pages for details and look out for flyers.

RESTAURANTS & CAFES

Al Aktham
Nr Muscat International Hotel
Al Khuwayr Al Janubiyyah **24 489 292**
alaktham.com
Map **2 F3**
Behind a rather run-down exterior hides a surprisingly large restaurant with an even larger menu. At Al Aktham you can choose from Arabian, Indian, Chinese and Filipino dishes or, if none of that appeals to the tastebuds, there's Continental too. It's a good place for a private dinner party in one of the screened rooms and you're sure to have an excellent value meal, served by polite and friendly staff. For lunch or dinner, Al Aktham is a hidden gem.

Al Bahar
Millennium Resort Mussanah
Al Musanaah **26 871 555**
millenniumhotels.com
Map **1 F4**
Give your taste buds a treat and feast on the mouth-watering dishes produced by the Chef Reiner Thieding and his team, in a tranquil, romantic setting over-looking the marina. The food Reiner and his team produce is nothing short of spectacular, as magnificently presented as it is absolutely scrumptious. As a starter, the lobster Carpaccio will fill your mouth with a burst of flavours so delicious you won't forget it. If something spicy is more your style, don't miss out on the Hara Bhara kebab. When it comes to the main course, the Lasooniachari Jhing (tiger prawns) are so lip-smackingly good you'll definitely want to go back for more. The 'swan in love' profiteroles are the perfect ending to a great evening out.

Al Barouk
Beach Hotel Muscat Shati Al Qurm
24 696 601
beachhotelmuscat.com
Map **2 G2**
A good option if you're in Shati Al Qurm and fancy Lebanese for lunch or dinner. The interior is simple yet thoughtfully decorated and the atmosphere conducive to a relaxed meal. A Lebanese musician and singer play gentle tunes on Monday nights. If you want to dine alfresco, the best spot is by the hotel pool – perfect for relaxing, taking in the view and enjoying some shisha. The menu includes all the

Lebanese favourites as well as a few extras, although prices aren't much more than at a regular takeaway joint, and Al Barouk is licensed to serve alcohol.

Al Diwan Restaurant
Ramada Muscat Shati Al Qurm
24 603 555
ramadamuscat.com
Map **2 G2**
Hungry but not entirely sure what you want? Then head down to the Ramada Hotel's Al Diwan dining area where you'll find Indian, Arabic, Chinese and international cuisine. The diversity of the menu is impressive, but like so many other places that try to be everything, overall quality and taste leaves a little to be desired. Sit on the terrace and you'll be tucking into your meal overlooking the car park and some of Muscat's flashiest cars.

Al Khiran Terrace Restaurant
Al Bustan Palace, A Ritz-Carlton Hotel
Haramil **24 799 666**
al-bustan.intercontinental.com
Map **2 L4**
A bright and open space with fantastic views of the garden and the beautiful bay is only the beginning – this is perhaps one of the friendliest restaurants in Oman. In addition to alfresco breakfasts, it serves up some of the most mouth-watering themed buffets in Muscat, but there's also an Italian a la carte menu available every night for those who prefer more restrained dining. The staff are attentive and will ensure your evening is one to remember.

FRUIT JUICES
A variety of fresh juices are widely available, either from shawarma stands, juice shops, coffee shops or cafes. They are uniformly delicious, healthy and cheap, and made on the spot from fresh fruits such as mango, banana, kiwi, strawberry, watermelon and pineapple – or the mixed fruit cocktail is a blessing for the indecisive. Fresh lemon mint juice is also very popular (ask for no sugar if you prefer), as is the local milk, laban, a heavy, salty buttermilk that's best drunk on its own (but doesn't go well in tea or coffee). Arabic mint tea is available, but it's probably not drunk as widely here as it is in other parts of the Arab world; however, Arabic coffee (thick and strong) is extremely popular and will have you on a caffeine high for days.

Al Mas
Bowshar Hotel Al Azaiba **24 491 105**
Map **2 G2**
Al Mas is located in the Bowsher Hotel, just north of the Ghubrah/Bowsher roundabout. The sleek hotel decor sets the pace for this fabulous little eatery. Open most hours, this is more of a restaurant than a quick coffee stop, and its menu is bursting with Indian, Chinese and Arabic dishes that will tempt you into staying longer. Those wanting just a quick coffee stop can choose from the small menu of snacks and quick bites. The staff are friendly and convivial and the prices are surprisingly reasonable.

Al Tajin Grill
Radisson Blu Hotel, Muscat Al Khuwayr
Al Janubiyyah **24 487 777**
radissonblu.com
Map **2 F3**
With a quality menu including black angus and wagu beef, this is the place to come to when you need a substantial meal at an affordable price. The price of your main course includes a selection of delicious starters from the buffet (local delicacies, fresh meats and fish) as well as a buffet dessert station. There is also a wide range of other meat, fish and vegetable dishes available, with the grilled lobster and the ovenroasted lamb rack being particular popular. For excellent value, try the all-inclusive offer – RO 7 is added to the price of your meal in return for an unlimited beverage selection. There is an extensive wine list and due to the fact that the restaurant hosts a wine and cheese club (first Tuesday of every month), there are always interesting choices.

Al Tanoor
Shangri-La's Barr Al Jissah Resort & Spa
Al Jissah **24 776 565**
shangri-la.com
Map **1 G4**
This vibrant restaurant offers an al la carte menu with something for everyone, including the kids. Available from noon to 22:45, there are several theme nights to dive into. Be sure to reserve a table on Thursdays as seafood night is the most popular; Tuesday's Indian theme night is also one not to be missed; an Omani buffet is served on Wednesdays. To end the meal, choose from the many mouth-watering desserts or, if you'd prefer, a selection of fine cheese and biscuits are on offer.

Alauddin Restaurant

Khalil Bldg Ras Al Hamra **24 600 667**
Map **2 J3**
You'll be hard pushed to find someone
who lives in Muscat and hasn't enjoyed
food from Alauddin, whether eating in
or taking away. It is, and deservedly so,
an enduring favourite. Don't expect the
decor to knock your socks off, and you're
not here for the booze either, because
this place is not licensed, but do arrive
with high expectations of a gastronomic
good time. Excellent Indian, superb
Arabic, mouth-watering Chinese and tasty
international cuisine is all available and
all served to deliciously high standards. A
Muscat must.

Arabic Oven

CBD Area, HSBC Junction Mutrah
24 797 276
Map **2 K2**
Located in the heart of the CBD, making
it convenient for office workers, Arabic
Oven is a nice change from the usual
sandwich at your workstation. The giant
water feature on the wall makes for
tranquil background noise while you
enjoy biryanis, curries, and shawarmas,
or pay per plateful for buffet salads. The
salads from the main menu are great

low-fat, carb-free lunch options (in other
words, they're not drowning in dressing).
For those who couldn't care less about
carbs, the home-baked Omani bread with
hummus or moutabel is delicious.

Atrium Tea Lounge

Al Bustan Palace, A Ritz-Carlton Hotel
Haramil **24 799 666**
al-bustan.intercontinental.com
Map **2 L4**
You'll be hard pressed to find a better way
to take in the splendour of the palatial Al
Bustan than with high tea at the Atrium.
Relax under the magnificent dome and
imposing crystal chandelier with a coffee
or tea and one of the delicious cakes
or pastries. The friendly service, plush
surroundings and the gentle music issuing
from the piano makes it terribly easy to
linger in the lap of luxury.

Automatic Restaurant

Nr SABCO Al Qurm **24 561 500**
Map **2 H2**
Automatic has established itself as the
benchmark for fast Arabic food, among
locals and expats alike. It's all about fresh
juices, mezze and large portions for very
reasonable prices. The waiters are efficient
and the food quick to your table. Those
with large appetites will be well-pleased
with the four daily specials, while the
range of traditional starters, salads, grilled
meats and locally caught seafood should
keep everyone happy. Friday brunch here
is also a must. Other locations: Al Khuwayr,
24 487 200; As Seeb, 24 424 343.

Bait Al Bahr

Shangri-La's Barr Al Jissah Resort & Spa
Al Jissah **24 776 565**
shangri-la.com
Map **1 G4**
If you fancy sampling some local delights
from the nearby sea, Bait Al Bahr is a
perfect choice. Standing alone from the
main hotels, a stop off the lazy river route
running throughout the resort, you are
made to feel as unique as the location you
are sitting in. Bag a table on the veranda
and cool off in the ocean breeze while you
select from the mouth-watering menu.
Obviously the emphasis is on succulent
seafood, but there are some vegetarian
choices too. Your chosen dish is presented
to you by elegantly dressed waiting
staff. Portions are on the small side, but
decadently rich.

Al Tajin Gril

Barista

SABCO Commercial Centre Al Qurm
24 571 531
Map **2 H2**
If you need a hit of good Italian coffee then Barista is the place. Situated in the SABCO Centre it's a bright, airy spot for a cup of caffeine with a pastry or some cooling icecream. The milkshakes are particularly good. It's a popular spot in the evenings and it is open from 09:00 until 22:00 throughout the week, with a later opening time of 16:30 on Fridays.

Beach Pavilion Restaurant & Bar

Al Bustan Palace, A Ritz-Carlton Hotel
Haramil **24 799 666**
ritzcarlton.com
Map **2 L4**
The seashore location of the Beach Pavilion makes this a delightful place to enjoy a light lunch, watching the waves crash onto the shore as you tuck into good food. Home-baked rolls supplement smallish portions and the staff are only too happy to adjust a dish to suit your needs. Service can be slow at weekends and holidays – in fact, it's so popular that you'll be lucky to get a table at all, so make sure you book in advance. Newly rebuilt, this restaurant now serves fresh seafood, and comforting dishes like risotto, year round.

The Beach Restaurant

The Chedi Muscat Al Ghubrah Ash Shamaliyyah **24 524 343**
chedimuscat.com
Map **2 E3**
The path to this glamorous beachside spot follows a candlelit walkway through the grounds of The Chedi. You can choose from outdoor dining or a table beneath the high ceilings, Colonial-style fans, modern wooden screens and rich burgundy silks of the restaurant. The well-chosen wine list allows you to order by the bottle or glass (try the delicious gavi di gavi white) and the menu is exclusively seafood, boasting chilled and cooked dishes with an undeniably Asian feel; think mussels in a spicy coconut broth and yellowfin tuna with a chilli and garlic risotto. The exotic flavours continue through to dessert with chocolate and coconut cheesecake served with Malibu sorbet. At the more expensive end of the scale, you're bound to leave this stunning spot feeling sated, de-stressed and spoilt.

Bellapais

Al Rusayl Centre Rusayl **24 521 100**
Map **1 F4**
This unpretentious gem of a restaurant is well worth the 40km drive from downtown Muscat. Don't be put off by the decor – the quality of the food surpasses all initial impressions. Known for the authentic moussaka, baked lamb, steaks and seafood, it also offers Chinese and Indian dishes. Try the mezze to start – it's an ideal introduction to your gastronomic journey, whichever route you choose to continue on. Bellapais comes alive at lunchtimes, is quieter in the evenings but no one has been known to leave hungry.

Bin Ateeq Restaurant

Nr Shell & McDonalds Al Khuwayr Al Janubiyyah **24 478 225**
binateeqoman.com
Map **2 F3**
One of the friendliest and most welcoming restaurants in Muscat, Bin Ateeq serves Omani food at its best. The takeaway queue is testament to the popularity with the locals but dining in is worth the experience. The cane-clad walls are reminiscent of a strange sort of jungle hut, but aircon keeps those jungle temperatures down. Simply spiced meat, chicken and fish, all still on the bone, and mountains of fried fluffy rice are brought to you as you recline on your majlis cushion. Prepare to get messy.
Other locations: Ruwi, CBD Area, 24 702 727; Nizwa, opposite Friday Market, 25 410 466; Salalah, near Souk Hafa, 23 292 380; near Al Saada Public Park, 23 225 652; 23rd July Road 23 292 384; Middle Town, 23rd July Road 23 290 232.

Blue Marlin

Marina Bander Al Rowdha Sidab **24 737 286**
marinaoman.net
Map **2 L3**
A haven of tranquility, intimacy and serenity, the Blue Marlin makes the most of its picturesque location. The alfresco breakfasts by the pool (including full English and buffet options) are incredibly popular at the weekend and booking is recommended, especially in the cooler months. Come evening, a sundowner watching the boats is also particularly enjoyable. The modern European fare is fantastically prepared and presented, surpassed only by the service. The menu

offers a good selection of seafood with a bit of a twist (the fish pie is fantastic), as well some unusual variations on non-fish dishes. This is one of the few restaurants where as much care is taken with the presentation as with the food itself.

Bollywood Chaat

Al Qurum Complex Al Qurm
24 565 653
Map **2 H2**
This vegetarian restaurant has a Bollywood-themed menu of light meals and snacks, in a bright fastfood-style setting. The heart-shaped potato cutlets (kajol cutlet) and the sweet and sticky dumplings (moon moon gulab jamun) are two dishes not to be missed. The fact that everything's so reasonably priced makes a meal here that little bit more special. Service is prompt and cheery and the staff willing to explain the ingredients of the dishes on offer.

Cafe Ceramique

Al Araimi Complex Al Qurm
24 566 617
cafe-ceramique.com
Map **2 H2**
Children and adults alike can unleash their inner artist at Café Ceramique, with a huge range of pottery pieces just waiting to be painted and glazed. Simply choose from the selection (which includes everything from dinner plates to jewellery boxes), pick your paints and get creative. Even if you're not in the artistic mood, Café Ceramique's extensive and well-priced menu, with an emphasis on healthy quick bites, makes it a worthwhile trip. The fantastic staff are on hand to recommend dishes while serving up great advice for your work of art, or showing customers the painting and firing process. The light, bright space is complemented by a large room downstairs for parties and events, making this a popular destination for birthdays and unique corporate days out.

Cafe Glacier

Al Qurum Complex Al Qurm
24 489 245
glaciercafe.com
Map **2 H2**
This spacious cafe is a welcome pitstop on a day of shopping, and it's long been a favourite of families and weary shoppers. Well-presented dishes and generous portions satisfy a hungry crowd. Free popcorn appeals to kids,

and high chairs are available. As well as serving Rombouts coffee, there are herbal teas, fruit smoothies and a menu that includes breakfasts, pasta, salads, soups, sandwiches and pancakes, all served by friendly and efficient wait staff. There is another branch at Zakher Mall, Al Khuwayr (24 694 245).

Capri Court

Shangri-La's Barr Al Jissah Resort & Spa Al Jissah **24 776 565**
shangri-la.com
Map **1 G4**
Guests will be charmed by the menu which is varied without being too busy. The dishes on offer are fresh and wholesome with a nice mix of pasta, meat and fish as well as quite an extensive selection of vegetarian options. If you choose to dine alfresco you can relax to the sounds of the waves gently lapping on the shore. Service is prompt and knowledgeable without being intrusive and the waiters have lots of friendly advice. For the sweet toothed, a treasure trove of treats is on offer with the traditional Italian tiramisu taking center stage. A well-researched wine list can turn any quiet dinner into a party and there is also a fresh and fruity mocktail menu to lend some zest to the occasion.

The Chedi Pool Cabana

The Chedi Muscat Al Ghubrah Ash Shamaliyyah **24 524 343**
chedimuscat.com
Map **2 E3**
This is one of those places you're unlikely to find unless someone has told you to look for it – and it's worth noting the tip. The Cabana at the glamorous Chedi hotel is a tranquil and intimate place to enjoy a cool evening breeze and a choice of set menus. The small number of tables ensures that each receives efficient service. The flavour is Mediterranean with an emphasis on seafood, served with finesse. An evening isn't complete without one of its wickedly decadent puddings. It's not a cheap night out, but it's definitely worth the splash.

Chili's

Muscat City Centre Al Mawalih Al Janubiyah **24 558 815**
chilis.com
Map **2 A3**
A real family favourite, Chili's has a great menu, a fun atmosphere and helpful, amiable staff. The menu caters to all

tastes – even those who are counting the calories, with 'guiltless' and 'low carb' options. Chili's burgers are famous and the lunchtime specials of soup and salad combos are popular, but to really get your taste buds going, try the steak and fish dishes. Shame there are no guilt-free versions of the sinful molten chocolate cake. Children are well catered for with activities and they get colouring pencils and sheets to keep them occupied and a varied menu to fill them up. It is also a good spot for kids' parties.

China Mood
Al Bustan Palace, A Ritz-Carlton Hotel
Haramil **24 799 666**
ritzcarlton.com
Map **2 L4**
Acknowledged locally as one of the finest Chinese restaurants in Muscat, China Mood excels on many levels. For a start, the atmosphere is decadent and the staff superbly attentive, ensuring that your plate is consistently filled with fabulous colours, tastes and textures. The meat dishes are tender and juicy and the vegetables perfectly cooked and refreshingly free from the usual greasy oil slick. A fantastic place to enjoy a Far Eastern meal, although an early reservation is essential if you want to bag a table.

China Town Restaurant
Al Qurum Complex Al Qurm
24 567 974
goldenspoongroup.com
Map **2 H2**
From the restaurant's decorated facade, it's easy to guess that the dinner that awaits you inside China Town is going to be nothing less than splendid Chinese cuisine. Much-loved and well-known dishes are served in a serene setting and expectations of fabulous fare are well met. A takeaway and delivery service is also available, but those dining in will enjoy excellent food presented in a 'no-fuss' manner by friendly and courteous staff.

Chinese Garden
Nr Oman Ice Rink Al Khuwayr Al Janubiyyah **24 489 414**
Map **2 F3**
Although a tad garish in design, Chinese Garden serves tasty and satisfying food in a no-frills, no big bills manner. Attached to Oman's only ice rink, in Al Khuwayr, the atmosphere within the small restaurant is friendly and the service is quick – the epitome of cheap and cheerful Chinese cuisine. It's a great place for a laidback supper but you can just make out the low rumblings coming from the generators that power the ice rink.

The Chedi Pool Cabana

CinnZeo Bakery Cafe
Al Masa Mall Shati Al Qurm
cinnzeo.com
Map **2 H2**
The smell of freshly baked cinnamon rolls will draw you into this bakery cafe. Not only does it have a lovely atmosphere, but you can watch the bakers at work in the open kitchen. Try the world-famous cinnamon rolls with different toppings, or splash out (calorie-wise) on one of the decadent chocolate twists. All of these naughty-but-nice delights come straight from the oven – you can choose fruity sauce instead of chocolate or caramel if you want to kid yourself that you are being healthy. It's perfect for a yummy sugar fix, a good cup of coffee and friendly service in comfortable surroundings.

Come Prima
Crowne Plaza Muscat Al Qurm
24 660 660
crowneplaza.com
Map **2 H2**
Inside or out, this establishment has some of the best views in town. Top these with garlic bread like it should be – hot, fresh, and very, very moreish – a traditional Italian menu with homemade pasta, pizza, meat and seafood dishes and you have yourself the making of an excellent night out. (And if you find yourself craving mamma's cooking during the day, it offers delivery at lunch time). Food is served at a relaxed pace, allowing time for plenty of chatting. Come Prima is not the most hip restaurant in town, so come here to enjoy the food and your friends – not to be seen.

Copper Chimney
CBD Area, Nr Central Bank of Oman Ruwi
24 780 207
Map **2 J3**
Behind the imposing copper door lies an impressive interior and a fabulous kitchen. Best of all, the fine Indian fare served perfectly meets the expectations the decor raises. A high, domed ceiling, complete with great copper lamps, means you eat your meal in an airy, spacious room. And once you've ordered from the mouthwatering selection of dishes, you can watch your meal being cooked in the vast clay oven in the kitchen. For excellent Indian food in a grand setting, with reasonable prices, look no further than Copper Chimney.

Curry House
Way 317, Bldg 1360 Al Wutayyah
24 564 033
Map **2 J2**
For some reason, food eaten with your fingers always seems to taste better. So, while you don't have to eat with your fingers, the Curry House near the Al Wattayah Roundabout, is a truly authentic North Indian dining experience and you'd do well to dive in hands first. The service is some of the best you'll find in Oman, and the delicious and cheap buffet has a superb selection of Indian cuisine. Many of the curries are served in 'karahi', lovely copper bowls imported from India, and all are accompanied by beautifully fragrant vegetable pilau. This is a cheap and very cheerful spot.

D'Arcy's Kitchen
Jawharat A'Shati & Oasis By The Sea Commercial Complex Hay As Saruj
24 600 234
Map **2 G2**
Overlooking the sea, this sunny cafe in the buzzing Shati Al Qurm area is a welcome stop for a late breakfast, lunch or a light dinner. Step inside and you'll feel as though you've walked into a farmhouse – a theme that's matched by the size of the servings. The interesting menu includes special salads, soups and burgers with a selection of delicious fruit smoothies, all served up by friendly staff. Whether you pop in for a light meal or just fancy a coffee while reading the newspaper, D'Arcy's treats you well. There is also a new branch in Madinat Al Sultan Qaboos – there, you'll find some extra dishes and a nice, fairy-lit outdoor area.

Fish Village
Nr Automatic Restaurant Al Khuwayr Al Janubiyyah **24 480 918**
Map **2 H2**
It's not quite a village, but it is a great little restaurant that is worth a visit for the view alone. It is located opposite the Radisson Blu, looking out over the Taimer Mosque and on towards 'White Mountain'. The outside seating area is large and merges with the other restaurants on either side. It's a bustling area, with lots of locals congregating over shisha and a shawarma. If your appetite permits, treat yourself to spicy squid, shish tawook or a sizzling tajin.

Four Seasons Restaurant
Haffa House Hotel Muscat Ruwi
24 707 207
shanfarihotels.com
Map **2 J3**
Four Seasons has an a la carte menu, but it's the favourably priced buffet that draws the diners in time and again. The choice of fare is international and simple but tasty. You'll be offered a soup starter, the choice of four or five salads, five main courses and a couple of desserts. It certainly makes for good value, but the ambience and setting is more business, less pleasure.

Golden Dragon
Nr Kargeen & Ziyara Madinat As Sultan
Qaboos **24 697 374**
Map **2 G3**
An upmarket and attractive Chinese restaurant in the quiet part of the Madinat Qaboos Shopping Centre, Golden Dragon has an extensive menu of Chinese and Thai dishes. Its interesting specialities are highly recommended – try the Dragon Boat, which consists of a range of starters served on a miniature wooden boat, or the sizzling dishes from the Chinese oven. This is the place to go for good value, fine Chinese cuisine served by friendly, experienced staff.

Golden Gate Cafe
Al Araimi Complex Al Qurm
24 571 644
Map **2 H2**
There's nothing fancy at the Golden Gate Cafe, but don't let that stop you from trying it out. The inexpensive food comes quickly and the venue is a good getaway from the hustle and bustle of Qurm. Located downstairs in the Al Araimi Complex, it has a fairly wide selection of quick meals to refuel the diehard shopper. Try the soup served inside a massive crusty roll. The service has to be beckoned but it comes with a smile.

The Golden Oryx
Al Burj St, CBD Area Ruwi **24 706 128**
thegoldenoryx.com
Map **2 J3**
The Golden Oryx is situated in the heart of the CBD. It's a bit of a drive, so the restaurant's popularity is a credit to the chefs. The decor is sumptuous and the service is impeccable, right down to the free water throughout your meal. The menu is Chinese, Thai and Mongolian,

and the Chinese crispy duck in plum or barbecue sauce is a particular favourite. Make sure someone in your party orders the Thai chicken satay starters (and that you get a bite) – they're delicious, with loads of crunchy, decadently rich sauce. Not to be missed.

Golden Spoon Restaurant
Nr Zawabi Mosque Al Khuwayr Al Janubiyyah **24 482 263**
goldenspoongroup.com
Map **2 F3**
This is a popular casual spot for good, inexpensive Chinese and Indian food. The decor is a bit dark, but the attentive and friendly staff more than make up for it. The menu is extensive and there are always excellent daily specials to be had. Servings are very generous and each dish is full of flavour. It's tempting to make a meal of the sweet and sour soup, but don't – save room for tasty dishes like the murj masala. There is another branch in As Seeb (24 424 214).

Green Cedar Restaurant
Nr Al Sarooj Centre Ruwi **24 601 199**
Map **2 J3**
This may just be a drive-through, nestled between Al Fair Supermarket and the petrol station, but the food is good enough to savour. There are a few tables outside if you wish to linger a little longer to fully appreciate your snack. You'll find the usual shawarma stand favourites like chicken or mutton sandwiches wrapped up with spicy sauce, in local bread. The real jewels though are the falafels, which are particularly tasty with lots of tahina sauce and crunchy vegetables. If you're lucky you may even come across a french fry in your sandwich – a local delicacy!

Grill House
Nr Centrepoint Al Khuwayr Al Janubiyyah
24 603 660
Map **2 F3**
At the Grill House, just a stone's throw from the Al Khuwayr Roundabout near Madinat Qaboos, the service comes faster than usual and with a smile. You'll feast on well-prepared dishes of the Indian, Chinese or Thai ilk and leave thrilled at the tiny total on your bill. An enjoyable experience from start to satisfying finish. You'll find another Grill House in Barka (24 541 502). Other branches: Near Muscat International Airport, Naseem Garden, Al Khoud and MBD, Ruwi.

Jade Garden
Al Qurum Resort Ruwi **24 605 945**
alhashargroup.com
Map **2 G2**
Even though it's located at the Al Qurum Resort on Qurm Beach, the Far Eastern restaurant just misses out on a sea view. Fortunately, the food is well worth your full attention. Choose from a selection of Chinese, Thai and teppanyaki dishes and all the takeaway classics, including lemon chicken and seafood noodles. The typical oriental puddings, from lychees to delicious ice creams, are fabulously indulgent. Service is prompt between courses and the atmosphere is peaceful; however, Thursdays are sushi nights and very popular.

Jean's Grill
Sultan Center Al Qurm **24 567 666**
sultan-center.com
Map **2 H3**
Located within the Sultan Center supermarket, Jean's Grill may seem like an unlikely destination for lunch or dinner; however, it actually offers an exciting and international spread that's well worth stopping by for. Your choices begin with soups and salads, and carry on through to pasta, curries, grilled meats, fish and even braised duck. Tuck into pastries from around the world, unlimited soft drinks, tea and coffee, and enjoy it all for a very reasonable set price. All-in-all, the perfect pit stop to refuel after a mammoth shopping excursion.

Karachi Darbar
Nr Zawabi Mosque Al Khuwayr Al Janubiyyah **24 479 360**
goldenspoongroup.com
Map **2 F3**
This is a fantastic fastfood joint and perfect if your lunch hour allows you just enough time to grab something quick and tasty.

BAKERIES
In addition to bread, Arabic bakeries offer a wonderful range of pastries, biscuits and Lebanese sweets. Look out for 'borek', which are flat pastries, baked or fried with spinach or cheese, or the biscuits filled with ground dates. All are delicious, and must be tried at least once. Omani Halwa is a sticky concoction of sugar, ghee (clarified butter), rosewater and saffron. It's made in huge batches and served in little dishes with a spoon.

A good sign is its popularity with the local community, particularly later in the day and around dinner time. The menu is limited and consists of curries and grilled dishes, but everything is delicious and the tandoori chicken is exceptional. Karachi Darbar is great value for money and casual dining – definitely one to try.

Kargeen Caffé
Madinat Al Sultan Qaboos Centre
Madinat As Sultan Qaboos **24 692 269**
kargeencaffe.com
Map **2 G3**
This is a quaint, tented cafe, full of quirky ornaments and furniture, which could easily be part of someone's home. The menu comprises hearty soups, salads and Arabic appetisers, as well as burgers, pizza and steak for mains and a range of cakes, desserts and fruity drinks. This outdoor cafe is a delightfully unusual way to enjoy a leisurely coffee-and-cake session or a complete meal within a great setting. Other locations: Centrepoint, 24 694 048; Al Harthy Complex, 24 560 531.

Khyber
CBD Area Ruwi **24 781 901**
Map **2 J3**
Khyber serves an extensive range of Indian food, with some Chinese options thrown in to boot, and boasts two licensed bars and separate dining areas. Its location, near the Central Bank of Oman in Ruwi's busy CBD, means it's well-placed to meet the demands of hungry business executives and it offers excellent specials that reflect this. Specialities include delicious Indian sweets and homemade frozen and fried icecream. The restaurant also boasts a mobile tandoori oven for outside catering events.

Le Mermaid
Nr Grand Hyatt Hotel Shati Al Qurm **24 602 327**
Map **2 G2**
In the shadow of the Grand Hyatt, you'll find one of the coolest cafes in Muscat. With a large outside seating area complete with majlis tents, shisha and great sea views, this popular cafe has people dropping by from all over town. Dishing up a wide range of seafood, grills and snacks, Le Mermaid is a hidden treasure. Indulge in a refreshing fruit cocktail or choose from the range of coffees and local hot drinks.

Naseem Lounge

The Lobby Lounge
The Chedi Muscat Al Ghubrah Ash Shamaliyyah **24 524 343**
chedimuscat.com
Map **2 E3**
Another string to the bow of the tranquil haven that is The Chedi is the Lobby Lounge. Situated just beyond the majlis area at the entrance, the cafe is an intimate arrangement of comfy seating areas in a brightly sunlit room. At night it's perfect for sundowners or after-dinner drinks. Guests spill outside to bag one of the sought-after tables around the giant gas fires in heavy black planters. You'll need to hover about to claim one – people don't give them up easily.

Majlis El Shams
InterContinental Muscat Hay As Saruj **24 680 000**
ichotelsgroup.com
Map **2 G2**
A relaxing light lunch or an indulgent coffee and cake session are on offer at this cafe in the InterContinental Muscat. Despite its grand surroundings, it's a surprisingly peaceful and intimate spot, and you could happily while away time here, musing over the range of delectable cakes and pastries. It also has freshly made sandwiches, fresh juices, and a selection of

teas and coffees. The service is extremely friendly and this, coupled with the comfortable sofas and chairs, means an afternoon here slips away very easily.

Marjan
Grand Hyatt Muscat Hay As Saruj **24 641 234**
muscat.grand.hyatt.com
Map **2 G2**
A restaurant with a split personality. By day, it's an extremely relaxed, child-friendly restaurant overlooking the pool and the sea. Families with young children will appreciate the kid's menu/activity booklet, high chairs and half portions. For lunch, you can choose from classics such as grilled tuna nicoise and club sandwich or try something authentically Indonesian such as the melt-in-your-mouth cumi goring (fried squid in a surprisingly tangy lime mayonnaise). By night, Marjan is a very grown up place. Start off your alfresco evening with a cocktail inspired by the colonial era while being serenaded by a duo of Indonesian musicians. Evening diners can discover a much wider range of Indonesian dishes representing all regions of this diverse country. The redang daging (dry beef curry in coconut milk) is a delight. Or, if sushi is your thing, Chef Yudi can offer you a large selection, freshly prepared.

Mokha Cafe

Grand Hyatt Muscat Hay As Saruj
24 641 234
muscat.hyatt.com
Map **2 G2**

The a la carte menu here has something for everyone in the form of seafood, pasta, steak and vegetarian dishes all served in both international and Arabic styles. If you are in town on a Wednesday evening, try not miss the seafood buffet; the barbecued lobster and prawns are outstanding and you can keep going back for more. Other theme nights include the British night on a Monday and, if you are looking for more authentic Arab fare while in Oman, then don't miss the Saturday night buffet when traditional Arabian food is served in a mouth-watering manner.

Mumtaz Mahal

Nr Al Qurum Natural Park Al Qurm
24 605 907
Map **2 H2**

Mumtaz Mahal is one of the most interesting dining experiences to be had in Muscat. Costumed waiters will ply you with baskets of poppadoms and dips (try the date chutney is a must try) while you're making your choice. Vegetarians will be very happy here – there are plenty of paneer and spicy vegetable dishes on the menu – while meat lovers will be equally impressed and satisfied. During peak season a traditional Indian band plays to the room and the atmosphere is lively and relaxed.

Musandam Cafe & Terrace Restaurant

InterContinental Muscat Hay As Saruj
24 680 000
ichotelsgroup.com
Map **2 G2**

A real winner for breakfast or brunch, the Musandam Cafe & Terrace is less of a sure thing for dinner, particularly during the off-season when you can expect typical hotel buffet fare. However, for a Friday family brunch, this is the spot. Fresh fish and salads, roast meats, an egg station and pancake making make this an ideal venue for a young and hungry family. On Fridays, children can have their faces painted and watch magic shows while you fill up at the buffet. And at this casual eatery, no one minds gaudily-daubed children running amok between the tables.

Mydan

Millennium Resort Mussanah
Al Musanaah **26 871 555**
millenniumhotels.com
Map **1 F4**

Overlooking the marina, this restaurant offers both indoor and terrace seating, and guests can choose from the buffet or the a la carte menu for breakfast, lunch and dinner. The international buffet is particularly good value and there is a wide range of mouth-watering dishes that change on a daily basis. Chefs at the cooking stations are happy to cook fish/meat to your liking; the coq au vin and beef tenderloin are firm favourites. Staff are friendly and helpful and the atmosphere is relaxed.

Nando's

Nr CCC Complex Al Qurm **24 561 818**
binmirza.com/nandos
Map **2 H2**

Put simply, at Nando's decent grub is served quickly. Diners enjoy something different: from main meals you eat with your hands, to the legendary chicken espetada, your appetite will be nicely satisfied. Nando's speciality is the marinated chicken, butterfly grilled on a naked flame and then spiced with the seasoning of your choice – from mild and lemony to hot-lips chilli. For a warm greeting at the door, rustic decor, the chance to watch your food being cooked and value prices, you just can't go wrong.

Naseem Lounge

Millennium Resort Mussanah
Al Musanaah **26 871 555**
millenniumhotels.com
Map **1 F4**

A delightful hideaway, where you can lap up the air-conditioned comfort of armchairs during the hot summer months, or enjoy the cane, cushioned outdoor seating that looks out over the marina. A wide selection of cakes and sandwiches delight taste buds and there's a fine selection of coffees and teas, including South African rooibos (bush) tea.

O Sole Mio

Jawharat A'Shati & Oasis By The Sea Commercial Complex Hay As Saruj
24 601 343
Map **2 G2**

The award-winning O Sole Mio is ideal for a candlelit dinner for two or an informal dinner with friends, thanks to its lively atmosphere, musical entertainment and delicious Italian food. The menu is extensive, with plenty of grilled options for the health-conscious, and servings are ample. The staff are attentive and offer quick, efficient service. O Sole Mio's popularity stems from its prime location and its ability to deliver good food at reasonable prices, making it advisable to book in advance.

Olivos Restaurant & Terrace

Radisson Blu Hotel, Muscat Al Khuwayr Al Janubiyyah **24 487 777**
radissonblu.com
Map **2 F3**
This all-day dining restaurant overlooks the hotel's swimming pool and gardens. It provides a nice enough, shaded setting for dining alfresco with themed nights and buffet style catering (although a wide range of international dishes is available off the a la carte menu too). With great service in a relaxed atmosphere, Olivos is a good value for money restaurant and the ideal location for a relaxed dinner with friends.

The Palm Restaurant

Palayok Restaurant

Nr OCC Ruwi **24 797 290**
Map **2 J3**
It's a bit of a challenge to find, tucked away in Ruwi, but the hunt is worth the effort. It looks a little dull on the outside but opens up into a bright, cheery little place. Mr Marlon will make you feel at home and offer you some excellent suggestions regarding the menu. Fresh vegetables, fish and meat are perfectly seasoned and dressed in delicious sauces to create some of the finest Asian eating in Muscat. Whether you decide to eat-in or take advantage of the home-delivery option, Palayok should be on your must-try list.

The Palm Restaurant

Park Inn By Radisson Muscat
Al Khuwayr Al Janubiyyah **24 507 888**
parkinn.com
Map **2 F3**
A bright, friendly all-day buffet restaurant, breakfasts offer everything from fruit and Danish to a halal fry up or waffles. The daily lunch buffet is served from 12:00-14:00, with all manner of hot dishes, salads and soups up for grabs, while for dinner the buffet is complemented by an a la cart menu that offers a wide variety of dishes to satisfy even the most international of palates. If a quiet, unrushed meal is what you are after, this place will do the trick.

Pane Caldo

Jawharat A' Shati, Nr InterContinental Hotel Al Qurm **24 698 697**
pane-caldo.ae
Map **2 G2**
This family-friendly restaurant errs just on the right side of bright, without being garish. The handy location next to Jawahat A'Shati Commerical Complex attracts customers, but the super thin pizzas, fantastic antipasti platters and fresh pastas keep the interest of food fans. With reasonable prices, lunch and dinner opening hours, and friendly service, Pane Caldo is a reliable Italian that you'll revisit again and again.

Passage To India

Hattat House Compound Al Wutayyah **24 568 480**
Map **2 J3**
Passage To India is one of Ruwi's finest. Located at the back of Hatat House, it's a truly special evening out. For most of the evening traditional Indian music plays

quietly in the background while you eat excellent food, but every now and then, dancers in exquisite costumes come out and perform beautifully synchronised dances from all over India. More than just a meal out, the combination of the relaxing ambience, efficient service, superb food and good value makes this an exceptional experience.

Pavo Real
Madinat Al Sultan Qaboos Centre
Madinat As Sultan Qaboos **24 602 603**
Map **2 G3**
Muscat is perhaps the last place in the world you'd expect to find a slice of real Mexico, but that's exactly what you get when you walk through the doors of Pavo Real. Don't over indulge in the complementary taco chips and salsa because you'll need room for the fabulous food and must-have margaritas (which are also available in non-alcoholic form). Pavo Real offers you all the ingredients for a great night out – awesome ambience, friendly service, absolutely delicious food and live music. Monday nights are for karaoke; the singers are pretty good and some take it very seriously. Oddly, dancing is only allowed by special licence. Still, you'd better book your table and your song early as the place fills up quickly.

Prince's Restaurant
Nr Zawabi Mosque Al Khuwayr Al Janubiyyah **24 482 213**
Map **2 F3**
Despite the rather gloomy interior, Prince's Restaurant serves up a wide and appealing range of Mughlai, Tandoori, Chinese and continental dishes at an appealing price. The decor is eclectic but the interior is comfortable and the service quiet and efficient. The smells from the kitchen encourage you to concentrate on the Indian specialities, such as the tandoori from the clay oven, which is delicious and filling. For a low price you can have a banquet fit for a prince.

RBG Bar & Grill
Park Inn By Radisson Muscat Al Khuwayr Al Janubiyyah **24 507 888**
parkinn.com
Map **2 F3**
If you want a great steak and a friendly service then the RBG Bar & Grill is the place to visit. This busy restaurant offers a tempting variety of international cuisine,

local specialities and signature grill dishes as well as great light bites. The spacious and stylish venue is unique in catering for those who wish to catch a football match while enjoying a great meal or indeed somebody looking for a quiet intimate meal for two. The presentation and quality of the food is superb, and it is no wonder the open-plan kitchen is located in the centre of the restaurant, showing off the chefs' culinary talents. Check the boards at the entrance for the great food and drink specials.

The Restaurant
The Chedi Muscat Al Ghubrah Ash Shamaliyyah **24 524 343**
chedimuscat.com
Map **2 E3**
The Restaurant boasts a fusion of contemporary Arabic and Far Eastern decor, aptly reflecting its menu. You can choose from sushi, tagine, fish or curries from one of the open kitchens, but leave room for the puddings, cakes and macaroons. You'll appreciate the warning as these are the best you'll ever taste in Muscat. Prices are high, especially for alcohol, but the wine list is extensive. After an excellent meal you can stroll around the tranquil garden or along the beach and enjoy your after-dinner coffee alfresco.

Safari Rooftop Grill House
Grand Hyatt Muscat Hay As Sarujz **24 641 234**
muscat.grand.hyatt.com
Map **2 G2**
If you're a fan of relaxed, open-air dining, succulent steaks and a good atmosphere, then you will definitely enjoy this rooftop restaurant. Overlooking the Gulf of Oman, the safari themed restaurant offers both buffet and al a carte dining; for an all-inclusive price, you can select from a range of salads, soups and starters on the buffet, and then take your pick from an al la carte menu featuring a selection of succulent steaks, specialty game meats and freshly caught seafood. An added bonus is that the excellent selection of beverages such as beer, wine and spirits are included in the all-inclusive price. The steak and lobster combination is a highlight and is highly recommended. Oktoberfest (each October) at the Safari Rooftop and Grillhouse features traditional Bavarian music, German delicacies and, of course, plenty of great tasting beer.

Samah

The Platinum Al Khuwayr Al Janubiyyah
24 392 500
theplatinumoman.com
Map **2 F3**

A great location for a pool party, this restaurant is perched on the roof top of The Platinum, with 360 degree views out over the city – truly amazing. Open from breakfast, there are two theme nights (BBQ buffet on Wednesdays, and a sizzler night on Sundays). The Sizzling Sunday is actually the signature evening, but there is also the Platinum Friday when visitors can pay RO 5.500 for a day at the pool, including a burger or pizza with a juice or some kind of soft drink. This restaurant is unlicensed.

Samba

Shangri-La's Barr Al Jissah Resort & Spa
Al Jissah **24 776 565**
shangri-la.com
Map **1 G4**

The South American theme has touched on all aspects of this restaurant, from the terracotta tiled floors to the splashes of vibrant colour, and of course, the food. The adventurous can try the cactus and date salad on the buffet or spicy seafood from the a la carte menu. While you can expect to be seated among families at Samba, the alfresco seating option is spacious and the service is excellent. Combined with a tequila bar, this can make for a very enjoyable evening.

Samharam Cafe

Haffa House Hotel Muscat Ruwi
24 707 207
shanfarihotels.com
Map **2 J3**

Far enough away from Muscat's bustling CBD to be relatively peaceful, this is still a convenient retreat for a lunch break from the office or a leisurely evening meal. The food is simple but tasty and quick to arrive. The grills, pasta, sandwiches and fruit juices all make for filling fare. After your meal, indulge in a headily pungent shisha, or sniff at the one being smoked near you.

Seblat Al Bustan

Al Bustan Palace, A Ritz-Carlton Hotel
Haramil **24 799 666**
ritzcarlton.com
Map **2 L4**

At Seblat Al Bustan, you'll be treated to dinner in a Bedouin tent set out under the stars. Traditional music and folk dancing, bread making, henna and handicrafts make this more a cultural experience than just a meal which, incidentally, is very tasty. And since you've come this far into the culture, be sure to try the shuwa, an Omani dish of slow-cooked meat. Finish the evening with traditional coffee and dates. Dinner is held every Wednesday night from September to May, from 19:30 to 23:00. A shuttle bus will take you from the hotel entrance to the tented village where your dinner awaits.

Second Cup

Al Qurum Complex Al Qurm
24 566 616
mysecondcup.com
Map **2 H2**

A bit of a Muscat stalwart, customers love the warm, friendly ambience and the contemporary coffee-shop setting in Second Cup. However, any fears that it is more about style than substance are quickly laid to rest when you sample the range of coffees, teas and fruit drinks, all of which are expertly prepared. To complement your choice of drink, Second Cup offers a delectable variety of delicious desserts that are freshly made each day. It's a great place to meet friends for a sociable 'coffee and cake' date, and if you're alone, you can keep busy by reading through the latest newspapers and magazines provided.

Senor Pico

InterContinental Muscat Hay As Saruj
24 680 000
ichotelsgroup.com
Map **2 G2**

An expat favourite, Senor Pico is nestled in the back corner of the InterContinental Muscat and is always busy with hotel guests and Muscat's legion of Mexican food fans. At first glance it's quaint and conducive to conversation, but don't be fooled. Come 22:00 and the arrival of the band, this is one of the most happening restaurants in the city. The decor is cool Aztec, the cuisine is hot Mexican – fajitas, enchiladas, and the most fantastic, must-try nachos. The hot, sweet and spicy tomato and saffron soup is an amazing way to start your meal. You will also find an excellent selection of succulent grills. The food is hearty, well presented and deserves to be complemented with the best margarita in Muscat.

Get your local Mobile Broadband Package from the leading mobile network

Connect starting from Rial 1 per day.

Pick the Mobile Broadband package that suits your lifestyle. Enjoy!

Visit www.omantel.om or call us on **1234**

Shahrazad

Shangri-La's Barr Al Jissah Resort & Spa
Al Jissah **24 776 565**
shangri-la.com
Map **1 G4**

The mix of traditional and contemporary decor exudes a sense of calm and tranquillity and you can almost imagine yourself under the stars in Marrakesh as you look up at the glittering ceiling. The Moroccan staff are only too happy to explain how the restaurant's authentic cuisine is prepared and cooked. The menu is delightful, with one of its signature dishes – Tanjin Marrakesha (braised lamb shanks with Moroccan olive oil, preserved lemon, garlic, cumin and ginger) – particularly worth trying. Moroccan wines are rare, so this is the opportunity to savour a Toual Red Syrah or one of the many others on the wine list. For a sweet ending, try the halaweyat, which is an interesting assortment of Moroccan pastries made with almonds, gum arabica and rose water.

Shiraz

Crowne Plaza Muscat Al Qurm
24 660 660
ichotelsgroup.com
Map **2 H2**

Shiraz offers a hearty menu of Iranian favourites. A tented ceiling and open bread preparation area add to the already-plush setting. It's definitely advisable to take along a huge appetite for the generous, and complimentary, portions of cheese, salad and Arabic bread you'll be given before your meal. Shiraz's starters and desserts are a particular treat, while the main courses, sadly, are a tad bland by comparison. During the cooler months, day and evening diners will enjoy eating on the terrace with its views of the coastline and the mountain backdrop.

Silk Route Restaurant

Al Noor Plaza, Nr SABCO Madinat As Sultan Qaboos **24 696 967**
Map **2 G3**

Silk Route is not inexpensive, but it is one of the better Chinese restaurants in Muscat. It draws fans from both the local and expat communities so you can expect it to get really busy in the evenings, particularly at the weekend. It's a great family restaurant too, so book in advance. Once there, the varied menu of Chinese, Cantonese and Szechwan cuisines includes some delicious dim sum and a particularly good crispy aromatic duck. There is also a Thai menu. Service is friendly and helpful and the atmosphere is warm and welcoming.

Sirj Tea Lounge

Grand Hyatt Muscat Hay As Saruj
24 641 234
muscat.grand.hyatt.com
Map **2 G2**

The scones, jam and cream here are a must, but, if afternoon (or morning) tea isn't your style (you must be mad), there is also a variety of light, delicious meals to choose from, as well as many different infusions and fruit juices, which are served throughout the day. In the afternoon and early evening, gentle music comes from the piano, thanks to the musical talents of the various pianists who play the striking black grand. Sitting in the air-conditioned comfort of this impressive lounge you can still take pleasure in the picturesque scenery through the giant glass windows forming the main wall of the impressive Hyatt Hotel, Muscat.

Spicy Village

Rusayl Commercial Complex, Nr Ministry of Defense Rusayl
24 510 612
spicyvillage.com
Map **1 F4**

With three outlets in Muscat, the Spicy Village in Rusayl serves authentic Indian and Chinese cuisine. It may lack atmosphere and a licence to serve alcohol, but its no frills approach offers customers generous portions of Asian food at very reasonable prices. Unfortunately, 'no frills' extends to the decor, atmosphere and ambience, but for cheap fare, this is the place. Other locations: Ruwi, 24 700 175; Nizwa, 25 431 694.

Sultanah

Shangri-La's Barr Al Jissah Resort & Spa
Al Jissah **24 776 565**
shangri-la.com
Map **1 G4**

Perched high above the Shangri-La's bay in Al Husn, Sultanah offers first-rate dining, fantastic views and impeccable service. Following the theme of a cruise ship visiting different ports every night, the international menu offers choices from locations such as New York, Singapore and Paris. Creative, contemporary international cuisine at its finest, the menu includes gamey choices such as rabbit, with fish and seafood. The dining room affords panoramic views of the bay from large windows, while the covered terrace and open patio overlook the resort from the edge of the cliff – a jazz trio also play here in the evenings. The stunning views get more romantic at night when the twinkling lights of the resort provide the perfect accompaniment to your meal. Sultanah has to be in the running for best restaurant in Oman.

Sumhuram
Salalah Marriott Resort Mirbat
23 268 245
marriott.com
Map **1 C11**
This agreeable all-day dining restaurant keeps the quality high, in spite of the long opening hours. The food is truly international – you'll find everything from Italian classics to must-try Omani delicacies – while there are both buffet and a la carte options. Breakfast too is a relaxed and diverse affair.

Tapas & Sablah
Shangri-La's Barr Al Jissah Resort & Spa
Al Jissah **24 776 565**
shangri-la.com
Map **1 G4**
Spread around the attractively lit and atmospheric 'Sablah' square outside Al Bandar Hotel, the alfresco Tapas & Sablah is the only chance to sample Spanish cuisine in Muscat. The range of dishes is good, all tasty and pretty authentic, and for some international twists on the tapas theme, they are complemented by some Arabic mezze and Asian tapas-style dishes. There are also specials, such as paella on offer, and the house sangria is worth sampling. Portions are generous – order less than you might normally, and top them up if your appetite isn't satisfied. For vegetarians, the selection of tapas is great, and the vegetable paella is one the best you'll find anywhere.

Tokyo Taro
Al Falaj Hotel Bayt Al Falaj
24 702 311
omanhotels.com
Map **2 J2**
This place is usually really vibrant, with the sights, smells and sounds of authentic Japanese food being prepared. Meat, vegetables and seafood all sizzle at the teppanyaki bar, and the green tea is on tap. If you're in a group, you can book one of the private dining rooms and sit at a traditional banquet table to enjoy your meal. The setting is serene and convincing enough for you to imagine that you actually are in the land of the rising sun – if only for an hour or two. Dining here affords you a tantalising – and delicious – glimpse of Japan.

Tomato
InterContinental Muscat Hay As Saruj
24 680 000
ichotelsgroup.com
Map **2 G2**
When it comes to tranquil restaurants, Tomato is the leader of the pack. Deep in the beautiful gardens of the InterContinental Muscat, getting there requires a picturesque walk along the palm tree-lined pathways near the swimming pool. All tables are located on a deck and there is no indoor option, making this a venue to be enjoyed when the weather is not too sticky. The food is the perfect combination of simple, wholesome classics and innovative flavours, and the funky cutlery and dazzling range of crockery wouldn't be out of place in any cutting-edge European eatery. Breakfasts are pleasant, and you can choose from three options – healthy, American or continental – while you enjoy another beautiful Muscat morning under the shade of a huge cream canopy. However, with live music, ambient lighting and some delectable Mediterranean fare, dinners are also good.

Trader Vic's
InterContinental Muscat Hay As Saruj
24 680 808
tradervics.com
Map **2 G2**
A popular venue, Trader Vic's is a dream for the indecisive diner. You'll find Caribbean cocktails, a Cuban band, an international menu and dishes prepared in a gigantic Chinese clay oven, all under one roof. It might sound like a bit of a mish mash but it's actually great and you would probably want to head here for the cocktail list alone. The service is excellent and, if nothing else, this is one of the only places that does a really good Irish coffee. Dining here isn't cheap, but for a good night out, it's worth it.

Tropicana

Crowne Plaza Muscat Al Qurm
24 660 660
ichotelsgroup.com
Map **2 H2**
Located at the poolside of the Crowne
Plaza hotel in Qurm, Tropicana has an
international menu ranging from Oriental
(with unlimited sushi and dim sum), Indian
and Mediterranean classics to the good
old American burger, and theme nights on
Wednesdays and Thursdays. Lunchtimes
see a loaded buffet and this tastefully
decorated restaurant is well frequented
in the afternoon hours. Appetising
dishes arrive in generous proportions,
accompanied by excellent service and a
reasonable price tag. The poolside location
offers a pleasant view, and outside seating
is available.

Tuscany

Grand Hyatt Muscat Hay As Saruj
24 641 234
muscat.grand.hyatt.com
Map **2 G2**
Dining alfresco just adds to the experience
at this charming Italian restaurant. As
you look out over the lush green gardens
of the Grand Hyatt, you'll feel utterly
pampered in every way. Service is very
efficient, with waiters providing lots of
good tips on the various dishes. The menu
offers interesting choices of fresh and
wholesome Italian food; all of the seafood
is locally sourced and is complemented by
wonderful seasoning while being expertly
presented. The wine list is extensive and
sourced from some of the best wine
regions of Italy. The dessert menu offers a
nice choice of both decadent and simpler
dishes. Try the torte semifreddo for the
perfect end to an evening.

Woodlands

Nr Europcar Bld, CBD Ruwi
24 700 192
Map **2 J3**
This place hits all the right spots: service
with a genuine smile, fabulously large
portions of delicious south Indian cuisine,
and an easy on your wallet bill to top it all
off. If you're having difficulty in deciding
what to order, allow one of the friendly
waiters to talk you through the menu, but if
you're not a fire-eater beware those brutal
south Indian chillies and spices. A good
place for an easy night out. There is another
branch at Salalah Airport (23 204 280).

Zuzana's Gallery

**Street 4014, Building 1076, Nr Mars
Hypermarket** Al Ghubrah Al Janubiyyah
92 020 299
zuzanas.com
Map **2 E3**
Zuzana's Gallery is an expat Muscat
experience; not only do you get to enjoy

Tuscany

a fresh coffee with friends, but you also get an insight into the family tradition of cookie-making, thanks to the wonderful display of cookie designs and gifts that is scattered throughout the shop. Little tummies are also catered for with Zuzana teaching children some fun cookie design while their parents enjoy their coffee. If you're looking for a great venue for group get togethers and celebrations, Zuzana's Gallery is also popular for its realxed vibe. The Gallery also caters for childrens birthday parties and fun filled afternoons of cookie and cupcake design activities. All of Zuzana's cookies are hand made from a traditional Slovak recipe and can be designed for any occasion such as baby showers, birthdays, weddings and many national and international holidays.

BARS, PUBS & CLUBS

Al Ghazal Pub
InterContinental Muscat Hay As Saruj **24 680 000**
ichotelsgroup.com
Map **2 G2**
Set within the five-star InterContinental Muscat, this pub offers a traditional pub experience that's second to none. With a friendly atmosphere, a huge selection of beverages, delicious pub grub and live entertainment, what more could you want? Tables are screened so diners can enjoy a meal of steak or fish and chips, or just a light sandwich, in privacy. Good

SHISHA CAFES
Relaxing with a juice or hot drink in a shisha cafe is an extremely popular pastime in Oman and there are several excellent places where you can enjoy the traditional delights of the hubbabubba. Try these for starters:
Al Barouk Beach Hotel, Shati Al Qurm
Al Deyar, Nr Shati Cinema, Shati Al Qurm
Al Madinat MSQ, Centre MSQ
Automatic, Nr Sabco Centre, Al Qurm
Fish Village, Nr Radisson BLU, Al Khuwayr
Japengo, Shatti Beach Road
Kargeeen Caffe MSQ, Centre MSQ
Layali Al Hilmya, Nr Zakher Mall, Al Khuwayr
Le Mermaid, Nr Grand Hyatt, Shati Al Qurm
Marjan Poolside, Grand Hyatt, Shati Al Qurm
Tche Tche Café, Shatti Beach Road

food, drinks, service and reasonable prices ensure this pub is nearly always crowded with regulars.

Chambers
Majan Continental Hotel
Al Ghubrah Al Janubiyyah **24 592 900**
majanhotel.com
Map **2 E4**
Chambers may be small in size but it's big in stature. With a pool table, large screen TV and a few gaming machines, it draws a regular crowd of local and Eastern European men. You won't find any draught beer here, but the rest of the beverage selection is very reasonably priced. An African band plays nightly and you'll receive friendly-enough service from the staff. The overall impression is one of a working man's pub.

Club Bar
Ruwi Hotel Ruwi **24 704 244**
omanhotels.com
Map **2 J3**
Located in the heart of the Ruwi business district, this is a small, no-frills hotel bar designed to serve the many businessmen in the area. It's friendly, low-lit and decked out with standard British pub paraphernalia but its identity as an unassuming bar gets a jolt when the lively band starts up. The service is quiet and efficient and while the menu is fairly basic, the food is good.

Copacabana
Grand Hyatt Muscat Hay As Saruj **24 641 234**
muscat.grand.hyatt.com
Map **2 G2**
On the ground floor of the Grand Hyatt hotel, this nightclub comes to life after midnight when people start to filter out of the pubs and restaurants. It is a large spacious venue with a good dance floor but if you would like some privacy, you can hire the VIP room. On Saturday, Monday and Wednesday nights, you can dance the night away to Arabic music. On Tuesday night, African music is played, while Thursday night is an international mix. Light meals are available including fish and chips, and sandwiches. There is an excellent beverages menu with champagne priced from RO 20 to RO 350. Opening times: closed Fri & Sun. Sat, Mon, Tues, Wed & Thurs 10:00-03:00. Entrance fee: RO 5 for men, free for women.

The Coral Bar

Radisson Blu Hotel, Muscat Al Khuwayr
Al Janubiyyah **24 487 777**
radissonblu.com
Map **2 F3**
This is a piano bar with acts that
change every few months and fabulous
underwater themed murals. The staff are
very friendly, and the beers, spirits and
wines are sold at standard hotel prices.
There's always a selection of nibbles at
your elbow to keep you thirsty. Coral Bar is
popular with local businessmen and hotel
guests, and appeals to the slightly older
customer or someone who's happy for a
chilled-out evening of something to drink
and conversation.

The Deck

Millennium Resort Mussanah
Al Musanaah **26 871 555**
millenniumhotels.com
Map **1 F4**
This modern and relaxed lounge bar has
a stylish interior based on the concepts
of water and wind – it's a theme that
lends itself perfectly to the bar's setting
overlooking the 54 berth private marina.
Guests have the option of sitting inside or
outside but, during the cooler months, the
balcony is the place to be. There is a good
selection of beers, spirits and cocktails,
and the menu features light meals and
snacks that include oysters, escargot and
risotto balls. Guests also have the option
of ordering from the more extensive menu
that is served at the Mydan restaurant
in the resort. One of the draws is the live
music that is played every night (19:00-
23:00) except Saturday.

Duke's Bar

Crowne Plaza Muscat Al Qurm
24 660 660
ichotelsgroup.com
Map **2 H2**
Given enough dark wood panelling,
brass fittings and cosy leather seats, you
can knock up an English theme pub
almost anywhere. But only Duke's has the
evocative rocky seascape view, framed by
a giant picture window. The regulars here
are a diverse bunch: locals and expats of
many nationalities adorn the bar stools
and tables, kept busy with quiz nights,
ladies' nights and various live music acts.
The food is typical pub-grub and can be
enjoyed on the terrace outside if you can
secure a sought-after table.

Feeney's Irish Pub

Al Qurum Resort Ruwi **24 605 945**
alhashargroup.com
Map **2 G2**
A comfortable little stop for a drink and
some decent pub grub. It's small but
somehow manages to pack a lot in – head
for one of the tables if you're eating,
or prop yourself up at the bar for a few
friendly drinks. There's a popular quiz night
on Tuesdays and live music every weekend.
And if you're looking for somewhere to
watch the big game, major Premiership
football matches are also shown here.

John Barry Bar

Grand Hyatt Muscat Hay As Saruj
24 641 234
muscat.grand.hyatt.com
Map **2 G2**
Servers buzz around dressed in naval attire
and there is plenty of memorabilia on the
walls from the original SS John Barry ship,
torpedoed off the coast of Oman in 1944.
The fish and chips, a simple but extremely
satisfying dish, is cooked to perfection
and should suit all seafarers. No visit here
would be complete without checking out
the tantalising cocktail and mocktail menu
which fizzes with fresh concoctions to
satisfy thirsty guests.

The Lazy Lizard

Radisson Blu Hotel, Muscat Al Khuwayr
Al Janubiyyah **24 487 777**
radissonblu.com
Map **2 F3**
After a long tiring day, this poolside venue
is the perfect spot to chill out at. Sit at the
bar and choose from its wide selection of
beers or relax at a candle-lit table under
the palm trees and enjoy a cocktail. Light
snacks are available, with the Lebanese
mixed grill a delicious option. Burgers,
spring rolls and samosas are also popular
and there is a good kids' menu with
'Aladdin's feast' (spaghetti in meat sauce)
a firm favourite. Every Wednesday and
Thursday, a DJ provides the chill out music
in this popular venue.

Left Bank

Nr Mumtaz Mahal Al Qurm
24 693 699
emiratesleisureretail.com
Map **2 H2**
Perched above Al Qurum Natural Park
(p.170) is one of the hottest bar-restaurants
in Muscat, with the slickest interior in

town. Left Bank has a fantastic reputation for serving up high quality fare and imaginative cocktails – and the applause is well deserved. The burgers, fish dishes and pastas are particularly recommended, as are the desserts which are alone worth the trip. While it's not a huge menu, each dish earns its place and everyone from gourmands to steak and veg fans are kept happy. The drinks list deserves special mention, with delicious martinis and a credible wine list just waiting to be sampled. It gets busy at weekends so reservations are essential if you want one of those coveted booths.

The Long Bar
Shangri-La's Barr Al Jissah Resort & Spa Al Jissah **24 776 565**
shangri-la.com
Map **1 G4**
Long Bar has one of the very best locations in Oman for enjoying happy hour indulgence. Although it is a little out of the way, it is certainly worth the drive to enjoy a beachfront sunset from the terrace as you work your way through the Martini menu and list of tropical cocktails. Be sure to pack your dancing shoes too when you visit Long Bar, as the venue transforms into Xyro Nightclub later on in the evening, a very popular dancing venue with expats and locals.

The Long Pool Cabana
The Chedi Muscat Al Ghubrah Ash Shamaliyyah **24 524 343**
chedimuscat.com
Map **2 E3**
After a hard day sun worshipping or sightseeing, this is the perfect place to unwind. During the cooler winter months (Oct- April), this alfresco venue is very popular, with people relaxing on plush cushions under the star filled Arabian sky. Enjoy the view of the 103 metre long pool, the longest in the Middle East, while listening to chillout contemporary music. The menu consists of reasonably priced light meals of authentic Japanese and Malaysian cuisine. Some of the starters, including the Kerabu Ayam (shredded chicken), are very spicy so you may wish to request a milder version. There is a nice selection of sushi rolls (Japanese eel, salmon, sako tuna, tempura prawn, Alaskan crab) and skewer dishes as well as stir fries. There is an extensive alcoholic and non-alcoholic beverages menu which includes beers from Thailand, Mexico and Japan as well as captivating cocktails. Open 18:00-00:00. Last food orders 22:30.

O'Malleys
Radisson Blu Hotel, Muscat Al Khuwayr Al Janubiyyah **24 487 777**
radissonblu.com
Map **2 F3**
With its dark wooden bar furniture specially made in Ireland and authentic photographs and memorabilia, this is the place to come for a taste of the Emerald Isle. Sit along the bar and savour the lively atmosphere or enjoy a quieter moment by the fireplace in the lounge area. There is a nice selection of light meals with the Leenane leek & potato soup (served with delicious Irish soda bread) and the Irish stew being particularly tasty. There is an assortment of draught beers available including the old country favourites Guinness and Kilkenny. The extensive beverage menu also includes several Irish malts – Jameson, Bushmills, Kilbeggan and Connemara. As with most Irish bars, the atmosphere is friendly and relaxed and the courteous staff are very professional. And, of course, it's where all the festivities abound for St. Patrick's Day in March. Opening times: Sat-Thurs 12:00-15:00 & 18:00-01:00, Fri 12:00-01:00.

Piano Lounge
Shangri-La's Barr Al Jissah Resort & Spa Al Jissah **24 776 565**
shangri-la.com
Map **1 G4**
With soft lighting, carpets, couches and cushions, Piano Lounge makes an elegant addition to an evening out at the Shangri-La Barr Al Jissah Resort (p.214). The bar doesn't serve meals, but does offer first class service and front row seats to the pianist every night from 20:00 to 23:45. The drinks menu has reasonably priced wine by the glass, beer and spirits, but this is definitely the place to treat yourself to a bottle of Moet or an aged malt whisky on the rocks.

The Pub
Al Falaj Hotel Bayt Al Falaj **24 702 311**
omanhotels.com
Map **2 J2**
The Pub is situated on the eighth floor of Muscat's second oldest hotel. Being so high up means you get the chance to drink in spectacular views over the Ruwi

area, especially at night, if you're lucky enough to get one of the two window booths. The bar is very quiet, frequented mainly by the hotel's guests and local men. There's live entertainment at night and, if you're peckish, you can order from a menu of light snacks.

Safari Pub
Grand Hyatt Muscat Hay As Saruj
24 641 234
muscat.grand.hyatt.com
Map **2 G2**
Set in the three-storey safari entertainment complex, the safari pub is located on the middle level of the venue. Standard 'pub grub' is available (chicken wings, potato skins, steak and pepper pie) and is reasonably priced. A resident band plays every night except Saturday. There is a 40% discount on beverages and ladies can enjoy free margaritas every day from 18:00-22:00. There is an indoor smoking room. Opening hours: 18:00-02:00.

Sama Terrazza
Park Inn By Radisson Muscat Al Khuwayr
Al Janubiyyah **24 507 888**
parkinn.com
Map **2 F3**
With panoramic views of the city, this stylish outdoor rooftop bar is the ideal venue to relax and unwind. Open during the cooler months (September to April) from 18:00 to 01:00, its chill-out vibe and laidback decor is the perfect antidote to a long day in the city. Take a seat by the pool, make yourself comfortable on the sofas or settle into a comfortable bean bag and enjoy the night. While the food menu is limited to a small selection of tapas, what is served is delicious and, at RO 6, it is great value for money. A wide range of wines, beers and sophisticated cocktails is available. On Wednesday and Thursday nights, a DJ expertly mixes the music and provides a chillout atmosphere. This is the perfect place to kick off or end a night.

Uptown
CBD Area, Nr Golden Oryx Restaurant
Ruwi **24 706 020**
Map **2 J3**
The decor at Uptown is a fairly unusual fusion of South East Asian and European, but this joint still sports all the swanky touches you would expect of a bar – the dim lighting and sofa seating. The latest sporting events play out on a large screen TV in one corner of the bar and the simple but moreish bar snacks will keep you ordering from the reasonably priced drinks menu. There's live entertainment every night and a happy hour. In other words, you've got all the ingredients for a good night out.

Safari Pub

334   **Oman Explorer**

Explorer Products

Residents' Guides

Mini Visitors' Guides

Mini Maps

Photography Books & Calendars

Maps

Adventure & Lifestyle Guides

Useful Numbers

Embassies & Consulates

Australian Embassy	
(Saudi Arabia)	00966 1488 7788
Bahrain Embassy	24 605 074
British Embassy	24 609 000
Canadian Consulate	24 788 890
Chinese Embassy	24 696 698
Czech Embassy	
(Saudi Arabia)	00966 1450 3617
Danish Consulate	24 526 000
Egyptian Embassy	24 600 411
French Embassy	24 681 800
German Embassy	24 835 000
Indian Embassy	24 684 500
Iranian Embassy	24 696 944
Irish Consulate	24 701 282
Italian Embassy	24 695 131
Japanese Embassy	24 601 028
Jordanian Embassy	24 692 760
Kuwaiti Embassy	24 699 626
Lebanese Embassy	24 695 844
Malaysian Embassy	24 698 329
Netherlands Embassy	24 603 706
New Zealand Consulate	24 694 692
Norwegian Consulate	24 526 444
Pakistani Embassy	24 603 439
Philippine Embassy	24 605 140
Qatar Embassy	24 691 156
Russian Embassy	24 602 894
Saudi Arabian Embassy	24 601 705
Spanish Embassy	24 691 101
South African Embassy	24 647 300
Sri Lankan Embassy	24 697 841
Swedish Consulate	24 708 693
Swiss Consulate	24 568 202
Thai Embassy	24 602 684
UAE Embassy	24 400 000
US Embassy	24 643 400

Useful Numbers

Friendi Mobile	98 400 000
Nawras Customer Service:	
From Nawras mobile	1500
From any phone	9501 1500
Renna:	
From Renna mobile	1240
From any phone	800 73662
Omantel Business Call Center	1235
Omantel Directory Enquiries	1318
Omantel Fixed & Internet Call Centre	1300
Omantel International Operator	
Connected Calls	1305
Omantel Marine & Coastal	
Radio Services	1302
Omantel Mobile Call Centre	1234
Omantel Payphone Faults & Complaints	1307
Omantel Telex Faults & Complaints	1301

Country & City Codes

Oman Country Code	968
Al Musanaah Area Code	26
Barka Area Code	26
Daba Area Code	26
Jabal Al Akhdar Area Code	25
Jebel Sifah Area Code	24
Khasab Area Code	26
Mirbat Area Code	23
Muscat Area Code	24
Nizwa Area Code	25
Salalah Area Code	23
Sur Area Code	25

Emergency & Other Services

AAA Oman	24 605 555
CID Services	24 569 501
Electricity Emergency	154
Emergency: Police / Fire / Ambulance	9999